# HESIOD AND CLAS

MW01265094

Hesiod was regarded by the Greeks as a foundational figure of their culture, alongside Homer. This book examines the rich and varied engagement of fifth-century lyric and drama with the poetic corpus attributed to Hesiod as well as with the poetic figure of Hesiod. The first half of the book is dedicated to Hesiodic reception in Pindaric and Bacchylidean poetry, with a particular focus on poetics, genealogies and mythological narratives, and didactic voices. The second half examines how Hesiodic narratives are approached and appropriated in tragedy and satyr drama, especially in the Prometheus plays and in Euripides' *Ion*. It also explores the multifaceted engagement of Old Comedy with the poetry and authority associated with Hesiod. Through close readings of numerous case studies, the book surveys the complex landscape of Hesiodic reception in the fifth century BCE, focusing primarily on lyric and dramatic responses to the Hesiodic tradition.

ZOE STAMATOPOULOU is an Associate Professor of Classics at Washington University in St. Louis. Her research focuses on Archaic and Classical Greek poetry as well as on Greek literature of the Imperial era, with an emphasis on the Hesiodic tradition and its reception in antiquity. She has authored several articles on Homer, Hesiod, Pindar, Euripides, and Plutarch.

# HESIOD AND CLASSICAL GREEK POETRY

## Reception and Transformation in the Fifth Century BCE

ZOE STAMATOPOULOU

*Washington University, St. Louis*

CAMBRIDGE
UNIVERSITY PRESS

# CAMBRIDGE
## UNIVERSITY PRESS

University Printing House, Cambridge CB2 8BS, United Kingdom

One Liberty Plaza, 20th Floor, New York, NY 10006, USA

477 Williamstown Road, Port Melbourne, VIC 3207, Australia

314-321, 3rd Floor, Plot 3, Splendor Forum, Jasola District Centre, New Delhi - 110025, India

103 Penang Road, #05-06/07, Visioncrest Commercial, Singapore 238467

Cambridge University Press is part of the University of Cambridge.

It furthers the University's mission by disseminating knowledge in the pursuit of education, learning and research at the highest international levels of excellence.

www.cambridge.org
Information on this title: www.cambridge.org/9781316615041

First published 2017
First paperback edition 2021

*A catalogue record for this publication is available from the British Library*

*Library of Congress Cataloging in Publication data*
NAMES: Stamatopoulou, Zoe, author.
TITLE: Hesiod and classical Greek poetry : reception and transformation in the Fifth Century BCE / Zoe Stamatopoulou, Washington University, St Louis.
DESCRIPTION: Cambridge, United Kingdom : Cambridge University Press, 2016. | Includes bibliographical references and indexes.
IDENTIFIERS: LCCN 2016034289 | ISBN 9781107162990 (Hardback)
SUBJECTS: LCSH: Hesiod–Criticism and interpretation. | Greek poetry–Criticism and interpretation.
CLASSIFICATION: LCC PA4011 .S73 2016 | DDC 881/.01–dc23 LC record available at https://lccn.loc.gov/2016034289

ISBN 978-1-107-16299-0 Hardback
ISBN 978-1-316-61504-1 Paperback

# Contents

# Acknowledgements

My interest in Hesiodic reception was born and nurtured during my graduate studies at the University of Virginia. I owe many thanks to the Faculty of Classics at UVa for their stimulating courses and their invaluable support. I am particularly grateful to Jenny Strauss Clay for opening my eyes to the beauty of Hesiodic and Pindaric poetry and for patiently teaching me how to be a researcher and a writer. As my dissertation advisor, Jenny encouraged me to explore the reception of Hesiodic poetry in Pindar's epinician odes and generously devoted time and effort to help me grow as a scholar. Although this book is very different from that early scholarly endeavor, her feedback shaped the trajectory of this project.

This book was written with support from the Fondation Hardt, the Loeb Classical Library Foundation, the College of the Liberal Arts at Penn State, and from Peter and Ann Tombros, who endowed the Early Career Professorship in Classical Studies that I held from 2013 to 2016. My ideas benefited greatly from exchanges I have had with my colleagues at the University of Georgia and at the Pennsylvania State University. I owe special thanks to Nancy Felson for our thought-provoking conversations about Greek poetry and to the participants of the 2011–12 Advanced Seminar in the Humanities at the Venice International University, especially Richard Hunter, David Sider, Ettore Cingano, Theodora Hadjimichael, Greta Hawes, and Enrico Prodi. I am most grateful to Ruth Scodel and Ian Rutherford, to Mark Munn and John Gilbert for reading parts of the manuscript, and to the anonymous readers of Cambridge University Press, whose generous comments improved this book in many ways. All errors are, of course, my own. Many thanks also to Michael Sharp and Sarah Lambert for all their help and to John Woodman, who allowed me to use his beautiful art on the cover of this book. I am indebted to Matthijs Wibier for challenging me intellectually and, above all, for being a wonderful partner. In addition to all the dear friends I have already mentioned, I would like to thank Pam and Milt Cole, Mary Lou Zimmerman Munn, Kathy Salzer, as well as my family.

Finally, I owe a debt of gratitude to Tony Woodman. Tony has been a patient and extremely helpful reader, but, more importantly, he has been a great mentor through thick and thin. This book would never have seen the light of day without his support.

# *Abbreviations*

The names of ancient Greek authors and works have been abbreviated according to the conventions familiar from the *LSJ*; for ancient authors and works outside the scope of the *LSJ*, I follow the conventions of the *Oxford Classical Dictionary* and the Duke papyrological *Checklist*. A few exceptions have been listed below. All translations of ancient passages in this book are mine, although I have consulted the Loeb and the Aris and Phillips series. Every Hesiodic fragment included in Hirschberger's edition is assigned two numbers: the one before the slash (/) corresponds to the fragment's number in Hirschberger's edition and the one after the slash to the edition by Merkelbach and West. If there is some significant discrepancy between the two editions, or if a fragment is included only in one of the two editions, I print the number(s) accompanied by the abbreviations 'H' or 'MW' accordingly. For the Pindaric scholia, I use the numbering in Drachmann's edition.

| | |
|---|---|
| Allen | T. W. Allen (1912). *Homeri Opera*, vol. V. Oxford. |
| Bernabé | A. Bernabé (1987–2007). *Poetae Epici Graeci. Testimonia et Fragmenta* (4 vols.).Berlin. |
| *Cat.* | Hesiod, *Catalogue of Women* |
| *CGFP* | C. Austin (1973). *Comicorum Graecorum Fragmenta: in Papyris Reperta*. Berlin. |
| Colonna | A. Colonna (1953). "I *Prolegomeni* ad Esiodo e la *Vita Esiodea* di Giovanni Tzetzes." *Accademia nazionale di Lincei: Bolletino del Comitato per la preparazione dell'Edizione nazionale dei Classici greci e latini* 2: 27–39. |
| Daremberg-Saglio | C. Daremberg, E. Saglio, et al. (1877–1919). *Dictionnaire des antiquités grecques et romaines, d'après les textes et les monuments*. Paris. |
| Davies | M. Davies (1988). *Epicorum Graecorum Fragmenta*. Göttingen |

| | |
|---|---|
| *Deipn.* | Athenaeus, *Deipnosophistae* |
| DF | M. Davies and P. Finglass (2015). *Stesichorus: The Poems.* Cambridge. |
| *DGE* | F. R. Adrados et al. (1980–). *Diccionario Griego-Español.* Madrid. |
| DK | H. Diels and W. Kranz (1951–52)[6]. *Die Fragmente der Vorsokratiker,* 6th edn. (3 vols.). Berlin. |
| Drachmann | A. B. Drachmann (1903–27). *Scholia Vetera in Pindari Carmina* (3 vols.). Leipzig. |
| *DTC*[2] | A. Pickard-Cambridge and T. B. L. Webster (1962)[2]. *Dithyramb, Tragedy and Comedy,* 2nd edn. Oxford. |
| *FGrH* | F. Jacoby (1923–58), *Die Fragmente der griechischen Historiker.* Berlin and Leiden. |
| Fowler | R. L. Fowler (2000–13). *Early Greek Mythography* (2 vols.). Oxford. |
| *GW* | Hesiod, *Megala Erga* |
| H | M. Hirschberger (2004). *Gynaikōn Katalogos und Megalai Ehoiai.* Munich and Leipzig. |
| KA | R. Kassel and C. Austin (1983–2001). *Poetae Comici Graeci* (8 vols.). Berlin. |
| Kannicht | R. Kannicht (2004). *Tragicorum Graecorum Fragmenta. Vol. 5: Euripides* (2 vols). Göttingen. |
| KRS | G. S. Kirk, J. E. Raven, and M. Schofield (1983)[2]. *The Presocratic Philosophers,* 2nd edn. Cambridge. |
| *LdfE* | (1955–2010) *Lexicon des frühgriechischen Epos.* Göttingen. |
| *LIMC* | (1981–2009) *Lexicon Iconographicum Mythologiae Classicae.* Zurich. |
| *LSJ* | H. G. Liddell, R. Scott, H. Stuart Jones, R. McKenzie, P. G. W. Glare (1996). *A Greek–English Lexicon, with a Revised Supplement,* 9th edn. Oxford. |
| Marzillo | P. Marzillo (2010). *Der Kommentar des Proklos zu Hesiods "Werken und Tagen": Edition, Übersetzung und Erläuterung der Fragmente.* Tübingen. |
| *ME* | Hesiod, *Megalai Ehoiai* |
| Most | G. W. Most (2006–07). *Hesiod* (2 vols.). Cambridge, Mass. |
| MW | R. Merkelbach and M. L. West (1967). *Fragmenta Hesiodea.* Oxford. |
| Obbink | D. Obbink (1996). *On Piety. Part 1: Critical Text with Commentary.* Oxford and New York. |

| | |
|---|---|
| Pertusi | A. Pertusi (1955). *Scholia Vetera in Hesiodi "Opera et Dies"*. Milan. |
| *PMGF* | M. Davies (1991). *Poetarum Melicorum Graecorum Fragmenta*, vol. I. Oxford. |
| Poltera | O. Poltera (2008). *Simonides lyricus, Testimonia und Fragmente: Einleitung, kritische Ausgabe, Übersetzung und Kommentar*. Basel. |
| Radt | Radt, S. (1985) and (1999)², *Tragicorum Graecorum Fragmenta. Vol. 3: Aeschylus* and *Vol. 4: Sophocles*. Göttingen. |
| *RE* | A. Pauly, G. Wissowa, and W. Kroll (eds.) (1893–1990). *Realencyclopädie der classischen Altertumswissenschaft*. Stuttgart and Munich. |
| RN | L. Rodríguez-Noriega Guillén (1996). *Epicarmo de Siracusa. Testimonios y Fragmentos. Edición crítica bilingüe*. Oviedo. |
| Rose | V. Rose (1886). *Aristotelis qui ferebantur librorum fragmenta*. Stuttgart. |
| Rzach | A. Rzach (1913). *Hesiodi Carmina*, repr. 1958. Stuttgart. |
| sch. | scholium |
| SM | Snell, B. and H. Maehler (1989). *Pindari carmina cum fragmentis. Pars II: Fragmenta. Indices*. Leipzig. |
| V | E.-M. Voigt (1971). *Sappho et Alcaeus: Fragmenta*. Amsterdam. |
| W | M. L. West (2003). *Greek Epic Fragments from the Seventh to the Fifth Centuries BC*. Cambridge, Mass. |
| W² | M. L. West (1989)². *Iambi et Elegi Graeci ante Alexandrum Cantati* (2 vols.), 2nd edn. Oxford. |
| *WD* | Hesiod, *Works and Days*. |
| Wehrli | F. Wehrli (1955). *Die Schule des Aristoteles: Texte und Kommentar. Vol. 8: Eudemos von Rhodos*. Basel. |
| West | M. L. West (2003). *Homeric Hymns, Homeric Apocrypha, Lives of Homer*. Cambridge, Mass. |

# *Introduction*

This study examines the reception of Hesiod's poetry and poetic authority in the fifth century BCE with particular focus on lyric poetry and drama. My aim is to explore how and to what effect major performative genres of this era invited their audiences to evoke the Hesiodic tradition. I have chosen to pursue this question through a series of case studies that demonstrate the richness and breadth of Hesiodic reception within a wide range of works composed for performance in diverse contexts. My analyses will expose the reader to varied, creative, and often critical engagements with the many aspects of the Hesiodic tradition that were culturally relevant to fifth-century audiences throughout the Greek world. This study does not aspire to offer an exhaustive survey of the topic or a taxonomy at the cost of nuance;[1] yet I hope that it contributes something new and useful to the ongoing exploration of Hesiodic reception in antiquity.[2]

Before delving into close readings, however, we need to understand what the Hesiodic tradition entailed for fifth-century audiences. Whether or not a poet named Hesiod ever existed is a question that cannot be answered and has no bearing upon the reception of the Hesiodic tradition.[3] For a fifth-century

---

[1] For a survey of Hesiodic reception in fifth-century literature, see Buzio 1938: chapter 4 and now Scully 2015: chapter 4 on the reception of (mainly) the *Theogony* in the archaic and classical eras. See also van der Kolf 1923 with focus on the Pindaric corpus, and Schwartz 1960: 549–608. On Solmsen 1949 regarding Hesiod and Aeschylus, see Chapter 4, p. 122.

[2] Musäus 2004 on the reception of Hesiod's Pandora from the Hellenistic scholars to Erasmus; Boys-Stones and Haubold 2010 on Hesiodic reception in Plato; Ziogas 2013 on Hesiodic reception in Ovid's *Metamorphoses*; Hunter 2014 on the ancient reception of the *Works and Days*; van Noorden 2015 on the Myth of the Races in Plato and later literature. See also Koning 2010a, who surveys Hesiodic reception in a broad literary corpus, including classical poetry and prose (chapters 1–6 and 9). Koning's study offers numerous excellent observations, not least with regard to Hesiodic reception in Parmenides, Empedocles, and Xenophanes, whose philosophical poetry is beyond the scope of my book. Koning, however, largely ignores the fragmentary part of the Hesiodic corpus and pays virtually no attention to the reception of Hesiodic poetry in drama. As for fifth-century lyric poetry, Koning's readings are limited in scope and, as I discuss in Chapter 1, somewhat problematic.

[3] Modern editors and commentators who discuss Hesiod as a historical figure include West 1966 and 1978, Colonna 1977: 9–12 and 37–38 with proposed dates, Marg 1984[2], Most 2006, Ercolani 2010.

audience, 'Hesiod' was the poetic figure that emerged from the self-referential statements of the narrator in the *Theogony* and the *Works and Days* and that was shaped further through related biographical fictions.[4] The 'autobiographical' passages within Hesiodic poetry present the narrator as a shepherd who was transformed into a poet by the Muses on Mount Helicon (*Th.* 22–34). It is in the context of this poetic initiation that the narrator reveals his name (Ἡσίοδον, *Th.* 22), which both ancient and modern readers have considered a *nomen loquens* although proposed etymologies and meanings vary.[5] In the *WD*, we learn that the speaker is the son of a man who migrated from Aeolian Cyme to Ascra, a wretched Boeotian town, in order to avoid poverty (*WD* 633–40).[6] We also hear that he had a dispute with his brother, Perses, which was overseen by corrupt local authorities (*WD* 27–41). Finally, while otherwise confident in his knowledge of human matters (*WD* 9–10), the narrator admits to having no expertise in sailing (*WD* 646–49) and recounts that his only trip on a boat was to Euboea, where he participated successfully at the poetic contest at the funerary games of Amphidamas in Chalcis (*WD* 650–62).[7] The account of his poetic victory, albeit brief, concludes with a reminder of his initiation by the Muses on Helicon (*WD* 658–59). This reference reaffirms the exceptional origins of his poetic skill and authority; it also establishes the continuity of the *persona loquens* and a temporal sequence between the two poems.[8]

The poetic *persona* that emerges only piecemeal in the *Theogony* and the *Works and Days* was developed into a fully fledged individual in the context of ancient biography. As recent scholarship has demonstrated, Hesiod's biographies are fictions based on material drawn from

Stoddard 2004: 1–33 offers a survey of biographical approaches towards the narrator of the *Theogony* and the *Works and Days*; cf. Koning 2010a: 31–32 with ample bibliography in n.24.

[4] Some of these biographical stories were circulating at least by the sixth century BCE. See Richardson 1981: 1–3; cf. Ibycus S151 *PMGF* with Steiner 2005: 353–54 and Chapter 1, pp. 49–51.

[5] On ancient etymologies of Ἡσίοδος, see T27–28 Most with Most 2006: xiv and Kivilo 2010: 9–10. The modern etymology of the name derives Ἡσίοδος from ἵημι and the root of αὐδή ("he who emits the voice"); the name is thus fitting for a poetic *persona* in the context of traditional oral poetry, as Nagy 1979: 296–97 and 1990a: 47–48, 58–59 has pointed out. See also Nagy 2009: 287–88 with a comparison between "Homer" and "Hesiod" as *nomina loquentia*; cf. Most 2006: xiv–xvi, who nonetheless prefers an historicizing approach.

[6] On the significance of the father's migration, see Martin 1992 and, differently, Clay 2003: 180–81.

[7] For an overview of the Hesiodic *persona*, see the seminal article by Griffith 1983a. See also Nagy 1990a: 36–82, esp. 44–61 and 63–82.

[8] Most 1993. Also establishing the continuity between the *Th.* and the *WD* is the revision of *Th.* 225–32 in *WD* 11–26.

the poetic corpus attributed to him with the addition of invented elements.[9] The (re)construction of Hesiod's family offers a good case study for the various degrees of invention that define ancient biographical traditions. The migration from Cyme, which became an intrinsic part of the poet's background in his biographies, is drawn directly from *WD* 633–40.[10] By the fifth century BCE, the poet's father was thought to be called Dios even though he remains anonymous in the *WD*; this name is almost certainly derived from a creative reading of *WD* 299 (Πέρση, δῖον γένος).[11] The figure of Hesiod's mother, by contrast, is based entirely on fabrication: since there is no information about her in Hesiodic poetry, the biographical tradition invented a woman called Πυκιμήδη. Judging by her *nomen loquens*, it appears that the woman who bore the wise poet was herself constructed as a wisdom figure.[12] At least one source grants Pycimede a divine pedigree: in *Cert.* 51–52 she is said to be Apollo's daughter, i.e. the product of a sexual union between a god and a mortal woman that evokes the core narrative of Hesiodic genealogical poetry (see below). By casting Hesiod as the grandson of Apollo, this tradition makes a strong statement about his skills, legitimacy, and authority as a poet. Moreover, the divine pedigree of Hesiod's mother indirectly confirms his superiority over Homer: even though both poets, who are envisioned as kinsmen in this biographical tradition, share a remote genealogical connection with Apollo through one parent, Hesiod has additional and more direct ties to the god of poetry. Already established by the fifth century BCE,[13] this genealogical link between Homer and Hesiod reconstructs them as roughly contemporary, thus probably encouraging the reception of their poetic corpora as complementary but also facilitating the fiction of their competition, to which I will return shortly. Evidently, the biographical traditions that transformed the narrative voice of Hesiodic poetry into a

---

[9] On biographical narratives about Hesiod, see extensively Kivilo 2010: 7–61 and 201–20, Lefkowitz 2012²: 6–13, and Nagy 2009; cf. Graziosi 2002: 168–80 and Stamatopoulou 2016 on the omission of the fraternal dispute in extant biographies.

[10] *Cert.* 2–6 and Tz. *Proleg. Hes. WD* 78–81 Colonna. Contrast Ephor. (*FGrH* 70 F 100), who accepts the migration story but assumes that it was motivated by a murder, not by an attempt to avoid poverty as the Hesiodic text claims.

[11] Proclus *Vit. Hom.* 4 West (= Hellanic. fr. 5b, Pherecyd. fr. 167 and Damastes fr. 11b Fowler).

[12] On her *nomen loquens*, see Kivilo 2010: 9.

[13] Proclus *Vit. Hom.* 4 West. On kinship and other personal ties in ancient biography, see the survey in Kivilo 2010: 212–13. According to Ephorus, Homer is born of the daughter of Hesiod's paternal uncle, and is thus one generation younger than Hesiod (*FGrH* 70 F 1, despite F 101b); cf. *Cert.* 51–53. For a different genealogy that envisions Homer and Hesiod as second cousins and traces their origins to Atlas, see Suda *s.v.* Ἡσίοδος.

full character use genealogy to establish poetic authority and make subtle
points about literary criticism.[14]

Hesiodic biography engages in literary criticism not only through
genealogy but also through its reception of *WD* 646–62, the account
of the poetic *agon* in Chalcis. The biographical tradition reconceptua-
lized this contest, which the Hesiodic narrator claims to have won, as a
contest between Homer and Hesiod. The *Works and Days* does not
reveal who competed against Hesiod; the fictional narrative that emerged
from *WD* 646–62, however, identified Homer as the other contestant,
possibly due to an interpretation of the Hesiodic passage as polemical
towards Homeric epic.[15] The story survives with some variation in post-
classical sources.[16] The most extensive account is embedded in the
second-century CE biographical compilation entitled *Certamen Homeri
et Hesiodi*, but can be traced back to the *Mouseion* by Alcidamas, a
fourth-century BCE sophist.[17] While Alcidamas used the story to support his own intellectual agenda, he almost certainly did not invent it,[18]
but worked with a preexisting narrative that was circulating in the fifth
century and perhaps as early as the sixth century BCE.[19] In addition to
the competition at Chalcis, the Hesiodic tradition preserves traces
of another poetic encounter of the two poets on the island of Delos.
In Hes. fr. 357 MW, the speaker, presumably Hesiod himself, recalls the

---

[14] Hesiod is also credited with poetic offspring: Stesichorus and Terpander. On Stesichorus, see Tz.
*Proleg. Hes. WD* 153–57 Colonna based on information found in the Aristotelian Constitution of
Orchomenus (fr. 565 Rose); cf. Philoch. *FGrH* 328 F 213 and Suda *s.v.* Στησίχορος. Cicero's *Rep.*
(2.20) seems to discuss whether Stesichorus was Hesiod's grandson (*nepos*); see Zetzel 1995: 176–77.
As for Terpander, according to the Suda *s.v.* other traditions make him the descendant of Homer.
See Kivilo 2010: 35 and 211–12, as well as Koning 2010a: 41.

[15] On the engagement with Homeric poetics in *WD* 646–62 and its immediate context, see Nagy
1982: 66 and 1990a, Rosen 1990 and 1996: 477–88 (whose discussion encompasses other passages
beyond *WD* 646–62), Graziosi 2002: 168–70, Tsagalis 2009: 152–55. I discuss anti-Homeric readings
of *Th.* 26–28 in Chapter 1, pp. 19–21.

[16] Koning 2010a: 259–66 offers a useful survey. Only Plutarch's version of the story in *Mor.* 153E–154C
deviates significantly from the other extant accounts of the story. Heldmann 1982: 53–57 has argued
that Plutarch's text reflects the original story of the poetic competition; see, however,
Stamatopoulou 2014: 534–48.

[17] On the biographical tradition surrounding the poetic competition between Homer and Hesiod,
see West 1967, Richardson 1981, Heldmann 1982, O'Sullivan 1992: 63–105, Rosen 1996: 473–77,
Graziosi 2002: 168–80, Kivilo 2010: 19–24, Koning 2010a: 245–68, Stamatopoulou 2014:
534–36.

[18] Contrast West 1967, who argued that the entire *Certamen* was Alcidamas' invention. Cf. O'Sullivan
1992: 63–105.

[19] Richardson 1981: 1–3 has suggested that the story is a product of the sympotic culture of the sixth
century BCE. Lamberton 1988: 6 also thinks that the story originates in the archaic period. On the
other hand, Graziosi 2002: 174–80 argues that the story reflects the rhapsodic culture of the fifth
century and its interaction with the sophists. On earlier scholarship, see Koning 2010a: 245 n.18.

time when he and Homer stitched together their song in the manner of rhapsodes and sang for Delian Apollo for the first time. The fragment replicates the first-person narrative style of *WD* 646–62, but it either disregards the narrator's commentary about his limited seafaring experience (*WD* 650–55) or defines itself as post-*WD*. The context of the performance is not explicitly defined, but it is very likely that Hes. fr. 357 MW recounts an *agon*.[20]

By the end of the fifth century BCE, therefore, Hesiod was established in people's imagination as a Boeotian man who was initiated to poetry by the Muses themselves and who won a poetic competition against Homer. As for his death, Thucydides (3.96.1) attests that there was already an established narrative that situated Hesiod's death in Locris and involved the misinterpretation of an oracle.[21] According to more extensive treatments of this biographical episode (including the one attributed to Alcidamas in *Cert.* 238–40),[22] Hesiod was thought to have been murdered in retaliation for the (actual or alleged) rape of a maiden. Discarded by the killers, the poet's body was miraculously recovered; furthermore, his murderers received harsh punishment, and the poet was buried in Locrian Oenoe.[23] Later, when the Orchomenians received refugees from Ascra after its destruction by the Thespians, Hesiod's bones were exhumed from Locris and reburied in Orchomenos. The Aristotelian *Constitution of Orchomenus* (Arist. fr. 565 Rose), the earliest attested source for the transference of Hesiod's bones, is said to have quoted an epigram that commemorated the poet's double burial.[24] While the attribution of this epigram to Pindar in later sources is probably invented,[25] the story about the poet's double burial may have been very old local lore and was possibly connected with hero-cult.[26]

---

[20] On Hes. fr. 357 MW, see Cingano 2009: 92 and, regarding the agonistic context, Martin 2000: 410–23 and Nagy 2010: 70–73; cf. Chapter 1, pp. 48–49. *Cert.* 54–55 report an *agon* between Homer and Hesiod in Aulis; this tradition stems from a (mis)interpretation of *WD* 651. If it was ever fully developed, it has left no other trace.

[21] This is a *topos* in ancient biography, as Kivilo 2010: 213–14 shows.

[22] It is quite possible that the story was already circulating by Alcidamas' time. The *Certamen* (240–47) also summarizes another version of the story, which is attributed to Eratosthenes.

[23] *Cert.* 215–54, Tz. *Proleg.* Hes. *WD* 163–54 Colonna; cf. Paus. 9.31.6, Plut. *Mor.* 162C–F, 969D–E, 984D, Pollux 5.42. Kivilo 2010: 25–35 surveys the stories of Hesiod's death.

[24] *Coll. proverb. cod. Vat. et Bodl.* (App. 4.92 ed. Gott. I p. 456) *s.v.* τὸ Ἡσιόδειον γῆρας.

[25] Tz. *Proleg.* Hes. *WD* 183–85 Colonna and the Suda (*s.v.* τὸ Ἡσιόδειον γῆρας). I am reluctant to follow Kivilo 2010: 25 in considering the epigram's attribution of the epigram to Pindar as evidence that the story of the double burial dates to the fifth century BCE.

[26] Brelich 1958: 320–22; cf. Nagy 1990a: 49–51, who suggests that rhapsodes organized around a poet's hero-cult, such as the Homeridae, may have contributed significantly to the expansion and the crystallization of certain poetic corpora. There is no evidence, however, that there ever was such a

Finally, there is evidence in fifth-century authors that there were already efforts to date Hesiod. For instance, Herodotus dates him jointly with Homer to no more than four hundred years prior to his own time (2.53.2). For the study of Hesiodic reception, however, the quest to pinpoint Hesiod in time is not as important as the relative dating of Homer and Hesiod. Aside from Herodotus' testimony, there are further indications that, in the classical era, the two poets were considered contemporaries. We have already discussed the circulation of stories about their agonistic encounter(s) as well as their alleged kinship. Judging by the sequence in which Hesiod and Homer are mentioned by Herodotus, Hippias, and Aristophanes, it is plausible to assume that, of the two contemporary poets, Hesiod was generally considered the older.[27] At any rate, the theory that the two poets were several generations apart seems to have emerged later, possibly in the third century BCE.[28]

## The Hesiodic Corpus

Just as the figure of Hesiod is a construct that evolved through time, the poetic corpus of dactylic hexameters attributed to him resulted from a gradual process of accumulation. An important catalyst in this process seems to have been the association of Hesiod's authority with certain themes and genres. The two poems that include the narrator's self-referential

---

guild of rhapsodes devoted to the performance of Hesiodic poetry. Furthermore, as Kivilo 2010: 35–36 points out, we cannot determine with certainty when Hesiod's cult was established, since there is no solid evidence for it before the Hellenistic times.

[27] Hdt. 2.53.2 and 4.32; cf. Hippias B 6 DK, Ar. *Av.* 1030–36, as well as Pl. *Ap.* 41a6-7 and *R.* 363a8–b1 and 377d4. Simonides is said to have viewed Hesiod as a predecessor of Homer (Sim. T91b Poltera), while the *Marmor Parium* (*FGrH* 239 A 28–29) considers Hesiod only a few decades older than Homer. On the other hand, according to Gellius *NA* 3.11.2, Xenophanes wrote that Homer was older than Hesiod. This is probably a later extrapolation from Xenophanes' poetry, esp. B 10 and 11.1 DK. Given Gellius' formulation (*in quis Philochorus et Xenophanes*), it is likely that this interpretation of Xenophanes' poetry belongs to Philochorus himself or a source of his, perhaps Heraclides of Pontus (third century BCE). On the relative dating of Homer and Hesiod, see also Graziosi 2002: 106–10 and Koning 2010a: 52–55.

[28] Tz. *Proleg.* Hes. *WD* 139–53 Colonna and Suda *s.v.* Ἡσίοδος; cf. Paus. 9.30.3 and T5–9 Most. In his commentary on the *Marmor Parium* (*FGrH* 239) and on Philochorus of Athens (*FGrH* 328), Jacoby suggests that the two poets were considered contemporaries until Heraclides of Pontus (third century BCE) argued that Homer was older in his Περὶ τῆς Ὁμήρου καὶ Ἡσιόδου ἡλικίας. This dating was subsequently adopted by Chamaeleon (cf. D.L. 5.92), Philoch. (*FGrH* 328 F 210), and others. Yet the old view of Homer and Hesiod as contemporaries persisted, as we can deduce from the continued popularity of the *Certamen* story attested by *P. Flinders Petrie* (third century BCE) and by the numerous treatments of the story during the Imperial Era (Plut. *Mor.* 153E–154A, 674A; Dio *Or.* 2.2–13; Philostr. *Her.* 43.7; Themist. *Or.* 30.348; Lib. *Decl.* 1.65; cf. the jibe in Lucian *VH* 2.22).

statements and thus present themselves as markedly "Hesiodic" belong to two different generic categories. The *Theogony* is formally a genealogical poem, enriched with embedded narratives that become extensive and consecutive after the emergence of Iapetus' progeny.[29] These narratives complement the poem's genealogies by integrating the various stages of the Succession Myth within the gradual population of the cosmos,[30] thus contributing significantly to the overall aetiological function of the poem. The *Works and Days*, on the other hand, can be described as a didactic epic in so far as the narrator has the explicit intent to instruct and admonish his audience, and this protreptic agenda lends structure and unity to the (admittedly varied) whole.[31]

The *WD* establishes Hesiod as an expert on human affairs and practices. Unambiguously didactic in his rhetoric and intent, the poet of the *WD* instructs his audience (internal and external) how to live their lives in a manner that guarantees their survival and pleases the gods, thus benefiting both the individual and the community.[32] While moral behavior is a central preoccupation of the *WD*, however, the poem also provides practical information and crucial advice about surviving in the natural world and exploiting its resources. In this context, the poem regularly incorporates elements of meteorology and astronomy, especially as it marks the appropriate time (καιρός) for specific agricultural and nautical activities by recourse to the movement of celestial bodies.[33] It is very likely that the inclusion of such information in the *WD*

---

[29] *Th.* 154–210, 386–403, 412–52, 459–506, 513–616, 617–725, 822–85; cf. the description of the underworld in *Th.* 726–819. See Schwenn 1934: 81–106, Philippson 1936: 7–42, West 1966: 31–34, Hamilton 1989: 23–40, Clay 2003: 13, and the overview in Pucci 2009. Unlike Hamilton 1989: 29–32, I do not consider the race of monsters in *Th.* 270–336 a digression and I read the brief proleptic accounts in *Th.* 289–94, 316–18, and 328–32 as an integral component of their respective genealogical entries.

[30] Ford 1996: 407.

[31] Clay 1994 offers an excellent discussion of the student–teacher constellation(s) in the *WD*. My (admittedly) minimalist definition of didactic poetry applies at least to the *WD*, to the *Chironos Hypothekai*, and to the *Megala Erga*, possibly also to the *Ornithomanteia* and the *Astronomia*. See West 1978: 3–25, who discusses the *WD*, the *Megala Erga*, the *Chironos Hypothekai*, and the *Astronomia* as "didactic poems" and contextualizes them within the broader category of wisdom poetry; cf., Most 2006: xlvi–xlvii, Ercolani 2010: 39–42, Scodel 2014, and Canevaro 2015: 123–42. On the *WD* as protreptic didactic through the lens of reception, see Hunter 2014 (esp. 40–122). However, 'didactic' as a generic category is not without problems, as Heath 1985 has shown in his discussion of both the *WD* and the *Theogony*. Broader discussions of didactic poetry as a genre and Hesiod's place in it can be found in Effe 1977: 1–26, Toohey 1996: 1–19, and Volk 2002: 34–43; cf. Fowler 2000 with useful observations even though his focus is on Roman didactic. For an alternative generic identification of archaic hexameter poems, including the *Th.* and the *WD*, see Pavese 1998: 85–86.

[32] See, e.g., Clay 2003: 31–48 and, much more extensively, Canevaro 2015.

[33] *WD* 383–87, 417–19, 479, 526–28, 563–67, 597–99, 609–10, 619–21, 663–65; cf. the effect of Sirius on men in *WD* 586–88. Signs in the *WD* are also drawn from the animal world: 448–51, 486–87, 524–25, 529–33, 568–69, 571–72, 582–84 (with a complementary detail from the world of plants), 679–81.

prompted the attribution of a poem entitled Ἀστρονομία (or Ἀστρολογία) to Hesiod. This hexameter poem was probably a catalogue of constellations enriched with details about their shape, location, and movement in the sky (frs. 288–90, 292–93 MW). Much like the *WD*, therefore, it divulged crucial information for the success of human activities such as agriculture and navigation, although it remains unknown whether the *Astronomia* made this point explicitly. It is possible – though not entirely certain – that this poem also included mythological information and aetiologies connected with the constellations, hence the inclusion of fr. 291 MW among its fragments.[34]

The didactic corpus attributed to Hesiod also encompassed a poem entitled Ὀρνιθομαντεία (*Bird Divination*) and another identified as Μεγάλα Ἔργα (*GW*). The *Ornithomanteia* must have been preoccupied with the interpretation of bird omens. The concluding lines of the *WD* (826–28) point out the importance of "discerning birds of omen" (ὄρνιθας κρίνων, *WD* 828) in the context of achieving happiness. It is possible that the *Ornithomanteia* was performed as a sequel to the *WD* at least until it was deemed spurious (cf. sch. Hes. *WD* 828a).[35] As for the *Megala Erga* (*GW*), very little is known.[36] The title suggests that the poem was similar to the *Works and Days* in content and form, but longer. Perhaps it was an expanded version of the *WD* or even an inclusive poem that encompassed other didactic poems of the Hesiodic corpus, possibly the *WD*, the *Ornithomanteia*, and the *Chironos Hypothekai*.[37]

---

[34] Cingano 2009: 129–30 entertains the possibility that this was not an independent poem but a section in an expanded version of the *WD*.

[35] Cf. the exhortation in *WD* 800–01. On the *Ornithomanteia* as the sequel of the *WD* and on its athetesis by Apollonius of Rhodes, see Schwartz 1960: 245–46, and Cingano 2009: 103 (cf. 130 on *WD* 828 as a transition to the *Ornithomanteia*). West 1966: 354–65 was rather skeptical about how much weight Apollonius' doubts could carry. The connection between Hesiod and μαντικὴ τέχνη in Paus. 9.31.5 may be a reference to the *Ornithomanteia* but also the *Melampodia*; see already Marckscheffel 1840: 89. No Hesiodic fragments can be identified as parts of the *Ornithomanteia* securely, although fr. 312 MW and especially fr. 355 MW may belong to it.

[36] Schwartz 1960: 245–46 and Cingano 2009: 129. Hes. fr. 286 MW offers a two-line formulation of the so-called *lex talionis*. Aristotle cites the second line and attributes it to Rhadamanthys (*EN* 1132b25); despite Cingano 2009: 129, however, it does not necessarily follow that Rhadamanthys featured as a didactic voice in the Hesiodic *GW*. Another fragment explicitly attributed to the *GW* traces the origins of silver to Ge herself (Hes. fr. 287 MW); cf. *Th.* 161–62 and the *Idaioi Dactyloi*, a poorly attested poem attributed to Hesiod that included origin stories pertaining to metallurgy (Hes. fr. 282 MW).

[37] Marckscheffel 1840: 89 and 188–89. The association of Hesiod with practical expertise underlies the attribution of a poem on preserved foods (Περὶ ταρίχων) to him. According to the only extant testimony for this poem (Ath. *Deipn.* 3.116b), the attribution is false; nonetheless, it reflects the prestige and legitimacy associated with Hesiodic authorship.

In the *Chironos Hypothekai,* Chiron, the legendary centaur and teacher of heroes par excellence, offers his wise teachings to young Achilles in the form of precepts (Hes. fr. 283 MW).[38] It is not certain that the poem included a Hesiodic sphragis; the fact that it was invested with Hesiodic authorship may be due mainly to the authoritative status of Hesiodic didactic. I discuss the *Chironos Hypothekai* extensively in Chapter 3, but here I want to draw attention to some additional factors that probably encouraged and solidified the association of this poem with Hesiod. To begin with, the *WD* and the *Chironos Hypothekai* do not simply belong to the same genre but, in fact, they can be viewed as complementary. The *WD* is firmly rooted in the poet's here and now, and the instructions aim at securing survival in the harsh world of the Iron Age. The *Chironos Hypothekai,* on the other hand, situates itself in the Heroic Age: the didactic voice belongs to a hybrid creature that no longer exists (Hes. fr. 283 MW; cf. Pi. *P.*6.19–27) and the precepts are meant to meet the needs of none other than Achilles. According to sch. Pi. *P.*6.22, the first three lines of the poem underlined the necessity for piety. Admittedly, in terms of content, this passage could have been part of the *WD,* but one would expect that, overall, the precepts of *Chironos Hypothekai* privileged values and ideals that would befit a heroic figure rather than an ordinary man laboring in the fields. At least by the time of Pindar's *Pythian* 6, the *Chironos Hypothekai* was circulating and consumed as part of the education of aristocratic men (see Chapter 3). One may argue, therefore, that the *Chironos Hypothekai* not only complemented the *WD* but also offered an excellent alternative to it in contexts that called for authoritative didactic but promoted aggressively the values of the aristocratic elite. It is worth noting that, as a poem featuring Chiron and Achilles, the *Chironos Hypothekai* also complements other parts of the Hesiodic corpus in which the Heroic Age is viewed through generic frames that are distinct from the grand-scale epic about war and *nostos* associated with the Homeric corpus. *Th.* 1006-07 recounts Achilles' birth (cf. *Cat.* frs. 98–100 H/211-13 MW), while the *Catalogue of Women* justifies his absence from the long list of Helen's suitors by pointing out that at the time he was still a child and under the tutelage of Chiron on Mount Pelion (Hes. fr. 110/204.87–92). The *Chironos Hypothekai,* then, explores an aspect of Achilles' life that the *Catalogue* only mentions in passing, and enriches the multifaceted Hesiodic perspective on the heroic era.

[38] The poem is included in Pausanias' list of Hesiodic works (παραινέσεις τε Χείρωνος ἐπὶ διδασκαλίᾳ δὴ τῇ Ἀχιλλέως, 9.31.5); cf. sch. Pi. *P.*6.22, Phryn. *Eclog.* p. 91 Lobeck, and esp. Quintilian *Inst.*1.1.15, according to which Aristophanes of Byzantium was the first to deny the poem's Hesiodic authorship. On *Chironos Hypothekai,* see Friedländer 1913: 571–72, Schwartz 1960: 228–44, and, more recently, Cingano 2009: 128–29. See also Chapter 3, pp. 114–15.

In addition to this cluster of didactic poems, there is another set of poems
that was invested with Hesiodic authorship in antiquity. Focusing exclusively on the mythical past, this group relates genealogical information
and stories pertaining to the divine realm and to the successive generations
of the heroic race. As mentioned earlier, the *Theogony* is a combination of
genealogical catalogues and narratives that reflects the gradual population of
the cosmos and the establishment of Zeus's rule. This poem was complemented by the *Ehoiai* or *Catalogue of Women* (*Cat.*),[39] a longer genealogical
poem that was either conceptualized from the beginning as the continuation of the *Theogony*, or was attached to it as a sequel at some later point
(*Th.* 1021–22 = *Cat.* fr. 1.1–2).[40] The *Catalogue* integrates and organizes
both chronologically and geographically a massive pool of traditional
genealogical information pertaining to the heroes, i.e. mortals born of
gods and mortal women, as well as their offspring.[41] The fundamental
structure of the poem is matrilinear and it is possible that the *Catalogue*
evolved partly from poetic aretalogies in honor of mythical women. In its
current form, however, the poem often uses the genealogical frame to
celebrate stories about men rather than women.[42] Through its interconnected genealogical catalogues,[43] this poem traces the various generations
of the heroic race from Deucalion, son of Prometheus, and his progeny
until the wooing of Helen (Hes. frs. 104–110.95/196–204.95) and the
impending Trojan War, a conflict that served Zeus's plan to exterminate
the heroes (Hes. fr. 110/204.96–123).[44] The genealogical catalogues

---

[39] According to the current scholarly consensus, the two titles in all their variations correspond to the
same poem, an idea first proposed by Leo 1894; see Cohen 1983: 111–13, Hirschberger 2004: 26 n.35
and 27 n.36. For a survey of the scholarship on this issue, see Hirschberger 2004: 26–30.

[40] See West 1966: 48–49 and 437, 1985a: 2–3, and Arrighetti 1998: 447–49. On the complementarity of
the two poems, see, e.g., Clay 2003: 162–67. Cingano 2009: 107 points out that the *Th.*, the *Cat.*,
and the *WD* were circulating widely as a set triad until the fourth century CE.

[41] On the symbolic value and the sociopolitical function of Hesiodic genealogical poetry, see
Chapters 2 (pp. 94–96) and 4 (pp. 170–78).

[42] On the generic archaeology of the Hesiodic *Catalogue*, see Rutherford 2000: 89–96; cf. 86 on
embedded male stories. Skempis 2011: 254–58 offers an illuminating juxtaposition between male
heroic epic and *ehoie*-poetry in terms of their themes and motifs; we should not overlook, however,
that Hesiodic genealogical poetry is infused with elements from heroic epic.

[43] On the ἢ οἴη formula and its function in the structure of Hesiodic genealogical poetry, see West
1985a: 167, Rutherford 2000: 83–85, Hirschberger 2004: 30–31, and Nasta 2006: 59–64.

[44] Cf. *WD* 161–68. The end of the Heroic Age in the *Cat.* also involves changes in the natural order of the
world (Hes. fr. 110/204.124–80). On the various visions regarding the past of humankind in the Hesiodic
corpus and the challenges involved in any effort to integrate them, see, e.g., Schmitt 1975, Koenen 1994,
Mayer 1996, Arrighetti 1998: 449–50 and 458–60, Cerutti 1998, Most 1998, and Clay 2005; cf. González
2010: 382–91. Even though it is not genealogical, the catalogue of Helen's suitors is consistent with core
elements and themes of the *Catalogue* as is shown by, e.g., Heilinger 1983, West 1985a: 114–19 and, more
recently, Cingano 2005. For a comparative study of the catalogue of ships in *Il.* 2 and the catalogue of

that comprise the five books of the *Catalogue* are occasionally enriched with non-genealogical catalogues: we find a catalogue of Helen's suitors in the final book (frs. 104–110.95/196–204.95) and a geographic catalogue of peoples embedded in the chase of the Harpyes by the Boreades, a passage also known as the Hesiodic Γῆς Περίοδος (Hes. frs. 62–64 H / 150–51 MW, cf. 152–53 MW).[45] The extant fragments also reveal longer narratives embedded in the genealogies, such as the story of Mestra (Hes. fr. 37/43a), of Salmoneus and Tyro (Hes. frs. 20–24 H / 30–32 MW), as well as of Atalanta and her race against Hippomenes (Hes. frs. *2–*4 H / 72–76 MW).[46] Another group of such narratives centers on events from Heracles' life and thus complements the substantial treatment of his birth (Hes. fr. 91/195.8–63).[47]

Besides the *Ehoiai* or *Catalogue of Women*, there is evidence that the Hesiodic corpus encompassed another genealogical poem that was entitled *Megalai Ehoiai (ME)*.[48] Judging by its title, this poem was longer than the *Catalogue* but included the same type of genealogical material; it also employed a core structural element of the *Catalogue*, namely the *ehoie*-formula.[49] Relatively few fragments can be ascribed to the *ME* with confidence,[50] and scholars have debated whether the poem was an expanded version of the *Catalogue of Women* or a different genealogical poem altogether.[51] In his 2005 piece on the *ME*, D'Alessio makes a

[45] Helen's suitors in the *Cat.*, see Cohen 1983: 437–40 and esp. Ziogas 2013: 21–27; cf. Nagy 1999[2]: 219–20 on Hes. fr. 110/204 as a convergence point between the Hesiodic and the Homeric tradition. Regarding the conclusion of the *Catalogue*, see esp. Clay 2003: 168–74 and 2005, as well as González 2010.

[45] Rutherford 2000: 85. On the titles applied to specific sections of Hesiodic genealogical poetry (Γῆς Περίοδος, Ἐπιθαλάμιον εἰς Πηλέα καὶ Θέτιν, Λευκιππίδων Κατάλογος), see Hirschberger 2004: 30.

[46] Hirschberger 2004: 458 is in doubt whether the extant Atalanta-*ehoie* belongs to the *Catalogue* or to the *ME*. D'Alessio 2005c, however, shows that the Atalanta-*ehoie* should be included in the *Catalogue*.

[47] Hes. fr. 16/25.20–33 (death and apotheosis of Heracles), 17/26.31–37 (sack of Oechalia), 25–26c/ 33–36 (sack of Pylos), 37.61–65/43a.85–89 (sack of Cos with a brief mention of the Gigantomachy), 72/165.8–13 (sack of Troy), 89/190.11–13 (mention of the labors), and 93/229 (Heracles and Iole; Heracles' apotheosis).

[48] Unlike the *Catalogue*, the *ME* is not always attributed to Hesiod in our sources. D'Alessio 2005a: 177–78 discusses Philodemus' distinction between Hesiod, the poet of the *Ehoiai*, and "the one who authored the *Great Ehoiai*" (ὁ τὰ]ς μεγάλας Ἡ[οίας ἀν]αγράψας, *De Piet.*, *P. Herc.* col. 263.7078–80 Obbink = Hes. fr. 363A.12–14 MW). Here Philodemus may be reiterating the view of Apollodorus of Athens (second century BCE).

[49] On the *ehoie*-formula, see above, n. 43.

[50] Hes. frs. 246–62 MW. However, as Cohen 1986 and D'Alessio 2005a: 205 point out, the attribution of fragments to the *ME* by Merkelbach and West is not without problems. For problematic attributions in Hirschberger's edition, see D'Alessio 2005c.

[51] On the *ME* as an expanded version of the *Cat.*, see Casanova 1979a (summarized in 192–93), and Rutherford (2000): 88; cf. already Wilamowitz 1905: 123–24. For Cohen 1986, the *Cat./Ehoiai* and the *ME* were identical; cf. Schwartz 1960: 22–23. On the other hand, both Hirschberger 2004 and D'Alessio 2005a consider the *ME* and the *Cat.* distinct poems; cf. Casanova 1979b and tentatively

persuasive case in favor of considering the *ME* and the *Catalogue* separate
and independent genealogical poems.[52] D'Alessio demonstrates that there
are substantial differences between the *Cat.* and the *ME* in terms of
content. Furthermore, he identifies two key problems in the theory that
the *ME* was an expanded version of the *Cat.*: not only would the creation
of such an extended poem entail large-scale tampering with the structure
of the *Cat.*, but it also would require adding material that was at times
incompatible with the preexisting content of the *Cat.*

Heracles appears to be a particularly important figure in the non-
didactic part of the Hesiodic corpus. The *Theogony* highlights Heracles'
role as a monster-slayer and as an agent of Zeus's order (*Th.* 289–94,
314–18, 328–32; cf. 526–32 and 950–55). In the *Catalogue*, on the other
hand, we find not only a rather extensive treatment of his birth in the *ehoie*
of Alcmene (fr. 91/195.8–63) but also references to his life and death,
especially to the acts of violence he committed after the completion of
the labors.[53] Along the same lines, several extant fragments of the *ME* are
preoccupied with the hero's life and progeny.[54] In addition, the manuscript tradition has preserved the *Shield of Heracles*, a rhapsodic elaboration
of the Alcmene-*ehoie* that recounted Heracles' violent encounter with
Cycnus and his father Ares at Pagasae.[55] It is likely that the preoccupation
with Heracles in Hesiodic genealogical poetry prompted the inclusion of
the *Wedding of Ceyx* (frs. 263–68 MW) and of the *Aegimius* (frs. 294–301
MW) in the Hesiodic corpus, since these hexameter poems center on two
sequential episodes of Heracles' life.[56] This intense engagement with
Heracles, however, should be contextualized within the broader interest
of genealogical and narrative Hesiodic poetry in the heroic world that
preceded the Trojan Expedition.[57] It is in this context that we can best

---

West 1985a: 167. Hirschberger 2004: 26–29 offers a thorough overview of the rich scholarship on
this issue.

[52] D'Alessio 2005a: 186–88.

[53] For an excellent study of Heracles in the *Catalogue of Women*, see Haubold 2005.

[54] A survey of fragments regarding Heracles and his descendants can be found in D'Alessio 2005a:
188–201, who concludes that Heracles and the Heraclidae are much more central in the *ME* than in
the *Catalogue*; for this reason, he suggests that the *ME* demonstrates pro-Laconian bias.

[55] On the *Shield*, see Russo 1965², Janko 1986, Martin 2005, Bing 2012, as well as Stamatopoulou 2013
and in press.

[56] The *Aegimius* was attributed to Hesiod or Cercops. Cingano 2009: 123–25 suggests that the
uncertain attribution may stem from the circulation of two different poems under the title
*Aegimius*. See also Robertson 1980, who argues that the poem included a *katabasis* of Heracles.
On potential allusions to the *Wedding of Ceyx* in Pindaric and Bacchylidean poetry, see
D'Alessio 2005b: 233 n.65.

[57] For example, the Hesiodic corpus incorporates the expedition of the Argonauts in *Cat.* 62–65 H /
150–57 MW, *ME* 14–15 H /253–56 MW, and, fr. 241 MW. The two sagas (Heracles and Argonauts)

appreciate the Hesiodic attribution of the *Katabasis of Peirithous*[58] and of the *Melampodia*.[59]

When considered as a group, therefore, the poems of the Hesiodic corpus that are not overtly didactic survey the cosmic history from the emergence of the first primordial beings to the establishment of Zeus's rule and from the first to the last generation of the heroic race. This survey is carried out through genealogical catalogues, yet some select episodes within the cosmic timeline have been isolated and developed either as embedded narratives or as individual poems. When concerned with mortals, these narratives tend to focus on heroes who preceded those who fought at Troy and Thebes (e.g. Heracles), thus reconstructing and exploring the world of the early Heroic Age.[60] Finally, it is fair to say that the two subsets of Hesiodic poetry, the non-didactic and the didactic, have complementary scopes: the former spans from the beginnings of the cosmos to the end of the Heroic Age, while the latter – with the exception of the *Chironos Hypothekai* – focuses on life in the post-heroic Iron Age.

## Hesiodic Poetry in the Fifth Century BCE

The fundamental working assumption of my project is that, by the beginning of the fifth century BCE, the Hesiodic corpus (or at least its major components)[61] was circulating on a Panhellenic level in a fairly stable form, which we can access through the extant Hesiodic text with reasonable confidence. In the predominantly oral culture of archaic Greece, it is highly unlikely that these poems circulated without

---

intersected; see, e.g., fr. 263 MW from the *Wedding of Ceyx* and tentatively D'Alessio 2005a: 195–200 on the *ME*.

[58] Cingano 2009: 126–28.

[59] The *Melampodia* was a genealogical poem featuring seers but it integrated within its genealogical frame an *agon* between Calchas and Mopsus (Hes. fr. 278 MW). Cf. the riddles in the sympotic setting of the *Wedding of Ceyx* (frs. 266–67 MW) and in the *agon* between Homer and Hesiod (*Cert.* 75–175). Cingano 2009: 123 suggests that this or a similar *agon* of seers was the model for the contest between Homer and Hesiod; for a more nuanced approach, see Collins 2004: 176–202. On the seers featured in the *Melampodia*, see Löffler 1963. I refrain from discussing here the obscure *Dirge for Batrachus* (Suda *s.v.* Ἡσίοδος), which is possibly a construct of the biographical tradition, and the equally obscure *Kaminos* or *Kerameis*, which Pollux (10.85) attributes to Hesiod but other sources to Homer (see the *testimonia* in Merkelbach and West 1967: 155).

[60] The relationship between Homeric and Hesiodic poetry is beyond the scope of this introduction. On the complementarity of the two poetic corpora, see the overview in Graziosi and Haubold 2005: 27–43.

[61] Namely the *Theogony*, the *WD*, the *Shield of Heracles*, and the two longer genealogical poems of the Hesiodic corpus (the *Catalogue of Women* and the *ME*).

variation, even if one were to trace their origin back to one individual poet.[62] Given the formulaic language of the Hesiodic corpus – and since the historicity of 'Hesiod' cannot be proven – we have to allow for the possibility that the poems invested with Hesiodic authorship evolved through several generations of oral poets. In fact, as Nagy has suggested, even the poetic *persona* identified as 'Hesiod' as well as the 'autobiographical' accounts embedded in Hesiodic poetry may be understood as a reflex of a tradition.[63] With their composition-in-performance, oral poets constantly reshaped, enriched, and varied the poetic (multi-)text as they tailored Hesiodic poetry to diverse audiences and occasions, including local and Panhellenic festivals, as well as more private, sympotic settings.[64] As a result, we may imagine that, at its earlier stages, the poetic tradition associated with Hesiod was in a flux, constantly evolving and changing, while preserving older elements both in content and in form.

Assuming it existed, this dynamic phase was probably over by the end of the sixth century BCE although different Hesiodic poems must have become fixed at different times.[65] Nagy has proposed that regular

---

[62] West 1966: 47–49 and 1978: 58–61, who maintains that Hesiod was one of the first Greek poets to commit his poetry to writing; cf. Solmsen 1982, Most 1993, Rossi 1997: 22, and Aloni 2008. Yet, as Nagy 1990a: 38–39 suggests, all the evidence (including *Th.* 22–34) points to a predominantly oral circulation of Hesiodic poetry. Furthermore, there is no evidence for the proliferation of written copies until the late archaic period; see, e.g., Pavese 1998: 72–73.

[63] Nagy 1990a: 36–82, and, from a different perspective, Judet de la Combe 1993: 38–39. Doherty's (2006) suggestion that the *Catalogue of Women* is informed by women's traditions is not unlikely but remains unverifiable.

[64] Hesiodic poems would have been performed in their entirety or partially; furthermore, as the *Shield of Heracles* demonstrates, genealogical entries could function as the introduction of small-scale narrative epics. Regarding the competitive performance of genealogical Hesiodic poetry at festivals, see Aloni 2008: 62–63. On performance in symposia, see Aloni 2008: 66–74 and 2010 for the *WD*, and Irwin 2005 for the *Catalogue*; cf. Hunter 2014: 123–66. See also Koning 2010a: 46–51, who adds education among the contexts in which Hesiodic poetry was consumed. On the performance of the *Catalogue* in the context of heroine cult, see Rutherford 2000: 88; cf. Tsagalis 2009: 171 with legitimate objections.

[65] This is not to say that the text became entirely rigid and fixed; see, e.g., Ercolani 2001. The *Theogony* and the *WD* are generally dated somewhere between the mid-eighth and the mid-seventh centuries BCE; see West 1966: 40, Marg 1984²: 6, Most 2006: xxv, and Ercolani 2010: 34–38. The extant form of the *Catalogue* is generally assumed to be later: Schwartz 1960: 489–91, Stiewe 1962: 291–99 and 1963: 27–29, West 1985a: 130–37, Fowler 1998: 1, Ormand 2014, and Irwin 2005 date the poem to the sixth century BCE. For a survey of the scholarship on the date of the *Catalogue*, see Hirschberger 2004: 45–51, who suggests a slightly earlier date (630–590 BCE). Regarding the *Shield*, Janko 1986 dates the poem to the first quarter of the sixth century BCE. As for the *ME*, D'Alessio 2005a: 200–01 suggests that the pro-Laconian and Boeotian bias he traces in some fragments may reflect Spartan and Boeotian politics in the late sixth century BCE. More recently, Janko 2012: 30, 41–43 has argued on the basis of language and content that the *Catalogue* predates the extant version of the *Theogony* and the *WD*.

performance in competitions hosted at Panhellenic festivals was a primary driving force for the stabilization of Hesiodic as well as Homeric
poetry.[66] It is possible that writing contributed to the crystallization of
the Hesiodic text towards the end of the archaic era. A vase painting
from the beginning of the fifth century BCE suggests that copies of
Hesiodic poetry were already in circulation at least in the context of
education.[67] The crystallization of the Hesiodic corpus may have taken
place in sixth-century Athens, but there is no reliable evidence for a
Peisistratean recension.[68] The question of provenance is particularly
challenging in the case of the longer genealogical poems. In its extant
version, the *Catalogue of Women* reflects a deliberate effort to amass,
integrate, and organize preexisting local traditions into a consistent
whole with Panhellenic aspirations. Where was this meticulously structured text put together? Depending on what sociopolitical and geographic biases scholars have traced in the *Catalogue*, its production has
been located in Athens, in north-central Greece, or Asia Minor.[69] Even
if the genealogical poems attributed to Hesiod do, in fact, reflect the
politics of specific communities at specific points in their history, I have
found no evidence that these particularities were underscored or even
acknowledged in the poetic reception of the Hesiodic corpus around the
Greek world. Much like the *Theogony* and the *WD*, therefore, Hesiodic

[66] Nagy 1990a: 36–82.

[67] Berlin 2322 = Daremberg-Saglio, fig. 2600. On this *kyathos*, a boy is reading a book-roll and on its
cylinder, which is lying nearby, we read ΧΙΡΩΝΕΙΑ, possibly an alternative title to the *Chironos
Hypothekai*. See Birt 1907: 148, Beazley 1948: 337, who dates the *kyathos* to 490 BCE or a little
earlier, and Schwartz 1960: 232.

[68] The only extant source is Hereas *FGrH* 486 F1 with Piccirilli 1975: 61–62. Since Hereas was
Megarian, the accusation that Peisistratus tampered with the Hesiodic text (fr. 298 MW) may
simply be anti-Athenian fabrication. Proponents of a Peisistratean recension include Evelyn-White
1924, Buzio 1938: 33–34 and 40, and Merkelbach 1952: 40–41. For arguments against the
Peisistratean recension, see Sinclair 1927, Schwartz 1960: 494–95, and West 1966: 50 n.1 with
more bibliography. The hypothesis of a sixth-century edition of Hesiodic poetry under the auspices
of Peisistratus has been fueled by the supposed Peisistratean redaction of Homeric poetry, yet that
too is a debated issue. See Koning 2010a: 47 n.98 with bibliography.

[69] In favor of Athens, see Schwartz 1960: 489–91 and esp. West 1985a: 164–71 with arguments based
on both content and language; cf. also Ormand 2014. Based on the prominence of the
Deucalionids, on the other hand, Fowler 1988 has suggested that the poet who produced the
extant version of the *Catalogue* was Thessalian and that the poem reflects the politics surrounding
the Delphic Amphictyony in the early sixth century BCE; cf. D'Alessio 2005c. Rutherford 2005:
114–17 offers a balanced discussion of the two positions and attempts to integrate them.
Hirschberger 2004: 49–50 accepts Fowler's hypothesis of an Aeolian poet but, less persuasively,
locates him in Asia Minor (eastern Aeolis). The *Shield* too reflects an interest in the politics of the
Delphic Amphictyony in the early sixth century BCE, albeit from a Theban perspective as Janko
1986 has demonstrated.

genealogical poetry appears to have been perceived and received as Panhellenic in scope and orientation.[70]

By the time of Xenophanes and Heraclitus, there is explicit evidence that Hesiodic poetry was circulating on a Panhellenic scale.[71] Performances continued throughout the classical period,[72] although, assuming that the corpus had reached a relatively fixed form by then, rhapsodes would recite rather than engage in composition-in-performance. At the same time, with the expansion of the book culture, the Hesiodic text was being consumed not only through copies of entire works but also through anthologies of excerpts (e.g. Hippias B 6 DK).[73] Given the wide circulation and authoritative status of the Hesiodic tradition, therefore, it is hardly surprising that fifth-century lyric and drama engaged intensely with it.[74]

---

[70] Cf. Rutherford 2005.
[71] See Xenoph. B 11 DK (cf. also B 12–16) as well as Heraclit. B 40 and 57 DK.
[72] Evidence for the performance of Hesiod in public festivals in the classical era can be found in Pl. *Ion* 531a–32a and *Lg.* 658d; cf. the public performance mentioned in Isoc. *Panath.* 18 and 33.
[73] Ford 2002: 194–97 and 2010; cf. Canevaro 2015: 17–21. For more on this topic, see Chapter 5, pp. 185–87.
[74] For a summary of Chapters 1–5, see Conclusion.

CHAPTER I

# Hesiod and the Poetics of Lyric

Any attempt to understand Hesiodic poetics must begin with the proem of the *Theogony* (1–115), where we find the most extensive exploration of poetic creativity and performance in the entire Hesiodic corpus. The *Theogony* defines good poetry as a mental diversion from the miseries of everyday life, a function best served when the subject matter pertains to the realm of the divine and/or the distant mythological past. The idea is introduced in *Th.* 53–62, as the birth of the Muses from Zeus and Mnemosyne establishes a genealogical connection that acknowledges the importance of memory in the composition and performance of oral poetry, but also evokes the cognitive process involved and underscores its commemorative aspect.[1] And yet, at the same time, the offspring of Memory are said to have been born "as forgetfulness of evils and as respite from worries" (λησμοσύνην τε κακῶν ἄμπαυμά τε μερμηράων, *Th.* 55). The poem develops this idea further in its portrayal of the ideal human poet in *Th.* 94–103. According to this passage, a successful poet is endowed by the Muses and Apollo with the gift to distract and soothe his human audience with his performance.[2] The language that describes the effect of poetry upon its audience here reiterates the tension between remembering and forgetting as well as the preoccupation with anxiety and its temporary relief expressed in *Th.* 53–62:[3]

> ... γλυκερή οἱ ἀπὸ στόματος ῥέει αὐδή.
> εἰ γάρ τις καὶ πένθος ἔχων νεοκηδέι θυμῷ
> ἄζηται κραδίην ἀκαχήμενος, αὐτὰρ ἀοιδὸς
> Μουσάων θεράπων κλεῖα προτέρων ἀνθρώπων

---

[1] Pucci 1977: 22–25, Clay 2003: 68–70, Stoddard 2003: 11–12; on the discourse of remembrance, see also Bakker 2002: 67–73. On the poetics of diversion, see Pucci 1977: 17–19 and, in response, Ferrari 1988: 55–56.
[2] On the parallel between divinely favored poets and kings in *Th.* 80–103, see, e.g., Duban 1980, Thalmann 1984: 139–43, Clay 2003: 69–70, Stoddard 2003, Blößner 2005.
[3] On the difficult syntax of this passage, see Rijksbaron 2009: 257–59.

ὑμνήσει μάκαράς τε θεούς οἳ Ὄλυμπον ἔχουσιν,
αἶψ' ὅ γε δυσφροσυνέων ἐπιλήθεται οὐδέ τι κηδέων
μέμνηται· ταχέως δὲ παρέτραπε δῶρα θεάων.
(Hesiod, Theogony 97–103)

... sweet flows the voice from his mouth. For, even if someone who has sorrow in his newly afflicted spirit is parched in his heart with grief, but if then a poet, the attendant of the Muses, sings of the glorious deeds of earlier men and of the blessed gods who inhabit Olympus, immediately this man forgets his anxieties and does not remember his worries at all. For quickly the gifts of the gods divert his mind (παρέτραπε).

Unsurprisingly, escapist poetry is not concerned with its audience's 'here and now' but focuses instead on gods and heroes. The Hesiodic text is vague, but *Th.* 100–01 probably encompasses not only heroic epic and hymnic poetry, as Clay has suggested,[4] but also theogonic and genealogical poems, as well as combinations of genealogical and heroic poetry, such as the Hesiodic *Shield of Heracles*.[5]

The lyric poets Pindar and Bacchylides are certainly familiar with the idea of poetry as diversion, as their poems occasionally envision their own soothing effect.[6] Yet the main focus of scholars who have studied the contribution of Hesiodic ideas regarding poets and poetry to fifth-century lyric has been on two other, interconnected elements: the ideal of a close relationship between the poet and the Muses, and Hesiod's claim to the truth. Early in the proem of the *Theogony*, the first-person voice, who identifies himself as 'Hesiod' (*Th.* 22), recounts the incident that transformed him from a shepherd into a poet, namely his encounter with the Muses on Helicon (*Th.* 22–34). After a brief initial utterance, the Muses gave Hesiod a staff of laurel (*Th.* 30–31) and breathed into him a divine voice (αὐδὴν / θέσπιν, *Th.* 31–32) that could divulge "what will be and was before," i.e. what lies outside the immediate experience and limited knowledge of a mortal man (*Th.* 31–32).[7] The Muses then

---

[4] Clay 2003: 70; cf. Marg 1970: 101. Contrast West 1966: 188.

[5] The formulation of *Th.* 101 (ὑμνήσει μάκαράς τε θεούς) echoes the Muses' mandate to Hesiod in *Th.* 33 (ὑμνεῖν μακάρων γένος). Nagy 1990a: 61.

[6] Ba. *Ode* 5.6–7 in a context that engages more broadly with the proem to the *Theogony* (see below), *Dith.* 19/5.35–36, Pi. *N.*1.1–5, fr. 124a–b SM; cf. *P.*1.5–12.

[7] Clay 1988: 330 with n.31, who takes the formula to mean exclusively eternal matters that pertain to the divine, and juxtaposes *Th.* 32 with *Th.* 38 (song of the Muses) as well as *Il.* 1.70 (Calchas' oracular power); cf. West 1966: 166 and Arrighetti 1998: 316–17. The Muses give Hesiod the capacity to sing of the past and the future (*Th.* 32), yet the latter is absent from the *Theogony*, as Lucian's fictional character complains in *Hesiodus* 1–3. Note, moreover, that the Muses are explicitly evoked as the divine source of the *Theogony* in *Th.* 114–15 (ταῦτά μοι ἔσπετε Μοῦσαι ... / καὶ εἴπαθ' ὅτι πρῶτον

ordered Hesiod to sing of the immortals, starting and ending with the goddesses themselves (*Th.* 33–34).[8] Though brief, this account succeeds at establishing the poetic authority of the Hesiodic voice.

The words with which the Muses address Hesiod before they bestow their material and immaterial gifts upon him are central to Hesiodic poetics:

> ποιμένες ἄγραυλοι, κάκ' ἐλέγχεα, γαστέρες οἶον,
> ἴδμεν ψεύδεα πολλὰ λέγειν ἐτύμοισιν ὁμοῖα,
> ἴδμεν δ' εὖτ' ἐθέλωμεν ἀληθέα γηρύσασθαι.
>
> (Hesiod, *Theogony* 26–28)

Field-dwelling shepherds, base disgraces, mere bellies, we know how to say many lies similar to genuine things, and we know how to utter true things whenever we wish.

Cryptic as it is,[9] the contrast between a full account that leaves out nothing (ἀληθέα < ἀ- + λανθάνω) and falsehoods that resemble what is genuine (ψεύδεα … ἐτύμοισιν ὁμοῖα) in *Th.* 27–28 has invited several interpretations.[10] For instance, the lines have been interpreted as a denunciation of the poetry that Hesiod produced before he met the Muses on Helicon.[11] The text, however, seems to indicate that, before his encounter with the goddesses, the narrator was just a shepherd and that the Muses' epiphany marked the beginning of his life as a poet, not just the improvement of his poetry (*Th.* 22–23, 30–31; cf. *WD* 658–59).[12] Other interpretations view the passage as Hesiod's attempt to justify fictional elements in his own poetry,[13] or, more recently, as an admission that the complex rhetoric of the *Theogony* includes a mix of

γένετ' αὐτῶν. "tell me these things, Muses … and say which of them came to being first") and in the proem to the *Catalogue* (fr. 1.1–2), also a poem about the mythical past. Even though the proem of the *WD* does not involve the goddesses as an authoritative source for Hesiod's advice to Perses (see below), the poetic voice does depend on them for the part of his teaching that falls outside his immediate experience (*WD* 646–49 on seafaring).

[8] For an analysis of the Muses' gifts, see Stoddard 2003: 6–9 with bibliography; cf. also Nagy 1990a: 52–53 and Clay 2003: 65–67.

[9] For a reading of the Muses' statement as a riddle, see Pratt 1993: 110–11.

[10] On the semantics of ἀληθής and ἐτήτυμος/ἔτυμος, see Krischer 1965. On ψεῦδος, see Luther 1935: 80–90 and Levet 1976: 201–14. For an overview of the various interpretative approaches to *Th.* 26–28, see Pucci 2007: 60–64 and 2009: 42–44; cf. Bowie 1993: 20–23 and Koning 2010a: 300–04.

[11] West 1966: 162.

[12] Cf. Arrighetti 1998: 312–13 and Nagy 2009: 307–08 with connection to hero-cult.

[13] See, e.g., Wilamowitz 1928: 48–49 and Mayer 1933: 682. By contrast, Wade-Gery 1949: 86 envisions Hesiod as a proto-scientist and sees in *Th.* 27–28 Hesiod's attempt to liberate his imagination in order to put forth his hypotheses regarding the cosmos. Verdenius 1972: 235 with n.1 offers further bibliography on this interpretative line as well as a reasonable refutation.

truths and falsehoods.[14] The passage has also been interpreted as a commentary on the human inability to determine the degree of truthfulness in divinely inspired poetic language.[15] Reading the lines as an introspective acknowledgement of fictionality or as a disclaimer regarding the truthfulness of Hesiodic poetry may be attractive to modern scholars, but it becomes problematic when we take into consideration the context of *Th.* 26–28, which is an attempt to establish poetic authority. Though not entirely impossible, it is highly unlikely that the account of the poet's initiation would begin by preemptively undercutting the truthfulness of Hesiodic poetry. Hence, another group of interpretations suggests that *Th.* 26–28 are polemical against other poets in general,[16] against poets who are dependent upon their patrons,[17] or, much more plausibly, against poets of rival theogonies.[18] Yet the most prominent polemical interpretation of these lines, which was already popular in antiquity and has left its mark on the biographical tradition,[19] views *Th.* 26–28 as an attack against Homeric heroic epic.[20] The reading of the passage as a contrast between Homer, through whom the Muses spread verisimilar lies, and Hesiod, the

---

[14] Stroh 1976; cf. Pratt 1993: 110–11 and Ferrari 1988: 70–71.

[15] Pucci 1977: 8–16 reads in *Th.* 26–28 the admission that the mortal poet "does not personally have any direct knowledge of that which he sings," and that humans do not have the ability to distinguish which of the Muses' accounts are truthful imitations of what is and which are distorted; cf. Pucci 2009: 42–44. On the ambiguity of language, see already Detienne 1973: 51–80; cf. Arthur 1983: 104–07, Thalmann 1984: 143–52, and Clay 2003: 62–64. For a thoughtful critique of Pucci's Derridean interpretation, see Ferrari 1988. For far less ambitious justifications of Hesiod's inability to know whether the content of his poem is true or not, see Walcot 1960: 36–37, who interprets *Th.* 26–28 as preemptive finger-pointing to the source of the poem in case a god becomes offended by it, and Harriott 1969: 113, who reads the passage as a warning that, should Hesiod offend the gods, he will produce poetry of lies without knowing it.

[16] Griffith 1983a: 48–49 interprets the lines as a generic reminder of the inferiority of poetry produced by poets who are not enjoying the Muses' favor as Hesiod does.

[17] Svenbro 1976: 59–61.

[18] According to Nagy 1990a: 45, Hesiod here asserts the superior, Panhellenic appeal of his theogonic narrative against local traditions; this view is reiterated in 2009: 277–78. Hesiod's proem includes also genealogical accounts similar to, but distinct from, the genealogies found in the theogony proper. Since they are ultimately (albeit subtly) refuted, these accounts can be read not only as foils for Hesiod's truthful account but also as representing the types of narratives described in line 27; see Clay 1989 and 2003: 54–56. For a reading of *Th.* 27–28 as a defense of originality and new material, see also Bowra 1952: 40–41. Paley 1889: xiii speaks of pre-Hesiodic poetry, but in his commentary on *Th.* 28 he reads a contrast between didactic (truth) and epic (lies).

[19] On the *Certamen* as a product of a polemical (anti-Homeric) interpretation of Hesiodic passages, see Graziosi 2002: 170 and Steiner 2005: 350; cf. Rosen 1990, esp. 100 and 112, as well as Nagy 1982: 66. See also Introduction, pp. 4–5. There is no reason to assume with West 1966: 44–45 that the *Theogony* was actually performed at the funerary games of Amphidamas and is thus tailored to such an agonistic performance; cf. the discussion in Arrighetti 1998: 280–81.

[20] Luther 1935: 124–26; Latte 1946: 159–62; Maehler 1963: 41–42; Verdenius 1972: 234–35; Murray 1981: 91; Cole 1983: 21–22.

truthful poet, has been particularly encouraged by the verbal proximity between *Th.* 27 and *Od.* 19.203, where the Homeric narrator refers to the false autobiographical tale that Odysseus tells Penelope while still in disguise as "many lies ... similar to genuine things" (ψεύδεα πολλὰ ... ἐτύμοισιν ὁμοῖα).[21]

However one may interpret *Th.* 26–28, it is safe to say that, as a whole, Hesiod's encounter with the Muses (*Th.* 22–34) establishes the poet's claim to a truthful account of material that lies beyond his own experience. This elaborate construction of authority comes in sharp contrast to the proem of the *WD* (1–10), where Hesiod promises to reveal ἐτήτυμα ("things as they are", *WD* 10) without recourse to any divine source.[22] The Muses are involved in this context only as a chorus invited to sing a hymn for their father Zeus (Δί᾽ ἐννέπετε, *WD* 2). Nonetheless, Hesiod emerges from both poems as a poet with access to truthful and genuine information about both the human and the divine realm. The authority that was bestowed upon the Hesiodic poetic voice in the *Theogony* still informs the *WD*, as the didactic voice admits his dependence on the Muses for matters of which he has no immediate experience (*WD* 646–62 on seafaring). After all, the narrator evokes his life-changing encounter with the Muses on Helicon when he recounts that he dedicated to the goddesses the trophy he won at the poetic competition in Chalcis (*WD* 658–59).

According to Hesiodic poetics, the Muses grant a truthful account to a poet only when they choose to (εὖτ᾽ ἐθέλωμεν, *Th.* 28). Therefore, singing ἀληθέα implies that the poet curries special favor with the goddesses and that his close relationship with them sets his poetry apart from fallacious competition (*Th.* 22–34). Scholars have occasionally linked these ideas to the persistent assertion of truthfulness found in the Pindaric corpus.[23] According to the most recent extensive iteration of this view, the reception of Hesiod in lyric poetry of the fifth century is supposedly framed through a distinction between the Hesiodic poetics of truth, to which Pindar and Bacchylides subscribe, and its Homeric counterpart that stands for

---

[21] Goldhill 1991: 45 and Lada-Richards 2002: 73–74. On *Th.* 27 and *Od.* 19.203, see Neitzel 1980: 389–90, who juxtaposes Homer's full awareness and control of the truths and lies of his narrative with Hesiod's lack thereof. See also Arrighetti 1996: 53–60.

[22] Pucci 1996: 192–93 and, similarly, Clay 2003: 77–80.

[23] E.g., Kirkwood 1982: 20 and Puelma 1989: 88 apropos of *O.*1.28–35; cf. also implicitly West 1966: 162. Contrast Hubbard 1985: 102, who reads *Th.* 27–28 as an assertion of the "ambivalent potential for both truth and lies" and draws a parallel with Pindar's discourse of selective remembrance and forgetting.

seductive yet false poetry.[24] It is certainly true that the *personae loquentes* of Pindar as well as Bacchylides often draw attention to their close connection with the divine, especially the Muses, but this connection is not an indispensable part of lyric poetics, since there are several odes where the divine patronage of the Muses is absent.[25] Furthermore, whenever it does surface, the relationship between the mortal voice and its immortal patrons is treated with considerable variation,[26] which incidentally does not include recourse to a single crucial moment of initiation in the poet's past. Overall, the lyric interaction with the Muses is not "Hesiod-like" at all, in that it is friendly and cooperative rather than hierarchical and abusive (*Th.* 26), and it allows the *persona loquens* an active role,[27] even when the latter presents itself as the Muses' mouthpiece.[28]

Pindar's discourse about truth and falsehood is rich and varied, as Komornicka has shown,[29] but a joint consideration with the Bacchylidean corpus reveals that his perceived preoccupation with the truth is, in fact, a *topos* rather than a piece of Boeotian heritage, as Kirkwood puts it,[30] or a form of Hesiodic reception. In the *Theogony*, both truthfulness and falsehood are dependent on the whim of the Muses (*Th.* 27–28). A survey of Pindaric and Bacchylidean poetry yields that ἀλάθεια is a concept important enough to be invested with agency[31] and addressed as a divinity,[32] but its dependence upon a divine source is only occasional.[33] E.g., when Pi. *O.*1 promotes its account of Pelops' story through polemics against

---

[24] Koning 2010a: 310–18, esp. 314–16.

[25] Among Pindar's epinician odes, the Muses are not mentioned in *O.*2, *O.*4, *O.*5, *O.*8, *O.*12, *O.*14 (addressed to the Charites), *P.*2, *P.*7, *P.*8, *P.*9, *P.*12, *N.*2, *N.*11, *I.*3, *I.*5; cf. Bacchylides' lacunose *Odes* 7, 8, 11, and 14. Cf. Harriott 1969: 53 n.2 for a list of the references to the Muses in the surviving poetry of Pindar and Bacchylides.

[26] See Harriott 1969: 52–70.

[27] Bowra 1964: 4, Calame 1995: 51, Mackie 2003: 47–48 and, more importantly, 64–67.

[28] For the *topos* of the Muses' προφάτας, see Ba. *Ode* 9.3 and Pi. *Pa.*6/52f.6; cf. Pi. fr. 150 SM, where *persona loquens* appears to be active or even proactive in its relationship with the Muse (μαντεύεο, Μοῖσα, προφατεύσω δ' ἐγώ). Notably Ba. *Ode* 10.28 employs προφάτας with no apparent connotation of oracular speech. On προφάτας Μοισᾶν as Hesiodic reception, see Koning 2010a: 310–11 (cf. Sperduti 1950: 230–33); for a more critical approach, see Ledbetter 2003: 62–68.

[29] Komornicka 1981 and, more recently, Park 2013. See also n.33 below.     [30] Kirkwood 1982: 20.

[31] Ba. *Ode* 13.204–05, *Hyp.* fr. 1.2–5.

[32] Pi. *O.*10.4, fr. 205 SM; cf. Ba. fr. dub. 57 (but see Maehler 1997: 314–15).

[33] On the contrast between Pindaric ἀλάθεια and Hes. *Th.* 27–28, see Park 2013: 21–22. Ἀλάθεια occurs with no explicit connection to divine sources in *O.*2.91–95, *P.*3.103–04, *I.*2.9–10 where the source is clearly a mortal, as well as in Ba. *Odes* 3.96, 8.20–21 (cf. also 9.85–86). For claims to the truth without a divine source, cf. Pi. *O.*11.4–6, *O.*13.98–100, where the evoked "truthful witness" is the mortal herald's shout (cf. *Parth.* 2.36–41), *N.*7.61–63, as well as *O.*4.17–18, *N.*18, and fr. 11 SM. As I mention above, *O.*1.28–35 does not attribute Pindar's revision of the Pelops story to any divine insight. Perhaps relevant to this discussion is also the straight-talking man of *P.*2.86 (cf. the ideal of the sincere leader in *P.*1.86). For associations of ἀλάθεια with non-human entities, see *O.*8.1–8,

competing versions (28–35), it does not establish its validity with recourse to some authoritative divine source. It does credit, however, χάρις for rendering even incredible stories credible in the context of bestowing τιμή (30–32). Lyric poetry, and especially praise-poetry, has a pronounced social dimension that one does not find in Hesiodic poetry. The public performance of ἀλάθεια in lyric is determined largely by what is deemed socially appropriate and expected. Pindaric and Bacchylidean odes weave narratives that aim to extoll the *laudandi* directly or indirectly and thus rescue their deeds from obscurity. These narrative accounts are selective and controlled rather than exhaustive, and the *personae loquentes* are constantly aware of what is fitting for the occasion and the genre, and what is not.[34] Perhaps one of the most illustrative contemplations of lyric ἀλάθεια and its limitations occurs in *Nemean* 5:

> στάσομαι· οὔ τοι ἅπασα κερδίων
> φαίνοισα πρόσωπον ἀλάθει᾽ ἀτρεκές·
> καὶ τὸ σιγᾶν πολλάκις ἐστὶ σοφώ-
> τατον ἀνθρώπῳ νοῆσαι.
> (Pindar, *Nemean* 5.16–18)

I will stop; for indeed not every truth is more advantageous when it shows its precise face; and often keeping silent is the wisest thing for a man to heed.

In this passage, the speaker not only acknowledges the conditional value of a full and complete account that leaves nothing out (ἀλάθεια), but also restrains the narrative in accordance with those considerations and draws attention to this elision. Reading the lyric ἀλάθεια as a reception of Hesiod's implicit claim to ἀληθέα in *Th.* 26–28, therefore, is reductive and misleading.

Finally, the argument that lyric associates Hesiod with its own poetics of truth in contrast with Homer, whose poetics supposedly represent deception, oversimplifies the reception of both poets in the lyric corpus.[35] Homer's association with deceptive and false poetry is based on *Nemean* 7:

where Olympia is called the mistress of truth probably in connection with empyromancy (cf. *P.*11.6) and *O.*10.53–55 with reference to Time (Χρόνος). In *O.*10.4 the *persona loquens* constructs Ἀλάθεια as the daughter of Zeus, and evokes her along with the Muse; cf. Pi. fr. 205 SM and the highly problematic Ba. fr. dub 57. For other concepts connected with ἀλάθεια (e.g. ἀτρέκεια) and its opposites (e.g. ψεῦδος), see Komornicka 1972 and 1981 as well as Pratt 1993: 115–29.

[34] For a nuanced discussion of ἀλάθεια as representation rather than reduplication, see Hubbard 1985: 102–04; cf. also Komornicka 1972, Gianotti 1975: 56–65, Puelma 1989: 87–88, Nagy 1990b: 65–72, and Park 2013, who examines Pindar's ἀλάθεια in the context of the *laudator*'s obligation towards the *laudandus*.

[35] A recent iteration of this argument can be found in Koning 2010a: 310–18, esp. 314–16, but see already Segal 1967: 441–42 on *N.*7, and Kirkwood (1982): 52.

ἐγὼ δὲ πλέον' ἔλπομαι
λόγον Ὀδυσσέος ἢ πάθαν
    διὰ τὸν ἁδυεπῆ γενέσθ' Ὅμηρον·
ἐπεὶ ψεύδεσί οἱ ποτανᾷ <τε> μαχανᾷ
σεμνὸν ἔπεστί τι· σοφία
    δὲ κλέπτει παράγοισα μύθοις. τυφλὸν δ'ἔχει
ἦτορ ὅμιλος ἀνδρῶν ὁ πλεῖστος. εἰ γὰρ ἦν
ἓ τὰν ἀλάθειαν ἰδέμεν, οὔ κεν ὅπλων χολωθεὶς
ὁ καρτερὸς Αἴας ἔπαξε διὰ φρενῶν
λευρὸν ξίφος

(Pindar, Nemean 7.20–27)

But I expect that the story of Odysseus became greater than his suffering thanks to Homer of sweet verses, since upon his lies and his winged resourcefulness there is some majesty; skill deceives, misleading with stories, and the majority of a crowd of men has a blind heart. For, if they could have seen the truth, mighty Ajax would not have planted a smooth sword through his midriff, angered over the arms (*sc.* of Achilles).

This is admittedly a challenging passage.[36] Lines 20–22 express the view that Homeric poetry has immortalized an enhanced account of Odysseus' experiences that does not correspond to the actual events. The following statements about the deceptive power of poetic skill and people's inability to see through it (22–24) offer commentary on Homeric epic, but they also amplify the ode's earlier point about accurate representation in the context of praise-poetry (11–20, also linking poetic language with vision and visibility).[37] Rather unexpectedly, the speaker then turns to the judgment of Achilles' arms in order to illustrate the noxious effects of partial and misleading narratives on glorious men such as Ajax (24–27). The text here either invites us to envision epic verses about the deeds of Odysseus and Ajax being performed in the Greek camp when the judgment of the arms was taking place or, more likely, it alludes to a debate in which Odysseus' accomplishments were inflated whereas those of Ajax were underrepresented.[38] The ode concludes its treatment of Ajax with an account of his

---

[36] On these difficult lines, see Köhnken 1971: 46–60, Most 1985: 148–56, Park 2013: 32–34 with comparison to *N*.8 and *I*.4. Cf. Nagy 1990b: 203 (with n.17) and 423–24.

[37] Köhnken 1971: 46; cf. Segal 1967.

[38] Cf. *Little Iliad* fr. 2 W (= sch. Ar. *Eq.* 1056a), which attests to a debate about the accomplishments of each warrior between two Trojan maidens; cf. Davies 1989: 61–62. A line from *N*.8 on the same subject may be pointing to a debate featuring Ajax, who proved to be an insufficient advocate of himself (*N*.8.24–25, ἤ τιν' ἄγλωσσον μέν, ἦτορ δ'ἄλκιμον, λάθα κατέχει / ἐν λυγρῷ νείκει); cf. Ovid *Met.* 13.382–83. The contrast between Odysseus and Ajax as orators is established already in *Iliad* 9. In the cyclic *Aethiopis*, which also included Ajax's suicide (fr. 6 W = sch. Pi. *I*.4.58b), the judgment of the arms depended on an athletic competition; see Procl. *Chr.* p. 106, 15–17 Allen and Ps.-Apollod. *Epit.* 5.6 with West 2013: 159–62.

valor in battle full of epic resonances (*N.*7.27–32).[39] Thus, by commemor-
ating the deeds that would have earned Ajax the arms and prevented his
suicide, if facts had been accurately represented, the ode compensates for
the failure of the epic tradition to do justice to Ajax.[40]

*N.*7 criticizes the epic tradition circulating under Homer's name for
misrepresentation, but we should not extrapolate from this ode that Pindar
consistently associated Homeric poetics with falsehood.[41] *Nemean 7* is one of
three Pindaric odes that dwell on Ajax's suicide. Much like *N.*7, *N.*8 mourns
Ajax mainly as a victim of envy and praises his great deeds (*N.*8.21–34). The
language of falsehood, deception, and obscurity resonates with that of *N.*7,
but in *N.*8 there is no explicit condemnation of Homer.[42] *Isthmian 4*, on the
other hand, commemorates the suicide as a widely known event and praises
Homer for honoring and immortalizing Ajax's deeds with his poetry
(*I.*4.35–39). Far from vilifying Homer, the Pindaric speaker considers his
epic poetry a model for the ode's own epinician poetics (*I.*4.40–45).[43] There
are, therefore, two distinct attitudes towards Homeric epic in these odes.
The crucial difference between *N.*7 and 8, on the one hand, and *I.*4, on the
other, is the performative context: the first group was intended for an
Aeginetan audience, whereas *I.*4 was composed for a Theban victor. The
Aeacidae, and especially Ajax, were central to the cult, culture, and identity
of the Aeginetans.[44] Therefore, by condemning the epic narrative of the
hero's defeat during the judgment of the arms and by 'restoring' his glory,
Pindar's epinician responds to the local culture and appeals to its primary
audience.[45] No such considerations apply to Thebes, thus no tension
between local and Panhellenic needs to be resolved in *I.*4.

In what follows, I examine first how epinician poetry appropriates
Hesiodic poetry to lend authority and support to its own commemorative
function, thus complementing its reception of heroic epic. Bacchylides'
*Ode* 5 evokes Hesiod's authoritative voice to justify celebration through
praise-poetry. Hesiodic poetics are particularly important in the context

---

[39] On verbal echoes of Homeric epic in *N.*7.25–30, see Most 1985: 153 with n.88.
[40] According to my reading, *N.*7.20–34 deal with the issue of adequate representation and
commemoration through poetry. For a different view, see Most 1985: 152–54, who argues that,
while Odysseus' case exemplifies false (exaggerated) commemoration through poetry, Ajax's plight
reflects insufficient reception of a narrative by a poor audience.
[41] On the Homeric tradition, including the epic cycle, in Pindaric poetry, see Nisetich 1989: 9–23 with
emphasis on context and occasion, as well as Nagy 1990b, esp. chapters 2 and 14.
[42] On the parallels, see, e.g., Park 2013: 33–34.
[43] Privitera 1982: 181 on *I.*4.43–5; cf. *P.*4.277–79, where Homer's authority is also evoked without any
reservation.
[44] See, e.g., Nagy 2011: 49–59 and 75–78, Athanassaki 2011 (esp. 279–93), Indergaard 2011 (esp. 317–20 on
the centrality of the Aeacidae in odes for Aeginetan victors), Hedreen 2011, and Irwin 2011: 405–10.
[45] Cf. Lloyd-Jones 1973: 130 on *N.*7 and *N.*8.

of negotiating the relationship between the *laudator* and a powerful *laudandus* not only in *Ode* 5 but also in *Ode* 3. After exploring how epinician appropriates ideas about poetry and power from the Hesiodic corpus, I turn to lyric that distances itself from Hesiodic poetics. I hope that my discussion of *Pa.*7b/52h in conjunction with Ibycus S151 *PMGF* will illuminate how poems can juxtapose Homeric and Hesiodic poetics only to reduce them to foils for their own poetic message.

### Fame and the Divine: Bacchylides' *Ode* 5

Composed for Hieron's Olympic victory in 476 BCE,[46] *Ode* 5 consists of a lengthy mythological narrative (56–175) framed by extensive praise for the *laudandus* (1–55; 176–200). In its laudatory conclusion, the ode reiterates the idea that praise is owed to Hieron:[47]

> Χρή] δ᾽ ἀλαθείας χάριν
> αἰνεῖν, φθόνον ἀμφ[οτέραισιν
> χερσὶν ἀπωσάμενον,
> εἴ τις εὖ πράσσοι βροτῶ[ν.
>
> Βοιωτὸς ἀνὴρ τᾶδε φών[ησεν, γλυκειᾶν
>     Ἡσίοδος πρόπολος
> Μουσᾶν, ὃν <ἂν> ἀθάνατοι τι[μῶσι, τούτῳ
>     καὶ βροτῶν φήμαν ἕπ[εσθαι.
> Πείθομαι εὐμαρέως
>     εὐκλέα κελεύθου γλῶσσαν οὐ[κ ἐκτὸς δίκας
> πέμπειν Ἱέρωνι· τόθεν γὰ[ρ
>     πυθμένες θάλλουσιν ἐσθλ[ῶν,
> τοὺς ὁ μεγιστοπάτωρ
>     Ζεὺς ἀκινήτους ἐν εἰρήν[ᾳ φυλάσσοι.
>                   (Bacchylides, *Ode* 5.187–200)

For the sake of the truth [one must] praise any mortal who succeeds, pushing away envy with both hands. Thus spoke the Boeotian man, Hesiod, the minister of the [sweet] Muses, that, whomever the immortals [honor, him] also the good repute (φήμαν) of mortals [follows]. I am easily persuaded to send Hieron a song of good fame without [straying from] the path [of justice]. For, from there do the tree-stocks of good things flourish; these [may] Zeus, the greatest father, [preserve] unshaken in peace.

---

[46] The same victory is celebrated by Pindar's *O.*1; on the evidence for dating, see Maehler 1982: 78–90 and Cairns 2010: 75–76.

[47] Assuming, of course, that Kenyon's χρή in 5.187 is correct. For the *topos* of obligation, see already Schadewaldt 1928: 278–79, Bundy 1962, esp. 10–11, 55–58.

The poetic agenda articulated here calls for a truthful account of Hieron's achievements and offers the victor not only commemoration of his glory but also protection against the malicious effects of envy.[48] In this context, the ode evokes the "Boeotian man," i.e. Hesiod,[49] as an established authority whose words and ideas are appropriated, reformulated, and reframed in a way that lends support and legitimacy to the poem's laudatory program.

Identifying the Hesiodic passage embedded in 5.191–94 has been a challenge, since there is no exact match to the Bacchylidean text in the surviving Hesiodic corpus. One proposed solution to the problem has been to declare the Hesiodic reference false. Along these lines, Jebb entertained the possibility of a memory slip, claiming that Bacchylides is actually citing Theognis:[50]

> Ὅν δὲ θεοὶ τιμῶσιν, ὁ καὶ μωμεύμενος αἰνεῖ·
> ἀνδρὸς δὲ σπουδὴ γίνεται οὐδεμία.
>                                    (Theognis, 169–70)

Even the fault-finder praises whomever the gods honor; but a man's effort amounts to nothing.

At first glance, Thgn.169 appears to overlap with 5.191–94 in its focus on divine favor as a prerequisite for human success and on positive human speech as a manifestation of divine approval. In addition, Bacchylides' ὃν <ἂν> ἀθάνατοι τι[μῶσι (193) bears close resemblance to the beginning of 169 (ὃν δὲ θεοὶ τιμῶσιν).[51] When considered more carefully, however, Thgn. 169 seems to be an inappropriate intertext for Ba. 5.191–94: depending

---

[48] For Bacchylides' ἀλήθεια as truthful commemoration, see Cairns 2010: 215 on Ba. 3.96–98 (with bibliography) and 245–46 on 5.187–90; see also Stenger 2004: 113, 158. Pratt 1993: 115–20 (cf. 17–22) rightly points out that ἀλήθεια is a claim to truthfulness, but goes too far in excluding any connotation of memory and commemoration; cf. Heitsch 1962 and Cole 1983. See also Hubbard 1985: 100–06 and Puelma 1989: 87–89, who much like Hubbard reads the epinician ἀλήθεια as a poetic truth that conveys what is appropriate in the context of a specific (aristocratic) value system.

[49] According to Bonifazi 2004: 405, the non-articular diction of Βοιωτὸς ἀνήρ indicates a figure well known to the audience. Βοιωτὸς ἀνήρ is itself a unique designation for Hesiod. The phrase may be modeled upon Simonides' reference to Homer as "the man from Chios" (Χῖος ... ἀνήρ , fr. 19.1 W²), which is itself informed by the *Homeric Hymn to Apollo* (*h.Ap.* 172–73); see Graziosi 2002: 63–64. Proponents of an historicizing interpretation have read Βοιωτὸς ἀνήρ as a teaser, suggesting that Bacchylides presents his audience with the possibility of a reference to Pindar – supposedly his great rival – only to dispel the deliberate ambiguity one line later by naming Hesiod. The most representative proponent of this reading is Steffen 1961, who is nonetheless refuted thoroughly and convincingly by Schmidt 1987. On the rivalry among the epinician poets (Simonides and Bacchylides vs. Pindar) as unreliable fiction created by the scholiasts, Lefkowitz 1991: 98–99.

[50] Jebb 1905: 293.

[51] On the textual problem of Thgn. 169, see Radermacher 1938: 1–2, who rejects Diehls' ὃ καί as well as ὃν καί, the reading adopted by Bergk, Blass, and others. Instead, he favors ὁ καί (already in Crusius), which Radermacher finds consistent with his reconstruction of the Hesiodic idea behind 5.191–94.

on how one reads it, it either eradicates malicious blame altogether or reinterprets it as praise.[52] By contrast, just before citing Hesiod, the epinician ode acknowledges the existence of blame and the need to push it away by means of praise (5.187–90). In other words, Bacchylides' *Ode* 5 makes a sharp distinction between those who praise the successful man and the envious lot who pose a threat. Furthermore, when viewed as a whole, the Theognidean couplet emerges as a commentary on the futility of human effort in the absence of divine favor and thus follows a different trajectory from the conclusion of the Bacchylidean ode(5.195–200). Finally, as I discuss below, variations of ὃν δὲ θεοὶ τιμῶσιν (Thgn. 169) are found elsewhere, so *Ode* 5.193 need not be paraphrasing Theognis in particular.[53]

Another interpretation that attempts to solve the problem of Ba. *Ode* 5.191–94 by undermining the Hesiodic reference was put forth recently by Stenger.[54] For Stenger, lines 193–94 are not a statement in indirect discourse ("that, whomever the immortals [honor, him] also the good repute of mortals [follows]"). Instead, he reads them as a reported exhortation ("that, whomever the immortals [honor, him] also the good repute of mortals [should follow]"), preceded by a prescriptive sentence in 5.187–90 (χρή ...) and followed by an admission of compliance in 5.195–98 (πείθομαι ...). Stenger argues that, if read as an indirect statement, 5.191–94 imply that successful men *are* in fact accompanied by good repute, at least according to Hesiod. The lines thus appear to contradict the immediately preceding passage (5.188–90) that articulates the obligation not only to praise but also to thwart envy.[55] Stenger's suggested reading

---

[52] I take the line to mean that whoever is favored by the gods is praised even by those who (generally) blame; for this interpretation, see Radermacher 1938: 1–2, and, more recently, Garzya 1958: 164. Van Groningen 1966: 66–67, on the other hand, prefers a more contrived interpretation: assuming blame is motivated by jealousy, it is a sign that one enjoys the favor of the gods, and it can thus be perceived as praise (cf. Harrison 1902: 214–15). The assumption that Thgn. 169 and Ba. *Ode* 5.191–94 convey the same idea has sometimes dictated the interpretation of the former; see, e.g., Friedländer 1913: 590 n.1, who equates ὁ καὶ μωμεύμενος to "everyone" on the basis of βροτῶν φήμαν in *Ode* 5.193–4.

[53] Márquez Guerrero 1992: 82–83 has traced verbal echoes of Thgn. 167–70 throughout Ba. *Ode* 5: in lines 50–55, 193–94, and (much less convincingly) 160–62. Márquez Guerrero readily assumes that Bacchylides took Thgn. 167–70 into account when he composed *Ode* 5, but he fails to justify the mention of Hesiod in 5.192. He does concede the alternative possibility, however, that both authors may be drawing from the same non-extant Hesiodic source; cf. already Jebb 1905: 293.

[54] Stenger 2004: 163–67.

[55] Stenger 2004: 163. Cf. the paraphrase in Steffen 1961: 16 ("a man who is esteemed by the gods should also obtain his fair share of praise from human beings") and, more recently, the translation of 5.193–94 in Cairns 1997: 38 = 2010: 169 ("that whoever the immortals honour, him should the voice of mortals also accompany"). In his commentary, however, Cairns 2010: 246 endorses Lefkowitz's interpretation of 5.193–94 as a "summary allusion" to *Th.* 81–97 rather than Stenger's idea of a fake reference.

of 5.191–94 is certainly attractive. We must admit, however, that if lines 193–94 are paraphrasing a Hesiodic exhortation in indirect discourse, they do it in a rather unmarked fashion. If we compare Ba. *Ode* 5.191–94 with the reception of Hesiodic instruction in the Pindaric corpus (*I.*6.66–73 and *P.*6.19–27), we observe an important difference. Both *Pythian* 6 and *Isthmian* 6 mark their appropriation of Hesiodic prescriptions with the verb παραινέω.[56] The verb φών[ησεν in Ba. *Ode* 5.191 has broader semantics, however, so the audience receives no unambiguous hint as to whether what follows is a Hesiodic statement or an injunction. Perhaps it is worth considering a more dynamic reading of the Bacchylidean text: 5.193–94 may be paraphrasing a gnomic statement from the Hesiodic corpus, which becomes invested with prescriptive force only in retrospect, once the *persona loquens* utters πείθομαι in line 195.

While Stenger's reading of an indirect exhortation in 5.191–94 merits serious consideration, his thoughts regarding the Hesiodic reference itself are innovative but far less persuasive. He proposes that the idea expressed in 5.193–94 is not actually drawn from the Hesiodic corpus, but that Bacchylides has only attributed it to an authoritative poet in order to give it additional *gravitas*;[57] Hesiod is preferred over other potential sources because the ode has already alluded to the *Theogony* earlier.[58] Of course, if Bacchylides fabricates a precept and simply attaches Hesiodic authorship to it, any attempt to recover the original Hesiodic passage behind the supposed allusion is futile. Perhaps the main counterargument to this suggestion is that there is no legitimate reason to doubt that this Hesiodic reference should be taken at face value. For Stenger, all utterances attributed to authoritative sources in epinician poetry are variations of the same poetic technique: by citing and paraphrasing these sayings, the lyric *personae loquentes* draw authority from widely accepted and established sources of wisdom, be it poets, mythological figures, or anonymous speakers representing tradition.[59] While this is by no means a false assessment, it fails to take into consideration what conventions or

---

[56] See Chapter 3, pp. 108 and 116.

[57] Cf. D'Alessio 2005b: 231 for the possibility that Bacchylides here attributes to Hesiod a traditional *sententia* in order to retroject the poetics of praise-poetry upon a significant poetic authority of the past.

[58] Stenger 2004: 166. On Hesiodic allusions earlier in the ode, esp. in 5.1–16, see Lefkowitz 1969: 48–51 and 1976: 44–45, followed by Goldhill 1983, and Cairns 1997: 37–38 with emphasis on the ring-composition.

[59] Stenger 2004: 164–66.

expectations determine a poem's interaction with a certain type of source. When we look at other lyric poems that, like Bacchylides' *Ode* 5, claim to quote or paraphrase lines attributed explicitly to ancient poets, we find that the allusions are indeed genuine.[60] Instead of inventing a Hesiodic utterance, then, it is much more likely that Ba. 5.191–94 reformulates an original Hesiodic passage in a manner that conforms to the expectations of the ode's audience(s) and invites them to recall the intertext.

It stands to reason, then, that we should approach *Ode* 5.191–94 as a genuine Hesiodic allusion. Yet, since no extant passage in the Hesiodic corpus corresponds precisely to these lines, tracking the reference depends largely on our presumptions regarding τᾶδε φών[ησεν (5.191): how loose a paraphrase would the audience expect or allow based on this phrase? Compared to other lyric passages that single out and draw attention to individual sayings, τᾶδε φών[ησεν seems to be vague.[61] Scholars who have assumed that line 191 sets the audience up for a near-quotation have concluded that Ba. 5.191–94 must allude to a part of the Hesiodic corpus that no longer survives;[62] given the gnomic nature of the evoked passage, some have even surmised that the lost intertext was part of the *Chironos Hypothekai*.[63] Others, however, maintain that the lines allude to an extant Hesiodic passage, namely the discourse about divinely favored kings and poets:[64]

> ὅντινα τιμήσουσι Διὸς κοῦραι μεγάλοιο
> γεινόμενόν τ᾽ ἐσίδωσι διοτρεφέων βασιλήων,
> τῷ μὲν ἐπὶ γλώσσῃ γλυκερὴν χείουσιν ἐέρσην,
> τοῦ δ᾽ ἔπε᾽ ἐκ στόματος ῥεῖ μείλιχα· οἱ δέ τε λαοὶ
> πάντες ἐς αὐτὸν ὁρῶσι διακρίνοντα θέμιστας
> ἰθείῃσι δίκῃσιν· ὁ δ᾽ ἀσφαλέως ἀγορεύων
> αἶψά τι καὶ μέγα νεῖκος ἐπισταμένως κατέπαυσεν·

---

[60] Simon. fr. 19.1–2W² – *Il.* 6.146; Pi. *I.*6.66–69 ~ *WD* 412, *P.*4.277–78 ~ *Il.* 15.207; cf. *O.*9.1–2 (Archilochus) with Pavlou 2008: 541–42.

[61] Simon. fr. 19.1–2W² (ἓν δὲ τὸ κάλλιστον Χῖος ἔειπεν ἀνήρ·) cf. Pi. *I.*2.9–11 (νῦν δ᾽ ἐφίητι <τὸ> τὠργείου φυλάξαι / ῥῆμ᾽ . . ., / "χρήματα χρήματ᾽ ἀνήρ"), *I.*6.66–69 (Ἡσιόδου. . . τοῦτ᾽ ἔπος) and *P.* 4.277–8 (τῶν δ᾽ Ὁμήρου καὶ τόδε συνθέμενος / ῥῆμα). See also *P.*6.20–27 (. . . ἐφημοσύναν / τά ποτ᾽ . . . φαντὶ / Φιλύρας υἱὸν . . . / . . . παραινεῖν, followed by precepts in indirect discourse) and *P.*9.94–96 (μὴ λόγον βλάπτων ἀλίοιο γέροντος κρυπτέτω· / κεῖνος αἰνεῖν καὶ τὸν ἐχθρόν / παντὶ θυμῷ σύν τε δίκα καλὰ ῥέζοντ᾽ ἔννεπεν). The degree to which these passages replicate the language of the text they allude to varies. Simonides quotes a line from *Iliad* 6 in its entirety, and Pindar's *I.*6 involves a close paraphrase of Hesiod's *WD* 412 (see Chapter 3, pp. 106–11). On the other hand, the Homeric allusion in Pi. *P.*4 can be linked to *Iliad* 15.207 only as a combination of loose paraphrase and interpretation.

[62] See, e.g., Jebb 1905: 293, Maehler 1982: 122 on Ba. *Ode* 5.191–93, and D'Alessio 2005b: 231.

[63] Snell and Maehler 1970: xxii. On the reception of *Chironos Hypothekai* in Pi. *P.*6, see Chapter 3, pp. 113–18.

[64] On *Th.* 97–103, see also above, pp. 30–33.

τοὔνεκα γὰρ βασιλῆες ἐχέφρονες, οὕνεκα λαοῖς
βλαπτομένοις ἀγορῆφι μετάτροπα ἔργα τελεῦσι
ῥηιδίως, μαλακοῖσι παραιφάμενοι ἐπέεσσιν·
ἐρχόμενον δ' ἀν' ἀγῶνα θεὸν ὣς ἱλάσκονται
αἰδοῖ μειλιχίῃ, μετὰ δὲ πρέπει ἀγρομένοισι.
τοίη Μουσάων ἱερὴ δόσις ἀνθρώποισιν.
ἐκ γάρ τοι Μουσέων καὶ ἑκηβόλου Ἀπόλλωνος
ἄνδρες ἀοιδοὶ ἔασιν ἐπὶ χθόνα καὶ κιθαρισταί,
ἐκ δὲ Διὸς βασιλῆες· ὁ δ' ὄλβιος, ὅντινα Μοῦσαι
φίλωνται· γλυκερή οἱ ἀπὸ στόματος ῥέει αὐδή.
εἰ γάρ τις καὶ πένθος ἔχων νεοκηδέι θυμῷ
ἄζηται κραδίην ἀκαχήμενος, αὐτὰρ ἀοιδὸς
Μουσάων θεράπων κλεῖα προτέρων ἀνθρώπων
ὑμνήσει μάκαράς τε θεοὺς οἳ Ὄλυμπον ἔχουσιν,
αἶψ' ὅ γε δυσφροσυνέων ἐπιλήθεται οὐδέ τι κηδέων
μέμνηται· ταχέως δὲ παρέτραπε δῶρα θεάων.

(Hesiod, *Theogony* 81–103)

Whomever of the kings who are nurtured by Zeus the daughters of great Zeus honor and look upon when he's born, upon his tongue they pour a sweet dew, and from his mouth flow soothing words. And all the people look at him as he settles disputes with straight judgments; and, speaking in the assembly without fail, he quickly and expertly ends even a great quarrel. For kings are prudent for this reason, namely that, when people are harmed in the assembly, they achieve restitution easily, appeasing them with gentle words. And as he comes up to the gathering place, they placate him like a god with soothing reverence, and he stands out among the gathered men. Such is the sacred gift of the Muses to humans. For poets and lyre-players upon the earth are from the Muses and far-shooting Apollo, but kings are from Zeus. And, whomever the Muses love, he is blessed. Sweet flows the voice from his mouth. For, even if someone who has sorrow in his newly afflicted spirit is parched in his heart with grief, but if then a poet, the attendant of the Muses, sings of the glorious deeds of men of old and of the blessed gods who hold Olympus, immediately this man forgets his anxieties and he does not remember his worries at all. For quickly the gifts of the gods divert his mind (παρέτραπε).

An allusion to *Th.* 81ff. was first proposed by Sitzler[65] and was subsequently noted by Rzach, even though he assigned the Bacchylidean lines to Hesiod's *incerta fragmenta* (fr. 202 Rzach). Likewise, Merkelbach and West classified lines 5.193–94 among the *dubia fragmenta* of the Hesiodic corpus (fr. 344 MW) but suggested an allusion to *Th.* 81–97 in their *apparatus criticus*. The idea has become increasingly popular in recent years. Lefkowitz, Goldhill, and Cairns have made a strong case for an

---

[65] Mentioned in Buchholz 1898[4]: 154.

intertextual connection between the Bacchylidean passage and the proem of the *Theogony*,[66] while in his 2004 commentary Maehler refers to lines 5.193–94 as a possible "approximate 'quotation'" of *Th.* 81–97.[67]

Proponents of this interpretation point out that the language of 5.193 (ὃν <ἂν> ἀθάνατοι τι[μῶσι) is a close paraphrase of the relative clause that introduces the ideal kings in *Th.* 81 (ὅντινα τιμήσουσι Διὸς κοῦραι μεγάλοιο). The Bacchylidean line has expanded its view of divine favor to include all gods; furthermore, it has divested the Hesiodic line of its specific reference to the βασιλεῖς (*Th.* 82) and has thus reformulated the idea in an all-encompassing manner that fits the epinician genre best, since not all *laudandi* are political leaders.[68] Given the particular context of *Ode* 5, however, the political dimension of the Hesiodic intertext inevitably remains active, since the *laudandus* in this case is, in fact, the man who rules Syracuse. In addition, the good repute of men that follows those favored by the gods in *Ode* 5.193–94 (τούτῳ] / καὶ βροτῶν φήμαν ἔπ[εσθαι) has been read as an adaptation of *Th.* 84–85, a passage in which the people watch their leader as he performs his duties, and (more persuasively) of *Th.* 91–92, namely the veneration of the people towards their king.[69]

The allusion to Hesiod's celebration of just kings, to whom the gods have granted the ability to resolve conflicts successfully with reconciliatory words rather than violence and whom men revere for their leadership, enriches the ode's praise of Hieron. Furthermore, the evocation of Hesiod's *Theogony* in 5.193–94 contributes to a ring-composition, as the first strophe is replete with allusions to *Th.* 81–103.[70] Most of these are drawn from the Hesiodic treatment of successful poets (*Th.* 97–103) and are woven into the ode's poetics: the prospect of setting aside one's worries at the sound of this song (5.6–8) recalls *Th.* 98–103, although epinician celebrates gods and heroes of the past (*Th.* 100–01) in the context of extolling the deeds of contemporary men. Moreover, the

---

[66] Lefkowitz 1976: 72–73, Goldhill 1983: 67–68, Cairns 1997: 34 and 2010: 246 on Ba. *Ode* 5.191–93.

[67] This is a departure from Maehler 1982: 122 with n.39.

[68] One could even argue that, by eliminating the particulars of *Th.* 82, line 193 plays with the similarities between good kings and divinely favored poet in the *Theogony*, given that the latter group is introduced with a similar clause (ὅντινα Μοῦσαι / φίλωνται, *Th.* 96–97). The evocation may be aided by the echo of *Th.* 100 (Μουσάων θεράπων) in 5.191–93 (γλυκειᾶν] / Ἡσίοδος πρόπολος Μουσᾶν). If read in this manner, the Bacchylidean passage seems to collapse momentarily the distinction between praiseworthy leaders and poets, and to invite praise for the poet as well as the victor. Nonetheless, the *persona loquens* immediately resumes the role of the *laudator* already in the following line (πείθομαι, 5.195).

[69] Lefkowitz 1969: 91 and Maehler 2004: 128.

[70] On the ring-composition in *Ode* 5, see Cairns 1997, esp. 38–39 on the Hesiodic allusions; cf. Lefkowitz 1969: 50–52 and 90–91, as well as 1976: 45–46 and 72–74.

poetic *persona* in *Ode* 5 describes himself as the χρυσάμπυκος Οὐρανίας / κλεινὸς θεράπων (lines 13–14), which adapts the phrase Μουσᾶν θεράπων (*Th.* 100); this Hesiodic line also underlies Bacchylides' [γλυκειᾶν] / Ἡσίοδος πρόπολος Μουσᾶν in the final strophe of *Ode* 5 (191–93). The "sweet-gifted adornment of the violet-crowned Muses" ([ἰ]οστεφάνων / Μοισᾶν γλυκ[ύ]δωρον ἄγαλμα, *Ode* 5.3–4) reiterates the sweetness that defines the voice of those favored by the Muses (kings in *Th.* 83; poets in *Th.* 97), while the metaphor of one pouring voice out of their chest (ἐθέλει γᾶρυν ἐκ στηθέων χέων / αἰνεῖν Ἱέρωνα) in *Ode* 5.14–16 may be adapting Hesiod's metaphor of voice flowing from one's mouth (kings in *Th.* 83 and poets in *Th.* 97, modeled upon the Muses themselves in *Th.* 39–40). In this context, it also seems likely that Hieron's εὐθύδικος φρήν (*Ode* 5.6) is informed by the Hesiodic portrayal of the divinely favored kings as administrators of justice (*Th.* 84–90, esp. ἰθείῃσι δίκῃσιν in *Th.* 86) and thus looks forward to the allusion to the same Hesiodic passage in *Ode* 5.191–94.

It is certainly plausible that the verbal echoes of *Th.* 81 in 5.193 trigger a condensed evocation of the *Theogony*'s ideal kings, which enriches and amplifies the ode's praise of Hieron. There is, however, a pending problem with this interpretation: lines 193–94 establish a correlation between divine favor and human speech that is not found in the proem of the *Theogony*. The Hesiodic poem envisions as a manifestation of divine favor the effective use of language, be it in the realm of public rhetoric or poetry. In *Ode* 5, on the other hand, those honored by the gods stand out not for what they say but for what is said about them. Lefkowitz attempts to by-pass this inconsistency by taking ἱλάσκονται of *Th.* 91 to mean "greet"; the semantics of the verb, however, do not necessarily privilege verbal over other sorts of interactions, and its use in *Th.* 91 underscores the god-like treatment of the ideal kings (cf. θεὸν ὥς, *Th.* 91) rather than their good reputation. It is certainly possible that the Bacchylidean lines allude to a version of the *Theogony* that no longer survives.[71] I propose, however, that Bacchylides' allusion to the good kings of the *Theogony* may be informed by the association between divine favor and reputation found elsewhere in the Hesiodic corpus, namely in the proem to the *WD*:

> Μοῦσαι Πιερίηθεν ἀοιδῇσι κλείουσαι,
> δεῦτε, Δί᾽ ἐννέπετε σφέτερον πατέρ᾽ ὑμνείουσαι
> ὅν τε διὰ βροτοὶ ἄνδρες ὁμῶς ἄφατοί τε φατοί τε,

---

[71] D'Alessio 2005b: 231.

ῥητοί τ' ἄρρητοί τε Διὸς μεγάλοιο ἕκητι.
ῥέα μὲν γὰρ βριάει, ῥέα δὲ βριάοντα χαλέπτει,
ῥεῖα δ' ἀρίζηλον μινύθει καὶ ἄδηλον ἀέξει,
ῥεῖα δέ τ' ἰθύνει σκολιὸν καὶ ἀγήνορα κάρφει
Ζεὺς ὑψιβρεμέτης, ὃς ὑπέρτατα δώματα ναίει.

(Hesiod, *Works and Days* 1–8)

Muses from Pieria, glorifying with songs, come here, tell in song of your father Zeus, through whom mortal men are obscure and famed alike, and spoken of and not spoken of, by the will of great Zeus. For easily he strengthens, and easily he crushes the strong, easily he diminishes the conspicuous and increases the inconspicuous, and easily he straightens the crooked and withers the proud – high-thundering Zeus, who inhabits the highest abode.

This short hymn celebrates Zeus's power to assign and control the relative importance of individuals in their communities, an apt introduction to a poem preoccupied largely with justice.[72] One's power and success are in the hands of Zeus (*WD* 5–8), but so is one's renown (ἄφατοί τε φατοί τε, / ῥητοί τ' ἄρρητοί τε, *WD* 3–4). The proem distinguishes between those who are known because they are talked about and those without reputation and thus obscure. Whether one belongs to the famous or the unknown depends entirely on Zeus, and the text underscores this fact by framing the two sets of opposite adjectives in *WD* 3–4 with reminders of the god's crucial role in the process (*WD* 3, ὅν τε διά "through whom" punning on Δί' in line 2; *WD* 4, Διὸς μεγάλοιο ἕκητι).[73] Much like *Ode* 5.193–94 (esp. βροτῶν φήμαν, 194), *WD* 3–4 seem to envision reputation exclusively as positive talk, and to regard its presence or absence as a manifestation of divine judgment.[74]

Bacchylides, therefore, may have grafted into his Hesiodic allusion to the ideal kings of the *Theogony* a view about reputation that is expressed in a different part of the Hesiodic corpus. While not a complete fabrication,

---

[72] On the hymn as a proem to the *WD*, see Ercolani 2010: 119–20.

[73] For ἄφατος and ἄρρητος meaning "not famous," "obscure" (cf. ἄδηλος in line 6) see sch. Hes. *WD* 3c, 4a, as well as West 1978: 139 (with emphasis on social status), Verdenius 1985: 4, Mancini 1986, Calame 1996: 171, Rousseau 1996: 98–99, and Ercolani 2010: 121.

[74] Note that in *WD* 760–64 βροτῶν φήμη stands exclusively for malicious gossip. The passage does not implicate the gods at all in the dispensation of bad reputation, thus indicating that this is a purely human phenomenon and not part of Zeus's dispensation of fame as seen in *WD* 3–4. On *WD* 3–4 and 760–64, see Clay 2003: 148 and Canevaro 2015: 133–34; cf. Arrighetti 1998: 397–98 and Ercolani 2010: 411. If Bacchylides' word choice in 5.194 is informed by *WD* 760–65, the epinician poet is redefining and rehabilitating Hesiod's pejorative concept of βροτῶν φήμη into something positive and desirable that lies at the heart of praise-poetry (cf. the unambiguously positive inclusion of Φήμη in Ba. *Odes* 2.1 and 10.1). Admittedly, though, weaving a 'correction' of *WD* 760–64 into the already dense fabric of *Ode* 5.193–94 may be somewhat implausible.

as Stenger has suggested, the Hesiodic reference in *Ode* 5.191–94 may be a
creative merging of two Hesiodic ideas rather than a close paraphrase of a
single passage. Through this complex Hesiodic intertext, *Ode* 5 not only
aligns Hieron with the idealized kings of the *Theogony* but also casts
epinician poetry as a conduit through which Zeus's dispensation of fame
and obscurity becomes part of human reality. In other words, lines
5.191–94 appropriate Hesiodic poetry into the song's epinician poetics by
casting the ode itself – and praise-poetry in general – as a specific application of the all-encompassing statement in *WD* 3–4.

## Birds of Song, Birds of Prey: Bacchylides' *Ode* 3

Bacchylides' *Ode* 3 was composed for the victory of Hieron's chariot at
Olympia in 468 BCE.[75] Even though the occasion for the performance of
Bacchylides' ode is an athletic achievement, the poem is preoccupied with
death and the inevitability of decay, perhaps in response to the tyrant's
deteriorating health.[76] Ultimately, in the final triad Bacchylides suggests
that poetry offers a path towards immortality both for its object and for the
poet himself. Immortality through poetic commemoration is, of course,
the quintessence of heroic epic; nonetheless, I argue that the construction
of Bacchylides' poetic *persona* in these closing lines is informed by the
Hesiodic representation of the poet in the *WD*. Here too, just as in *Ode* 5,
Hesiodic poetics help the lyric speaker define and shape the relationship
between the poet and the *laudandus*.

After a long mythological section that commemorates the miraculous
rescue of Croesus and his daughters from the pyre as a reward for his
piety and concludes with a statement about the unpredictability of mortal
life uttered by Apollo to Admetus, his pious protégé,[77] the *persona loquens*
returns to the 'here and now' and approaches the theme of mortality from
a different perspective:

> φρονέοντι συνετὰ γαρύω· βαθὺς μὲν
> αἰθὴρ ἀμίαντος· ὕδωρ δὲ πόντου

---

[75] Hutchinson 2001: 328, who points out that the song also celebrated Hieron's dedications to Delphi;
Cairns 2010: 63.

[76] Hieron died the following year and it is possible that he was already sick when he celebrated this
Olympic victory. However, Hutchinson 2001: 329–30 is right to recommend caution when it comes
to biographical assumptions and historicizing interpretations.

[77] On the mythological section of *Ode* 3 and how the featured characters (esp. Croesus) relate to
Hieron, see Cairns 2010: 65–74 and 202–11. On 3.83–84 and the problem of the speaker Cairns
2010: 210–11 on 3.81; cf. Maehler 1982: 58 and Stenger 2004: 89–90, 93, 95–96.

οὐ σάπεται· εὐφροσύνα δ᾽ ὁ χρυσός·
ἀνδρὶ δ᾽ οὐ θέμις, πολιὸν τ[αρ]έντα

γῆρας, θάλ[εια]ν αὖτις ἀγκομίσσαι
ἥβαν. ἀρετᾶ[ς γε μ]ὲν οὐ μινύθει
βροτῶν ἅμα σ[ώμ]ατι φέγγος, ἀλλὰ
　　Μοῦσά νιν τρ[έφει.] Ἱέρων, σὺ δ᾽ ὄλβου

κάλλιστ᾽ ἐπεδ[είξ]αο θνατοῖς
　　ἄνθεα· πράξα[ντι] δ᾽ εὖ
οὐ φέρει κόσμ[ον σι]ω-
　　πά· σὺν δ᾽ ἀλαθ[είᾳ] καλῶν
καὶ μελιγλώσσου τις ὑμνήσει χάριν
　　Κηΐας ἀηδόνος.
　　　　　　　　　　　　(Bacchylides, Ode 3.85–98)

I utter things that can be comprehended by one who understands. The deep sky is undefiled, the water of the sea does not rot, and gold is merriment. But it is not right for a man to bring back again flourishing youth, having pushed aside grey old age. However, the light of men's excellence does not diminish along with their body, but the Muse nourishes it. Hieron, you have displayed to mortals the most beautiful flowers of prosperity. To one who is successful silence bears no adornment; but, along with the truthful account of fine deeds, one will praise also the grace of the honey-tongued nightingale from Ceos.

The asyndeton in line 85 marks a new direction in the poem, and the speaker engages in an elaborate priamel that contrasts the eternal elements (sky, sea, gold) with the decaying nature of mortals, but also brings up the complementarity of wealth and poetry.[78] Wealth offers solace in merriment (3.87, 92–94), while poetry rescues one's excellence from his physical decline (3.90–92) and commits a full account of his deeds to immortality (3.96–98).

The complicated priamel is introduced with a first-person statement that demands the attention and active intellectual participation of the audience in the final triad: φρονέοντι συνετὰ γαρύω (3.85). We find similar statements in epinician poetry, in which the audience's insight is somehow marked as a prerequisite for full access to the poetic message. Take, for instance, the following passage in Pindar's *Olympian* 2, an ode composed in 478 BCE. The poem offers a long account of the afterlife that includes

---

[78] Modern interpretations of 3.87 vary greatly. For gold as one of the eternal elements, see already Kenyon 1897: 28, Jebb 1905: 264–65; more recently, Race 1982: 85–86 and Crane 1996: 68–69. On gold in relation to the human condition, see Segal 1976: 111–12, Carey 1977/78, Capra 1999: 168–72, Maehler 2004: 97. For an inclusive reading of the line as looking both backward and forward, see Carson 1984: 117–19 and Cairns 2010: 211–13 with a very perceptive interpretation of the priamel.

the judgment of Rhadamanthys and even the prospect of joining heroes like Achilles on the Isle of the Blessed after several transmigrations of the soul (*O.2.56–83*). After this *katabasis*, the ode breaks off into a different direction with the following statement:

> πολλά μοι ὑπ'
> ἀγκῶνος ὠκέα βέλη
> ἔνδον ἐντὶ φαρέτρας
> φωνάεντα συνετοῖσιν· ἐς δὲ τὸ πᾶν ἑρμανέων
> χατίζει. σοφὸς ὁ πολλὰ εἰδὼς φυᾷ·
> μαθόντες δὲ λάβροι
> παγγλωσσίᾳ κόρακες ὥς ἄκραντα γαρύετον
>
> Διὸς πρὸς ὄρνιχα θεῖον. (Pindar, *Olympian* 2.83–88)

In the quiver under my arm, I have many swift arrows that speak to those who understand, but for the crowd there is need of interpreters. One who knows many things by nature is wise, but those who have learned (things), boisterous in their babbling, they cry out in vain like a pair of crows against the divine bird of Zeus.

The meaning of lines 85–86, which is crucial for our understanding of the entire passage, is unclear and often debated.[79] Yet it seems likely that the *persona loquens*, presumably the poet (83–85), makes a distinction between those who are συνετοί and understand his poetry (φωνάεντα συνετοῖσιν, 85), and those who are not συνετοί and thus cannot access the poetic message directly. This distinction is followed by another contrast between the one who knows a lot by nature and those who know only by learning. The language (σοφός, παγγλωσσίᾳ, γαρύετον) and the bird-simile imply that this is a juxtaposition between Pindar, a superior poet by nature, and lesser poets.[80] While *O.2.86–88* point to poetic rivalry relatively clearly,

---

[79] Ever since antiquity, lines 83–85 have been read as a contrast between the few who know and the crowd (ἐς δὲ τὸ πᾶν) who need interpreters: see sch. Pi. *O.2.152b* (attributed to Aristarchus), 153a–b, as well as Gildersleeve 1885: 152, Farnell 1932: 21 (who equates τὸ πᾶν with οἱ πολλοί while acknowledging that the meaning is unattested), and Kirkwood 1982: 75. Race 1981 has objected to the traditional interpretation, arguing that ἐς δὲ τὸ πᾶν means "for the whole subject." Most 1986 proposed that ἐς δὲ τὸ πάν is a synonym of πάντως and that ἑρμηνεύς stands for a performer; lines 83–85, therefore, express the *topos* that the poet has many ways of praising the *laudandus*, even if he cannot include all of them in this ode (cf. sch. *O.2.153c*). In defense of the traditional view, see Gentili et al. 2013: 408–10 (cf. Lavecchia 2000).

[80] See the discussion in Gentili et al. 2013: 411; on the metapoetic dimensions of arrows, birds, and flying, see also Arrighetti 1987: 104–08. Steiner 2007 sees here a transformation of the Hesiodic *ainos* of the hawk and the nightingale, whereby the conflict is not between a power-figure and a poet but between different poetic *personae* representing different moral and aesthetic perspectives. While her study of Pindar's avian metaphors for poetry and poetics is sharp, I am not entirely convinced that the conflict between the eagle and the crows is an instance of Hesiodic reception rather than Pindar's version of a *topos*. Steiner argues in passing that *O.2.83* alludes to Hesiod's *WD* 202 but

the commentary on knowledge in the previous lines (83–86), including the formulation σοφὸς ὁ πολλὰ εἰδὼς φυᾷ in 86, is vague enough to encompass both the poet and the συνετοί.[81] Another convergence between the epinician speaker and the συνετοί is explicit in Pindar's *Pythian* 5:[82]

> ἄνδρα κεῖνον ἐπαινέοντι συνετοί·
> λεγόμενον ἐρέω.
>
> (Pindar, *Pythian* 5.107–08)

Those who know praise that man; I will report what is said.

In this passage, the speaker voluntarily channels the voice of the συνετοί, so that it may be commemorated and proliferated through song, and may thus reach even those who do not belong to that exceptional group. Finally, sometimes lyric draws attention to the capacity of its audience to appreciate the poet's work in a less convoluted manner; see, for instance, the *captationes benevolentiae* in Bacchylides' *Ode* 5.3–5 (esp. γνώσῃ, 3) and Pindar's *O.*1.103–105 (esp. ἴδριν, 104).[83]

The study of these passages has yielded several interpretations for Bacchylides' φρονέοντι συνετὰ γαρύω in *Ode* 3.85. The way in which the Bacchylidean line privileges one group among the audience, much like *Ode* 5.3–5 and Pindar's *O.*1.103–05, has been identified as an epinician convention: praise-poetry requires that a poet construct the *laudandus* as erudite and sophisticated.[84] On the other hand, Nagy has interpreted Ba. 3.85 in conjunction with Pi. *O.*2.85 and *P.*5.107, and he has traced in these passages that appeal to the intellect of their audience a different generic trait of the epinician, namely the poetics of exclusivity. In Nagy's opinion, these passages are programmatic in so far as they reiterate the idea that praise-poetry is a coded message (ἔπ-αινος) meant to be deciphered and understood by a specific social group (κῶμος) consisting of comrades (ἑταῖροι) bonded by φιλότης.[85] More recently, Currie has

---

does not dwell on the problems surrounding the meaning of the Pindaric line. On the subject, see also Morgan 2015: 123–32.

[81] Cf. Kirkwood 1982: 75 and Lavecchia 2000.

[82] Contrast Pi. *N.*4.30–32, where the *persona loquens* isolates a certain kind of audience for lack of understanding.

[83] Cf. also Pindar's praise of Thrasyboulus in *P.*6.47–49, although the passage may be reiterating the idea that Thrasyboulus has gained wisdom from poetry (cf. 19–42, esp. 19–27), rather than celebrating "his sophistication in the ways of the Muses" as Bundy 1962: 25 reads it.

[84] For the elite audience's presumed sophistication, see already sch. *O.*2.152c and 153a; cf. Maehler 1982: 58 for Ba. 3.85. See also Bundy 1962: 24–26, on the conventional combination of the appreciation of poetry with other elements of praise as a reflection of social values, and Arrighetti 1987: 115–16.

[85] Nagy 1999: 222–42. On συνετός, a term used in aristocratic self-description, see Battisti 2011.

suggested that the exclusionary poetics are not based on social networks but on cult. Currie points out that language of understanding (συνίημι, συνετός/ἀσύνετος) is often associated with mysteries and initiation. Therefore, he reads in Ba. *Ode* 3.85, Pi. *O*.2.83–5, and in two other Pindaric passages addressed to Hieron (*P*.2.80 and fr. 105a.1 SM) a direct engagement with the tyrant's involvement in mysteries.[86] Finally, there is a literary interpretation of *Ode* 3.85 which dates back to the nineteenth century and does not take into consideration any of the other passages.[87] According to this view, φρονέοντι stands for literary expertise and the line invites its audience (and especially Hieron) to recall the priamel in Pindar's *O*.1.1–2 in preparation for Bacchylides' own priamel in the immediately following lines(3.85–87).

There is little doubt in my mind that Bacchylides' φρονέοντι συνετά γαρύω in 3.85 is informed by exclusionary aristocratic poetics, which are only reinforced by the subsequent emphasis on χρυσός (3.87), ἀρετά (3.90), and ὄλβος (3.92). Unlike similar passages discussed above (Pi. *O*.2.85 and *P*.5.107), however, 3.85 isolates an exceptional individual rather than a group, thus establishing a rapport between the speaker and this insightful man who has the intellectual capacity to understand the message of the priamel. While Hieron's name does not appear here, the speaker addresses him directly and by name after the priamel has come to a conclusion (3.92). I suggest that, with the singular φρονέοντι in line 85, the speaker implicates Hieron and thus engages with him already from the very beginning of the last triad, before addressing him directly in line 92. In 3.85–92 the *persona loquens* not only singles out a powerful figure as the primary addressee of the coded poetic message but also underscores his capacity to access and appreciate its meaning, namely the value of commemorative poetics: praise-poetry can save a man's excellence from his inevitable physical decline and death. In the final three lines the ode decodes this message, as it explicitly underscores the poet's commitment to securing Hieron's immortality by linking

---

[86] Currie 2005: 389–90; his discussion of mystical elements in Bacchylides' *Ode* 3, however, is admittedly only tentative (386–87). Cf. Krummen 1990: 258, Hutchinson 2001: 352–53. On the mystical elements in *O*.2 in particular, see Lloyd-Jones 1990: 88; contrast, however, Willcock 1995: 157–58, who views the Homeric (*Od*. 4.561–69) and Hesiodic (*WD* 166–73a) elements as predominant.

[87] On the priamel in *Ode* 3 as a creative allusion to the opening priamel of *O*.1, see Kenyon 1897: 27, Jebb 1905: 264, Gentili 1958: 92–93, Maehler 1963: 93 and 1982b: 58 on 3.85, Wind 1971, and Morrison 2007: 87–88. In the light of Simonides 256.3–5 Poltera, however, Cairns 2010: 212 objects that the common imagery of the Pindaric and the Bacchylidean priamels may actually be a matter of convention rather than intertextuality.

inextricably the fame and reputation of the *laudator* and the *laudandus* (3.96–98).[88]

In the concluding *sphragis*, Bacchylides is identified as the "nightingale from Ceos." Early Greek poetry associates the nightingale with song and springtime, and it is a bird a poet may compare himself to (e.g. Thgn. 939).[89] In *Odē* 3, however, the bird stands for the poet himself. The only precedent for the nightingale as an embodiment of a poetic figure is Hesiod's *ainos* in the *WD*:

> Νῦν δ' αἶνον βασιλεῦσιν ἐρέω φρονέουσι[90] καὶ αὐτοῖς·
> ὧδ' ἴρηξ προσέειπεν ἀηδόνα ποικιλόδειρον
> ὕψι μάλ' ἐν νεφέεσσι φέρων ὀνύχεσσι μεμαρπώς·
> ἣ δ' ἐλεόν, γναμπτοῖσι πεπαρμένη ἀμφ' ὀνύχεσσι,
> μύρετο· τὴν ὅ γ' ἐπικρατέως πρὸς μῦθον ἔειπεν·
> "δαιμονίη, τί λέληκας; ἔχει νύ σε πολλὸν ἀρείων·
> τῇ δ' εἶς ᾗ σ' ἂν ἐγώ περ ἄγω καὶ ἀοιδὸν ἐοῦσαν·
> δεῖπνον δ', αἴ κ' ἐθέλω, ποιήσομαι ἠὲ μεθήσω.
> ἄφρων δ', ὅς κ' ἐθέλῃ πρὸς κρείσσονας ἀντιφερίζειν·
> νίκης τε στέρεται πρός τ' αἴσχεσιν ἄλγεα πάσχει."
> ὣς ἔφατ' ὠκυπέτης ἴρηξ, τανυσίπτερος ὄρνις.
>
> (Hesiod, *Works and Days* 202–12)

And now I will tell a fable (αἶνον) to the kings who themselves understand: a hawk addressed a nightingale with a colorful neck in this way, as he was carrying her very high in the clouds, having snatched her with his talons, and she was weeping pitifully, pierced by the curved talons. To her he spoke forcefully: "Silly one, why are you screaming? Someone much superior holds you now; you are going wherever I may take you, even if you are a singer. I will make (you) my dinner if I want, or I'll let you go. Whoever wishes to contend against those who are stronger is stupid. He is both deprived of victory and suffers pains in addition to humiliations." Thus spoke the swift-flying hawk, the long-winged bird.

Bacchylides involves a variety of animals in the context of his poetic self-representation: he is the rooster of Ourania in *Ode* 4.7–8 and a bee

---

[88] The syntax of 3.96–98 is not without problems. See Hutchinson 2001: 356–58, Maehler 1982: 60–61, Stenger 2004: 113–15, and Cairns 2010: 214–15.

[89] Thgn. 939: οὐ δύναμαι φωνῇ λίγ' ἀειδέμεν ὥσπερ ἀηδών. Nightingales are mentioned as songbirds in Hom. *Od.* 19.518–19 and Alcman *PMGF* 10a.6–7 and fr. 224 Calame (who reads the ἀηδών as the chorus' reference to the *choragos*); cf. Lesb. inc. auct. 28.5–7V. Nightingales are mentioned as the herald of spring in Sapph. fr. 136 V; Alcaeus fr. 307c V; Simon. F 294 Poltera. For a survey of all passages linking birds with poetry and song in early Greek poetry, see Nünlist 1998: 39–60. The nightingale as a metaphor for poets occurs often in Hellenistic and post-Hellenistic poetry, especially in epigrams; see Maehler 1982: 62–63 nn.97–98 and Nünlist 1998: 351 with n.54.

[90] On the preference of φρονέουσι over the *varia lectio* νοέουσι, see West 1978: 205.

in *Ode* 10.10. I suggest that the choice of the nightingale in the *sphragis* of *Ode* 3 alludes to the fate of the nightingale/poet in the Hesiodic poem. Through the evocation of *WD* 202–12, the ode defines more sharply the relationship it envisions between Hieron and the epinician poet. The *ainos* is part of Hesiod's elaborate effort to persuade Perses and the corrupt kings that *dike* is preferable to *hybris*. Its meaning is the subject of an ongoing debate among scholars, but, according to the most straightforward interpretation found already in the scholia, the anthropomorphic interaction between the two birds demonstrates vividly the suffering of the helpless nightingale/poet in the hands of those who wield power in an arbitrary and overwhelming fashion.[91] The primary intended audience for this *ainos* is not Perses but the kings, and the introductory line requires special attention because it bears similarities to *Ode* 3.85. Much like Bacchylides' φρονέοντι συνετὰ γαρύω, the Hesiodic line νῦν δ' αἶνον βασιλεῦσιν ἐρέω φρονέουσι καὶ αὐτοῖς involves a first-person statement by the poet that marks the upcoming lines as intellectually challenging (αἶνος, cf. συνετά); it also employs a participle of the verb φρονέω to herald the exceptional capacity of the primary intended audience to comprehend the message.[92] Ba. 3.85 thus emerges as the first allusion to the Hesiodic *ainos* in the final triad of the ode.[93]

I suggest here that *Ode* 3 alludes to the Hesiodic *ainos* in order to intensify the bond it forges between the poet and Hieron. Both poems imply that poet and ruler share some knowledge: in the *WD* it concerns the abuse of power, while in the epinician ode it revolves around the mortality of the flesh and the immortality of poetry. The Hesiodic passage casts poet and ruler as opponents and laments the helplessness of the poet;

---

[91] The hawk and the nightingale stand for the corrupt kings and Hesiod according to sch. *WD* 202, 202a, 207–12 and, more recently, Wilamowitz 1928: 64, Sellschopp 1934: 83–86, Nicolai 1964: 50–53, Verdenius 1985: 117. For a different modern approach that interprets the fable as a commentary on the relationship between Zeus (hawk) and the kings (nightingale), see Jensen 1966 and Nelson 1997. For a reading of the fable as pertaining to poetics, see Puelma 1972, Hubbard 1995, Mordine 2006, Steiner 2007 and 2012. Cf. also the survey in Ercolani 2010: 204–05.

[92] Mordine 2006: 365; cf. Wilamowitz 1928: 64. There is little point in taking the participial phrase φρονέουσι καὶ αὐτοῖς as concessive, especially since the fable is left open-ended and the kings are actually invested with the task of interpreting it; cf. the appeal to the kings' intellect in *WD* 248 (καταφράζεσθε καὶ αὐτοί). Notice also that the belated "commentary" on the fable in *WD* 274–81 is addressed to Perses, not the kings, who have presumably already gotten the message. I am not convinced that the kings to whom Hesiod addresses his fable are the ones praised in the proem to the *Theogony*, as in Nicolai 1964: 51, Griffith 1983a: 59, and Mordine 2006: 365 assume. The bribe-eating kings are in a perfect position to interpret the abusive behavior of the hawk; cf. Puelma 1972: 87–88, Nelson 1997, Steiner 2012: 5–6. For a different interpretation, see Dalfen 1994: 163 who reads the nightingale as the arrogant challenger but presupposes that the audience would supply a lot of crucial information not included in the Hesiodic version of the fable.

[93] Cf. Race 1982: 85 n.127 who states that the "correct parallel" for *Ode* 3.85 is *WD* 202, not Pindar's *O*.2.85, but does not justify or elaborate on this statement.

the ode, on the other hand, reconfigures this relationship into a celebration of the ruler. The poetic voice endorses the powerful man and promises to provide immortality after death; more than that, the praise-poet acknowledges that his own reputation is bound to the successful commemoration of the ruler's excellence. In sum, through juxtaposition to the Hesiodic *ainos*, the alignment between Bacchylides and Hieron becomes even clearer; the Hesiodic allusion, therefore, enriches the poetics of praise in *Ode 3* and contributes a foil for the poem's negotiation of the relationship between *laudator* and *laudandus*.

## Homer and Hesiod in Pindar's *Paean* 7b

Pindar's *Paean* 7b/52h, a song composed for performance at Delos, is woefully lacunose, but what survives attests to a direct and explicit engagement with Homer. The poem opens with an address to Apollo and a reference to a mother, probably Leto (*Pa.*7b/52h.1–3); in the following lines, the extant text preserves the word παιαν[, possibly a "generic signature" of the song, and some reference to garlands (*Pa.*7b/52h.4–6). After marking the beginning of its song (ἀρχομ[, *Pa.*7b/52h.8),[94] the chorus goes on to elaborate on the poetics of their song:[95]

> κελαδ᾿ ἤσαθ᾿ ὕμ᾿νους,
> Ὁμήρου [ ~4 τρι]πτον κατ᾿ ἀμαξιτὸν
> ἰόντες, ᾀ[ ~5 ἀλ]λοτρίαις ἀν᾿ ἵπποις,
> ἐπεὶ αυ[ ~6 π]τανὸν ἅρμα[96]
> Μοισα[ ~10 ]μεν.
> ἐ]πεύχο[μαι] δ᾿ Οὐρανοῦ τ᾿ ἐυπέπλῳ θυγατρὶ
>      Μναμ[ο]σύ[ν]ᾳ κόραισί τ᾿ εὐ-
>      μαχανίαν διδόμεν.
> τ]υφλα[ὶ γὰ]ρ ἀνδρῶν φρένες
> ὅ]στις ἄνευθ᾿ Ἑλικωνιάδων
> βαθεῖαν ε᾿᾿[᾿᾿] ων ἐρευνᾷ σοφίας ὁδόν.
>
> ἐμοὶ δὲ τοῦτο[ν δ]ιέδω-
>    κ᾿ ᾿ ν] ἀθάνατ[ο]ν πόνον
>                          (Pindar, *Paean* 7b/52h.10–22)

---

[94] On the reference to some hero or something pertaining to hero-cult (ἥρωϊ[, *Pa.*7b/52h.9), see Rutherford 2001: 246.

[95] I print the text of Rutherford's 2001 edition.

[96] See D'Alessio 1995: 175 for a discussion of πο]τανόν instead of π]τανόν.

Sing hymns, going on the ... [trodden] wagon-track of Homer ... on the mares of another since [we?] ... the winged chariot [of] the Muse[s]. I pray to Mnemosyne, the fair-robed daughter of Ouranus and to her daughters that they grant poetic resourcefulness. [For] blind are the minds of men, whoever may seek the deep path of skill without the Heliconian (Muses). [They?] have given me this immortal task ...

After a substantial hiatus, the text resumes with the story of Asteria, daughter of Coeus and sister of Leto (*Pa.*7b/52h.42–52).[97] Asteria evaded Zeus's advances and was turned into a small wandering island. The chorus relates with some reservation her metamorphosis and concludes the story with the name that humans have long assigned to her new form (Ortygia). The immediately following lines indicate that the context of this tale is the birth of Apollo: Ortygia acquired a firm spot in the sea in return for giving refuge to Leto when she was about to give birth. The extant text does not complete the aetiological story with the final transformation of the wandering rock to the fixed and holy island known as Delos,[98] but perhaps it was mentioned in the final five lines that are missing.

Apollo's birth, as well as Delos' crucial aid to Leto and the ensuing reward were treated extensively in the *Homeric Hymn to Apollo* (*h.Ap.* 25–90);[99] it is reasonable, therefore, to assume that the paean's engagement with Homer's poetry in lines 11–12 refers primarily to that Homeric Hymn.[100] But what is the relationship that these lines establish between the lyric poem and the authoritative Homeric voice? Is the chorus treading the wagon-track of Homer or not? It all depends on how we supplement the missing text. Di Benedetto suggests Ὁμήρου [πολύτρι]πτον κατ' ἀμαξιτόν / ἰόντες, ἀ[λλ' οὐκ ἀλ]λοτρίαις ἀν' ἵπποις ("going on the much-worn wagon-track of Homer but not on the mares of another"), a reading that declares the paean's dependence on the Homeric tradition.[101] However, the mythological narrative of the paean's extant epode departs significantly from the Homeric Hymn.[102] To begin with, in the *h.Ap.*

---

[97] The genealogy is found already in Hes.*Th.* 404–10. According to the *Theogony*, Asteria is the mother of Hecate. However, there is no trace in Hesiodic poetry of the story regarding Asteria that is recounted in Pi. *Pa.*52h/52h.

[98] The poem plays with the etymology of Δῆλος / δῆλος already in lines 46–47 (esp. 47, φανῆναι).

[99] Cf. also *h.Ap.* 14–18 and the description of the festival at Delos (146–78), which vividly exemplifies the reward that Delos earned.

[100] Treu 1967: 151 and n.11; Rutherford 1988: 65–70. For the authorship of the *h.Ap.*, cf. Thuc. 3.104.4–6 who also attributes it to Homer. On the Delian part of the *h.Ap.* in particular as representative of the Homeric tradition, cf. Martin 2000: 411–24.

[101] Di Benedetto 1991.     [102] Rutherford 2001: 252.

Ortygia and Delos are two separate entities: Leto gives birth to Artemis on the former and to Apollo on the latter (*h.Ap.* 14–18). Furthermore, in the Homeric Hymn the reward that Delos receives consists in honor and wealth through the cult of Apollo (*h.Ap.* 51–65, 79–89; cf. 146–76). It is much more likely, therefore, that lines 11–12 conveyed a statement of departure from the Homeric tradition.[103] Along these lines, Snell supplemented a negation in 11 ('Ομήρου [δὲ μὴ τρι]πτὸν κατ' ἀμαξιτόν / ἰόντες, "not going on the much-worn wagon-track of Homer"),[104] while D'Alessio proposed 'Ομήρου [ἑκὰς ἄτρι]πτον κατ' ἀμαξιτόν / ἰόντες ("going on an untrodden wagon-track far from Homer").[105]

The metaphor of the voyage that immediately follows lines 11–12 reinforces the poem's declaration of independence from the Homeric tradition. Once again, we encounter textual difficulties. The chorus envisions a poetic journey on the winged chariot of the Muses (*Pa.*7b/ 52h.13–14),[106] but whom do the horses of this poetic chariot belong to (line 12)? Lobel's reconstruction implies that the horses are not the chorus' (ἀ[λλ' ἀλ]λοτρίαις ἀν' ἵπποις). Yet D'Alessio has demonstrated conclusively that line 12 should include a negative statement[107] and proposes ἀ[εὶ οὐκ ἀλ]λοτρίαις.[108] While on the winged chariot of the Muses, then, the chorus seems to be propelled by its own poetic horses. In addition, D'Alessio has drawn attention to some similarities between this passage and Parmenides B 1 DK. In the Parmenidean fragment, the speaker

---

[103] Rutherford 1988: 65–70 as well as 2001: 248 and 252. According to D'Alessio 1995: 178–81, the paean underscores that it differs from the Homeric tradition in terms of genre (form), but Rutherford 2001: 252 rightly points out that the statement of lines 11–14 must also include the divergences in content. On the ἀμαξιτός established by previous poets, contrast *N.*6.53–54, where the first-person voice readily follows the wagon-road of the heroic epic tradition.

[104] Maehler 1989: 37.

[105] D'Alessio 1995: 169 and 172–74. D'Alessio reconstructs the line based on Parm. B 1.27 DK (ἣ γὰρ ἀπ' ἀνθρώπων ἐκτὸς πάτου ἐστίν), thus expanding the number of verbal correspondences that he traces between Pi. *Pa.*52h/52h.10–20 and the poem of Parmenides (primarily B 1.21–28 DK and B 6.3–7 DK). Cf. the reception of the road metaphor later by Callimachus. In *Aetia* fr. 1.25–28, the programmatic announcement of Callimachean aesthetics includes a divinely ordained preference for the narrow untrodden path (κελεύθους / [ἀτρίπτ]ους, 27–28) rather than the wide road. Massimilla 1996: 219 points out the passage's debt to *WD* 286–92 as well as the metaphors of the poetic chariot in Pindaric poetry; cf. also Reinsch-Werner 1976: 334–37. Nonetheless, it is worth noting that, while it is very likely that the two roads in Callimachus' *Aetia* are informed by the two paths in the *WD*, Pindar's *Paean* 7b/52h sets up a different contrast, since driving on a road is juxtaposed to flying on a winged divine chariot.

[106] Snell-Maehler supplement line 14 as Μοῦσα[ν or Μουσα[ῖον ἐζεύξα]μεν or ἀνέβα]μεν. Di Benedetto 1991 prefers ἐλαύνο]μεν.

[107] D'Alessio 1992: 363–66; cf. Di Benedetto 1991, who nonetheless argues that *Pa.*7b/52h.11–14 claim Homer as the song's model.

[108] D'Alessio 1995: 167–69.

recounts his ride on the winged chariot of the Heliades as they flew together to the house of the Night, where he was initiated into privileged knowledge. D'Alessio is right in pointing out that both poems involve mortals riding flying chariots that belong to divinities,[109] but he downplays a crucial difference: in the Parmenidean passage, the Heliades accompany the young man (B 1.4–21 DK), whereas in *Paean 7b/52h* the chorus appears to ride the chariot of the Muses alone.[110]

Lines 12–14, therefore, introduce a crucial aspect of the paean's poetics, namely the relationship between the *persona loquens* and the Muses. Ultimately, the ode appears to claim that it defies mortality (τοῦτον ... ἀθάνατον πόνον, *Pa.*7b/52h.21–22),[111] but only after it has fashioned itself as the product of a synergy between human poetic skill and divine patronage. In *Pa.*7b/52h.15–20, the speaker prays to Mnemosyne and the Muses for poetic resourcefulness (εὐμαχανίαν, *Pa.*7b/52h.16–17), and criticizes those who seek poetic skill without the support of the Muses:

> ἐ]πεύχο[μαι] δ' Οὐρανοῦ τ' ἐυπέπλῳ θυγατρὶ
> Μναμ[ο]σύ[ν]ᾳ κόραισί τ' εὐ-
> μαχανίαν διδόμεν.
> τ]υφλα[ὶ γὰ]ρ ἀνδρῶν φρένες,
> ὅ]στις ἄνευθ' Ἑλικωνιάδων
> βαθεῖαν ε . . [ . . ] . ων ἐρευνᾷ σοφίας ὁδόν.
>
> (Pindar, *Paean* 7b/52h.15–20)

I pray to Mnemosyne, the fair-robed daughter of Ouranus, and to her daughters that they grant poetic resourcefulness. [For] blind are the minds of men, whoever may seek the deep path of skill without the Heliconian (Muses).

The reference to the Muses as the "Heliconians" is rare in Pindar and used only here in connection with poetics and poetic competence.[112] In this

---

[109] D'Alessio 1995: 170, who also underlines the shared use of ἀμαξιτός (Parm. B 1.21 DK; Pi. *Pa.*7b/52h.11). On Parm. B 6 DK and *Pa.*7b/52h.11–20, see note 110.

[110] Cf. Pi *O.*6.22–27, in which the *persona loquens* invites the victorious charioteer Phintis to yoke the mules so that they may embark the chariot (βάσομεν, 24) and that the *persona loquens* may arrive at the victor's kin (ἵκωμαι, 24). The epinician text blurs the boundaries between reality (Phintis and the victorious chariot) and the figurative trajectory of poetry, but the *persona loquens* envisions riding that chariot with the mortal charioteer, not some divinity. For a careful and intriguing reading of *O.*6 in light of Parmenides B 1 DK, see D'Alessio 1995: 146–67 with ample bibliography. I assume the *persona loquens* in Pa 7b/52h.14 still represents the chorus based on the assumption that the extant ]μεν is the ending of a first-person plural verbal form.

[111] The person of the verbal form in 21–22 is unclear, as is its subject, but it is possible that the paean envisions itself as a commission of the Muses themselves. Cf. δέλτου (l.24), sadly without context.

[112] There are only two other instances. *I.*8.56a–58 recounts that the "Heliconian maidens" stood by Achilles' pyre and grave, and sang their dirge. On the other hand, in *I.*2.33–34 (οὐ γὰρ πάγος οὐδὲ προσάντης ἁ κέλευθος γίνεται, / εἴ τις εὐδόξων ἐς ἀνδρῶν ἄγοι τιμὰς Ἑλικωνιάδων), the *persona loquens* declares that nothing can obstruct a man determined to honor glorious men with poetry.

context, the adjective is particularly significant, as it evokes the geographic location where the goddesses encountered Hesiod and initiated him into poetry (*Th.* 22–34).[113] The Heliconian Muses are marked as Hesiodic not only in the proem of the *Theogony* but also in the *WD*: in lines 658–59 the narrator recounts the dedication of the tripod he won at a competition to the goddesses in commemoration of their transformative encounter on Helicon (τὸν μὲν ἐγὼ Μούσησ' Ἑλικωνιάδεσσ' ἀνέθηκα / ἔνθα με τὸ πρῶτον λιγυρῆς ἐπέβησαν ἀοιδῆς). The evocation of Hesiod's poetic initiation in *Pa.*7b/52h is further facilitated by the invocation of Mnemo-syne and the Muses through the frame of their genealogical connection (Μναμ[ο]σύ[ν]ᾳ κόραισί τ', *Pa.*7b/52h.16) since the *Theogony* recounts the Muses' birth shortly after the narrative of their encounter with Hesiod on Mount Helicon (*Th.* 53–63).[114] Finally, if indeed they cast the Pindaric paean as a labor that the Muses have bestowed upon the *persona loquens*, lines 21–22 reinforce the allusion to Hesiod's poetic initiation, given that the idea of poetry as a divinely assigned task resonates with his experience in *Th.* 30–34.[115] In *Pa.*7b/52h.18–20, therefore, the decisive role of the Heliconian Muses in the attainment of poetic *sophia* is informed by their active involvement in Hesiod's transformation into a poet. On the other hand, the element of blindness that is central to the criticism of those who seek poetic skill without the Muses' help (τ]υφλα[ὶ γὰ]ρ ἀνδρῶν φρένες, 18) seems to resume the paean's polemics against Homer, since he is the blind poet par excellence, albeit in a strictly physical sense.[116] Thus, while the *persona loquens* of *Pa.*7b/52h claims an active poetic role in cooperation with the Muses, poetic authority is established not only by declaring independence from the Homeric tradition but also by

Accessibility is a theme shared between *I.*2.33–34 and *Pa.*7b/52h.18–20. However, the latter refers clearly to poetic skill, while the former underscores the idea that great deeds lead effortlessly to praise: a poet's access to praise is easy when he celebrates famous men (cf. *N.*6.45–46).

[113] Cf. already Gianotti 1975: 61.

[114] Mnemosyne's birth of Gaia and Ouranos is recounted in *Th.* 135.

[115] On poetry as a gift that the Muses bestow upon mortals, cf. also *Th.* 103–04 (ταχέως δὲ παρέτραπε δῶρα θεάων. / Χαίρετε, τέκνα Διός, δότε δ' ἱμερόεσσα ἀοιδήν).

[116] See already *h.Ap.* 172. On blindness in Homer's biographical tradition, see Graziosi 2002: 125–63. D'Alessio 1995: 170–72 draws attention to a possible intertextual connection between *Pa.*7b/52h.18–20 and Parmenides' B 6.3–7 DK: ἀμηχανίη γὰρ ἐν αὐτῶν / στήθεσιν ἰθύνει πλακτὸν νόον· οἱ δὲ φοροῦνται / κωφοὶ ὁμῶς τυφλοί τε, τεθηπότες, ἄκριτα φῦλα. While the idea of some intertextual engagement is intriguing, Parmenides' discourse is purely epistemological, whereas in Pi. *Pa.*7b/52h it is most likely that both the εὐμαχανία and the σοφία that comes from the Muses pertain to poetics (even if one concedes that at least the latter may include some epistemological aspects).

appropriating the foundation of Hesiod's poetic authority, namely his poetic initiation.

How are we to interpret the Hesiodic resonances in this paean? It has been argued that the passage iterates the contrast between Hesiod, the poet upon whom the Heliconian Muses have bestowed access to the truth, and Homer, whose poetry does not enjoy this divine privilege.[117] According to this reading, the passage condemns the Homeric tradition as false and, by coopting the Hesiodic poetics, establishes the paean's own claim to a truthful account. Although the polemical tone of the lines is undeniable, I am reluctant to interpret σοφία in line 20 as pertaining primarily to epistemology rather than poetics, given that resourcefulness (εὐμαχανία, lines 16–17), which the Pindaric speaker hopes to receive from Mnemosyne and the Muses, almost certainly stands for poetic skill. That *Pa.7b/52h.15–20* discuss poetic competence rather than truth is all the more evident when they are compared to Pindar's *Isthmian 4*:

> Ἔστι μοι θεῶν ἕκατι μυρία παντᾷ κέλευθος,
> ὦ Μέλισσ᾽, εὐμαχανίαν γὰρ ἔφανας Ἰσθμίοις,
> ὑμετέρας ἀρετὰς ὕμνῳ διώκειν.
>
> (Pindar, *Isthmian* 4.1–3)

Thanks to the gods, I have countless roads in every direction to pursue in song your (pl.) achievements, Melissus, for you revealed (to me) much resource at the Isthmian Games.

The ode opens by pointing out that, with his Isthmian victory, the *laudandus* has facilitated the poetic praise of his glorious clan. The passage combines the idea of ample access to a poetic subject (εὐμαχανία) with the metaphorical path of song (κέλευθος; cf. ὕμνῳ διώκειν), while linking inextricably the gods (θεῶν ἕκατι, *I.4.1*)[118] not only with the athletic victory but also with the poetic ingenuity involved in its celebration.

---

[117] Koning 2010a: 316 with Bowra 1964: 33–34. Differently Rutherford 2001: 249–50, who traces an emphasis on "Muses as bestowers of wisdom, particularly in matters of religion" and interprets the choice of the Heliconian Muses "not just as reflecting Pindar's specially Boeotian allegiances, but also, perhaps, as an allusion to the didactic nature of Hesiodic poetry."

[118] The path of poetry is a fairly common metaphor in Pindaric and Bacchylidean poetry; see the parallels cited in Privitera 1982: 172–73. Note that Koning 2010a: 315–16, who discusses *Pa.7b/52h.11–20* without consideration of its textual problems, reads in these lines a contrast between the well-trodden avenue that needs to be avoided (ἁμαξιτός) and the path (βαθεῖα ὁδός) that is hard to follow but leads to something valuable. According to his reading, this juxtaposition alludes to the contrast between the paths of virtue and sloth in the *WD* 287–92. However, the road metaphor in the *WD* applies strictly to ethical matters, not poetics; more importantly, the role of the gods in the *WD* is to make the desirable path difficult (*WD* 289–90), not to provide exclusive

The juxtaposition between Hesiodic and Homeric poetics in lines 15–20 enhances the ode's programmatic rejection of the Homeric tradition, but the interpretation of this passage could be taken further if we consider the intended location of the paean's performance. In the context of a poetic celebration of Apollo at Delos, the juxtaposition between Hesiod and Homer is more than a means to establish poetic authority: it invites the audience to recall the biographical tradition that envisioned these two great poets performing together in Delos. According to the Pindaric scholion to N.2.1:

> δηλοῖ δὲ ὁ Ἡσίοδος λέγων·
> "ἐν Δήλῳ τότε πρῶτον ἐγὼ καὶ Ὅμηρος ἀοιδοὶ
> μέλπομεν, ἐν νεαροῖς ὕμνοις ῥάψαντες ἀοιδήν,
> Φοῖβον Ἀπόλλωνα χρυσάορον, ὃν τέκε Λητώ" (= Hes. fr. 357 MW)

And Hesiod reveals (sc. the etymology of 'rhapsode' from 'rhaptein') when he says: "In Delos then for the first time I and Homer, bards, stitching a song with new hymns, were singing of Phoebus Apollo with the golden sword, whom Leto bore."

The context of these lines is unknown, but the speaker was clearly understood by the scholiast to be Hesiod himself. The first-person account resembles, and is probably modeled upon, the account of the poetic contest at Chalcis in the WD (650–62).[119] Unlike the *agon* at Amphidamas' games, however, which is well attested in the biographical tradition,[120] this is the only extant testimony of a poetic meeting, or rather a poetic competition, at Delos.[121] These lines have rightly been interpreted as a retrojection produced by rhapsodes in order to appropriate Homer and Hesiod and to create a prototypical agonistic rhapsodic performance.[122] It is tempting to think of the first-person narrative in Hes. fr. 357 MW as a response to the *sphragis* embedded in the Delian part of the *Homeric Hymn to Apollo* (h.Ap. 169–76),

---

access to it (cf. *I.*2.33–34 with n.112). I do not see, therefore, how Pa.7b/52h.11–20 would have been perceived as a reception of WD 287–92.

[119] Hes. fr. 357 MW disregards WD 649–53, according to which the poet never sailed except for his (short) trip to Euboea for the funerary games for Amphidamas. See Bassino 2013: 14–18.

[120] On the *agon* of Homer and Hesiod in Chalcis, see Graziosi 2002: 168–80, Kivilo 2010: 19–24, Koning 2010a: 245–68, and Bassino 2013: 11–52. See also Introduction, pp. 4–5.

[121] Although in Hes. fr. 357 MW the context of performance is not explicitly competitive, it is very likely that the passage refers to a contest; see Martin 2000: 410–23 and Nagy 2010: 70–73. For competitive performances at Delos, cf. *h.Ap.* 149–50.

[122] See Martin 2000: 410–23, Graziosi 2002: 33–34, who reads the passage as an aetiological tale, and Collins 2004: 181 and 194, who emphasizes that the two poets are envisioned in a performance that is not only competitive but also amoebic.

where 'Homer', identified only as a blind man from Chios, asserts his poetic superiority, thus suggesting an agonistic occasion.[123] If the Delian meeting of the two poets was indeed envisioned as competitive, its outcome remains unknown; yet the consistency with which Hesiod wins in all extant versions of the contest at Chalcis (sometimes even against expectation) suggests that in the biographical tradition competitions may have had a set outcome in favor of the Boeotian poet.[124] However that may be, I suggest that, in the context of dissociating the Pindaric poem from the *Homeric Hymn to Apollo*, the *persona loquens* in *Pa.*7b/52h.15–20 evokes this legendary competition at Delos and aligns itself with the poet who challenged Homer at the same location and in a similar ritual context, i.e. the cult of Delian Apollo. In other words, by inviting its audience to recall the *agon* between Homer and Hesiod, the paean reinforces its polemical attitude towards the Homeric tradition.

We find a similar creative appropriation of the competitive relationship between Homer and Hesiod in the context of lyric poetics in Ibycus' *Ode to Polycrates* (S151 *PMGF*). This highly allusive ode engages intensely with the *Cypria* and the *Iliad* in an extensive *praeteritio*, in which the *persona loquens* expresses his desire to avoid the martial tales of the Homeric tradition.[125] When the narrative reaches the arrival of the Greek army at Troy (S151.15–22 *PMGF*), the poem offers a variation of this narrative strategy:[126]

κοὶ τὰ μὲν ἂ[ν] Μοῖσαι σεσοφι[σμ]έναι
εὖ Ἑλικωνίδ[ες] ἐμβαίεν †λογω[ι
θνατ[ὸ]ς† δ' οὔ κ[ε]ν ἀνὴρ
διερ[ὸς. . . .] τὰ ἕκαστα εἴποι,

ναῶν ὅ[σσος ἀρι]θμὸς ἀπ' Αὐλίδος
Αἰγαῖον διὰ [πό]ντον ἀπ' Ἄργεος
ἠλύθο[ν ἐς Τροία]ν
ἱπποτρόφο[ν, ἐν δ]ὲ φῶτες

χ]αλκάσπ[ιδες, υἷ]ες Ἀχα[ι]ῶν.
(Ibycus, S151.23–31 *PMGF*)

---

[123] Cf. Martin 2000: 411–24 and earlier Else 1957: 30–31, who reiterates Crusius' idea that the two parts of the *HH to Apollo*, the Delian and the Pythian, represent the poetic contributions of Homer and Hesiod respectively during the performance at Delos mentioned in Hes. fr. 357 MW.

[124] The *Certamen* mentions Homer's voyage to Delos (315–22), but makes no reference to a contest on that island. After his performance of the *Homeric Hymn to Apollo* (*Cert.* 318= *h.Ap.* 1), Homer receives great honor from the Ionians and from the Delians in particular.

[125] See, e.g., Steiner 2005: 350–54, Péron 1982, Wilkinson 2013: 56–57 and 72–73.

[126] I use the text in Wilkinson 2013.

And on these the Heliconian Muses, who have expertise, would embark well in speech, but no living mortal could tell … one by one the ships, as many as they came from Aulis through the Aegean sea, from Argos to horse-rearing [Troy], and the bronze-shielded men inside, the sons of the Achaeans.

The evocation of the Muses in the context of a catalogue of ships, coupled with the emphasis on the mortal's inability to perform what the goddesses can with ease, blatantly evokes the proem of the Homeric Catalogue of Ships in *Il.* 2.484–93.[127] In Ibycus' text, human inadequacy is not remedied by divine aid, and the catalogue that the ode actually offers in subsequent lines (33–37) is brief and highly selective. The speaker not only distances himself from the Iliadic narrator, but also undermines him by weaving into S151.23–26 *PMGF* allusions to *WD* 646–62. The Hesiodic passage explains the poet's limited experience with seafaring (οὔτε τι ναυτιλίης σεσοφισμένος οὔτε τι νηῶν, *WD* 649). The only trip he ever made by boat was when he traveled the short distance from Aulis, the place where the Greek army gathered once upon a time before sailing to Troy (*WD* 651–53), to Chalcis, where he competed in a poetic contest and won (*WD* 654–62).[128] In antiquity, the brief engagement with the Homeric world in *WD* 651–53 as well as the contrast between the epic journey to Troy and Hesiod's brief trip to Euboea were interpreted as polemical against Homeric epic and fostered the biographical fiction that Hesiod's opponent at Chalcis was Homer.[129] Ibycus' ode is attuned to the metapoetic dimension of the two journeys juxtaposed in *WD* 650–62, namely the grand, epic expedition across the Aegean and Hesiod's short trip: when the fleet of the Greeks is first introduced, the ships are described as πολυγόμφοι (S151.18 *PMGF*), the adjective used in *WD* 660 (τόσσον τοι νηῶν γε πεπείρημαι πολυγόμφων).[130] The allusions to the Hesiodic *Nautilia* continue: the ode not only implicates the

---

[127] Hutchinson 2001: 244–47 with a useful discussion of the textual problems; cf. Wilkinson 2013: 71–72 and Hardie 2013: 32–33, who suggests οὐ παρεὼν δέ κεν ἀνήρ or οὐ δὲ παρὼν κ' ἀνήρ for line 25 and διερὸς τὰ ἕκαστα ἂν εἴποι for 26.

[128] On the Hesiodic allusions in Ibycus' ode, see Barron 1969: 134, Péron 1982: 53, and Steiner 2005: 347–50, who suggests further intertextual connections in the use ὕμνος/ὑμνῆν for poetry (S151.12 *PMGF* ~ *WD* 657, 662), the metaphor for poetic activity in ἐπέβησαν (*WD* 659) ~ ἐμβαίεν (S151.24 *PMGF*), and the Aeolism Μοῖσαι (a nod to the origins of Hesiod's father, *WD* 636). Cf. also Hardie 2013, esp. 9–19.

[129] See Introduction, pp. 4–5 and Chapter 5, pp. 181–83.

[130] Hardie 2013: 18–20 suggests that Ibycus "conflates Hesiod's programmatic contrast of short (personal) and long (Homeric) sea-voyage" to set up a foil for his own arrival on Samos, which was presumably a dominant theme in the non-extant beginning of the ode.

distinctly Hesiodic (and thus anti-Homeric) Muses of Helicon[131] as
potential performers of a Catalogue of Ships,[132] but also captures their
Iliadic omniscience (*Il.*2.485–86) with the same word that Hesiod
employs to renounce any expertise in seafaring (σεσοφισμέναι ~ οὐ
σεσοφισμένος). By mixing these particular aspects of Homeric and Hesiodic poetics, the ode clearly undermines the former, yet it is important
to acknowledge that it also distances itself from the latter. Once established in lines 23–26, the gap between the Heliconian Muses and the
mortal poetic voice is never bridged: they remain two separate voices.[133]
In addition, the ode's celebration of Troilus' beauty (S151.41–45 *PMGF*)
is as much un-Hesiodic as it is un-Homeric.

I hope to have demonstrated that the appropriation of Hesiodic
poetics in Pindar's *Pa.*7b/52h contributes to the distance that the paean
puts between itself and the *Homeric Hymn to Apollo*. Hesiod's Muses are
evoked in a song that resonates thematically with Hesiodic poetry in its
focus on Zeus' union with Leto (cf. *Th.* 918-20) and the consequences of
his desire for another goddess. Still, to the best of our knowledge,
Asteria's story is non-Hesiodic as much as it is non-Homeric. Not unlike
Ibycus' Ode, then, Pindar's paean dissociates its celebration of Apollo
from the Homeric tradition but remains rather distinct in its content
from the Hesiodic tradition too. Lines 10–22, furthermore, acknowledge
the need for the Muses' aid but the goddesses do not appear to interact
with the first-person speaker,[134] and they seem to be absent from their
own chariot. Unlike Hesiod, whose poetry and poetic authority are a
result of his personal encounter with the Muses, and unlike Parmenides'
young man, who acquires true knowledge through divine revelation,[135]
the *persona loquens* in the (extant) text of *Paean* 7b/52h is not defined by
such transformative experiences. Thus the paean forges a relationship
between the speaker and the Muses that is cooperative but rather remote
or, at least, not intensely interactive.

---

[131]  See above, n.120.

[132]  Hardie 2013: 24–25 suggests that S151.20–22 and 32–45 *PMGF* are the direct utterances of the
Muses, but I find no compelling argument in support of his suggestion. On the contrary, I agree
with Hutchinson 2001: 245–46 and Wilkinson 2013: 72 that the ode is more interested in exposing
human (including Homeric) inadequacy.

[133]  For a very different approach to the relationship between the Muses and the poet in Ibycus' *Ode to
Polycrates*, see Hardie 2013.

[134]  Unless the Muses are the subject of the verb in line 22, in which case they would have some
interaction with the *persona loquens*.

[135]  On the reception of Hesiodic poetry in the poem of Parmenides, see, e.g., Jaeger 1947: 92–94,
Dolin 1962, Schwabl 1963, Pellikaan-Engel 1974, Northrup 1980, and Koning 2010a: 210–13.

# CHAPTER 2

# Hesiodic Narratives in Lyric

Composed primarily for public and semi-public performances, fifth-century lyric poems include rich mythological narratives that relate to the primary audiences of these songs as well as to the occasions and locations of their premieres. Often aetiological, these narratives incorporate genealogical information also featured in the hexameter genealogical poetry that was circulating in the Greek world under the name of Hesiod. Given the fragmentary state of the *Catalogue* and the *Megalai Ehoiai* today, it is not easy to draw conclusions about how these lyric narratives engaged with Hesiodic poetry. In fact, in cases such as *Pythian* 3 and *Pythian* 9, we are almost entirely dependent upon the testimony of ancient scholia to assess Pindar's reception of the relevant Hesiodic material.[1] Although we are hampered not only by the lacunose state of the Hesiodic corpus but also by the lack of information regarding competing mythological accounts (especially local ones), there is still value in investigating the reception of Hesiodic narratives in the extant lyric poetry of the fifth century, as this inquiry reveals a complex and creative engagement with the Hesiodic tradition.

The intention of this chapter is not to offer an exhaustive survey but to examine carefully a few select case studies that illustrate the variety and complexity involved in lyric receptions of Hesiodic narratives.[2] First, I take a close look at Pindar's subtle appropriation of Hesiod's Typhonomachy in

---

[1] I discuss the pertinent scholia below. Nünlist 2009: 257–61 offers a useful overview of the literary criticism embedded in ancient scholia on mythological narratives; he also discusses the compilation of genealogical and other mythological information found in the scholia. Cf. also Cameron 2004: 89–123 on source references in compilatory (esp. mythographical) writings and the ancient scholia that draw material from them.

[2] For such a survey, one should turn to D'Alessio 2005a, and especially 2005b, as well as the extensive (albeit somewhat outdated) study by Schwartz 1960: esp. 138–47 and 562–70. I have chosen not to include in my case studies the reception of Deucalion's progeny in Pindar's *O.9*, because it has been analyzed thoroughly by D'Alessio 2005b: 220–26; cf. also Pavlou 2008: 554–60. On Pindar's reworking of Hesiod's *Theogony* in the *First Hymn*, see D'Alessio 2005b: 228–29, cf. Scully 2015: 99.

*Pythian* 1 in order to explore the relatively understudied Hesiodic dimension of Typhos in this ode. Then I turn to *Pythians* 2, 3, and 9 with a particular interest in Pindar's treatment of the female figures he receives from Hesiodic poetry. Ultimately, I hope to show that Pindar develops these rather simple and formulaic Hesiodic characters into multidimensional figures who expand beyond the limits of the genealogical script and dominate their stories.

## Pindar's Typhos (*Pythian* 1): Between the Local and the Panhellenic

*Pythian* 1 celebrates the victory of Hieron's chariot at the Pythian Games of 470 BCE, only a few years after the Syracusan tyrant had expelled the inhabitants of Catane (a Chalcidian colony on the slopes of Mount Aetna), renamed the city Aetna, and repopulated it with Dorian settlers under the leadership of his son, Deinomenes.[3] The ode clearly engages with Hieron's political agenda regarding his newly founded city. For instance, while evoking Aetnaean Zeus (*P.*1.29–30),[4] the text underscores Hieron's active role in the foundation and naming of Aetna (*P.*1.30–32); furthermore, the poem commemorates the announcement of Hieron's victory at Delphi as an occasion for the celebration of his newly founded city in a Panhellenic context (*P.*1.32–33).[5] Later, Hieron's son, Deinomenes, is called Αἴτνας βασιλεύς (*P.*1.60; cf. 67–68),[6] and Hieron is praised for Aetna's pure Dorian institutions (*P.*1.61–70).[7] Given the prominence of Hieron's

[3] For Hieron's policy of doricizing the eastern coast of Sicily by moving the population of Naxus and Catane to Leontini, refounding Catane as Aetna, and settling new inhabitants of Doric origin there, see Luraghi 1994: 335–46 and 358–65. For the eruption of Aetna sometime between 480 and 475, see, e.g., Vallet 1985: 293.

[4] On the cult of Ζεὺς Αἰτναῖος, see Gentili et al. 1995: 339; cf. *O.*6.96 and *N.*1.6. For the Aetnaean festival as a potential context for the premiere of *P.*1, see Morrison 2007: 67, who nonetheless explores the possibility that Hieron may have celebrated the festival in Syracuse rather than Aetna. On the Deinomenids' use of religion and poetry for political purposes, see, e.g., Privitera 1980 and, more recently, Morgan 2015: 87–132.

[5] Ba. *Ode* 4, which celebrates the same victory, connects Hieron to Syracuse, not Aetna (1–3). It is possible that at Delphi Hieron was identified as Syracusan rather than Aetnaean, and that *P.*1 is deliberately manipulating the details in order to promote his role as the founder of Aetna to a local audience; see Maehler 1982: 64–65 and 2004: 100–01.

[6] On βασιλεύς as a poetic attribute rather than a reflection of a real title, see Gentili et al. 1995: 349 (*contra* Oost 1976, esp. 227–29); cf. Privitera 1980 on the ideology involved. On the plural βασιλεῦσι in line 68, see Morrison 2007: 68.

[7] On the return of the Heraclidae and the establishment of the Dorian world as a mythical prototype for Aetna's foundation (*P.*1.61–6), see Athanassaki 2003: 119–21, as well as Malkin 1994: 41 and Miller 1997: 269–70 (cf. 214–23 on *P.*1 and the foundation of Aetna). On *P.*1 and Hieron's political agenda, see already Kirsten 1941.

Aetna in *Pythian* 1, it is plausible to assume that the city was the intended
location for the ode's premiere. This hypothesis is supported further by
the fact that lines *P*.1.33–35, which immediately follow the poem's reference to the victory's announcement at Delphi (*P*.1.32–33), express the idea
of a successful *nostos*, thus implying a first performance in the victor's
home territory.[8]

    Although it is the focal point for the contemporary politics embedded
in the ode, Aetna is first introduced not as a human community, but as a
volcano, a particularly violent part of Sicily's natural landscape that is
inextricably connected with Zeus and the establishment of his order in
the cosmos. The poem opens with the juxtaposition between the calming
effect that music and song have even upon the most aggressive elements of
Zeus's rule, and the terror that the same sound inspires to Zeus's foes
(*P*.1.1–14).[9] In this context, Typhos is singled out as a paradigmatic enemy
of the Olympians (*P*.1.13–28). After a brief mention of the monster's form
and origin (*P*.1.15–17), the Pindaric text focuses on Typhos' current state of
captivity under Mount Aetna and on the spectacular volcanic activity that
results from the monster's painful imprisonment (*P*.1.17–28). The text thus
transforms the landscape of Hieron's city into a monument of Zeus's
supremacy. Iterating the monster-slaying motif that is often linked to
city-foundation,[10] the subjugation and incarceration of Typhos symbolize
the victory of order and civilization over chaos. At the same time, however,
the volcanic eruption, this extraordinary and threatening natural phenomenon that dominates the natural landscape, offers a metaphor for the violence
and cruelty involved in Hieron's 'foundation' plan; as Athanassaki points
out, in this ode "[c]olonial violence and disruption are simultaneously
reflected and sanctioned in the myth of Typhos."[11] The treatment of
vanquished Typhos, therefore, weaves a parallel between the cosmic and
the mortal ruler as agents of justified violence, which not only anticipates
the praise of Hieron's military victories against barbaric and hybristic

---

[8] See, e.g., Gentili et al. 1995: 9. Morrison 2007: 66–69 suggests tentatively that the premiere may not
have taken place in Aetna based on the deixis entailed in τοῦτ' ... ὄρος (*P*.1.30) and πόλιν κείναν
(*P*.1.61), as well as on the inclusion of broader Sicilian elements. He examines the possibility that the
ode was performed in Syracuse instead, and proposes that perhaps it was intended for re-
performance in different Sicilian locations (Morrison 2007: 98–102).
[9] On harmony as a major theme in *P*.1, see Kirkwood 1982: 125; cf. Kirsten 1941: 62–66 on συμφωνία
in relation to the Dorian institution evoked later in the ode (*P*.1.61–70).
[10] Trumpf 1958. On the Typhonomachy in the context of the dragon-slaying motif, cf. Fontenrose
1959: 70–93, Watkins 1995: 448–59, Ogden 2013: 69–80.
[11] Athanassaki 2003: 120.

enemies (*P*.1.71–80) but also informs his celebration as Aetna's founder throughout the ode.[12]

At first glance, Pindar's treatment of Typhos' confinement under Aetna in *Pythian* 1 seems to be very different from the Hesiodic account of the Typhonomachy (*Th*. 820–80). Neither the localization of the monster's punishment under Sicily and the shores of Cuma (*P*.1.18–19) nor his birth in Cilicia (*P*.1.16–20; cf. *P*.8.16) can be found in the extant Hesiodic text.[13] Furthermore, unlike the *Theogony* that recounts events of the distant mythical past, *Pythian* 1 focuses on the current state of affairs. Most importantly, perhaps, these two poems reserve a different fate for Typhos after his defeat. In the *Theogony*, Typhos is confined in Tartarus (*Th*. 868) and seems to sink into complete inaction, leaving behind him only a legacy of destructive winds (*Th*. 869–80). The Hesiodic text refrains from making an explicit aetiological connection between Typhos and volcanoes, even though the duel itself abounds in volcanic imagery: not only does the battle involve earthquakes (*Th*. 842–43, 849) and a veritable conflagration (*Th*. 844–47), but also the moment of Typhos' collapse under the debilitating force of the thunderbolt is punctuated by a release of fire from the monster (*Th*. 859–61) and the melting of the earth (*Th*. 861–67).[14] In *Pythian* 1, by contrast, Aetna stands as a monument of Zeus's victory, but, inside his prison, the monster remains a dynamic presence since he manifests himself every time he causes the volcano to erupt (*P*.1.25–26). Ultimately, while the *Theogony* celebrates Zeus's *aristeia* against the monster and his victory over a potential usurper in the mythical past (*Th*. 836–38), the Pindaric ode communicates in vivid terms the contemporary experiences of its local, Sicilian audience(s) and it is likely to be informed by local lore.

---

[12] The correspondences between the two conflicts in the Ode (Zeus/Typhos and Hieron/barbarians) are pointed out by all commentators (e.g., Gentili et al. 1995: 357–58). For a close (and at times exaggerated) reading of the verbal and thematic correspondences, see also Lefkowitz 1976: 119–20. Cf. Gantz 1978: 143–45 and 148, who offers an interesting study of the problems arising from the juxtaposition between Zeus's and Hieron's violence, and Carey 1978: 25, who argues that the correspondence leads to retrospective interpretation.

[13] On the political significance of Typhos' location in *P*.1, see Morgan 2015: 316–20. *P*.1 offers the earliest surviving association of Typhos with the western Greek terrain of Cuma and Sicily; as Gentili et al. 1995: 14 point out, however, later occurrences of the western Greek version treat the two regions as mutually exclusive. Pindar's *O*.4.6–7 and fr. 92 SM also envision Typhos as imprisoned under Aetna. Pindar's fr. 93 SM, on the other hand, follows the Homeric tradition (*Il*. 2.783) by situating the battle between Zeus and (fifty-headed) Typhos ἐν Ἀρίμοις. Hes. *Th*. 304–07 locates Echidna's lair and probably also her coupling with Typhos εἰν Ἀρίμοισιν. As West 1966: 250–51 points out, the exact meaning of the phrase ἐν Ἀρίμοις was debated in antiquity.

[14] Cf. West 1966: 393.

While distinct from the Hesiodic Typhonomachy, the treatment of Typhos under Aetna in *Pythian* 1 displays remarkable similarities to the description of the monster's punishment in the *Prometheus Bound* (*PV* 351–72). Comparative readings of the two accounts have yielded undeniable resonances, some of which I discuss in Chapter 4. A few scholars have assumed that *Pythian* 1 was influenced by the *PV*; yet, even though the date of the play's composition is debated, it seems much more likely that it was composed after *P.*1 and was informed by it.[15] Regarding the association of Aetna with Typhos, an element that Pindaric poetry and the *PV* share, Severyns has suggested that it may have been established already in an archaic epic poem that no longer survives, possibly the *Titanomachy*.[16] Severyns based his hypothesis on a scholion to *Il.* 2.783 that juxtaposes the Homeric tradition, according to which Typhos is under Arima of Pisidia, with more recent poets (οἱ μ(έν)τοι γε νεώτεροι), who situate him under Sicilian Aetna; of these poets, the ancient commentator names only Pindar.[17] Unfortunately, the term νεώτεροι is so open-ended and inclusive that we can neither exclude nor confirm the existence of an archaic epic situating Typhos under Aetna on the basis of this scholion.[18] More recently, however, Debiasi revived the idea of an archaic epic source, arguing that the association between Aetna and Typhos should be traced back to Hesiod's *Theogony*.[19] Debiasi proposed this engagement with the Hesiodic tradition on the basis of a long list of previously overlooked verbal parallels among *Th.* 820–68, *P.*1.15–28, and *PV* 351–72.[20] Debiasi finds echoes of the

---

[15] E.g., Bowra 1964: 476–78, Griffith 1977: 9–10 and 1978: 117–20, Ardizzoni 1978, Griffith 1983b: 149–53, Gentili et al. 1995: 13. I should add here that there is a verbal echo between *PV* 365 (ἱπούμενος) and *O.*4.8 (ἵπου), an ode that features a hundred-headed Typhos (like *P.*1 and the *PV*) and was composed late, probably in 452 BCE. This echo may be an indication of a common source, or it may be an allusion of one poem to the other, possibly an allusion of *O.*4 to the *PV*. See Griffith 1978: 120. On the composition of the *PV*, see Chapter 4, pp. 123–25.

[16] Severyns 1928: 170–71. Before Severyns, von Mess 1901 had formulated a different hypothesis regarding a lost epic source for *P.*1 and *PV*. Based on a mistaken attribution of Typhon's Cilician birth to Hesiod in sch. *PV* 351a, he concluded that the epic source belongs to the pseudo-Hesiodic corpus. For a thorough refutation of von Mess' arguments, see Griffith 1978: 117–20.

[17] sch. *Il.* 2.783 *ap. P. Oxy.* 1086 II 49 = *Titanomachy* fr. dub. 15 Bernabé.

[18] On the difficulties involved in the term νεώτεροι, see Davies 1986: 109–10, whose edition of the fragments of Greek epic does not include sch. *Il.* 2.783 *ap. P. Oxy.* 1086 II 49. Cf. D'Alessio 2015: 209 n.48.

[19] Debiasi 2008: 79–94 and, regarding Severyns' argument, 2004: 106. On considering Hesiod one of the νεώτεροι, see already Severyns 1928: 39–40.

[20] Debiasi 2008: 90–91. Cf. Kollmann 1989: 98–106, who, in his discussion of *P.*1.13–15, compares the relevant passages from the *Theogony*, *P.*1, and the *PV*, but does not argue explicitly for Hesiodic allusions in Pindar. Note that Burton 1962: 98 tentatively admits that the *Theogony* may be a source for Pindar's treatment of Typhos, because he "provides a good example of the habit of describing natural phenomena in terms of a conflict between living creatures." However, there has been a

Hesiodic text throughout the Pindaric account of Typhos' imprisonment under Aetna, and views them as supporting evidence for a broader argument, to which I will return, namely that Aetna was explicitly associated with Typhos already in the Hesiodic narrative (*Th.* 860).

Debiasi's analysis leaves no doubt that *P.*1 does indeed take into consideration the Hesiodic Typhonomachy, but not all of the parallels he proposes can be read as Hesiodic allusions. In fact, I argue that the strongest and most unambiguous evocations of the Hesiodic account are clustered in the very beginning of the Pindaric passage (*P.*1.15–16). Upon closer examination, the resonances traced by Debiasi outside *P.*1.15–16 seem dubious. For instance, he associates ἑρπετόν in *P.*1.25 with the hundred snake-heads in *Th.* 825, but the word probably alludes to a full animal form, most probably a snake as Debiasi himself points out.[21] As such, however, it differs from the Hesiodic form of Typhos, who has an anthropomorphic body below the hundred snake-heads (*Th.* 823–24).[22] Moreover, Debiasi suggests that *P.*1.26 (θαῦμα δὲ καὶ παρεόντων ἀκοῦσαι, "a wonder even to hear about from those present") corresponds to the comment that the Hesiodic narrator embeds in his description of Typhos emitting puppy-like sounds in *Th.* 834 (ἄλλοτε δ' αὖ σκυλάκεσσιν ἐοικότα, θαύματ' ἀκοῦσαι, "and then at other times they (*sc.* Typhos' snake-heads) emitted sounds resembling puppies, a wonder to hear").[23] While at first glance the connection seems strong, it weakens once one realizes that θαῦμα δὲ καὶ παρεόντων ἀκοῦσαι in *P.*1.26 complements the immediately preceding phrase τέρας μὲν θαυμάσιον προσιδέσθαι ("a portent wondrous to behold"). Thus it should be read as the second half of a bipartite appeal to the audience's vision and hearing that has no counterpart in the Hesiodic text; also non-Hesiodic is the emphasis on eyewitnesses and their role in the dissemination of information. Furthermore, even if one were to consider an allusion to *Th.* 834 in *P.*1.26, one would have to concede that the soundscapes constructed in the two passages are completely different: in the *Theogony*, the wild variety of articulate and inarticulate bestial sounds that Typhos emits, much like his mixed physical appearance, reflects his chaotic and monstrous nature.[24] On the other hand, *P.*1 dwells on the

---

general reluctance to trace Hesiodic allusions in *P.*1, which is aptly epitomized by the pronouncement in Griffith 1978: 117 that "whereas *Prom.* shows unmistakable echoes of Hesiod, Pindar yields none."

[21] Debiasi 2008: 90 n.66. Gentili et al. 1995: 338 (cf. 335) suggest that the word ἑρπετόν in *P.*1.25 alludes to Typhos' representation as a reptile in art.

[22] I also find it likely that ἑρπετόν evokes the crippling effect of the thunderbolt in *Th.* 858.

[23] On the narrator's comment in *Th.* 834, see Stoddard 2004: 57.     [24] Blaise 1992: 359–63.

natural sounds of the eruption: *P.1.23–24* evoke the crash that resounds when lava meets the sea (σὺν πατάγῳ), while *P.1.26* draws attention to the wondrous sight and sound of the fire emitted from the monster. If *P.1.26* evokes *Th.* 834 at all – and I doubt that it does – it only underscores how different the Pindaric approach to Typhos is from the Hesiodic one. Finally, Debiasi draws a connection between τέρας μὲν θαυμάσιον (*P.1.26*) and δεινοῖο πελώρου ("of the terrible monster," *Th.* 856), as well as between Ἀφαίστοιο κρουνούς ("springs of Hephaestus," *P.1.25*) and the reference to "the hands of Hephaestus" in the context of smelting iron ore (ἠὲ σίδηρος ... τήκεται ἐν χθονὶ δίῃ ὑφ' Ἡφαίστου παλάμῃσιν, "or (as) iron ... melts inside the divine earth by the hands of Hephaestus," *Th.* 864–66). However, there is no verbal overlap to trigger an allusion in the first pair, whereas in the second pair Hephaestus is not even involved in the same context.[25]

Nonetheless, Debiasi is right to identify allusions to the Hesiodic Typhonomachy in the first few lines of the ode that are dedicated to the monster:

> ὅσσα δὲ μὴ πεφίληκε Ζεύς, ἀτύζονται βοάν
> Πιερίδων ἀΐοντα, γᾶν τε καὶ πόν-
>       τον κατ' ἀμαιμάκετον,
> ὅς τ' ἐν αἰνᾷ Ταρτάρῳ κεῖται, θεῶν πολέμιος,
> Τυφὼς ἑκατοντακάρανος· τόν ποτε
> Κιλίκιον θρέψεν πολυώνυμον ἄντρον· νῦν γε μάν
> ταί θ' ὑπὲρ Κύμας ἀλιερκέες ὄχθαι
> Σικελία τ' αὐτοῦ πιέζει
>       στέρνα λαχνάεντα· κίων δ' οὐρανία συνέχει,
> νιφόεσσ' Αἴτνα, πάνετες χιόνος ὀξείας τιθήνα·
>                       (Pindar, *Pythian* 1.13–20)

But all the creatures that Zeus dislikes are terrified when they hear the voice of the Pierian (Muses), all over the land and the unyielding sea, and the one who lies in dreaded Tartarus, an enemy of the gods, hundred-headed Typhos. Him did the famous Cilician cave nurture once upon a time, but now Sicily and the sea-fenced cliffs above Cuma press upon his shaggy chest; and a sky-high column confines him, snowy Aetna, nurse of biting snow all year round.

Despite its pivotal importance for *Pythian* 1, Typhos' localization in the western Greek terrain is postponed until after the monster is first

---

[25] Contrast, however, the close resonance between τέρας μὲν θαυμάσιον in *P.1.26* and δάιον τέρας in *PV* 352, as well as the association of fire with metallurgy that *PV* 366–67 shares with *Th.* 864–67.

depicted as a resident of Tartarus (*P.*1.15). This defining detail, which precedes all others regarding Typhos in the ode, even his name, evokes the conclusion of the Hesiodic Typhonomachy, according to which Zeus threw Typhos into Tartarus ([*sc.* Zεὺς] ῥῖψε δέ μιν θυμῷ ἀκαχὼν ἐς Τάρταρον εὐρύν, *Th.* 868).[26] The engagement with the Hesiodic tradition is reinforced by Typhos' description as hundred-headed (*P.*1.16) since, in the extant archaic literary corpus at least, Hesiod's *Theogony* is the only text that depicts him as a hundred-headed monster (*Th.* 824–25).[27] In fact, far from being a passing detail, the heads are an important focal point in Hesiod's description since they become the most conspicuous manifestation of Typhos' monstrous nature.[28] After elaborating on their number (*Th.* 824–25), the text of the *Theogony* focuses on the fire that comes out of Typhos' many eyes (*Th.* 826–28) as well as the sounds – sometimes articulate and sometimes bestial – emitted from his many mouths (*Th.* 829–35). The terrifying and chaotic sounds that define the version of Typhos evoked in *P.*1.13–15 contrast sharply with the peaceful soundscape that the ode constructs in the immediately preceding strophes (*P.*1.1–12). The ode opens with a hymn to the soothing *phorminx* of Apollo and the Muses, whose music fosters merriment (*P.*1.1–4) and puts to sleep even the most aggressive elements (*P.*1.5–12). The harmonious sound of the *phorminx* reflects the peace and order that both mortals and immortals enjoy in an era when all enemies of the

[26] Debiasi 2008: 91; cf. Kollmann 1989: 98. Pindar's use of Tartarus here as a feminine noun is unique and striking; contrast *Pa.*4.44, where it is masculine (the grammatical gender is undetermined in fr. 207 SM). I suggest that the gender choice in *P.*1 prepares the localization of the monster under Aetna, a grammatically feminine toponym. Furthermore, the exceptional gender of Tartarus in *P.*1.15, while not attested in Hesiodic poetry, still evokes the flexibility with which the noun is used in the *Theogony* (neuter plural in lines 119 and 841, masculine singular in 682, 721, 723a, 725, 736, 807, 868, and, of course, personified as the father of Typhos in 822). Cf. Tartarus as masculine singular in *Sc.* 255 and Hes. fr. 20/30.22; Hes. fr. 6.2 H (*ME*) = fr. 54.6 MW (*Cat.*) is too lacunose for a conclusive reading.

[27] Debiasi 2008: 90. The depiction of the Typhos as a hundred-headed monster is also unattested in art. On his representation as an anguiped, see Vian 1952: 12–16 with an unsuccessful attempt to read that physical form in Hesiod's *Theogony*. See also Kollmann 1989: 104–05, Carpenter 1991: 70–71, and Touchefeu-Meynier 1997.

[28] By contrast, the rest of Typhos' body receives a mere two-line mention of his strong arms and untiring feet (*Th.* 823–4). Typhos has one hundred heads also in Pindar's *O.*4.7 and *P.*8.16, two odes composed for victors of different provenance (Camarina and Aegina respectively). For a one-hundred-headed Typhos after *P.*1, see also *PV* 353 and the dithyrambic excerpt embedded in Ar. *Nub.* 336, which was composed, according to the scholia, by Philoxenus of Cythera; cf. Dover 1968: 145. Note that Pi. fr. 93 SM, which engages with the Homeric tradition in that it locates the Typhonomachy ἐν Ἀρίμοις, envisions the monster with fifty heads. It appears, therefore, that the number of Typhos' heads can be read as an indicator for the presence or absence of engagement with the Hesiodic tradition.

Olympian rule have been defeated and confined, and when there is no need for the "warring thunderbolt" (καὶ τὸν αἰχματὰν κεραυνὸν σβεννύεις / ἀενάου πυρός, "you quench even the warring thunderbolt of ever-flowing fire," *P*.1.5–6). Having elaborated on the soothing effect of music within the world that Zeus oversees (*P*.1.1–12), the ode then demonstrates further the intrinsic connection between the Olympian order and musical harmony by exploring the negative reception of the Muses' song among those elements that Zeus does not like (*P*.1.13–14). Singled out as a paradigmatic "enemy of the gods" (θεῶν πολέμιος, *P*.1.15), Typhos in his Hesiodic form embodies a monster of confounded and terrifying voices, and yet he is one of those beings who are themselves distraught (ἀτύζονται, *P*.1.13) by the song of the Muses, a sound that expresses and reflects the order of Zeus.

However, there is more to the ode's evocation of Hesiod's Typhos in *P*.1.13–15 than just a subtle play between the harmony of the world under Zeus and the chaotic voices of the Hesiodic monster. After introducing the monster's Hesiodic form and residence in Tartarus, the ode unfolds its vivid treatment of Typhos' presence in the western territory and of the volcanic eruptions caused by the vexed monster (*P*.1.16–28). As I argued earlier, Pindar's treatment of Typhos no longer engages with the Hesiodic tradition after lines 13–15. Yet the ode uses these early Hesiodic allusions to recall an episode of the mythical past that the ode itself does not dwell on but certainly presupposes, namely the clash between Zeus and Typhos. Inviting the audience to recall the Hesiodic Typhonomachy by means of a few allusions serves the poem's narrative economy and strengthens its celebration of Zeus, since the Hesiodic Typhonomachy is a successful *aristeia* that confirms Zeus's competence as a leader and a defender of order against chaos.[29] Finally, the fleeting evocation of the Hesiodic background story in *P*.1.13–15 allows the text to avoid an explicit account of the violent clash that has led to the harmonious and orderly status quo celebrated in the first two stanzas. The poem implicitly justifies the violence that Zeus brought upon Typhos in the past by presenting the volcanic activity as a terrifying reminder of the monster's destructive potential; however, it does not dwell on that ancient conflict. The ode's reluctance to recount the clash in detail is best understood in the context of its engagement with Hieron's politics, especially given the parallel it draws between him and Zeus. In the interest of eliding the violence which the

---

[29] *Pace* Morgan 2015: 316, this is not the victory that earns Zeus the cosmic throne in the *Theogony* (see *Th.* 881–82), even though his enthronement follows the Typhonomachy in the Hesiodic narrative.

*laudandus* inflicted in the region with the foundation of Aetna, *Pythian* 1 relegates the description of violent conflict and opposition to another text.

*Pythian* 1, therefore, not only prefaces the local, Sicilian aetiology for Aetna's volcanic eruptions with the Panhellenic account of the conflict between Zeus and Typhos in Hesiod's *Theogony*, but in fact links the two accounts in a continuous storyline. Several scholars, including most recently Debiasi, have attempted to read Aetna into the Hesiodic text, thus arguing that the aetiological connection between Typhos and the Sicilian volcano was already established in the Hesiodic tradition. This hypothesis is fostered, of course, by the fact that the Hesiodic Typhonomachy involves imagery dominated by fire that can be interpreted as volcanic. Even more tantalizing is the detail that, when Typhos succumbs to the violence of Zeus's thunderbolt and releases fire, he is located on a mountain:

> φλὸξ δὲ κεραυνωθέντος ἀπέσσυτο τοῖο ἄνακτος
> οὔρεος ἐν βήσσῃσιν ἀιδνῆς παιπαλοέσσης
> πληγέντος
>
> (Hesiod, *Theogony* 859–61)

And from the thunderstruck lord a flame rushed forth in the dark, rugged dales of the mountain when he was hit.

The rare adjective ἀιδνή (*Th.* 860) is attested unanimously in the manuscript tradition, although in two alternative readings: ἀιδνῆς παιπαλοέσσης and ἀιδνῆς παιπαλοέσσης. However, a scholion by Tzetzes on Lycophron's *Alexandra* 688, according to which Hesiod situates the thunderstruck Typhos in Sicily, has led to the assumption that, instead of ἀιδνῆς/ἀιδνῆς, *Th.* 860 included Αἴτνης or rather, given the metrical position, Ἀίτνης, an unattested form as of yet.[30] In his recent argument in favor of emending the Hesiodic text to Ἀίτνης παιπαλοέσσης,[31] Debiasi points out that the reading *Αἴτνης παιπαλοέσσης would not only be consistent with Tzetzes' scholion but, more importantly, would normalize the use of παιπαλόεις in this context. The emendation is certainly attractive since ἀιδνῆς παιπαλοέσσης presents the problem of gender agreement with οὔρεος, and the use of παιπαλόεσσα with βῆσσα is unparalleled. In fact, παιπαλόεις often modifies the names of mountains and mountainous islands,[32] and the reading κ[αὶ Αἴτν]ην

---

[30] sch. Lycophron *Alex.* 688: ἕτεροι δὲ τὴν Σικελίαν, ὅπου καὶ τὸν Τυφῶνα κεραυνοῖ ὡς καὶ Ἡσίοδος, "but others (understand) Sicily, where (Zeus) also strikes Typhos with the thunderbolt, as Hesiod too (attests)". Cf. the gloss ἀιτνῆς that West (1966) reports in his *apparatus criticus*.

[31] Debiasi 2008: 79–94.    [32] For a list of passages, see Debiasi 2008: 83–84.

παιπαλόεσσαν has been plausibly supplemented in Hes. fr. 63/150.25. Despite Debiasi's argument to the contrary,[33] however, the diaeresis does not make Ἀίτνης a more obscure word than ἀιδνῆ(ι)ς, especially since the diaeresis is not a particularly exceptional phenomenon, as Debiasi himself admits.[34] There is no doubt that ἀιδνῆ(ι)ς is the *lectio difficilior* in *Th.* 860; furthermore, while παιπαλοέσσης remains somewhat problematic, perhaps its use to modify mountain-dales can be explained through analogy, given that elsewhere the adjective modifies mountain-tops (σκοπιὴν ἐς παιπαλόεσ- σαν, *Od.* 10.97, 148, 194) and paths on the mountains (*Il.* 12.168 ὁδῷ ἔπι παιπαλοέσσῃ; *Il.* 17.743, κατὰ παιπαλόεσσαν ἀτραπόν; *Od.* 17.204, ὁδὸν κατὰ παιπαλόεσσαν). I should add here that some scholars have attempted to read Aetna in *Th.* 860 without emending the text. Wilamowitz suggested reading Ἀιδνῆς in *Th.* 860 as an otherwise unknown toponymic, which he associated (albeit hesitantly) with Mount Aetna.[35] More recently, Ballabriga revived Wilamowitz's emendation in order to argue that Ἀιδνή was a mythological projection of Mount Aetna and that Pindar and his contem- poraries would have understood it as such.[36]

Overall, it seems to me that there is not sufficient evidence linking Typhos with Aetna in the extant Hesiodic text. However, as I discuss in the Introduction, the *Theogony* at this time still circulated primarily through oral performances. Even if the text had become relatively stable, rhapsodes performing Hesiodic poetry throughout the Greek world were presumably still in a position to generate or reiterate variations in order to appeal more to local audiences. One obvious way to please a community would be to incorporate its local aetiologies. Manipulating the text of *Th.* 860 so as to associate Typhos with Aetna, therefore, does not seem implausible in the context of Sicilian performances. In other words, even though it is not a compelling emendation for the transmitted text of *Th.* 860, Debiasi's suggested reading *Αἴτνης παιπαλοέσσης may be tenable as an alternative version of the Hesiodic line that originated in performances tailored for Sicilian audiences (cf. Hes. fr. 63/150.25, if indeed supplemented correctly). If we entertain this possibility, we may perhaps trace a nod towards both versions in the concluding lines of the Typhos-passage in *P.*1: Αἴτνας ἐν μελαμφύλλοις ... κορυφαῖς (*P.*1.27) may reflect not only the dark landscape of the mountain envisioned in the

[33] Debiasi 2008: 88.    [34] Debiasi 2008: 86–88.
[35] Wilamowitz 1922: 225 n.2. Cf. West 1966: 393, who admits the possibility that *Th.* 860 may have included a reference to a real mountain, although he does not think it could have been Aetna.
[36] Ballabriga 1990: 21–23, whose argument presupposes that the imagery in *Th.* 859–67 took the Sicilian volcano into consideration.

extant version of *Th.* 860 (ἀιδνῆς) but also the explicit reference to Aetna in an alternative version of the line featuring *Αἴτνης παιπαλοέσσης. When it first recalls Hesiod's Typhonomachy in *P.*1.13–15, however, the Pindaric ode refrains from committing to a markedly local version of the Hesiodic tradition. Thus, for Sicilian audiences, *P.*1.13–15 may have evoked a Hesiodic text that already associated Typhos with Aetna, but audiences elsewhere in the Greek world who were familiar with the Hesiodic Typhonomachy in its extant version could still appreciate the Hesiodic allusions in *P.*1.13–15 and involve them in their interpretation of the Pindaric poem. By linking the Sicilian narrative surrounding Aetna's eruptions with the Panhellenic Hesiodic tradition regarding the mythical past, the ode facilitates its subsequent circulation and appreciation outside Sicily.[37]

## Hesiodic Women in Epinician Poetry

In this section, I look closely at two Pindaric female figures, Coronis in *Pythian* 3 and Cyrene in *Pythian* 9. Any discussion of Hesiodic reception in these two poems is bound to have as its starting point the exegetical scholia to the Pindaric odes, since they are our primary source of information on this topic. The Pindaric scholia preserve a rich collection of ancient scholarship drawn mainly from the works of Hellenistic (mostly Alexandrian) scholars with some added material from the early Imperial era.[38] Even though this corpus in its extant form is the product of a long process that involved selection, abridgment, and reformulation at several stages, it contains virtually no material from late antiquity and the Byzantine era. The Alexandrian provenance of most information preserved in this collection inspires considerable confidence about the quality of this material, although one should still exercise caution, as Lefkowitz has amply demonstrated. The Pindaric scholia provide us with invaluable clues regarding literary traditions that are almost entirely lost today but were part of a Panhellenic cultural horizon shared by audiences throughout the Greek

---

[37] Regarding the circulation of *P.*1 outside Sicily, cf. Morrison 2007: 116–17, who points out the overlap in language and themes between *P.*1 and *P.*8, an ode composed for an Aeginetan victor in 446 BCE. This overlap brings into relief the theme of changeability that is found in *P.*8 but not in *P.*1. Assuming that the optimal reception of *P.*8 by its Aeginetan audience presupposes familiarity with *P.*1, Morrison sees here evidence for the Panhellenic circulation of Pindaric poetry.

[38] On the ancient Pindaric scholia, see Deas 1931, Lefkowitz 1975 and 1985, Wilson 1980, and summarily Dickey 2007: 38–40. I was unable to consult Tom Phillips' *Pindar's Library* (Oxford, 2016) before the submission of this manuscript.

world. In other words, these ancient commentaries contribute to a fuller reconstruction of the literary framework within which audiences in the fifth century were consuming and interpreting contemporary lyric poetry. In the case of Coronis and Cyrene, the scholia to *P.*3 and 9 report that both mythological figures were treated in Hesiodic genealogical poetry and that Pindar drew his mythological narratives from their *ehoiai*. Unfortunately, our attempt to explore the validity of these statements is dependent mainly upon extremely short Hesiodic fragments preserved by the same scholia. While acknowledging the methodological problems inherent in this setting, I pursue the question of Hesiodic reception in *P.*3 and 9 in hopes that my discussion will enrich and expand our current appreciation of Pindar's engagement with the Hesiodic corpus.

## Coronis (*Pythian* 3)

*Pythian* 3, an ode of uncertain date and occasion,[39] opens with the unattainable wish that Chiron, the long-dead Centaur, were alive;[40] if that were the case, he could produce another healer like Asclepius, and the *persona loquens* could offer Hieron, the addressee, not only an epinician for a Delphic victory but also the means to unfailing health (*P.*3.1–76). Of course, that is all a fantasy: in reality, what the speaker can offer Hieron is a prayer (*P.*3.77–79), a reminder that suffering is part of human nature (*P.*3.80–109), and a promise of immortality through poetry (*P.*3.110–15). The unattainable wish regarding Chiron includes a lengthy narrative that elucidates how Asclepius came to Chiron's tutelage and how he himself perished, leaving humankind without an exceptional healer. Chiron emerges as Asclepius' surrogate parent (*P.*3.45–46) after his mother, Coronis, is killed for betraying Apollo. Asclepius' miraculous rescue from the womb of his mother's burning corpse offers undeniable proof of his

---

[39] It is unclear whether *P.*3.72–76 (esp. στεφάνοις in line 73) refer to one or two Pythian victories and, more importantly, whether the ode was composed around the time of victory or several years later. Further problems arise from the ode's consolatory tone, an unusual choice for epinician poetry that encouraged Wilamowitz and others to read the poem as a "poetic epistle." On the ode's date and occasion, see sch. *P.*3 *inscr.* a + b, Gaspar 1900: 77–80, Schroeder 1922: 24, Wilamowitz 1922: 280 and 283, Burton 1962: 78–81, Lefkowitz 1976: 142, Young 1968: 27 with n.2 and, more importantly, 1983: 35–42, Robbins 1990 with a lengthy discussion of suggested dates and occasions, as well as Cingano 1991, Schade 2006: 375–76, and Morgan 2015: 268–72; cf. also Gentili et al. 1995: xli and 78–79. On the accommodation of subsequent performances in the text of *P.*3, see Morrison 2007: 97–98.

[40] On the complexities and problems involved in the unattainable wish of *P.*3, especially regarding lines 1–3, see Young 1968: 28–34, Pelliccia 1987, Slater 1988, and Morgan 2015: 272–75.

divine pedigree, while his tutelage under Chiron and his subsequent medical career also attest to Apollo's favor towards his son.

The mythological narrative that justifies and complements the wish uttered by the *persona loquens* is rather lengthy, occupying eight strophes in a poem of five triads. Against the expectation established in lines 1–7, however, Asclepius' medical apprenticeship under the legendary Centaur is mentioned only in passing (*P.*3.45–46); instead, the text focuses extensively on the hero's extraordinary healing skills and his eventual downfall (*P.*3.47–58). Even more surprising is that four of these eight strophes are dedicated neither to Chiron nor to Asclepius, but instead to Coronis, the hero's mother (*P.*3.8–40).[41] The inclusion of Coronis in the ode is expected in so far as it completes Asclepius' genealogical profile and paves the way to the account of his miraculous birth. The extensive treatment of her betrayal and punishment, on the other hand, is harder to justify, since Coronis' choices are hardly relevant to Asclepius' success as a doctor. Scholars intent on confirming Pindar's piety and his special relationship with Apollo have explained his interest in Coronis as an attempt to represent the god as an agent of justice.[42] Yet others have rightly pointed out that Coronis has an important paradigmatic function in the ode as a figure who provokes the deadly wrath of a god because she scorns what she has and desires what is unavailable (*P.*3.19–26). Her transgression and demise anticipate and mirror those of her son (*P.*3.54–60); furthermore, her story dramatizes and comments subtly upon the poem's broader preoccupation with unattainable wishes and desires.[43]

As it shapes its own version of the Coronis-story, *Pythian* 3 appropriates and revises circulating traditions surrounding the heroine. In extant sources, Coronis appears consistently as the mother of Asclepius when the roots of the mythical healer are situated in Thessaly or at least when the accounts retain some trace of this Thessalian tradition.[44] Coronis' betrayal

---

[41] On the structure of the mythological narrative, see Illig 1932: 47–54 and Young 1968: 64–65.

[42] See Wilamowitz 1886: 57–62, van der Kolf 1923: 16–17, Farnell 1932: 137–39, Illig 1932: 51–52, Duchemin 1955: 106–12 and 156–57, as well as 1967: 33–35, Stefos 1975: 58–64, and, more recently, Kyriakou 1994: 33 and 38–39.

[43] Luppino 1959, Burton 1962: 81–85, and Young 1968: 34–40, who discusses extensively and carefully the thematic relevance of the Coronis-story and points out (among other things) that the narrative introduces the importance of song that is also central to the ode; cf. briefly Erbse 1999: 19. On the paradigmatic function of Coronis and Asclepius in relation to Hieron and Sicily and in comparison to Tantalus in *O.*1, see, e.g., Morgan 2015: 275–82.

[44] *Homeric Hymn to Asclepius* 2–3, Pherecydes fr. 3 Fowler (= sch. Pi. *P.*3.59), Acusilaus fr. 17 Fowler (= sch. Pi. *P.*3.25c), Epimenides fr. 4 Fowler (=Diod. Sic. 5.74.6 cf. 4.71.1), *Pa.*37.5 Käppel (Erythraean

and punishment, however, do not seem to be a standard and intrinsic element of Asclepius' story. For instance, the *Homeric Hymn to Asclepius* celebrates the birth of the healer to Coronis and Apollo without even hinting at her death or at the infant's miraculous rescue (*h.Ascl.* 1–3).[45] In fact, the scholia to *Pythian* 3 indicate that Coronis' transgression and punishment were associated with a particular poetic tradition circulating under Hesiod's name. According to sch. *P.*3.52b, Artemon of Pergamum (*FGrH* 569 F5) praised Pindar because in *Pythian* 3 Apollo does not learn the bad news from a crow but perceives Coronis' indiscretion on his own, as is appropriate for the god of prophecy (*P.*3.27–30).[46] Artemon associates the detail of the crow with Hesiodic poetry:

τὸν δὲ περὶ τὸν κόρακα μῦθόν φησι καὶ Ἡσίοδον μνημονεύοντα λέγειν οὕτως:

"τῆμος ἄρ' ἄγγελος ἦλθε κόραξ ἱερῆς ἀπὸ δαιτὸς
Πυθὼ ἐς ἠγαθέην, καί ῥ' ἔφρασεν ἔργ' ἀίδηλα
Φοίβῳ ἀκερσεκόμῃ, ὅτι Ἴσχυς γῆμε Κόρωνιν
Εἰλατίδης, Φλεγύαο διογνήτοιο θύγατρα" (=Hesiod fr. 71/60)
(sch. Pindar, *Pythian* 3.52b)

And he (*sc.* Artemon) says that Hesiod too, when he mentions the story about the crow, speaks thus:

"then a crow came as a messenger from the sacred feast
to most holy Pytho, and revealed the unseen deeds
to long-haired Phoebus, that Ischys, Elatus' son, married Coronis,
the daughter of Phlegyas born of Zeus."

An alternative, slightly abbreviated version of this Hesiodic fragment appears also in sch. *P.*3.14, after a discussion of the two distinct traditions regarding the identity of Asclepius' mother:

---

Paean), *Pa.*41.11 Käppel (Macedonius' Paean). For Roman sources, cf. also Edelstein and Edelstein 1945: 1–25. On the Hesiodic Coronis *ehoie*, see below in this chapter. On the limited cult of Coronis, see Larson 1995: 63–64. Isyllus' *Paean*, a poem dating to the late fourth or to the third century BCE, weaves an Epidaurean genealogy for Asclepius, in which he is the son of Apollo and Aegle, the daughter of an Epidaurian Phlegyas. This genealogy aims at making Asclepius indigenous to Epidaurus, but it marks its appropriation of the Thessalian tradition not only by including Phlegyas as Asclepius' maternal grandfather but also by granting Aegle the nickname 'Coronis' (lines 44–45); see Kolde 2003: 151–59. On the alternative genealogical connection of Asclepius with Arsinoe, daughter of Leucippus, see below.

[45] Cf. Isyllus' *Paean* 48–50, where Aegle gives birth to Asclepius in a sanctuary with divine assistance. Artemis, who is almost certainly the unspecified Διὸς παῖς in 49–50, is facilitating the birth of Apollo's son. Isyllus' *Paean* therefore, overwrites Artemis' murderous intervention in *P.*3.8–11 and replaces the transgressive story of the Thessalian Coronis with the harmonious tale of Epidaurian Aegle.

[46] On Artemon, see Deas 1931: 12–13, Irigoin 1952: 62, and Hummel 1997: 68.

ἐν δὲ τοῖς εἰς Ἡσίοδον ἀναφερομένοις ἔπεσι φέρεται ταῦτα περὶ τῆς Κορωνίδος·
"τῇ μὲν ἄρ' ἦλθε κόραξ, φράσσεν δ' ἄρα ἔργ' ἀΐδηλα,
Φοίβῳ ἀκερσεκόμῃ, ὅτ' ἄρ' Ἴσχυς γῆμε Κόρωνιν
Εἰλατίδης Φλεγύαο διογνήτοιο θύγατρα."

(sch. Pindar, Pythian 3.14)

These things are said about Coronis in the verses attributed to Hesiod:
"there a crow came and revealed the unseen deeds
to long-haired Phoebus, that Ischys, Elatus' son, married Coronis,
the daughter of Phlegyas born of Zeus."

Unfortunately, the Pindaric scholia do not specify from which poem of the
Hesiodic corpus they draw these lines. They also do not mention explicitly
that Hesiod's treatment of Coronis included the birth of Asclepius. Nonetheless, it is possible that the Hesiodic fragment belongs to a genealogical
poem; note that it is embedded in a survey of Asclepius' genealogies (sch.
*P.*3.14). There is, in fact, a papyrus fragment that preserves what is most
probably the beginning of a Coronis-*ehoie* (Hes. fr. 70/59, see below). It is
plausible, then, that a version of Coronis' story which included her
marriage to Ischys, her punishment, and the miraculous birth of Asclepius
was circulating as part of a genealogical poem attributed to Hesiod, either
the *Catalogue of Women* or the *Megalai Ehoiai*.[47] But which one? Determining which of the two poems included the Coronis-*ehoie* is challenging
not only because the evidence is lacking but also because there was another
genealogy of Asclepius attributed to Hesiod, according to which the
healer's mother was Arsinoe, a Leucippid.[48] It has been suggested that
both *ehoiai* were part of the same poem.[49] Yet, judging by the careful
overall structure that emerges from the fragments of the *Catalogue*, this
hypothesis is rather implausible; in addition, there is no parallel case of
conflicting genealogies within the *Catalogue* or the *Megalai Ehoiai* to
support it. On this issue, I follow D'Alessio, who offers a lucid, careful,
and thorough consideration of the evidence, and concludes that the most

---

[47] Differently West 1985a: 69–72, who suggests that Coronis may not have been featured in the
*Catalogue* at all, and that, if she was, she had nothing to do with Asclepius. As for Hes. fr. 71/60, he
argues that it may have been part of the Hesiodic *Ornithomanteia* or even the *Astronomia*. Cf.
Most's reluctance to assign Hes. fr. 71/60 to a specific poem (Most 2007: 310–11 with n.24).

[48] Pausanias 2.26.7 attributes the version involving Arsinoe either to Hesiod or to an interpolator who
is promoting the interests of the Messenians. For an attempt to conflate Arsinoe with Coronis, see
Aristeides (*FGrH* 444 F1, "she (*sc.* Arsinoe) used to be called Coronis when she was a maiden").

[49] Wilamowitz 1886: 72–83 situated both *ehoiai* in the *Catalogue* based on his hypothesis that the poem
was growing "like a snowball" through the accretion of genealogical entries (cf. Wilamowitz 1905:
123). See also Casanova 1979a: 239–40 and Merkelbach and West, whose 1967 edition of the
Hesiodic fragments incorporates both Arsinoe and Coronis in the *Catalogue* (frs. 50–61MW).

economical solution to the problem is to assign Coronis to the *Catalogue* and Arsinoe to the *Megalai Ehoiai*.[50]

Let's take a closer look at the longer version of Hes. fr. 71/60 quoted above. The sacred feast from which the crow arrives in line 1 is almost certainly that of Coronis' wedding;[51] the Hesiodic text thus draws attention to the tension between the sanctity of the wedding ritual (ἱερῆς ἀπὸ δαιτός) and the offense Apollo is about to take from it. While there is no explicit reference to the repercussions of the crow's message, its revelatory power is clearly brought to the forefront with the phrase ἔφρασεν ἔργ' ἀίδηλα. The formula ἔργ' ἀίδηλα draws attention to Apollo's newly gained insight, but may also capture a negative assessment of the events that is focalized through the offended god and forebodes the upcoming punishment and ruin.[52] Next, the fragment offers a line-up of all the important characters of the story: Apollo, defined here by his perennial youth (ἀκερσεκόμη; cf. *P*.3.14), Ischys, the subject of the verb γῆμε and Apollo's replacement in Coronis' bed, as well as Coronis herself, who has just crossed the threshold to maturity through marriage. Finally, the extensive identification of the couple with an entire line of patronymics in line 4 has led to the assumption that, in the original context of these lines, this would be the first mention of Coronis and Ischys.[53] It is equally possible, however, that the line simply reflects the fullness and accuracy of the crow's report. Besides, if Pherecydes (fr. 3 Fowler) follows the Hesiodic *ehoie* when he recounts that Apollo killed not only Coronis but also Ischys,[54] then Hes. fr. 71/60.3–4 identify with precision the targets of the divine punishment that will follow immediately after the revelations of the crow.

---

[50] D'Alessio 2005a: 208–10; cf. Dräger 1997: 84–86 and Hirschberger 2004: 439–40 with D'Alessio 2005c. For the reverse attribution of the two *ehoiai*, see, e.g., Leo 1894: 351 and, more recently, Most 2007; for the problems involved in this arrangement, see D'Alessio 2005a: 208.

[51] Hirschberger 2004: 337. For ἱερῆς δαιτός standing for a wedding feast, see *LdfE* s.v. δαίς B.1a.

[52] For ἔργ' ἀίδηλα in the sense of "hidden/unseen deeds" in this passage, see *LdfE* s.v. ἀίδηλος B.I.2 and cf. *WD* 756 (μωμεύειν ἀίδηλα). Elsewhere, however, the formula ἔργ' ἀίδηλα has a different meaning: in Hes. fr. 20/30.16–17 and Tyrtaeus fr. 11.7W², it is used for deeds that are "terrible to look at", i.e. "hateful," "abominable" (*LdfE* s.v. ἀίδηλος B.II). Nonetheless, there is evidence that the adjective was understood in antiquity as "destructive" (*LdfE* s.v. Σχ c α, ε, ζ, η, cf. also γ), hence *LSJ* s.v. I ("making unseen, annihilating, destructive") and *DGE* s.v. II ("que hace desaparecer, destructor, aniquilador"). It is tempting to assume a double entendre in ἔργ' ἀίδηλα of Hes. fr. 71/60.2 ("unseen"/"destructive").

[53] West 1985a: 71.

[54] Pherecydes' fr. 3 Fowler agrees with *P*.3 in several details: Coronis' location, her execution by Artemis, and Asclepius' delivery to Chiron by Apollo; cf. also the collateral casualties in the local community. Unlike *P*.3, however, fr. 3 Fowler includes the death of Ischys as well as the crow, an element also featured in the *ehoie*. It is possible that Pherecydes' version of the story was informed extensively by the Hesiodic tradition.

While the fragment embedded in the scholion to *P.*3.52b seems to set up the denouement of the Hesiodic *Coronis-ehoie*, a different fragment (*P.Oxy.* 2490 = 2483 fr. 3, ed. Lobel) may be preserving its beginning:

$$
\begin{array}{c}
].\text{ηος} \\
\text{ἢ οἵη Διδύμους ἱεροὺς ναίουσα κολωνούς,} \\
\text{Δωτίωι ἐν πεδίωι πολυβότρυος ἀντ' Ἀ}\text{,μύροιο} \\
\text{νίψατο Βοιβιάδος λίμνης πόδα παρθέ}\text{,νος ἀδμής} \\
].[..]\text{s} \\
\text{ἄρ]ουρα} \\
\text{ἄ]λσος} \\
]\text{α καλά} \\
\textit{desunt versus quinque (9–13)} \\
]\text{s} \\
.] \ \text{Ἑρμῆς} \\
]\text{s} \\
\text{ἄ]κοιτιν} \\
]\text{ου} \\
]\text{ν ἔχουσα} \\
].\text{α} \\
]\text{εντι} \\
\text{(Hesiod, fr. 70/59)}
\end{array}
$$

2–4 Strabo 9.5.22 and 14.1.40
. . . or such as the one inhabiting the sacred Twin Hills in the Dotian plain facing Amyrus of many grapes washed her foot in Lake Boebias, an unmarried maiden, . . . land . . . grove . . . beautiful . . . Hermes . . . wife . . . having . . .

It is clear that line 2 marks the beginning of an *ehoie*, but it is impossible to identify the παρθένος ἀδμής with certainty. The only hints available to us are the geographical details, which point to Coronis.[55] Strabo quotes Hes. fr. 70/59.2–4 as evidence that the Dotian field was right in the middle of Thessaly next to Lake Boebias (9.5.22 and 14.1.40). That is exactly where both Pherecydes (fr. 3 Fowler) and, more importantly, Pindar locate Lacereia, the home town of Coronis (*P.*3.34). If Hes. fr. 70/59 is indeed an *ehoie* of Coronis, the word ἄκοιτιν of line 17 probably indicates a reference to the marriage between Coronis and Ischys; if so, then the maiden's relationship with Apollo should occupy the preceding lines, and fr. 71/60 should follow fr. 70/59 closely. While most extant textual clues are compatible with the hypothesis that fr. 70/59 is a Coronis-*ehoie*, the presence of Hermes in line 15 poses a challenge since it does not

---

[55] Hirschberger 2004: 334–35, esp. 334 on other possible identifications of the παρθένος ἀδμής.

conform to any (known) early version of the maiden's story. Fitting the god in the storyline is all the more problematic if he plays a role *before* the marriage of Coronis and Ischys (perhaps recounted in lines 17–19).[56] Still the god's inclusion, however puzzling, does not suffice to undermine the view that this fragment is part of the Coronis-*ehoie*.

In fact, I suggest that the Pindaric ode alludes to fr. 70/59 at a crucial moment in its narrative:

καὶ τότε γνοὺς ᾿Ίσχυος Εἰλατίδα
ξεινίαν κοίταν ἀθέμιν τε δόλον, πέμ-
ψεν κασιγνήταν μένει
θυίοισαν ἀμαιμακέτῳ
ἐς Λακέρειαν, ἐπεὶ παρὰ Βοιβιάδος
κρημνοῖσιν ᾤκει παρθένος
(Pindar, *Pythian* 3.31–34)

And then, after he (*sc.* Apollo) found out about (her) sleeping with a foreigner, Ischys, son of Elatus, and about her impious deceit, he sent his sister raging with irresistible force to Lacereia, since the maiden used to live next to the banks of Boebias.

Both the Hesiodic fragment and the Pindaric passage privilege a close association between the παρθένος and her local landscape.[57] The *ehoie* uses the geographic details to construct a *locus amoenus* in which it situates the girl's carefree maidenhood (νίψατο Βοιβιάδος λίμνης πόδα παρθέ᾿νος ἀδμής, fr. 70/59.4); the Hesiodic narrative may also have located her union with Apollo there.[58] The ode, on the other hand, evokes the same landscape in a much bleaker context: Coronis, a παρθένος but no longer ἀδμής, is about to die, killed at the behest of her immortal lover due to another union (*P.*3.34–35). Through juxtaposition with its Hesiodic intertext, the Pindaric text puts a dark spin on its reception of the *ehoie*.

While reiterating the geography of Hes. fr. 70/59 and exploiting its connotations, Pindar's *Pythian* 3 also engages creatively with Hes. fr. 71/60.

[56] Dräger 1997: 73–76 suggests that Hermes is the god who rescues the infant Asclepius from the burning corpse of his mother in the Hesiodic account. Hermes' involvement in the story of Coronis, however, is found only in one late source (Paus. 2.26.6); more importantly, if Coronis has already mated with Apollo, married Ischys, and died by line 15, there is no plausible way to combine Hes. fr. 71/60 with fr. 70/59. We could assume that the two fragments belong to different treatments of the story in the Hesiodic corpus. Alternatively, one could suppose that we have two different variations of the same *ehoie*.

[57] On the παρθένος as a maiden at the age of marriage without any connotations of virginity, see Sissa 1990 and Rigoglioso 2009: 40–42.

[58] See ἄρ]ουρα, 6 and especially ἄ]λσος, 7, possibly the *locus amoenus* in which the girl's rape takes place. Cf. *Pythian* 9, in which Apollo falls for Cyrene after spotting her in the countryside although there the landscape is constructed as much more wild.

As the Hesiodic crow disappears from the picture, the ode draws our attention to its omission:

> οὐδ' ἔλαθε σκοπόν· ἐν δ' ἄρα μηλοδόκῳ
> Πυθῶνι τόσσαις ἄϊεν ναοῦ βασιλεύς
> Λοξίας, κοινᾶνι παρ' εὐθυτάτῳ γνώμαν πιθών,
> πάντα ἰσάντι νόῳ·
> ψευδέων δ' οὐχ ἅπτεται, κλέπτει τέ μιν
> οὐ θεὸς οὐ βροτὸς ἔργοις οὔτε βουλαῖς.
>
> (Pindar, *Pythian* 3.27–30)

She (*sc.* Coronis) did not escape the watcher; for the lord of the temple, Loxias, who happened to be at sheep-receiving Pytho, heard, having convinced his judgment by consulting his most unerring partner, his all-knowing mind. He does not cling to lies, and no god or mortal deceives him with deeds or counsels.

As is often pointed out, Pindar has crafted a text that misleads his audience:[59] anyone familiar with Hes. fr. 71/60 would expect that the deliberately vague σκοπός of line 27 is the Hesiodic crow rather than Apollo himself. False expectations are further fostered by ἄϊεν, a verb used regularly for auditory perception, and by the emphasis on the physical distance between Apollo and Coronis, a detail that justifies the necessity for an eyewitness and messenger in the Hesiodic account (fr. 71/60.1–2). Line 28 (κοινᾶνι παρ' εὐθυτάτῳ γνώμαν πιθών) delivers the final misleading clue: just as ambiguous as the earlier σκοπόν, Apollo's "most unerring partner" in counsel is presented at first as an agent external to the god himself, thus hinting at the crow. Only the final word of this long sentence reveals that in this version Apollo, being omniscient, has no need for a messenger (πάντα ἰσάντι νόῳ, *P*.3.29). Not only does the ode construct Apollo in opposition to the Hesiodic *ehoie*, then, but it also manipulates the audience, lulling them into a false sense of familiarity with details known from the Hesiodic tradition, only to defamiliarize the entire passage with a few concluding words.

While celebrating the omniscience of Apollo,[60] *Pythian* 3 also enhances the image of Delphi. The ode replaces the Hesiodic phrase "most holy Pytho" (Πυθὼ ἐς ἠγαθέην, fr. 71/60.2) with a more elaborate reference to Delphi as a cultic and oracular center. Unlike the trite ἠγαθέη ("most holy"), which is used for Delphi elsewhere in the Pindaric

---

[59] On *P*.3.27–29, see Burton 1962: 83–84, Young 1968: 37–38, Gentili et al. 1995: 75–76 with n.4.

[60] By omitting the crow, the ode also elides the impulsive and unfair punishment that the god inflicts upon the feathered messenger according to some extant versions. On the story of Coronis as an *aition* for the crow's black feathers, see Ps.-Apollod. *Bibl.* 3.10.3, Hyg. *Astr.* 2.40 and *Fab.* 202, Ovid *Met.* 2.542–47 and 596–632.

corpus (*P.*9.71, *N.*6.34), the epithet μηλοδόκος (*P.*3.27) is a striking *hapax legomenon* that constructs Delphi more concretely as a place of ritual and sacrifice (cf. *h.Ap.* 535–37). Furthermore, the phrase ναοῦ βασιλεύς (*P.*3.27) evokes the oracular function of the god's temple at Delphi, subtly preparing the ground for Pindar's revisionist representation of Apollo. While the poem's association of Delphi with cult and prophecy paves the way for the overt affirmation of Apollo's omniscience in line 30, it also celebrates the only geographic and cultic space in which *Pythian* 3 situates athletic victory (*P.*3.73–74).

While reconfiguring the Hesiodic narrative in order to enhance the divine figure of Apollo, however, *Pythian* 3 also reshapes the Hesiodic figure of Coronis in a profound way, an aspect of the poem's engagement with the Hesiodic genealogical tradition that has not been adequately studied. As far as we can tell from Hes. fr. 71/60,[61] in the Hesiodic *ehoie* Coronis and Ischys are wedded (Hes. fr. 71/60.3)[62] with proper ritual (ἱερῆς ἀπὸ δαιτός, 1) and presumably with her father's permission. Furthermore, the language of marriage in the fragment casts Ischys in an active role (ὅτι Ἴσχυς γῆμε Κόρωνιν, 3), thus defining the relationship in accordance with traditional gender roles. When she is first introduced in *Pythian* 3, Pindar's Coronis appears to conform to the narrative expectations established by her *ehoie*; soon, however, she proves to be a more complex and rather subversive version of her Hesiodic self.

The story of Coronis in *Pythian* 3 begins at the end of its thread.[63] The first details revealed about her are consistent with the Hesiodic narrative: she is the daughter of Phlegyas and, having provoked the wrath of Apollo, she was killed before she could give birth to Asclepius (*P.*3.8–12).[64] Here too Coronis dies because of her union with Ischys; nonetheless, as her transgression gradually unfolds, it clearly departs from the Hesiodic tradition:

> ἁ δ' ἀποφλαυρίξαισά νιν
> ἀμπλακίαισι φρενῶν,
> 　　　ἄλλον αἴνησεν γάμον κρύβδαν πατρός,
> πρόσθεν ἀκερσεκόμᾳ μιχθεῖσα Φοίβῳ,

---

[61] cf. ἄκοιτιν, Hes. fr. 70/59.17.

[62] Unlike μείγνυμι which unambiguously points to a sexual union (cf. τὴν Ἴσχυος μίξιν δήλωσεν in sch. *P.*3.52b), the primary connotation of γαμέω is marriage (*LfgrE s.v.* B.1a on Hes. fr. 71/60).

[63] On the ring-composition that defines the structure of the Coronis story in *Pythian* 3, see Illig 1932: 50–53 and Young 1968: 64–65.

[64] On the involvement of Artemis see, e.g., Bernardini 1983: 72 and Tsitsibakou-Vasalos 2010: 32–33.

καὶ φέροισα σπέρμα θεοῦ καθαρόν·
οὐκ ἔμειν' ἐλθεῖν τράπεζαν νυμφίαν,
οὐδὲ παμφώνων ἰαχὰν ὑμεναίων, ἅλικες
οἷα παρθένοι φιλέοισιν ἑταῖραι
ἑσπερίαις ὑποκουρίζεσθ' ἀοιδαῖς·
(Pindar, *Pythian* 3.12–19)

But she (*sc.* Coronis) disparaged it (*sc.* Apollo's anger) in the folly of her mind and agreed to another union, hiding it from her father, even though she had sex with long-haired Phoebus previously and was carrying the pure seed of the god. And she did not wait for the wedding feast to come or for the sound of full-voiced wedding songs, such as unwedded companions of the same age like to utter softly in evening songs.

ἐλθόν-
τος γὰρ εὐνάσθη ξένου
λέκτροισιν ἀπ' Ἀρκαδίας.
(Pindar, *Pythian* 3.25–26)

for (Coronis) slept in the bed of the stranger who came from Arcadia.

*Pythian* 3 portrays Coronis as a transgressor in the eyes of gods and men alike. There is no doubt that she recklessly disregards Apollo by sleeping with another man while being pregnant with the god's child. Yet the Pindaric text adds another layer of blame by highlighting her disrespect towards the social norms and expectations for a woman of her age. Coronis hides her affair with Ischys from her father and consummates her desire before the relationship receives legitimation and communal approval through public ritual.[65] Significantly, her relationship with Ischys is introduced as an ἄλλος γάμος (line 13), a phrase that immediately evokes their marriage in the Hesiodic account (cf. γῆμε, Hes. fr. 71/60.3). While fostering the false expectation that the ode will offer a simple iteration of the *ehoie*, ἄλλος γάμος also exploits masterfully the semantics in order to suggest that this relationship was reproachable. The sequence implied by the adjective ἄλλος points to Coronis' previous affair with Apollo, which was (and could only have been) a sexual encounter. The text thus hints at a pattern of γάμος without matrimony with which her new relationship is consistent as the ode soon reveals. In the narrative that follows, the ode underscores repeatedly the sexual nature of Coronis' relationships (ἀκερσεκόμᾳ μιχθεῖσα Φοίβῳ, *P*.3.14, εὐνάσθη ξένου / λέκτροισιν, *P*.3.25–26, Ἴσχυος Εἰλατίδα / ξεινίαν κοίταν,

[65] Cf. Sissa 1990: 346–48.

*P*.3.31–32); marriage, on the other hand, is brought up only to be negated as an unfulfilled expectation (*P*.3.16–19).[66]

Pindar's version of Coronis' relationship with Ischys divests the maiden of the passive and probably guiltless role she would have held in her *ehoie*. Coronis now operates with guile and deceit (κρύβδαν πατρός, *P*.3.13; ἄθεμιν δόλον, *P*.3.32),[67] and the ode assigns her full responsibility for the course of events that leads to her death. The syntactical arrangement of the text consistently casts Coronis in an active role and grants her complete control of her pursuit of Ischys. In fact, Ischys is barely present in the narrative. The only aspect of his identity that receives considerable attention is that he is a foreigner, a guest from Arcadia (*P*.3.25–26, cf. 32); his name and patronymic are revealed relatively late in the narrative (*P*.3.31).[68] Far from being coerced, Coronis throws herself into a ξεινία κοίτα (*P*.3.32) that is not only a scandalous secret but also, in all likelihood, a short-lived union. Reversing the traditional gender dynamics featured in Hes. fr. 71/60, *Pythian* 3 constructs Ischys as a passive figure, a character that remains undeveloped and simply supports Coronis' negative portrayal. His minimal and ancillary presence in the narrative could justify the fact that the ode does not mention his punishment; this omission may even imply that, in Pindar's version of the story, Ischys is too passive to be blamed by the god.[69] One may contrast the elision of Ischys' death to the several innocent people who are said to have perished on account of Coronis' transgression in *P*.3.35–37, a passage that brands her as a bane to the entire community and furthers her vilification.[70]

---

[66] On the ritual language of *P*.3.16–23 and on Coronis' resistance to participating in the rite of passage that is marriage, see Tsitsibakou-Vasalos 2010: 34.

[67] Cf. Gentili et al. 1995: 76 n.4 continued and 413 on *P*.3.32. I do not think that ἄθεμις δόλος implies that Ischys is transgressing the limits of *xenia*, as Kyriakou 1994: 34–35 tentatively suggests. The text shifts all blame onto Coronis for her sexual desire.

[68] On the significance of the late revelation of his name and patronymic, see Kyriakou 1994: 39, who points out that these details are part of Apollo's realization and thus underscore his omniscience. We do not know whether Hesiod's Ischys was an Arcadian or a Thessalian (cf. Ps.-Apollod. *Bibl.* 3.10.3, where Ischys is said to be a Lapith, the brother of Caeneus). Therefore, it is possible that *P*.3 departs from the Hesiodic tradition in giving Ischys a non-Thessalian identity. If that is the case, then, by postponing the name of Coronis' mortal lover, the Pindaric text sets the audience up for a surprise at the mention of an (untraditional) Arcadian lover. The prominence of Arcadia may have been particularly popular with the ode's primary audience in Syracuse, given the city's Arcadian population, on which see Luraghi 1994: 292–96.

[69] In other versions of the story, Apollo kills Ischys (e.g. Pherecydes fr. 3 Fowler); it is possible that this detail is already Hesiodic.

[70] While commenting on the demise of innocent people in lines 35–36, sch. *P*.3.64b quotes Hes. *WD* 240 ("often even the entire polis suffers on account of a bad man"). If the scholiast assumes here an extended engagement with the Hesiodic corpus that goes beyond the *ehoie* of Coronis, he does not make it explicit.

The ode, therefore, lays the blame exclusively on Coronis[71] – but why and to what effect? Those who read Pindar's version as a pious "correction" of the Hesiodic tradition are content to argue that, by disparaging Coronis, the ode makes Apollo's reaction come across as a justified punishment rather than an irrational act of jealousy.[72] Such readings, however, do not address the complexities of Coronis' transgression. While her guilt is unambiguous in *Pythian* 3, the exact nature of her crime resists a clear and straightforward definition. Take, for instance, the question of marriage: the ode draws attention to the public wedding ritual that never happened, but, in a completely un-Hesiodic twist, the text seems to imply that, in the case of Coronis' affair with Ischys, a wedding would have been an appropriate course of action (*P*.3.16–19). Furthermore, while at first Coronis is blamed for having disrespected the pure "seed of the god" inside her by sleeping with another man (*P*.3.15), later the text defines her delusion (αὐάτα, *P*.3.24) in different terms, as she is said to be in love with what is not present (ἀλλά τοι ἤρατο τῶν ἀπεόντων, *P*.3.19–20).[73] The ode establishes Coronis as a paradigm for the destructive consequences of unattainable desires, thus linking her to one of the main themes of the entire poem. Yet how can Coronis be a fool for desiring that which is "far away" when she sleeps with (a very present) Ischys? Given that Ischys' Arcadian provenance almost exclusively defines his identity (*P*.3.25–26, 31–32), we are led to conclude that the most alarming and unpardonable aspect of Coronis' desire was that she slept with a visitor who was bound to leave and thus become unavailable; without the prospect of marriage, Ischys would soon become a permanent absence. In *Pythian* 3, therefore, Coronis does not provoke Apollo because he has lingering

---

[71] Gentili et al. 1995: 413 suggest that Coronis suffers because she has inherited the hubristic nature of her father Phlegyas (cf. 408–09); nonetheless, the ode does not make the slightest mention of Phlegyas' past misconduct. In *Pythian* 3 Coronis emerges as fully responsible for her action, and, even though her son shares her self-destructive desire for what should not be desired, the text does not represent this fatal fault as his mother's legacy (*P*.3.54–58).

[72] For the idea that *P*.3 is supposed to be an expression of Pindar's heavy bias in favor of Apollo, see the literature in n.59.

[73] The ancient scholiast (sch. *P*.3.38c) finds *P*.3.21–23 similar in content to a line which, based on other sources, we can identify as Hesiodic (νήπιος, ὃς τὰ ἑτοῖμα λιπὼν ἀνέτοιμα διώκει, "foolish is he who abandons the things that are within reach and chases unattainable things," Hes. fr. *24/61). Despite Blumenthal 1914, there is no reason to assume that this gnomic statement belongs to the *ehoie* of Coronis (cf. Schwartz 1960: 403 n.4). As Hirschberger 2004: 483 points out, given the lack of *gnomai* in the extant fragments of Hesiodic genealogical poetry, it is more likely that the quoted line originates in a didactic poem attributed to Hesiod, perhaps the *Chironos Hypothekai* or the *Megala Erga*, on which see Introduction, pp. 8–9.

feelings of affection and possessiveness, nor simply because she sleeps
with another man while pregnant with the god's son. Instead, I argue,
she invites the god's wrath because, without the prospect of legitimation
through marriage, her son would be considered the bastard child of a
random Arcadian passer-by. In other words, Coronis' affair with Ischys
does not simply cast a shadow upon Asclepius' divine pedigree but
completely undermines his status in society. Along these lines, Asclepius' miraculous rescue from the pyre not only promotes Apollo as a
just and merciful god, but also counterbalances Coronis' insult by
offering an open and indisputable confirmation of the baby's divine
origins.[74]

I hope to have shown that Pindar's Coronis presents a complex case
of Hesiodic reception. Pindar departs significantly from the Hesiodic
tradition in the way he shapes both the character of Coronis and the
plot of her story. At the same time, however, he expects his audience to
evoke the Coronis-*ehoie* and encourages them to interpret *Pythian* 3
through juxtaposition to the Hesiodic tradition. In this context, Pindar's Coronis emerges as a better-developed and more complex character. *Pythian* 3 transforms the passive and inconspicuous heroine of the
*ehoie* into a strong female figure who is in charge of her sexuality and in
active pursuit of her desires. Far from being a simple circumlocution as
the ancient commentator (sch. *P*.3.43a) claims, the phrase καλλιπέπλου
λῆμα Κορωνίδος in *P*.3.25 epitomizes the heroine's radical transformation:
while καλλίπεπλος conveys her appealing femininity, λῆμα invests her with
the kind of willfulness that Pindar elsewhere associates exclusively with
men.[75] Unambiguously overbearing and transgressive, this enhanced version of Coronis is central to this poem as a showcase of humankind's self-
destructive tendency to desire what is beyond reach (*P*.3.19–25). Intrinsically linked to the core theme of unattainable wishes and the harm they can
cause, Pindar's Coronis emerges as a universal paradigm that not only

---

[74] On the parallel between the births of Asclepius and Dionysus, see Burgess 2001. Cf. Tsitsibakou-
Vasalos 2010: 32 and 37 on the role of Artemis and the ambivalence of language in the context of
Coronis' death (*P*.3.8–15, 31–37). Note that the Hesiodic corpus included an account of Asclepius'
death by Zeus's thunderbolt as well. Hes. fr. 52 MW indicates that the story was recounted in the
*ME* (cf. D'Alessio 2005a: 208–10), but it was probably part of the *Catalogue* too. See D'Alessio
2005c, who argues against Hirschberger's choice to include frs. 51, 54–58, and 106 MW in the
Arsinoe-*ehoie* of the *ME* (frs. 3–9 H) instead of the Coronis-*ehoie* of the *Catalogue*. Since we do not
have any details about the Hesiodic treatment of Asclepius' crime, there is no way to assess its
reception in *Pythian* 3. Wilamowitz 1886: 60 assumes that Asclepius' avarice is a Pindaric invention.
[75] Pindar uses the word λῆμα for male characters with a positive connotation (*P*.8.44–45, *N*.1.56–58,
*N*.3.83–84). On λῆμα Κορωνίδος, see Xanthou 2013.

informs the subsequent representation of her son Asclepius (P.3.54–60), but also offers an important lesson both to the poem's *persona loquens* and to its audience(s), including Hieron himself.

Much like Coronis in *Pythian* 3, Cyrene undergoes a spectacular transformation from a conventional Hesiodic maiden to an intrepid huntress in *Pythian* 9, to which I now turn.

## Cyrene (*Pythian* 9)

*Pythian* 9 was composed for the victory of Telesicrates, a *hoplitodromos* from Cyrene, at the Pythian Games of 474 BCE. Intended most probably for a first performance at Cyrene,[76] the ode opens with a long mythological narrative that recounts the union of Apollo and Cyrene (*P.9.5–70*) and thus celebrates the origins of the victor's home town. The poem introduces the story with a brief summary of Cyrene's relocation from Thessaly to Libya and of her union with Apollo (*P.9.5–14*). The narrative then seamlessly traces the genealogical pedigree of Cyrene (*P.9.14–16*), before delving into the maiden's exceptional qualities and recounting how she attracted Apollo's erotic interest (*P.9.17–28*). In this context, and while Apollo considers how to approach Cyrene (*P.9.29–37*), Chiron the Centaur offers some advice but also a prophecy regarding the birth of Aristaeus and the foundation of Cyrene (*P.9.38–65*). The narrative concludes with the marriage of Cyrene and Apollo where the city that bears her name now lies (*P.9.66–70*).

The prominence of marriage in the mythological account has been interpreted in the broader context of Pindar's discourse of colonization. The story begins with the god abducting Cyrene on his chariot;[77] the rape, however, is quickly reframed as a mutual union and a legitimate marriage presided over by Aphrodite (*P.9.9–13*). Once redefined as conjugal, their relationship is consistently presented as such (*P.9.51–52, 55–56a, 66*).[78] In the context of this aetiological narrative that celebrates the foundation of

---

[76] The poem points at the location of its (first) intended performance in line 91 (πόλιν τάνδ᾽), but the identity of this city is an object of debate. For arguments supporting the ode's Cyrenean premiere, see D'Alessio 1994: 131–32 with n.47 and 2004: 290–91; cf. also Carey 1981: 65–66 and Gentili et al. 1995: 237–39. Others, however, have suggested Thebes as the location of the poem's premiere; see esp. Péron 1976, followed by Danielewicz 1990: 12–13 with n.18. The debate focuses on *P.9.87–96*, since there have been different opinions regarding the textual integrity of the passage, the interpretation of future verbs (κωμάσομαι, 88; cf. δέξεται, 73), and the identity of the first-person voice (see Hubbard 1991a: 22–26 with bibliography).

[77] For the motif, cf. *h.Dem.* 16–20; cf. Dougherty 1993: 141.

[78] Cf. the emphasis on the pleasure that Cyrene's grandmother experiences in Peneus' bed (ὅν [sc. Ὑψέα]. . ./ Ναῒς εὐφρανθεῖσα Πηνειοῦ λέχει Κρέοισ᾽ ἔτικτεν, *P.9.15–16*).

Cyrene, the transformation of rape into marriage as well as the bride's welcome reception in Libya diffuse the violence involved in colonization and rewrite the narrative of invasion as a peaceful integration between indigenous and foreign elements.[79] In fact, marriage as a metaphor for harmonious assimilation frames the entire poem since it recurs in the ode's closing lines, where Alexidamus, an ancestor of the victor, receives praise for winning an indigenous Libyan bride in a footrace (*P.*9.101–25). Consistent with the programmatic account of Cyrene and Apollo, the story of Alexidamus reiterates the theme of peaceful integration through intermarriage, even though it involves a strong competitive element and ultimately underscores the superiority of the Greeks.[80]

While directly relevant to the politics of colonization and its representation, marriage in *P.*9 is also linked to athletics. To begin with, the mythological narrative of the first seventy lines introduces physical strength as an alluring feature. Cyrene prefers hunting wild animals to gender-appropriate activities (*P.*9.18–25), but, far from being disruptive, her unconventional behavior attracts the attention of Apollo, who falls in love as he watches her fight a lion with her bare hands (ἄτερ ἐγχέων, *P.*9.28). Furthermore, when the love-struck god praises her, he draws attention exclusively to her physical strength and her courage (*P.*9.30–35). Defying gender expectations, Cyrene's strength prefigures the prowess of the Cyreneans, and especially of their athletes, such as the *laudandus*, but also marks it as an attractive feature with erotic connotations. Notice that marriage and athletic excellence also converge in the story of Alexidamus: out of his many athletic victories (*P.*9.125), Pindar narrates extensively only the footrace in which he earned his wife (*P.*9.104–25). The appeal of physical strength, finally, is central to the ode's treatment of the *laudandus* himself, since the text links inextricably his many victories to his reception as an object of female desire – albeit not always of sexual desire (*P.*9.97–100).[81]

---

[79] Dougherty 1993: 136–56.

[80] Athanassaki 2003: 96–98. It is unclear whether the ode situates Alexidamus in the mythical past or in a more recent phase of Cyrenean history; see Carey 1981: 100, cf. Köhnken 1985: 104–10 and Calame 1990: 302–04 with astute observations on the parallel between the two narratives (Cyrene–Apollo, Alexidamus) as well as their relevance to the victor. For the parallel between marriage and athletic competition in *Pythian* 9, see also Carson 1982; on marriage and exchange in *Pythian* 9, see Kurke 1991: 127–34.

[81] On Cyrene as an athletic figure and the parallel between her and Telesicrates, see Carson 1984: 124, Köhnken 1985: 74–76 (cf. 97–98), and Dougherty 1993: 139 with a discussion of the verbal parallels between *P.*9.30–35 and Pindar's discourse on victors in other odes. On Apollo as *laudator* of an athlete in *P.*9.30–37, see Felson 2004: 370–72. On the desirability of the victor, cf. also Boeke 2007: 111–30.

The mythological narrative of Cyrene and Apollo, therefore, celebrates the victor's city and identity, but also introduces important themes that recur throughout *Pythian* 9. The ancient scholia inform us that Pindar draws the story from the Hesiodic corpus:

> ἀπὸ δὲ Ἠοίας Ἡσιόδου τὴν ἱστορίαν ἔλαβεν ὁ Πίνδαρος, ἧς ἡ ἀρχή·
> "ἢ οἵη Φθίῃ Χαρίτων ἄπο κάλλος ἔχουσα
> Πηνειοῦ παρ' ὕδωρ καλὴ ναίεσκε Κυρήνη." (= Hes. fr. 101/215)
> (sch. Pindar, *Pythian* 9.6a)

> Pindar took the story from Hesiod's *Ehoiai*, the beginning of which is:
> "or such as beautiful Cyrene used to live in Phthia
> by the water of Peneus, having beauty from the Graces."

Whether the Cyrene-*ehoie* belonged to the *Catalogue* or the *Megalai Ehoiai* is an open question.[82] The reference to the Ἠοῖαι in sch. *P*.9.6a is unique among the Pindaric scholia; elsewhere, the scholia refer to the Μεγάλαι Ἠοῖαι.[83] As D'Alessio has suggested, it is possible that Cyrene was mentioned in the context of the *Catalogue* but that the extensive treatment of her *ehoie* belongs to the *ME*.[84]

In addition to the opening of the *ehoie* preserved in the Pindaric scholia, we may also have traces of its concluding lines in a papyrus (*P. Oxy.* 2489):

> Ἀρι]σταῖον βαθυχαίτην
> ]  σὺν Ἑρμῆι Μαιάδος υἱεῖ
> ]  ἐπίσκοπος ἠδὲ νομήων
> ]ι δώματα καλά
> τε]θνηότα πορσανέουσαι
> (Hesiod fr. 102/217.1–5)[85]

---

[82] Cf. also the extensive discussion of the problem in Hirschberger 2004: 387–90, who considers the Cyrene-*ehoie* part of the *Catalogue*, as does Most 2007: 242–43. As for whether the Cyrene-*ehoie* took place exclusively in Thessaly or included her abduction to Africa, thus prefiguring the foundation of the eponymous city, I assume the latter. As West 1985a: 87 points out, it is very unlikely that the scholiast to *P.*9 would have considered Hesiod as the source of Pindar's mythological narrative if there was a significant difference between the two accounts; cf. Drexler 1931 and Janko 1982: 86 with 248 n.38 (contrast, however, Janko 2012: 41–42). For the opposite view, see the extensive discussion in Dräger 1993: 221–28 with bibliography. If the *ehoie* of Cyrene took into consideration the city's foundation in 631 BCE, that would provide a *terminus post quem* for whichever Hesiodic poem contained the *ehoie*; see, e.g., West 1985a: 132 and Hirschberger 2004: 48.

[83] sch. *I.*6.53 = Hes. fr. 250 MW (*ME*); sch. *P.*4.36c = Hes. fr. 14/253 (*ME*).

[84] D'Alessio 2005a: 206–07.

[85] Cf. Servius on Verg. *Georg.* 1.14 (= Hes. fr. 216 MW). It is almost certain that in the remaining three lines of *P. Oxy.* 2489 the poem turns to a different story. For possible reconstructions, see Lobel 1962: 36–37, West 1985a: 87–89, Hirschberger 2004: 392–93.

... Aristaeus with the rich hair ... with Hermes, son of Maia ... and guardian of shepherds ... beautiful abode ... in order to prepare him when he is dead.

The fragment seems to summarize the life of Aristaeus, the son of Cyrene and Apollo: his birth (presumably line 1),[86] his association with Hermes (line 2), his role as a guardian of herdsmen (line 3), and probably his death (line 5).[87] Aristaeus features in the prophecy that Chiron gives to Apollo in *Pythian* 9:

> τόθι παῖδα τέξεται, ὃν κλυτὸς Ἑρμᾶς
> εὐθρόνοις Ὥραισι καὶ Γαίᾳ
> ἀνελὼν φίλας ὑπὸ ματέρος οἴσει.
> ταὶ δ᾽ ἐπιγουνίδιον θαησάμεναι βρέφος αὐταῖς,
> νέκταρ ἐν χείλεσσι καὶ ἀμβροσίαν
>     στάξοισι, θήσονταί τέ νιν ἀθάνατον,
> Ζῆνα καὶ ἁγνὸν Ἀπόλλων᾽, ἀνδράσι χάρμα φίλοις
> ἄγχιστον ὀπάονα μήλων,
> Ἀγρέα καὶ Νόμιον, τοῖς δ᾽ Ἀρισταῖον καλεῖν.
>
> (Pindar, *Pythian* 9.59–65)

There she will bear a son, whom famous Hermes will take from under his dear mother and bring to the Horae of beautiful thrones and to Gaia. And, having seen the infant on their knees, they will drip nectar and ambrosia on his lips and will make him immortal, Zeus and holy Apollo, a delight to men dear (to him), the nearest guardian of sheep, called (by some) "Agreus" and "Nomius," by others "Aristaeus".

Indeed, the Pindaric ode is consistent with the Hesiodic fragment in linking Hermes to the establishment of Aristaeus as a pastoral divinity, but Pindar's Aristaeus emerges as a much greater figure. The ode evokes Aristaeus' cult titles as well as his identification with Zeus and Apollo; furthermore, with the mediation of Hermes, he is immortalized already as an infant by the Horae as well as Gaia, the primordial goddess who features in *Pythian* 9 both as Cyrene's ancestor (*P*.9.17) and as a deity honored by a local festival (*P*.9.101–02).[88] It is very unlikely that an apotheosis was ever included in the Hesiodic treatment of Aristaeus: if he ever became immortal in the

---

[86] Cf. Lobel 1962: 37 on line 4, Hirschberger 2004: 391 on line 1.

[87] Lobel 1962: 36–37 finds it unlikely that τεθνηότα could refer to Aristaeus, since he was immortal; therefore, Lobel argues, the story of Cyrene ends in line 3. West 1985a: 88, however, has suggested that lines 4–5 refer to the death of Actaeon, Aristaeus' son, whose story may have preceded the fragment (cf. Hes. fr. 103 H). According to West's reconstruction, lines 1–3 may narrate how Aristaeus was carried off by Hermes immediately after birth or they may identify Hermes as a god who assists Aristaeus in his role as a pastoral divinity. However, the immediate transition from Aristaeus' youth to the death of his son seems very difficult and therefore unlikely.

[88] Nonetheless, no evidence for an actual cult of Gaia/Ge in Cyrene has been discovered; Gentili et al. 1995: 615.

*Catalogue*, it would almost certainly have been recounted after his death, but Hes. fr. 102/217 bears no trace of immortalization.[89] Thus, while the inclusion of Aristaeus in *Pythian 9* supports – or at least does not undermine – the scholiast's suggestion that the mythological narrative is informed by the Hesiodic *ehoie* of Cyrene, it is clear that certain details of Aristaeus' portrayal in the ode are not drawn from the Hesiodic corpus but from other sources, possibly local Cyrenean lore.[90]

How about the treatment of Cyrene herself? Based on the two lines (Hes. fr. 101/215) preserved in sch. *P.9.6a*, it is possible to argue that Pindar's construction of the heroine may have struck his audience as markedly different from the Hesiodic *ehoie*. To begin with, the *ehoie*-fragment underscores Cyrene's beauty. Although we cannot exclude the possibility that the maiden was invested with additional qualities in subsequent lines, the beginning of the *ehoie* draws attention exclusively to her good looks. Cyrene's beauty, moreover, derives from the Graces; in the Hesiodic corpus, these divinities are associated consistently with the seductive appeal of women.[91] There are further indications that the Hesiodic Cyrene may have been more like the average pretty girl of the *Catalogue* than the huntress of Pindar's narrative. The *ehoie* mentions that Cyrene used to inhabit (ναίεσκε) the vicinity of the river Peneus, thus situating the girl in Thessaly just as *Pythian 9* does. The reference to Peneus almost certainly alludes to a genealogical connection: Peneus is mentioned in *P.9.14–18* as Cyrene's paternal grandfather, and it is very likely that Pindar drew her genealogical tree from the Hesiodic tradition.[92]

---

[89] In addition to the (admittedly inconclusive) participle τεθνηότα in Hes. fr. 102/217.5, consider also the brief appearance of Aristaeus in the *Theogony* (Αὐτονόην θ' ἣν γῆμεν Ἀρισταῖος βαθυχαίτης, *Th.* 977). The poem mentions the apotheosis of Dionysus and Semele (*Th.* 940–43), Ariadne (*Th.* 949), and Heracles (*Th.* 950–55), but not of Aristaeus.

[90] Notice also that, in *Pythian 9*, Aristaeus is a true native of Libya: he is not simply born after Cyrene is transported to Africa but he is conceived there (*P.9.68–69*). Contrast the *ehoie* of Mestra: Poseidon rapes the maiden in Thessaly, where she lives, but brings her to the island of Kos, where she gives birth to his offspring (Hes. fr. 37/43a). The comparison is, of course, not conclusive but it is indicative. On the cult of Aristaeus, see Cook 1984. Köhnken 1985: 79 rightly points out that Aristaeus inherits his mother's earlier role as the protector of herds.

[91] The formula Χαρίτων ἄπο κάλλος ἔχουσ- occurs only here in the extant Hesiodic corpus but see Hom. *Od.* 6.18 (Nausicaa's attendants). Compare, however, the recurrent formula Χαρίτων ἀμαρύγματ' ἔχουσ- (Hes. frs. 31/70.38, 37/43a.4, 82/185.20, 104/196.6, and *2/73.3); see Aguirre Castro 2005: 21. On beauty and the Charites, cf. Χ[αρ]ίτεσσιν ὁμοίας (Hes. fr. 5/10a.33), Χ. ὁμοίην (Hes. fr. 5/10a.49), and Χ. ὁμοῖα Hes. fr. 291.1 MW. In the *Theogony*, the Graces are born of Zeus and an Oceanid and are primarily associated with erotic desire (*Th.* 907–11). They are Aphrodite's steady companions (*Th.* 64) and, together with seductive Persuasion (Πειθώ), they contribute to the adornment of Pandora in *WD* 73. Cf. Ahlert 1942: 6–7 and Köhnken 1985: 99.

[92] In an effort to find in *Pythian 9* a genealogical connection between Cyrene and Chiron (through a common ancestor, Oceanus) as a deliberate and meaningful Pindaric invention, Robbins 1978: 94

At the same time, however, by situating her abode by the streams of Peneus, the Hesiodic fragment also associates Cyrene with a landscape that is significantly tamer than Pindar's Mount Pelion, the habitat of wild beasts.[93] The inclusion of rivers and their progeny in the mythical past of Greek communities is, of course, a way to integrate the local landscape into communal identity. In genealogical poetry, however, riverbanks, lakes, and waterholes also function as *loci amoeni* in which maidens are exposed to the gaze of male suitors and are eventually subjected to their sexual desire.[94] Sch. Ap. Rh. *Arg.* 2.498–527c reports that Apollo fell for Cyrene when he saw her by the river Peneus, and it is not inconceivable that this was the place of Apollo's seduction already in the Hesiodic text. Hes. fr. 101/215, in other words, appears to situate the girl in a space associated with the rape of maidens, not with the hunt of wild beasts.

The two lines preserved in sch. *P.*9.6a, therefore, suggest that the Hesiodic corpus constructed Cyrene first and foremost as an attractive maiden; the reiteration of her physical beauty as well as the space she inhabits in Hes. fr. 101/215 imply that the Hesiodic Cyrene was well within the parameters of femininity that genealogical poetry endorses and celebrates. This hypothesis becomes even stronger if one compares Cyrene's introduction in Hes. fr. 101/215 with the opening of the *ehoie* of Atalanta, an unconventional maiden who roamed the wilderness in an attempt to evade marriage.[95] The

n.11 thinks it is unlikely that the Hesiodic Cyrene was a descendant of Peneus. His arguments are based on (a) the lack of any explicit genealogical connection between Cyrene and Peneus in Apollonius Rhodius (*Arg.* 2.500–02), and (b) sch. Ap. Rh. *Arg.* 2. 498–527a, according to which those who consider Peneus as Cyrene's father are mistaken. It is very likely that *Arg.* 2.500–02 is not only alluding to the opening of the Hesiodic *ehoie* but also interpreting it. The *Argonautica* never mentions Cyrene's father; for the two competing versions, see sch. Ap. Rh. *Arg.* 2.498–527a and sch. Ap. Rh. *Arg.* 2.498–527c (which Robbins ignores): λέγουσι δὲ τὴν Κυρήνην οἱ μὲν Πηνειοῦ, οἱ δὲ Ὑψέως τοῦ Πηνειοῦ. Peneus appears as Cyrene's father only in later sources (Hyg. *Fab.* 161; cf. Verg. *G.* 4.353–56).

[93] Cf. Köhnken 1985: 98. For the banks of Peneus as pastureland, cf. Ap. Rh. *Arg.* 2.500–02 with sch. Ap. Rh. *Arg.* 2.498–527a. Cf. Herodotus's geographical description of Thessaly (7.129). Herodotus brings into relief the sharp contrast between the Thessalian plain and the high surrounding mountains; Peneus traverses the Thessalian plain from west to east and, augmented by four tributary rivers, flows into the sea through a narrow strip of flat land between Olympus and Ossa.

[94] On the *locus amoenus*, cf. Poseidon in Hes. fr. 20/30, who sleeps with Tyro by the river (line 35; cf. Hom. *Od.*11.240–5); cf. also the lacunose Hes. fr. 82/185, esp. lines 11–25, with Hirschberger 2004: 349 on line 25, as well as Hes. fr. 70/59.3, where an unwedded maiden (most likely Coronis) dips her foot into the lake.

[95] Cf. Fränkel 1951: 561 n.2, who finds similarities in thought and diction between Apollo's portrayal of Cyrene in *P.*9 and the treatment of Atalanta in Theognis (1287–94), which, Fränkel adds, in turn "held on to the type of young huntress described in the *Ehoiai*." Fränkel points out that both maidens roam in the wilderness (Thgn. 1291–92; *P.*9.34) having left their families (νοσφισθεῖσα, Thgn. 1291; ἀποσπασθεῖσα, *P.*9.33); in his view, both strive to avoid the *telos* of a woman's life, i.e. marriage (ἔργ' ἀτέλεστα τέλει, Thgn. 1290; γεύεται δ᾽ἀλκᾶς ἀπειράντου, *P.*9.35). The Theognidean

*ehoie* of Atalanta, which includes an extensive narrative of the footrace that led to her marriage (frs. *3-*4/75–76) and ends perhaps with her metamorphosis into a lion,[96] opens with the following lines:

> ἢ οἵη Σχ[οινῆος ἀγακλε]ιτοῖο ἄνακτος[97]
> ]σι ποδώκης δῖ᾽ Ἀταλάν[τη
> Χαρί]των ἀμαρύγματ᾽ ἔχο[υσα
> πρὸς ἀνθρώπων ἀ]παναίνετο φῦλον ὁμιλ[εῖν
> ἀνδρῶν ἐλπομένη φεύγ]ειν γάμον ἀλφηστάων
> ] τανισφύ[ρ]ου εἵνεκα κού[ρης
> (Hesiod, fr. *2/73.1–6)

3 Hopfner  4 Snell  5 ἐλπομένη West, cetera Rzach

or such as [the daughter of Schoeneus, the greatly famous] lord ... swift-footed godlike Atalanta ... having the radiance of the Graces ... she was refusing to mingle with the tribe [of human beings, hoping to avoid] marriage with bread-eating men ... on account of the long-ankled maiden ...

Just as in the case of Cyrene, Atalanta's beauty features prominently and repeatedly (lines 3 and 6), and it is enhanced by its association with the Graces. But unlike the *ehoie* of Cyrene, beauty is neither the first nor the only quality of the heroine as she is introduced in the text. The first two lines of this fragment draw attention to the maiden's speed, the quality that defines her as a mythological figure and largely determines the plot of her story. In fact, her swiftness is incorporated in the formula of her name (ποδώκης δῖ᾽ Ἀταλάντη),[98] and it is reiterated whenever her name is mentioned in the extant lines of her *ehoie*.[99] This core element of Atalanta's identity comes to the foreground even before her aversion to marriage and the footrace. With remarkable economy, therefore, the opening of Atalanta's *ehoie* uses one word (ποδώκης) to highlight the heroine's distinctive characteristic and pave the way for the narrative that follows. In sharp contrast to

passage does not draw Atalanta's genealogy from the Hesiodic tradition, since her father is Iasius, not Schoeneus (cf. Ps.-Apollod. *Bibl.* 3.10.9); nonetheless, it may still be engaging in part with the Atalanta-*ehoie* (see especially Thgn. 1289–90 and Hes. fr. *2/73.4–5).

[96] Sch. Theocr. 3.40–42b; Ovid *Met.* 10.560–704. Cf. Hirschberger 2004: 459.

[97] Hes. fr. *2/73.1 = *1/71a.12. Regarding the first line of the Atalanta-*ehoie*, see Parsons 1974: 1–2 and Hirschberger 2004: 457. On the place of the Atalanta-*ehoie* within the Hesiodic corpus, see D'Alessio 2005c in response to Hirschberger 2004: 458, as well as D'Alessio 2005b: 213–16.

[98] On the emergence of this formula, see West 2001: 132–33. On the juxtaposition between the Hesiodic formula ποδώκης δῖ᾽ Ἀταλάντη and the Iliadic ποδάρκης δῖος Ἀχιλλεύς, see Ziogas 2011: 258–61, who traces in the *ehoie* a polemical stance towards Homeric epic. On Atalanta and Achilles, see also Ormand 2014: 119–51, esp. 138–51.

[99] Hes. fr. *4/76.20; cf. Vitelli's suggestion for line 5 of the same fragment.

this passage, the introduction of the Cyrene-*ehoie* bears no indication that the maiden possesses some extraordinary feature. There is not even the slightest hint of the remarkable physical ability and courage expected of someone who can wrestle with lions (*P*.9.26–28)! Admittedly, the comparison between the two *ehoiai* must ultimately remain inconclusive, since there is no need to assume that all *ehoiai* displayed the same narrative structure and techniques. Nonetheless, we can at least note that, when juxtaposed with the beginning of Atalanta's *ehoie*, Hes. fr. 101/215 introduces Cyrene as a very attractive but otherwise ordinary maiden. Even if the non-extant part of her *ehoie* portrayed her as a virginal huntress, given her introduction it is highly unlikely that she was a Heraclean lion-wrestler.[100]

As the opening lines of the *ehoie* draw attention to Cyrene's looks, they construct her as a visual object rather than an agent, and invite the audience to envision precisely the attractive image that caught Apollo's eye. *Pythian* 9 also reconstructs Cyrene as a spectacle: after all, Apollo falls in love when he watches her fight a lion, a visual experience he shares with Chiron the Centaur (*P*.9.30–31).[101] Contrary to the Hesiodic text, however, the epinician ode elides Cyrene's beauty almost completely. The only hint about her physical appearance is given in *P*.9.17, where she is described as an εὐώλενος παῖς, a fair-armed girl. The adjective is rare and it may have been associated with Hesiodic genealogical poetry in particular. In the extant corpus of Greek literature predating *Pythian* 9, εὐώλενος occurs only once in Hes. fr. 110/204.81 (κούρης εὐ[ω]λ[ένο]υ) from the *Catalogue of Women*, where it modifies Helen in the context of her wooing. In the case of Pindar's Cyrene, however, the girlish beauty conveyed by

---

[100] Cf. Diod. Sic. 4.81.1 (Ἀπόλλωνα, περὶ τὸ Πήλιον τρεφομένης κόρης ὄνομα Κυρήνης κάλλει διαφερούσης, ἐρασθῆναι τῆς παρθένου). Cyrene the lion-wrestler originates probably in local Cyrenean lore. Malten 1911: 26–40 (cf. 55–56 on *P*.9) and Chamoux 1953: 80–81 hold the view that the fight with the lion was already part of Cyrene's *ehoie*, but they fail to make a persuasive case. West 1985a: 86 sees no compelling reason to assume that the Hesiodic *ehoie* included the lion; cf. Zagdoun 1992: 170, who points out that no extant representation of Cyrene fighting a lion dates to the Archaic era, with one possible (yet unlikely) exception.

[101] Cf. Illig 1932: 35–36. One may be tempted to draw a connection between Cyrene's wrestling with the lion in *P*.9, which is constructed as an athletic spectacle (see n.81 above), and the Hesiodic Atalanta, whose footrace against Hippomenes is also fashioned as an athletic spectacle, albeit a public one (Hes. fr. *3/75.6–11). As, e.g., Aguirre Castro 2005 and Ormand 2014: 119–51 have pointed out, Atalanta is eroticized under the male gaze even as she assumes a male role; so is Cyrene in *P*.9. Finally, both narratives conclude with the taming of the wild girl through marriage. However, the similarities do not go further than this; in fact, there are significant differences that prevent me from claiming that Pindar's Cyrene is informed by the Hesiodic Atalanta. Unlike Atalanta, who shuns marriage at all cost (Hes. fr. *2/73.4–5), Pindar's Cyrene never explicitly rejects marriage and men, even though her activities – much like Atalanta's – do not conform to norms of femininity. Cyrene does not resist her union with Apollo nor is any deception involved in the Pindaric narrative, as in the case of Atalanta (Hes. fr. *3/75).

εὐώλενος παῖς is undercut by her rather unfeminine behavior in the immediately following lines (*P*.9.18–28).

Instead of her good looks, the epinician ode focuses on Cyrene's actions. After the initial introductory summary of the aetiological myth, in which Cyrene appears to be a passive participant in her own story (*P*.9.5–13), the narrative begins anew.[102] As the narrative reboots, so does the character of Cyrene, who is now constructed as a figure of restless action (*P*.9.18–28). Shunning the loom and the pleasant interaction with age-mates within the safe confinement of domestic space, Cyrene prefers to hunt wild animals. In fact, the narrative of the maiden's unconventional behavior escalates: the lone huntress is first said to chase beasts with weapons,[103] but when she catches Apollo's eye, she is fighting a lion with her bare hands.[104] Some scholars have read her marriage as the catalyst for her complete transformation from a wild being to a civilized and nourishing figure.[105] Any marriage undeniably entails the taming of the maiden on a symbolic level,[106] but Cyrene's wild maidenhood does not simply amplify this transformative and restrictive effect of marriage. In the Pindaric text, the figure of Cyrene is informed by a typically male heroic ideal which, nonetheless, does not appear to exclude the idea of marriage and procreation. While her pursuits place her outside conventions and gender-bound expectations, they do not necessarily connote a complete lack of culture. On the contrary, Cyrene is constructed as a civilizing force, and this point

---

[102] On the structure of the mythological narrative with its multiple reiterations of the union between Apollo and Cyrene, see Köhnken 1985: 79 and Kurke 1991: 128–32, who analyses the three variations as exchanges of a different kind. Cf. already Illig 1932: 31–34.

[103] *P*.9.20–21, perhaps a parallel to the armed footrace that Telesicrates, the *laudandus*, has won.

[104] The landscape becomes gradually wilder as well. The text does not reveal where Cyrene hunts in order to protect her father's herds, but the association with the cattle points to space that is certainly not domestic but not entirely wild either. When Apollo sees her wrestling with the lion, however, he remarks that she dwells in the hollows of shadowy mountains, i.e. wild outdoors space (*P*.9.34).

[105] Robbins 1978: 97–98 oversimplifies the text when he argues that it portrays Cyrene as an "enfant sauvage." Cf. Dougherty 1993: 142–43, who describes Cyrene as a "wild and precultured nymph." Dougherty claims that "Pindar characterizes Cyrene prior to her marriage to Apollo as a wild nymph of nature, the child of Ocean and Earth, a veritable Artemis," but ignores *P*.9.22–23 (similarly Stéfos 1975: 49). Cyrene's pedigree is certainly remarkable (*P*.9.14–17), but her connection to Ocean and, especially, Earth does not necessarily mark her as savage. Instead, it elevates and glorifies her; moreover, it facilitates the identification of Cyrene with the local land and supports the metaphor of vegetation. On the last point, see Marshall 1998: 106; cf. Dougherty 1993: 143–44. Cyrene's connection with Gaia also prepares the latter's involvement in the immortalization of Aristaeus (*P*.9.60), and her association with athletic competitions (*P*.9.102).

[106] On the metaphor of taming embedded in the vocabulary of marriage, see, e.g., Aguirre Castro 2005: 22 who focuses exclusively on genealogical poetry.

becomes particularly clear when her hunting is framed as protection of her father's cattle (*P.*9.22–23). Cyrene is no savage; she is no Atalanta either. Cyrene never expresses aversion towards men or matrimony, nor does she resist Apollo's advances. In other words, this extraordinary and unconventional maiden behaves like a man but does not disavow all aspects of her femininity. This feature of her character renders her mutual union with Apollo and her transformation into a nourishing maternal figure somewhat less drastic, even though there is no doubt that the marriage marks some sort of transition.[107]

Cyrene's characterization through her actions continues even after she becomes the object of Apollo's gaze and speech (*P.*9.26–37). Based on the spectacle he witnesses, Apollo finds Cyrene admirable as he assesses her great physical strength (μεγάλαν δύνασιν, *P.*9.30) and, much more emphatically, her fearlessness (*P.*9.30–33 and 35).[108] The god's speech weaves vocabulary reserved for the male realms of war and games (νεῖκος, μόχθος, ἀλκά) with explicit reminders of Cyrene's gender (γυναικός, *P.*9.30; νεᾶνις, *P.*9.31a). This unconventional combination is never problematized in the ode; on the contrary, it causes admiration and arousal. After Apollo addresses Chiron, the maiden's actions recede into the background as Chiron shifts our attention from the ongoing spectacle of Cyrene to a prophetic vision of her impending union with Apollo and the fate of their son, her smooth integration in Libya, and the foundation of her eponymous city (*P.*9.51–65). Chiron's prophecy thus mirrors the summary with which the mythological narrative began (*P.*9.5–13) not only in content but also in portraying Cyrene as the passive beneficiary of others' actions rather than a figure with agency.

So far, I have argued that *Pythian* 9 departs significantly from the Hesiodic tradition in its construction of Cyrene. In the extant lines of the *ehoie*, Cyrene seems to be remarkable only in terms of her beauty. The Pindaric text underscores its divergence from the Hesiodic *ehoie* by consistently avoiding the emphasis on Cyrene's external appearance. Pindar's Cyrene is an unconventional maiden, a civilizing hero who catches the eye of a god with her masculine qualities but enters into a mutual marriage with him without resistance.

---

[107] Cf. Marshall 1998: 98–103, who focuses mainly on Cyrene's transformation into a nourishing and fecund mother through the *hieros gamos* with Apollo, but points out that her femininity is not entirely absent before her union with the god nor do her masculine qualities disappear entirely afterwards.

[108] On Cyrene's ἀνδρεία as a primarily masculine characteristic, see, e.g., Woodbury 1982: 251; cf. Ahlert 1942: 9–13, who reads in *P.*9 Pindar's admiration for a Doric ideal of femininity.

The engagement of *Pythian* 9 with the Hesiodic *ehoie*, however, involves much more than the reconfiguration of Cyrene. The ode's mythological account includes all the core information that makes up an *ehoie*: the identity and pedigree of the maiden, the circumstances of her sexual union with the god, and the offspring born as a result. Yet, at the same time, this information is scattered throughout the various distinct parts of the narrative. Pindar fractures the linear trajectory of the *ehoie*, frustrating his audience's expectations as he rearranges the genealogical narrative.[109] When Cyrene's story is first introduced (*P.*9.5–13), the text appears to be following the narrative pattern of an *ehoie* closely but some un-Hesiodic twists quickly emerge: the maiden's pedigree is not revealed in the beginning but deferred until later (*P.*9.12–18), rape becomes a sacred marriage, and, more importantly, there is no mention of the couple's offspring. Much like the introductory summary, the conclusion of the mythological narrative (*P.*9.67–70) reiterates Cyrene's integration in Libya without mentioning her son. Only in the dialogue between Apollo and Chiron[110] is the genealogical thread of Cyrene's story brought to completion as Chiron's prophecy includes not only Cyrene's union with Apollo but also the birth and extraordinary fate of their son, Aristaeus (*P.*9.59–65).[111] Notice that, when asked to reveal Cyrene's pedigree (*P.*9.32–33), Chiron

[109] For structural patterns in Hesiodic genealogical poetry, see Rengakos 2009: 215–16 and Tsagalis 2009: 162–66, esp. 163–64. Cf. also Davies 1992: 88–93.

[110] Some scholars have speculated that the prophecy that Chiron gives to Apollo in *Pythian* 9 was originally part of the *ehoie*, and that Pindar has shaped the exchange between the two (*P.*9.37 and 43–35) so as to criticize Hesiod for presenting the god of oracles as the recipient of a prophecy. See, e.g., Studniczka 1890: 41, Malten 1911: 9, Schroeder 1922: 80–81, van der Kolf 1923: 20, Drexler 1931: 461–63, and Illig 1932: 40–43. Contrast Köhnken 1985: 100, who argued that, if Chiron served as Aristaeus' trainer in the *Catalogue* (cf. Ap. Rh. *Arg.* 2.509–10), his inclusion in *P.*9 as a counselor to Apollo could be viewed as mirroring the role he holds in the *ehoie*. However, Chiron's prophecy regarding Aristaeus may be engaging with the Hesiodic tradition in a different way altogether. According to a dictionary of metamorphoses (*P. Mich. inv.* 1447 verso, col.ii 1–6 = Hes. fr. 217A MW), the *Catalogue* recounted that Actaeon, the son of Aristaeus, was turned into a deer by Artemis and killed by his own dogs because he wooed Semele, the woman who would eventually bear Dionysus to Zeus. Part of this Hesiodic account may be preserved in *P.Oxy.* 2509 (= Hes. fr. 103 H). The fragment opens with a prophecy about the birth and apotheosis of Dionysus, which is revealed to Chiron by a goddess identified only as Διὸς κούρη (line 13). In the meantime, Actaeon is being ripped apart by his dogs. After she has delivered the prophecy, the goddess lifts the madness from Actaeon's dogs (line 14) and departs. Chiron remains silent and, in the remaining extant lines, the dogs lament their dead master. Janko 1984: 302 has suggested that Chiron's prophetic announcement of Aristaeus' birth and apotheosis in *Pythian* 9 is a creative reception of the prophecy in Hes. fr. 103 H that privileges Dionysus at the expense of Actaeon; cf. Casanova 1969. Since Actaeon is Aristaeus' son, it is possible that *P. Oxy.* 2509 was part of the Cyrene-*ehoie*. It is possible, however, that the passage was not part of the Hesiodic corpus; see, e.g., Debiasi 2013 who recently attributed the fragment to Eumelus.

[111] On Chiron's prophecy and Delphic oracles involved in colonization, see Dougherty 1993: 147–49 as well as Athanassaki 2003: 98–101.

evades the question (*P.9.42–44*). By not repeating the genealogy that was
mentioned earlier in the poem (*P.9.12–18*), the Centaur misses the opportunity to present a full account of the genealogical material arranged in a
linear sequence (Cyrene's pedigree → union in Libya → birth of Aristaeus).[112] Chiron thus reinforces the ode's dismantling of the *ehoie*'s simple
structure. With this rearrangement of information, Pindar brings the
aetiological aspect of the story to the forefront and privileges it over
genealogy.

Finally, upon close examination Chiron's prophecy not only completes
Cyrene's transition from maidenhood to motherhood, but also offers a
commentary on the poetic tradition to which Cyrene's *ehoie* belongs.
When Apollo asks:

> ὁσία κλυτὰν χέρα οἱ προσενεγκεῖν
> ἦρα καὶ ἐκ λεχέων κεῖραι μελιαδέα ποίαν;
> (Pindar, *Pythian* 9.36–37)

Is it right to lay my glorious hand upon her and cut the honey-sweet flower from
the bed?

Chiron responds by revisiting the terms in which gods and mortals engage
in sex:

> κρυπταὶ κλαΐδες ἐντὶ σοφᾶς
> Πειθοῦς ἱερᾶν φιλοτάτων,
> Φοῖβε, καὶ ἔν τε θεοῖς τοῦτο κἀνθρώποις ὁμῶς
> αἰδέοντ᾽, ἀμφανδὸν ἀδεί-
> ας τυχεῖν τὸ πρῶτον εὐνᾶς.
> (Pindar, *Pythian* 9.38–41)

Wise Persuasion's keys to sacred acts of sex are hidden, Phoebus, and, among gods
and humans alike, (individuals) shy away from this, namely to make sweet love
openly for the first time.

Building on Chiron's traditional role as the educator of heroes par excellence,[113] *Pythian* 9 transforms the Centaur into Apollo's advisor about love,
sex, and desire, thus highlighting the (non-Hesiodic)[114] detail that Cyrene
is Apollo's first love. Yet the exchange also allows the ode to comment on a
core element of Hesiodic genealogical poetry, namely the non-consensual

[112] Cf. Wilamowitz 1922: 267–68.
[113] Cf. Studniczka 1890: 41 and, more recently, Woodbury 1972: 561–62.
[114] Philodemus' list of Apollo's loves (*P.Herc.* 243 III), presumably drawn from Hesiodic genealogical
poetry, includes Cyrene but it does not place her first in the sequence of lovers nor does it explicitly
mark her as the god's first love. See West 1985b and D'Alessio 2004a: 206–07 (cf. 210–13).

nature of erotic relationships between mortals and immortals. When Apollo is aroused by the sight of Cyrene, his first reaction is to consider rape (*P.*9.36–37).[115] Apollo's reaction reflects precisely the frame of sexual domination through which Olympian gods approach mortal women in the Hesiodic genealogical tradition, where consent is optional and may even be the product of deception (cf. *P.*9.42–43), as the cases of Tyro (Hes. frs. 20–24 H/ 30–32 MW) and Alcmene (Hes. fr. 91/195.8–63 = *Sc.*1–56) demonstrate. In his response Chiron offers an alternative: he recommends seduction by persuasion instead of rape (*P.*9.38–41; cf. 51–52), thus paving the way for the couple's mutual union (*P.*9.66–67; cf. 13, ξυνὸν . . . γάμον).[116] In addition, with his discussion of αἰδώς, he defines an emotional experience that is commonly shared by mortal and immortal lovers alike (*P.*9.40–41, esp. 40 ὁμῶς; cf. *P.*9.12–13).[117] Chiron, therefore, draws attention to the fact that *Pythian* 9 revises a Hesiodic *ehoie*[118] not only by enhancing the figure of Cyrene but also by revising the terms of her relationship with Apollo. The potential of rape quickly gives way to a mutual and legitimate bond between god and mortal of the kind that does not exist in the world of Hesiodic genealogical poetry.[119]

---

[115] Cf. the misleading ἅρπασ' in the beginning of the mythological narrative (*P.*9.6).

[116] Köhnken 1985: 89–90 has suggested that the union of Cyrene and Apollo as envisioned by Chiron is informed by the *hieros gamos* between Zeus and Hera in Hom. *Il.* 14.

[117] Capra and Gilardi 2002: 126–27 argue by recourse to the language of Hes. fr. 1.5–7 that *P.*9.13 emphasizes not the mutual but the mixed nature of the union, since a god is sleeping with a mortal woman. Unfortunately, they ignore line 12, which I think adds a layer to the relationship between Apollo and Cyrene that is not typical of the Hesiodic tradition. *P.*9 prompts its audience to recall the Hesiodic intertext, but also draws attention to its complex engagement with it.

[118] Cf. the potentially metapoetic adjective in εὐκλέα νύμφαν, *P.*9.56.

[119] While Pindar's *Pythian* 9 deals with colonization through the union between Apollo and Cyrene, his *Pythian* 4 explores the foundation of Cyrene from a different mythological vantage point. It is possible that the treatment of this topic in *P.*4 may also be informed by Hesiodic genealogical poetry, but the evidence is scant. In *P.*4.13–56, Medea explains to the Argonauts how Thera emerged from the clot of land which Euphemus, one of the Argonauts, received from Triton when the legendary crew was stranded in Lake Tritonis. Even though the clot of Libyan earth fell off the ship accidentally and created Thera, Triton's gift was an irrevocable promise of future colonization in Libya and, Medea prophesies, one day a descendant of Euphemus will be encouraged by the Delphic oracle to found Cyrene. Sch. *P.*4.36c (=Hes. *ME* fr. 14/253) informs us that the birth of Euphemus was recounted in the *Megalai Ehoiai*; in the Hesiodic poem, however, Euphemus is the son of Poseidon and Mekionike, the daughter of Eurotas, not of Europa, the daughter of Tityus, as in Pi. *P.*4.44–46. On the Mekionike-*ehoie*, see also Schwartz 1960: 466–68 and D'Alessio 2005a: 196–99. Since Hes. fr. 125/78 of the *Catalogue* preserves Tityus' name, Hirschberger 2004: 437 has tentatively suggested that perhaps Euphemus featured also in the *Catalogue* with a pedigree that was consistent with *P.*4. On the possibility that the *ME* recounted the Libyan adventures of the returning Argonauts, see West 1985a: 87 with Hes. fr. 241 MW; cf. Wilamowitz 1922: 386 n.2. Whether or not *P.*4 appropriates the lore of the earth clot from the Hesiodic corpus is debated; for a thorough discussion, see Dräger 1993: 228–34 (cf. D'Alessio 2005a: 196–97). Given the lack of textual evidence, however, opinions are bound to remain speculative.

To conclude: while the scholiast claims that Pindar received the story of Cyrene from Hesiod, the treatment of this female figure in *Pythian* 9 seems to depart significantly from the Hesiodic *ehoie*. Pindar constructs Cyrene as a strong and exceptional figure invested with a rich combination of qualities, yet he omits almost entirely the only feature that defines her in the extant introduction of her *ehoie*, namely her beauty. The ode attributes Cyrene's appeal not to her physical appearance but to her strength and courage, characteristics that are predominantly male and regularly associated with athletes. *Pythian* 9 revises the Hesiodic tradition also in its representation of Cyrene's union with Apollo. The ode departs from the Hesiodic script of divine control and domination through sex, and opens the possibility of a different type of relationship.

When read against one another, *Pythians* 3 and 9 shed additional light on Pindar's creative and adaptive reception of the Hesiodic genealogical poetry. As Floyd has amply demonstrated, there are several correspondences in content, structure, and language between the two odes.[120] Instead of rehearsing Floyd's observations here, I would like to look at the broader picture that emerges from comparing the reception of the Hesiodic tradition in the two mythological narratives. Both odes reformulate and rearrange the Hesiodic narrative of sex and birth in ways that depend largely on developing and enriching the female figures. In *Pythian* 3, Coronis becomes the author of her story, an active agent ultimately punished for her choices and actions; as a transgressive figure, she not only prefigures her son's failings but also contributes an important negative exemplum to the ode's exploration of what is humanly possible and appropriate. *Pythian* 9, on the other hand, invests Cyrene with male strength that resonates with the athletic culture to which the epinician genre belongs. The maiden emerges as a heroic figure whose union with Apollo is framed in terms of matrimony and thus revisits the nature of sexual unions between gods and mortals recounted in the *Catalogue*, even as it leads to the birth of a son destined to become immortal. It is noteworthy that both female figures outgrow their Hesiodic counterparts by renouncing gender-bound expectations and norms: Coronis is vilified for consummating her union with Ischys without consideration for proper ritual (*P.*3.13–20), while Cyrene clearly does not conform to the social

---

[120] Floyd 1968. While his conclusion regarding a common first performance in Thebes (186–90) is untenable, his close comparative reading remains useful. On the similarities and differences between the two mythological narratives in particular, cf. already Burton 1962: 81.

norms of maidenhood (*P.*9.18–25), even though she does not become disruptive nor does she renounce her femininity.

## Ixion and His Progeny in *Pythian* 2

*Pythian* 2, a poem addressed to Hieron of Syracuse, offers an extensive account of Ixion's story.[121] Ixion is a repeat offender, a transgressor who gets a second chance and wastes it. First he murdered his father-in-law, a crime for which he was pardoned by the gods; subsequently, he was granted a good life with access to Olympus but, thankless to his divine benefactors, he attempted to rape Hera. The ode mentions Ixion's first crime very briefly and leaves out crucial details including, notoriously, Zeus's pardon (*P.*2.31–32); this narrative strategy has been interpreted as an indication that Ixion's story was widely known to Pindar's Sicilian audience.[122] The second transgression, however, receives a thorough treatment in this ode, as the text dwells on Ixion's passion both as a desire (*P.*2.26–28) and as an act (*P.*2.33–40), while repeatedly drawing attention to its consequences. Ixion's mythological narrative reiterates the ode's engagement with the theme of gratitude, and complements the two positive examples of honored benefactors that occupy the preceding lines (*P.*2.13–20)[123] with a negative example of transgression and ingratitude. Notice that in *P.*2.21–24 the hero is said to have been ordered by the gods to offer humans admonition against ingratitude, while his punishment provides a spectacle that reinforces the same message; the didactic dimension of Ixion's story, therefore, is established already in its opening lines.[124] However, the mythological narrative also has an extensive programmatic function in the ode. For instance, it raises the issue of self-destructive behavior (*P.*2.40–41), an important theme that resurfaces later in the

---

[121] The occasion and date of *P.*2 have been notoriously elusive. The debate dates to antiquity and involves the question of genre classification as well. See Burton 1962: 111–15, Kirkwood 1982: 137–38, Most 1985: 61–68, Gentili et al. 1995: 43–47, Morrison 2007: 94–96, and Morgan 2015: 172–75. On the mythological story of Ixion in relation with Hieron and the ode's Syracusan audience, see Morgan 2015: 180–88.

[122] See sch. *P.*2.40b for the basic details, including the identity of Ixion's victim, the motive, occasion, and plot of the murder, as well as Zeus's pardon. On the story's popularity in the fifth century BCE, see Most 1985: 76–77, who posits an Italian origin for the myth based on archaeological evidence (77 n.30).

[123] The two examples of proper gratitude are Cinyras the mythical king, who is honored by the Cyprians through song (*P.*2.15–17), and Hieron himself, the tyrant of Syracuse, who is said to have the gratitude of the Locrians for keeping them safe (*P.*2.18–20).

[124] On the thematic correspondence between the mythological narrative and its context in *P.*2, see Burton 1962: 115–19 and Most 1985: 69–70.

context of Archilochus' self-inflicted ἀμαχανία in *P*.2.54–56, the reckless-
ness of envious men in *P*.2.88–90, and the metaphor in *P*.2.94–96.[125]
Ixion's story is programmatic also in exploring the contrast between
human limitations and divine omnipotence (*P*.2.34; cf. 49–52 and
88–89), and in exemplifying the divine punishment of the insolent
(*P*.2.28–30; cf. 51–52). My interest in the Ixion narrative of *Pythian* 2 lies
in the distinctly Hesiodic elements appropriated both in its content and
its structure. In this ode, I suggest, Pindar engages creatively with Hesiodic
genealogical narratives but also experiments with distinctly Hesiodic
female figures.

Viewed in its entirety, the mythological narrative of *Pythian* 2 is a
carefully structured ring-composition: Ixion's punishment occupies the
outer frame (*P*.2.21–24; 40–41), while the extensive account of his desire
for Hera and his intercourse with her cloud substitute functions as an inner
frame (*P*.2.25–30; 34–40); the center is occupied by the summary account
of Ixion's double criminal record (*P*.2.30–34).[126] After the completion of
this concentric movement in line 41, however, the narrative unexpectedly
shifts into a linear genealogical account:

> ἄνευ οἱ Χαρίτων τέκεν γόνον ὑπερφίαλον
> μόνα καὶ μόνον οὔτ' ἐν ἀν-
>        δράσι γερασφόρον οὔτ' ἐν θεῶν νόμοις·
> τὸν ὀνύμαζε τράφοισα Κένταυρον, ὅς
> ἵπποισι Μαγνητίδεσσιν ἐμείγνυτ' ἐν Παλίου
> σφυροῖς, ἐκ δ'ἐγένοντο στρατός
> θαυμαστός, ἀμφοτέροις
> ὁμοῖοι τοκεῦσι, τὰ μα-
>        τρόθεν μὲν κάτω, τὰ δ' ὕπερθε πατρός.
>
>                  (Pindar, *Pythian* 2.42–48)

Without the Graces she, a solitary mother, bore him, a single son, (who was)
overbearing and respected neither among men nor in the ways of the gods. She
who reared him called him Centaurus; he used to mate with Magnesian mares in
the foothills of Pelion, and from them a wondrous folk was born, similar to both
parents, having the mother's features below, the father's above.

---

[125] Cf. Schadewaldt 1928: 328–29.

[126] Cf. Burton 1962: 117 and Most 1985: 69–70, who sets aside lines 42–48 and regards them as a
supplement to the ring-composition. In my analysis of the ode's structure, I follow Most with one
exception. Most places at the heart of the ring-composition the murder alone (*P*.2.31–32) rather
than the summary of Ixion's transgressions; in my view, however, lines 30–34 must be read
together. Given that the gnomic statement in *P*.2.34 reflects exclusively on Ixion's desire for
Hera, it marks the transition from the collective summary of Ixion's criminal record to the
exclusive focus on his second crime alone (cf. *P*.2.35).

The passage covers two successive generations of progeny (Centaurus, *P*.2.42–44; his monstrous offspring, *P*.2.45–48) that resulted from the coupling of Ixion and the cloud-*eidolon* of Hera. Thematically it defines insolent nature as a hereditary quality that manifests itself in subsequent generations. Ixion's son is an arrogant and isolated being who exists at the margins of the human and the divine (*P*.2.42–43), and resorts to bestiality to procreate (*P*.2.44–46); accordingly, his offspring are a hybrid species that embodies insolence and savageness.[127] The genealogical account, therefore, develops further the theme of sexual transgression that begins with Ixion: while Centaurus is the result of Ixion's attempt to cross the line between man and god, his biform progeny emerges from his crossing the (much more base) line between man and animal.[128] Furthermore, procreation in this narrative defies all expectations and natural limitations. Ixion beds with a cloud figment that gives birth in spite of her nature;[129] in fact, she commemorates this unconventional and unnatural conception of their son in the name she gives him.[130] Subsequently, the child of this impossible union staged by Zeus spawns a new hybrid race, a remarkable and wondrous tribe (cf. στρατός θαυμαστός, *P*.2.46–47). With its extraordinary features, Ixion's progeny offers a clear demonstration of the unfailing and absolute power of the gods, thus leading up to the gnomic statement that celebrates in hymnic style the omnipotence of the divine (*P*.2.49–52).

While complementary to Ixion's own story in terms of its themes, however, the account of Ixion's progeny is structured as a self-contained section. The genealogical information is presented in a linear fashion and it

---

[127] The two civilized Centaurs, Chiron and Pholos, have different origins than the rest, a distinction that further underscores the violent and transgressive nature of the Centaurs as a race; see, e.g., Roscher 1890–94: 1032–33. On the Centaurs as the embodiment of sexual violence and rape in particular, cf. Zeitlin 1986: 131–35.

[128] Most 1985: 81 argues that Centaurus' isolation is an element displaced from the story of his father's miasma and the madness that afflicted him after the murder of his father-in-law (for the madness, see Pherecydes fr. 51 Fowler). Cf. Carey 1981: 34, who reads an allusion to that earlier madness embedded in the erotic language of line 26 (μαινομέναις φρεσί); similarly, Lefkowitz 1976: 17–19 on ἀνήρ (*P*.2.29). However, the isolation of Centaurus has a function of its own in the narrative, since it creates the perfect conditions for his bestiality. In addition, while evoking Ixion's madness, Centaurus' marginality also invites a comparison between the father, who was given the chance to escape isolation, and his son, who was born into it and was never granted the opportunity of integration.

[129] Given line 36 (ἐπεὶ νεφέλᾳ παρελέξατο, "after he slept with the cloud/Nephele"), the interpretation proposed in sch.*P*.2.78a that ἄνευ Χαρίτων (*P*.2.42) means without sex (ἀντὶ τοῦ ἔξω συνουσίας) is unlikely.

[130] On the *figura etymologica*, see von der Mühll 1968: 226–29; cf. Gentili et al. 1995: 382 on the suggested etymologies of Κένταυρος.

is attached to – rather than included in – the perfectly concentric narrative of Ixion's transgressions. The genealogical account stands out also for its representation of Centaurus. In all other extant sources that connect Ixion to the Centaurs, there is no intermediate figure: the biform creatures are born directly from the sexual union between Ixion and Nephele (the "Cloud-Woman"), and owe their equine half to their mother, since clouds are often perceived as assuming the shape of horses.[131] Pindar appears to have reshaped the aetiological story by reinventing Centaurus as the single, anthropomorphic offspring of Ixion and the cloud-woman. Pindar's revision has been interpreted as an attempt to rationalize the mythological story[132] and to produce a version that demonstrates more effectively the hereditary evil that has permanently afflicted Ixion's progeny.[133] We should not disregard, however, that this new version is communicated through a specific type of narrative in which basic genealogical information is arranged in a quick linear succession and supplemented by a select and concise commentary with an aetiological function. I suggest that Pindar's account of the successive generations of Ixion's progeny is constructed in a manner that deliberately evokes the genre of catalogic genealogical poetry.

If the presentation of Ixion's progeny evokes genealogical poetry, then it also invites the audience to compare the outcome of Ixion's sexual union to the heroes celebrated in well-known genealogical poems such as the *Catalogue* and the *ME*, thus bringing the perverted nature of Ixion's offspring into sharper relief. In its programmatic proem, the *Catalogue* defines itself as a poem that celebrates the race of heroes born of the sexual encounters between gods and mortal women:

> τάων ἔσπετε Μ[οῦσαι
> ὅσσ[αι]ς ἂν παρέλ[εκτο πατὴρ ἀνδρῶν τε θεῶν τε
> σ͵περμ͵αί͵νων τὰ ꓕπρῶτα γένος κυδρῶν βασιλήων
> .]ς τε Π[ο]σειδάω[ν
> . . . . . .]ν τ' Ἄρης [

(Hesiod fr. 1.14–18)

14 Μ[οῦσαι Lobel, West : μ[οι MW  15 αν Π : δὴ Lobel
ἂν παρέλ[εκτο πατὴρ ἀνδρῶν τε θεῶν τε Hirschberger : δὴ παρελ[έξατ'
Ὀλύμπιος εὐρύοπα Ζεὺς MW

---

[131] Roscher 1890–94: 1032–33 with sources.    [132] Wilamowitz 1922: 288.
[133] Bowra 1964: 295 and Most 1985: 86.

Of these (women) tell, [Muses] ... all those with whom used to lie [the father
of men and gods], sowing at first the race of glorious kings, and ... Poseidon ...
and Ares ...

Progeny is the pivotal principle that advances Hesiodic genealogical poetry
both vertically and horizontally, thus fulfilling the text's function as a
charter myth that provides a narrative of origins, but also retrojects and
justifies relationships between various groups.[134] The "race of glorious
kings" (γένος κυδρῶν βασιλήων) whose birth and progeny are recounted
in the *Catalogue* and the *ME* include the eponymous heroes of the Greek
tribes as well as of smaller communities. These figures were considered
forefathers not in a biological sense but in political terms; in other words,
they were perceived as founders and legendary leaders.[135]

I suggest that the genealogical catalogue of Ixion's progeny in *P.*2 offers
a distorted version of the heroic genealogical branches commemorated
and celebrated in genealogical poetry. To start with, Pindar constructs
his Centaurus as a mortal man born of a union which inverts the sexual
pattern that engendered the entire heroic race. While the vast majority of
ἡμίθεοι were born of women raped by gods, Centaurus was born of the
semblance of a goddess raped by a man. Furthermore, while clearly
invested with an aetiological function just like the eponymous heroes of
the *Catalogue*, Pindar's Centaurus differs from those ancestral figures in
that his ties to the community that bears his name are based on biology
rather than leadership. Centaurus is no leader: not only does he exist
outside society, but the new "people" (στρατός) he generates through
bestiality is savage and unruly. His role as a biological progenitor is not
only dominant but also exaggerated, since he is responsible for the birth of
an entire race. The preeminence of his procreative role mirrors his father's
uncontrollable and transgressive sexual desires[136] but, since it involves
bestiality, it also marks Centaurus as subhuman. Thus genealogical poetry,
such as Hesiod's *Catalogue* and *ME*, contributes to Pindar's new version of
the Ixion story elements from its poetics, especially regarding the structure
of genealogical information.[137] More than that, however, it provides the

---

[134] See West 1985a: 1–11 (with parallels from other cultures in 11–30), Hall 1997: 40–51, Fowler 1998:
with bibliography, Finkelberg 2005: 24–41, and Cingano 2009: 113–14; cf. Rutherford 2000: 83–89
and, for a different reading of the ideology embedded in the Catalogue, Irwin 2005.

[135] See, e.g., Hall 1997: 40–51, Bertelli 2001: 73–76, and Larson 2007: 17–66 with particular emphasis
on Boeotia.

[136] Gentili et al. 1995: 383.

[137] On the appropriation of structural elements from catalogic genealogical poetry in epinician odes, cf.
D'Alessio 2005b: 237 on the catalogue of Asopus' daughters in Ba. *Ode* 9.

foil against which Ixion's son emerges as a distorted heroic figure, one who is born from the attempted rape of an immortal by a mortal (rather than the other way around) and who produces monsters instead of killing them. Unlike the monster-slayers celebrated in the Hesiodic corpus for eliminating such destructive agents and for enforcing the order of their Olympian fathers, Centaurus engenders a new breed of transgressive hybrids.[138]

While the linear genealogical account of lines 42–48 engages with genealogical catalogues both in its structure and its content, it is likely that the text invites a reading of Ixion's story through a distinctly Hesiodic lens earlier, before the concentric narrative of Ixion's transgression even comes to its conclusion. In *Pythian* 2 Ixion earns his eternal torture and paradigmatic status because he had the insolence to desire Hera (whom the text explicitly reserves for the conjugal bed of Zeus, *P.*2.27–28), but also because he acts on this desire, attempting to rape the wife of his divine benefactor in his own house (*P.*2.33–34). However, the man who once killed a family member "not without deception" (οὐκ ἄτερ τέχνας, *P.*2.32) falls for a trick himself, as Zeus substitutes a cloud simulacrum for his wife.[139] It is possible that this account of Ixion's crime and punishment may have struck Pindar's audience as distinctly Hesiodic. Although there are no extant sources for Ixion's crimes that predate *Pythian* 2,[140] according to a scholion to Apollonius' *Argonautica* the basic plotline of his sexual transgression and Hera's substitution was also found in the Hesiodic treatment of Endymion:[141]

τὸν δὲ Ἐνδυμίωνα Ἡσίοδος μὲν Ἀεθλίου τοῦ Διὸς καὶ Καλύκης, παρὰ Διὸς εἰληφότα τὸ δῶρον ἶν αὐτῷ ταμίαν εἶναι θανάτου, ὅτε θέλοι ὀλέσθαι· ... ἐν δὲ ταῖς Μεγάλαις Ἡοίαις λέγεται τὸν Ἐνδυμίωνα ἀνενεχθῆναι ὑπὸ τοῦ Διὸς εἰς οὐρανόν, ἐρασθέντα δὲ Ἥρας εἰδώλῳ παραλογισθῆναι νεφέλης, καὶ διὰ τὸν ἔρωτα ἐκβληθέντα κατελθεῖν εἰς Ἅιδου.

(sch. Apollonius Rhodius, *Argonautica* 4.57–58 = Hesiod fr. 260 MW)

---

[138] The birth of hybrid beings is not completely absent from the *Catalogue of Women*: we find the Satyrs listed along with the mountain Nymphs and the Curetae among the children of Iphthime (Hes. fr. 5/10a.18). These three groups complement each other, as Hirschberger 2004: 182–83 points out, and, since it is rather exceptional, their inclusion in the *Catalogue* does not annul the poem's programmatic focus on the emergence of the heroic race. It is significant that Hes. fr. 5/10a.18 makes no mention whatsoever of the bestial elements in the Satyrs' form. Unlike *P.*2, where the hybrid nature of the Centaurs is a reflex of Ixion's moral depravity and an extension of his punishment, the Satyrs of the *Catalogue* (albeit naughty) are not the result of an ancestral crime.

[139] The language of copulation in *P.*2.36 (ἐπεὶ νεφέλᾳ παρελέξατο) is found in the programmatic proem to the *Catalogue of Women* (Hes. fr. 1.15 MW; ὅσσ[αι]ς ἂν παρέλ[εκτο]. Cf. Hes. *Th.* 278–79, where the verb is applied to Poseidon sleeping with Medusa, the only mortal of the Gorgons. Note that this passage marks the first sexual union between an Olympian and a mortal female figure in the *Theogony* and, in fact, in the entire sequence *Theogony–Catalogue of Women*.

[140] Lochin 1990.

[141] Cf. Acusilaus fr. 36 Fowler, Epimenides fr. 12 Fowler, and Pherecydes fr. 121 Fowler.

"Hesiod (says) that Endymion, the son of Aethlius, son of Zeus, and Kalyke, died when he wanted, having received from Zeus the gift to be the manager of his own death ... But in the *Megalai Ehoiai* it is said that Endymion was brought up to the sky by Zeus, but, after he fell in love with Hera, he was fooled by a cloud-simulacrum and, having been thrown out (of Olympus) on account of his desire, he descended to Hades."

Endymion's genealogy and his special god-given privilege to determine the time of his death has been identified in a fragment from the *Catalogue* (Hes. fr. 5/10a.60–62). Sch. Ap. Rh. *Arg.* 4.57–58, however, is our only evidence for the treatment of Endymion's illicit desire for Hera and its consequences in the Hesiodic *ME*.[142] A comparative survey of extant sources regarding Endymion reveals that he was not associated with an (attempted) rape of Hera outside the *ME* and Epimenides (fr. 12 Fowler), but the cloud-simulacrum of the goddess was featured exclusively in the *ME*.[143] There is, therefore, a version of Endymion's assault and of the ruse involved in his demise that is exclusive to the Hesiodic corpus. It is tempting to assume that audiences familiar with the *ME* would interpret Pindar's Ixion as a figure informed by the Hesiodic version of Endymion. However, we must not lose sight of the fact that the overlap is limited to the circumstances of the rape and to the involvement of an *eidolon*. The two heroes receive different punishments and, more importantly, Endymion's union with Hera's substitute (unlike Ixion's) remains barren.

It is possible, then, that Ixion's sexual transgression in *P.*2 has been entirely invented on the basis of Endymion's narrative in the *ME* or, at least, that it draws some fundamental details from it. And yet the cloud-simulacrum appears better integrated in the story of Ixion, since her nature is reflected upon the name of her offspring as well as the equine form of

---

[142] For the difficulties in reconciling the Endymion story of the *Catalogue* and that of the *ME*, see Hirschberger 2004: 189, who distinguishes between a Latmian version embedded in the *Cat.* and an Elian one with which the *ME* engages; cf. D'Alessio 2005a: 180–81, who concludes that "the two versions look contradictory rather than complementary." Differently Mele 2001: 262–64. For a completely different and far less persuasive approach, see Cohen 1986: 129 and 135–37, who allows for contradictory accounts within the same poem and makes the tangential suggestion that the title *Megalai Ehoiai* refers to a part of the *Catalogue*, not to a separate poem altogether.

[143] Epimenides (fr. 12 Fowler) discussed Endymion's desire for Hera, but his overlap with the Hesiodic version of the *ME* is limited, since there is no simulacrum in his story and Endymion's punishment involves eternal sleep (cf. the summary in sch. Theocr. 3.49–51b). While eternal sleep is an element firmly associated with the story of Endymion in the extant sources (with the exception of the *ME*), his sexual transgression against Hera is not. On Epimenides' engagement with the *ME*, see Mele 2001: 262–64 and D'Alessio 2005a: 204 n.116.

the Centaurs. Based on the popularity of Ixion's punishment in late-sixth-century vase painting, D'Alessio has tentatively suggested that his story was older than *Pythian* 2 and may have been included already in the genealogical poetry circulating under Hesiod's name.[144] In this case, the genealogical entry that included Ixion may also have included the birth of the Centaurs, which would render the Hesiodic mode of the linear genealogical account in *P.*2.42–48 all the more direct and evident to Pindar's audience. It is also possible that the Hesiodic account would include the rape of Ixion's wife by Zeus. Sch. D *Il.* 1.263 reports that Zeus impregnated Ixion's wife while in the form of a horse, and etymologizes Centaurus' name as reflecting the circumstances of his conception. No source is cited in the scholion, but the story would be at home in an *ehoie*. We must not exclude the possibility, then, that the Pindaric account of Ixion's sexual aggression was interpreted against a Hesiodic story of his wife's rape, and that the monstrosity of Ixion's progeny as well as the ode's commentary on the liberties enjoyed by divine agents (*P.*2.49–52) may have been qualified by an evocation of Zeus as a theriomorphic rapist.[145]

Whether both Endymion and Ixion were featured in the Hesiodic corpus or only Endymion, there is little doubt that the cloud-simulacrum of *Pythian* 2 emerges as a female figure constructed in Hesiodic terms. Substitutions through *eidola* are fairly rare in archaic poetry but, to the extent that our extant sources can be reliable witnesses, their distribution in Panhellenic hexameter poetry is gendered. While Homeric poetry uses *eidola* exclusively for men (Aeneas in *Il.* 5 and Heracles in *Od.* 11), the Hesiodic corpus features female *eidola*: in addition to the cloud-simulacrum of Hera that Endymion rapes (fr. 260 MW), the Hesiodic corpus seems to have included a substitute for Helen, as attested in the scholia to Lycophron's *Alexandra* (Hes. fr. 358 MW)[146]

---

[144] D'Alessio 2005a: 204.

[145] Cf. Most 1985: 82, who suggests that *P.*2 invites a comparison between Ixion's story and the rape of his wife by Zeus, but focuses on the version of the story hinted at in Hom. *Il.* 14.317–18. In this passage, Ixion's wife is the first item on Zeus's catalogue of past mortal lovers, and the result of that rape is said to be the birth of Peirithous. Most rightly argues that the juxtaposition between the two rapists (Zeus and Ixion) underscores the abysmal gap between gods and men regarding the outcome of their sexual advances towards mortal and immortal females respectively.

[146] Hes. fr. 358 MW = sch. Lykophr. *Alex.* 822. Cf. the commentary on Stesichorus in *P.Oxy.* 2506 fr. 26 col. i (Stes. fr. 193 *PMGF* = 90 DF), which informs us that the lyric poet assumed a polemical stance towards Helen's representation in both Homeric and Hesiodic poetry. His double palinode situated the real Helen in Egypt and her fake substitute in Troy. Assuming Hes. fr. 358 MW is reliable, Hesiodic poetry (unlike Homeric epic) did feature an *eidolon* for Helen, so Stesichorus must have objected to the

and perhaps in Hes. fr. 15/23a.21 if the first word was indeed εἰδώ[λου. It is possible, however, that fr. 15/23a.21 began with εἴδω[λον, thus referring to a simulacrum of Iphimede, sacrificed in her stead at Aulis (fr. 15/23a.17–18).[147] Both versions of fr.15/23a.21 are possible; it is even conceivable – albeit by no means verifiable – that both alternatives circulated among Greek audiences. The Pindaric *eidolon* of Hera in *P.*2, then, may have been perceived by the ode's audience as a particularly Hesiodic feature not only because of its common ground with the Endymion story in the *ME* but also because female *eidola* may have been distinctly Hesiodic elements.

Yet the Hesiodic associations of Pindar's cloud-woman are not exhausted in her nature as Hera's fake double. The ode's account of her construction is informed by a unique female figure within the Hesiodic cosmos and the prototype of all mortal women to come, namely Pandora. Let's take a close look at the lines that introduce Hera's cloud-*eidolon* to the Pindaric ode:

> ἐπεὶ
> νεφέλᾳ παρελέξατο
> ψεῦδος γλυκὺ μεθέπων ἄϊδρις ἀνήρ·
> εἶδος γὰρ ὑπεροχωτάτᾳ πρέπεν Οὐρανιᾶν
> θυγατέρι Κρόνου· ἅντε δόλον αὐτῷ θέσαν
> Ζηνὸς παλάμαι, καλὸν πῆμα· τὸν δὲ τε-
> τράκναμον ἔπραξε δεσμόν
> ἑὸν ὄλεθρον ὅγ᾽·
>
> (Pindar, *Pythian* 2.36–41)

because he lay with a cloud,[148] an ignorant man pursuing a sweet lie, for it resembled in appearance the most eminent of heavenly goddesses, the daughter of Cronus. Zeus's cunning set this as a trap for him, a beautiful bane. And the man made the binding to the four spokes his own destruction.

Nephele is the instrument of Zeus's ruse, a figure created ad hoc from a malleable and shape-shifting substance appropriately indigenous to the sky. This fabricated woman is defined as successfully deceptive, a "sweet lie" (ψεῦδος γλυκύ, *P.*2.37), and her deceptive quality is immediately

---

geographic arrangement involved. On the possibility that the Hesiodic *eidolon* of Helen was in Sparta rather than Troy, see Hirschberger 2004: 212 with bibliography.

[147] See, e.g., Austin 1994: 104–10 and Hirschberger 2004: 212.

[148] The noun νεφέλᾳ invites a double interpretation, since the cloud-simulacrum was traditionally called Nephele, aptly named after her material substance.

attributed to her external appearance, i.e. her resemblance to Hera, the object of Ixion's desire (*P.*2.38–39). The penultimate sentence of this passage emphasizes the active role that Zeus holds in the design and the creation of this *eidolon* (*P.*2.39–40); notice especially the subject of the sentence, Ζηνὸς παλάμαι, a phrase that is meaningful both literally ("the hands of Zeus") and metaphorically ("the devices of Zeus").[149] Finally, the apposition καλὸν πῆμα, "a beautiful bane" (*P.*2.40), reiterates the intrinsic bond between the pleasing, even arousing, effect Nephele has as an object of the male gaze and the destructive mission of deception and entrapment that she is designed to carry out through that beautiful appearance.

As many readers of *Pythian* 2 have pointed out, this passage bears several allusions to the creation of Pandora in the Hesiodic corpus. Already the ancient scholiast explicates καλὸν πῆμα by comparing it to a Hesiodic phrase used in the *Theogony* to describe Pandora:

ὡς καὶ Ἡσίοδος· καλὸν κακόν (=*Th.* 585)· καλὸν μὲν διὰ τὸ ὠμοιῶσθαι τῇ Ἥρᾳ, πῆμα δὲ ὡς πρὸς τὸ ἀποτέλεσμα.

(sch. Pindar, *Pythian* 2.72)

Just like Hesiod: "a beautiful evil." It is beautiful because it resembles Hera, but a bane in terms of the outcome.

The scholiast simply notes the similarity between the structure of the two oxymora. Given its context, however, Pindar's καλὸν πῆμα can be read as an echo of *Th.* 585 (αὐτὰρ ἐπεὶ δὴ τεῦξε καλὸν κακὸν ἀντ' ἀγαθοῖο) and can be even approached as a complex allusion that encompasses both the *Theogony*'s description of the first woman and the recurrent reference to Pandora as a πῆμα in the *WD*.[150] Further encouraging the evocation of Hesiod's Pandora in this ode, Pindar's ἑὸν ὄλεθρον in *P.*2.41 paraphrases ἑὸν κακόν, the phrase with which Zeus programmatically describes women in *WD* 58 as he plans mankind's punishment after Prometheus stealthily returns the fire to them.[151] Most interprets Pindar's allusions to Hesiod's Pandora exclusively as a means of characterizing Ixion himself; in his view, the allusions are meant to create a comparison between Prometheus and Ixion as two figures who failed to outsmart Zeus. His conclusion is that "Ixion combines within himself the roles of both the

---

[149] *LSJ s.v.* παλάμη.

[150] *WD* 56, μέγα πῆμα; *WD* 82, πῆμ' ἀνδράσιν ἀλφηστῇσιν; cf. *Th.* 592, where the whole female race that stems from the first woman is called πῆμα μέγα θνητοῖσι.

[151] Most 1985: 82–83. On the Hesiodic echoes of δόλος/πῆμα combination, see also Gentili et al. 1995: 380 on *P.*2.39–40.

crafty Prometheus and the stupid Epimetheus" (83). While I agree that
the story of Ixion in *Pythian 2* explores the limitations of human intelligence, I suggest that the main purpose of these Hesiodic allusions is to
provide a familiar model for the *eidolon* herself and for the type of sly and
vindictive divine plan she is created to serve.

Through these verbal echoes, then, the Pindaric text evokes the Hesiodic versions of Pandora's creation (*Th.* 570–612 and *WD* 53–105) and
invites an interpretation of Pindar's *eidolon* through the Hesiodic figure
of the first woman/wife. Much like *Pythian 2*, both Hesiodic accounts
represent women as instruments of divine retaliation and punishment:
they are designed and created by Zeus to seduce, lure, and ultimately bring
inescapable suffering to mortal men. Their appearance is of pivotal importance for the success of Zeus's ruse, given that in these texts the female
figure is crafted to be received first and foremost as an alluring spectacle.[152]
It is hardly surprising, therefore, that godlike looks are the defining
characteristic in the description of Pindar's Nephele too.[153] Both Pandora
and Nephele are explicitly marked as deceptive, since the *eidolon* is
conceived and constructed as a δόλος for Ixion (*P.*2.39; cf. ψεῦδος γλυκύ,
*P.*2.37) and Pandora is called a δόλος in both Hesiodic versions (δόλον
αἰπύν ἀμήχανον in *Th.* 589 and *WD* 83). Even the structure of *Pythian*
2.39–40 (ἄντε δόλον αὐτῷ θέσαν / Ζηνὸς παλάμαι) seems to mirror the
structure of *Th.* 600–01 (ὡς δ' αὔτως ἄνδρεσσι κακὸν θνητοῖσι γυναῖκας
/ Ζεὺς ὑψιβρεμέτης θῆκε). Both sentences use τίθημι with the fabricated
females as objects complemented by a sinister predicate (δόλον / κακὸν),
while the men for whom these women are made appear as datives of
disadvantage (αὐτῷ / ἄνδρεσσι). Furthermore, the subject in both
clauses is Zeus, although the more elaborate phrase Ζηνὸς παλάμαι in

---

[152] Hes. *Th.* 570–84, esp. 575 and 581; cf. her reception as a visual object in *Th.* 585–89, esp. 588–89
(θαῦμα δ' ἔχ' ἀθανάτους τε θεοὺς θνητούς τ' ἀνθρώπους, / ὡς εἶδον δόλον αἰπύν, ἀμήχανον
ἀνθρώποισιν). The *WD* too is concerned with Pandora's external looks (*WD* 70–76; cf. 62–63),
but in that version the gods endow her with other qualities as well (*WD* 77–80; cf. 67–68). Note
that the ambivalence regarding νεφέλα in *P.*2.36 combines Hesiod's diverse attitudes towards
naming the first woman in his poetry. In the *Theogony*, the female figure remains unnamed,
whereas the *WD* uses the *nomen loquens* as a reflection of Pandora's creation and function (*WD*
80–82). *Pythian 2* does not explicitly designate a name for the *eidolon*, yet line 36 could be
understood as a reference to her proper name (Νεφέλη). Cf. Tzetzes' rationalizing interpretation
of Nephele in response to Pindar's *P.*2 (*Chil.* 7 (99) 27–35).

[153] In *WD* 62–63, Zeus orders Pandora's appearance to be modeled upon the ideal of divine female
beauty. When *Pythian 2* underscores that the *eidolon* has the form of the "most eminent"
goddess of all, therefore, it not only signals that this is a perfect replica of Hera, and thus the
perfect trap for enamored Ixion, but it also evokes the ideal of divine beauty that determined
Pandora's looks too.

*P.2* may be evoking Hephaestus' manual labor in the context of the woman's creation and adornment in *Th.* 580 (ἀσκήσας παλάμῃσι χαριζόμενος Διὶ πατρί). Notice that Ixion, who was earlier called a ἥρως (*P.2.31*), is now reduced to an ἄϊδρις ἀνήρ, an "ignorant man" (*P.2.37*), a good match for *Theogony*'s equally clueless ἄνδρεσσι. Ultimately, both women are utterly successful in fulfilling Zeus's plans and in bringing evil upon the mortal men he has targeted: Ixion fulfills his desire for Hera through her replica only to receive an eternal punishment, while Pandora and her womankind become an inescapable evil that plagues men ever after.

By evoking the familiar paradigm of Hesiod's Pandora, then, Pindar adds yet another layer to his complex engagement with the Hesiodic corpus in *Pythian 2*. As I hope to have shown, Hera's *eidolon* emerges as a Pandora-like figure in so far as she embodies Zeus's deceptive manipulation of men's sexual desires in order to subdue them. Yet, as the ode transforms Nephele from a barren cloud to a mother, defying all expectations set by nature and tradition,[154] she becomes evocative of the women featured in Hesiodic genealogical poetry.[155] Unlike the kings born of the unions commemorated in the *Catalogue of Women* and the *ME*, however, the progeny that Nephele produces through her intercourse with Ixion is subhuman and marginalized, thus framing lines 42–48 of *Pythian 2* as a twisted version of a Hesiodic genealogical entry.

---

[154] On the parallel of Endymion's story, see above, pp. 96–98.

[155] On the representation of women as begetters and its importance for the structure of Hesiodic genealogies, cf. Davies 1992: 88–93. On Pandora's significance as the first heroine of the *Catalogue*, see Osborne 2005: 8–10; cf. Casanova 1979a: 135–55.

CHAPTER 3

# *Lyric Reception of Hesiod's Didactic Poetry*

Gnomic statements and precepts explicitly identified as Hesiodic are rarely woven into the poetic fabric of (extant) fifth-century lyric. In fact, only Pindar's *Isthmian 6* and *Pythian 6* engage directly with Hesiodic didactic. In this brief chapter, I explore how these epicinians appropriate Hesiodic precepts in their laudatory contexts and how they integrate distinct didactic voices. In both odes, Hesiod's wisdom emerges as a foundation of education and civic ethics, and as an indispensable source of success for the individual and the community. Beyond *I.6* and *P.6*, however, lyric poets refrain from invoking Hesiod's didactic authority, even when their *gnomai* overlap in content with those found in the Hesiodic corpus. As I discuss in the last section of this chapter, the scholiasts too refrain from identifying Hesiodic sources for lyric *gnomai*, even when they quote Hesiodic precepts as parallel passages. In other words, the scholia do not engage in *Quellenforschungen* for *gnomai* as they occasionally do for mythological narratives and genealogies.

## Works and Games: *Isthmian 6*

The only explicit reference to Hesiod in the extant corpus of Pindaric poetry occurs in *Isthmian 6*. The ode celebrates the first victory of Phylacidas, a boy from Aegina, in the contest of *pancration* at the Isthmian Games.[1] The poem extends its praise to other members of the victor's family who were successful athletes, specifically his maternal uncle, Euthymenes, and his brother, Pytheas, who had already achieved a victory in the

---

[1] Pfeijffer 1995 dates the ode no later than 480 BCE; cf. extensively Fearn 2007: 342–50, Cairns 2007 and 2010: 132–33. See also Indergaard 2011: 295–96, who argues that *I.6* was composed shortly after the new pediments of the Temple of Aphaea had been completed. On the performative context of the ode, see the discussion in Indergaard 2011: 298–300 and Morrison 2011: 322–24.

Nemean Games. Given that epinician rhetoric treats excellence as hereditary, it is not unusual for Pindaric poetry to celebrate other athletes in the
family of the *laudandus*.[2] What is unusual about this ode, however, is the
amount of attention it pays to the victor's father, Lampon, even though
he appears never to have participated in athletic games. This treatment
of the father of the *laudandus* in *Isthmian 6* is exceptional and remains
unparalleled even among the other epinician odes composed for Lampon's
sons (*I.5* for Phylacidas; *N.5* and Ba. *Ode* 13 for Pytheas).[3] In effect,
*Isthmian 6* obscures the boy-victor almost entirely and treats his father as
a *laudandus*.

It is precisely in the context of praising Lampon that the ode evokes
Hesiod (*I.6.66–73*). In order to appreciate fully how the poem appropriates
Hesiod's poetry and authority in this laudatory frame, we need to survey
first how it constructs the paternal figure of Lampon up until that point.
The first strophe (*I.6.1–9*) already establishes Lampon as a focal point
not only by merging the accomplishments of Phylacidas and his brother,
but also by treating the boys collectively as the victorious progeny of
their father (Λάμπωνος εὐαέθλου γενεᾶς ὕπερ, 3). Thus the text refrains
from focusing on the boy-victor as an individual, directing our attention
towards his father instead. Note that the *persona loquens* wishes for a third
victory, an Olympic one, but leaves the identity of the victor unspecified:
either one of the boys will do. What matters is the impact of that victory
upon their father.[4] The long gnomic statement that follows (*I.6.10–18*)
praises deeds of excellence (θεοδμάτους ἀρετάς, 11) that one achieves

---

[2] On the praise of the victor's family in epinician poetry, see Thummer 1968: 49–54 and, more
recently, Fenno 2005: esp. 294 with n.1. On Pindar's praise of this particular family in *I.5*, *I.6*, and
*N.5* see Silk 1998: 56–70, 75, 79–85, and Fenno 2005.

[3] Cf. Privitera 1982: 90; cf. Gärtner 1978: 39–40, who argues that Lampon's centrality in *I.6*
compensates for his marginal treatment in the earlier Pindaric ode for Pytheas (*N.5*). Building on
D'Alessio 1994, Indergaard 2011: 300–03 notes that the *persona loquens* clearly encompasses not only
the Aeginetan performers but also Pindar the Theban poet, who poses in the ode as Lampon's *xenos*
(see the *sphragis* in *I.6.74–75*; cf. 19–21). *Xenia* certainly functions as a justification for praise in
epinician poetry; it cannot explain adequately, however, the unparalleled degree to which the praise
for Lampon obscures the celebration of his son. On the particular characteristics of Aeginetan *xenia*,
see Kowalzig 2011, esp. 145–63; cf. already Figueira 1981: 326–32, Hubbard 2001: 393–94 (see also
Hornblower 2007: 297–302).

[4] On *I.6.7–16*, see Thummer 1968: 104. Largely influenced by Bundy's approach to Pindar, Thummer
attempts to categorize every element of the odes as some form of praise, but such a formalistic
approach often misses the subtleties of the text. For instance, his interpretation of *I.6.10–16* as "ein
Lob des bereits erreichten und des erbetenen Glückes (v. 10–16)" (*ibid.* 104; cf. Thummer 1969:
101–02) fails to point out that Pindar deliberately marginalizes the boy-victor. For a historicizing
approach, see Kirkwood 1982: 291, who extrapolates from the wish that one of the boys was about to
compete at the Olympic Games.

through expenditure, toil, and divine favor.[5] The lines appear to extoll hard-earned athletic victories, thus hinting that they refer to Lampon's victorious sons; the passage could be interpreted as a commentary on the boys' accomplishment or as admonition for the future, given that the speaker just wished for a third victory. Yet this impression soon proves to be misleading: as lines 14–16 reveal, the preceding *gnome* is meant to capture the mentality of Lampon himself, for whom the *persona loquens* expresses affection and prays to the Fates (*I.*6.16–18).[6]

Even when Lampon is not in the forefront, the text does not let the audience forget his importance. The mythological narrative that occupies the middle part of this tripartite poem celebrates the Aeacidae, and in particular Telamon and Ajax.[7] *Isthmian 6* recounts an incident that took place when Heracles came to recruit Telamon for his expedition against Troy (*I.*6.26–56).[8] Ajax was not yet born, but, thanks to Heracles' mediation, Telamon received reassurance from Zeus that he would have a strong son, whose name was bound to memorialize precisely that divine intervention (*I.*6.49–54). Given the extraordinary treatment of Lampon earlier in the ode, it is significant that, in the father–son constellation that emerges in the mythological narrative, the paternal figure is dominant. The text draws attention to Telamon as a hopeful father but also to Heracles as a father-like figure who shapes and defines the unborn hero.[9] Ajax, on the other hand, is only a passive presence, an infant yet to be born, whose name and character are formed through the interactions among the father-to-be, his guest-friend, and the gods.

When *Isthmian 6* returns from the mythological past to the present time (*I.*6.56), it praises the victor in the same collective manner it employed in the first strophe; this time, however, the praise extends not only to Phylacidas and Pytheas but also to maternal kin who have been successful athletes.

---

[5] For a concise assessment of the significance of these three themes for Pindar's poetry, see Willcock 1995: 15–16.

[6] For a different interpretation, see Kurke 1991b.

[7] The connection between Aeacus and Aegina is not attested in the *Iliad* but is already evident in the *Catalogue of Women* (Hes. fr. 95/205). On the Aeginetan appropriation of Aeacus already in the sixth century BCE, see Mann 2001: 204–12 and Fearn 2007: 100–05 with bibliography (cf. 96–100 for the representation of the Aeacidae on the Aphaea pediments); cf. Nagy 2011, esp. 41–60, Indergaard 2011: 307–08. On Heracles, Telamon, and the *ME* (Hes. fr. 250 MW), see below, p. 112.

[8] The bond of *xenia* between Heracles the Theban hero and Telamon offers a parallel for the *xenia* bond between Pindar the Theban poet and Lampon, but also a parallel to the close political relations between the city-states of Thebes and Aegina at the time of the ode's composition. See D'Alessio 2005a: 232 and Indergaard 2011: 318. On *xenia*, see also n.26.

[9] Cf. Indergaard 2011: 318, who points out that Heracles obscures Telamon as a father figure in *I.*6. On Heracles in this mythological narrative, see also Burnett 2005: 82–86.

The poem celebrates jointly the victories of Phylacidas, his brother, and their maternal uncle Euthymenes (*I.6.56–62*); subsequently, their accomplishments are assessed in terms of their positive contributions to the *patra* of the Psalychiadae and the *oikos* of Themistius, who was the boys' maternal grandfather and an athletic victor himself (*I.6.63–66*).[10] The praise of maternal relatives establishes Phylacidas' place within a long family tradition of athletic victories before the remaining lines of the poem shift our focus back to Lampon, who receives a final round of laudation. The juxtaposition between the well-justified praise of athletes and the ode's preoccupation with Lampon reveals how exceptional the latter is, since there is not even a hint that he ever participated in – let alone won – athletic competitions.

How does the epinician construct Lampon's praise so that the latter can counterbalance the eminence of a family of victors and not be obscured by it? The ode associates him with an established authority of Panhellenic renown, namely Hesiod:

> Λάμπων δὲ μελέταν
> ἔργοις ὀπάζων Ἡσιό-
>   δου μάλα τιμᾷ τοῦτ᾽ ἔπος,
> υἱοῖσί τε φράζων παραινεῖ,
> ξυνὸν ἄστει κόσμον ἑῷ προσάγων·
> καὶ ξένων εὐεργεσίαις ἀγαπᾶται
> μέτρα μὲν γνώμᾳ διώκων, μέτρα δὲ καὶ κατέχων·
> γλῶσσα δ᾽ οὐκ ἔξω φρενῶν· φαί-
>   ης κέ νιν ἄνδρ᾽ ἐν ἀεθληταῖσιν ἔμμεν
> Ναξίαν πέτραις ἐν ἄλλαις χαλκοδάμαντ᾽ ἀκόναν.[11]
>                                            (Pindar, *Isthmian* 6.66–73)

In devoting industry to his deeds, Lampon honors greatly this saying of Hesiod, and he admonishes his sons by quoting it, bringing to his own city an adornment shared by all. He is also beloved for his acts of kindness to guest-friends, pursuing due measure in judgment and holding fast to due measure. His tongue does not

---

[10] sch. *N.*5.91, 94b and e. Privitera 1982: xxxviii seems to think that the Psalychiadae are Lampon's *patra*; see, however, Fenno 2005: 311 who argues persuasively that Lampon was not a member of the *patra* to which Euthymenes and Themistius belonged. Cairns 2010: 135 n.23 misreads Fenno and suggests that Pytheas and Phylacidas may be Psalychiadae both on their paternal and their maternal side "given Greek habits of moderate endogamy." For a study of the Aeginetan *patrai*, see Morrison 2011, esp. 315–21 on the Psalychiadae; cf. Mann 2001: 200–02.

[11] The punctuation of the passage is debated. Snell-Maehler and the majority of commentators (e.g. Bowra, Thummer) favor a strong pause after προσάγων (69), κατέχων (71), and φρενῶν (72); cf. Kirkwood (1982) 290, who places a comma rather than a semicolon after κατέχων (71). On the other hand, Privitera 1982: 213–14 argues for a different tripartite structure with strong pauses after παραινεῖ (68) and ἀγαπᾶται (70). Cf. Race 1997b: 192, who punctuates with commas after παραινεῖ (68) and ἀγαπᾶται (70) but places a semicolon after κατέχων (71).

stray from his thoughts. You would say that as a man he is among athletes a bronze-taming whetstone from Naxos among other stones.

This passage underscores Lampon's virtues in relation to his *oikos*, his city, and his *xenoi*. It highlights the work ethic he adopts and passes on to his sons, his contributions to fellow citizens as well as foreigners, his sense of measure, and the consistency in content and quality between his words and his wise thoughts. Lampon thus emerges as an exemplary father, citizen, and host, who brings a ξυνὸς κόσμος to his community with his own behavior but also by being a good teacher and role model to his sons.[12] The catalogue of Lampon's virtues concludes with his contribution to the shaping of good athletes. Lines 66–73, then, reframe his broader civic qualities in order to emphasize their relevance in the realm of athletics and compensate for Lampon's non-existent athletic résumé by casting him in the role of a trainer.[13] While the victor's maternal family has contributed good pedigree to the gene pool, his father's admonition and upbringing have groomed Phylacidas and Pytheas for victory.

At the heart of this claim lies Lampon's explicit and extensive appropriation of Hesiod's wisdom and authority. The Ἡσιόδου ἔπος of *I.*6.66–68 is identified already in the ancient scholia as an allusion to μελέτη δέ τοι ἔργον ὀφέλλει (*WD* 412), a gnomic statement about the benefits of diligence that is embedded in a brief exhortation against procrastination:

> μηδ' ἀναβάλλεσθαι ἔς τ' αὔριον ἔς τ' ἔνηφιν·
> οὐ γὰρ ἐτωσιεργὸς ἀνὴρ πίμπλησι καλιὴν
> οὐδ' ἀναβαλλόμενος· μελέτη δέ τοι ἔργον ὀφέλλει·
> αἰεὶ δ' ἀμβολιεργὸς ἀνὴρ ἄτῃσι παλαίει
> (Hesiod, *Works and Days*, 410–13)

Do not postpone (work) until tomorrow and the day after, for the man who works in vain does not fill his granary, nor does the one who postpones; industry makes work thrive, and the man who postpones work is always wrestling with calamities.

The complexities of Pindar's paraphrase deserve a close look. The epinician ode echoes the original Hesiodic language with μελέτα (*I.*6.66) and ἔργοις (*I.*6.67),[14] but it does not immediately mark the Hesiodic reference. Rather,

---

[12] Koning 2010a: 175.
[13] On the Naxian whetstone analogy and its implications for Lampon's representation as an athletic trainer, see Privitera 1982: 214 and Kirkwood 1982: 296. Whether and to what extent the poem's representation of Lampon as a trainer is historically accurate is of minor importance.
[14] The context in which Lampon himself applies the Hesiodic motto is left unspecified, although it is bound to encompass a greater scope of ἔργα than the agricultural activities it stands for in the *Works*

the text opts to dramatize first the implementation of the precept through Lampon's own actions (Λάμπων δὲ μελέταν ἔργοις ὀπάζων, *I*.6.66–67) before his behavior is cast as homage to Hesiodic advice.[15] In other words, the ode does not offer a direct quote from the *WD*;[16] instead, it weaves a partial paraphrase into the description of Lampon's habitual behavior and prompts the audience to reconstruct the Hesiodic precept in retrospect. The full appreciation of the ode, then, presupposes familiarity with the Hesiodic text. It seems that at least the song's primary intended audience was expected to have some knowledge of Hesiod's precepts.

While the phrase τοῦτ' ἔπος redefines the preceding words as an echo of a Hesiodic gnomic statement, the immediately following line (υἱοῖσί τε φράζων παραινεῖ, *I*.6.68) incorporates this *gnome* in Lampon's advice to his sons. The ode, therefore, receives and adapts not only a Hesiodic precept but also its didactic context. As *I*.6 appropriates the dramatic framework of the *WD*, it adjusts it to its own agenda of privileging the victor's father; thus Lampon is said to appropriate the Hesiodic voice in the context of paternal instead of fraternal admonition.[17] As D'Alessio points out in his perceptive reading of *I*.6.66–69, the ode's appropriation of Hesiod's didactic voice is underscored and solidified by the marked verb παραινεῖ.[18] The poem grants Lampon an active role in the implementation but also in the proliferation of Hesiod's precept with great results both for his own *oikos* and for the city (*I*.6.69). The unambiguously positive assessment of Lampon's choices confirms the validity of Hesiodic authority, but, more importantly, it draws attention to Lampon's own wisdom in picking such an excellent source of advice. Cast as a Hesiodic man in both words and deeds, Lampon emerges as an exemplary father and a model citizen.

---

*and Days*. Kurke 1990: 89 entertains the possibility of a double entendre of ἔργοις as Lampon's own works and as the title of the Hesiodic *Works and Days*, the source of the ἔπος.

[15] Mace 1992: 183–191 cannot tolerate a partial paraphrase but also finds the mechanics of paraphrasing *WD* 412 incongruent with the system she has produced to describe Pindar's allusive technique. Therefore, she explores the possibility that the Hesiodic motto in *I*.6.66–68 may refer to *WD* 441–45, 314–16, or, more plausibly in her view, 381–82 (with an "associative reminiscence" of 380). There is no reason to assume with Mace that Pindar follows an ironclad formula for his allusions; and, even if we made that assumption, Mace's alternatives are thoroughly unsatisfactory.

[16] For the expectation of a verbatim quotation linked to the phrase τοῦτ' ἔπος, see Thummer 1969: 110; cf. Kurke 1990: 89. D'Alessio 2005b: 231 with n.57 observes that Pindar's reformulation and paraphrase of *WD* 412 resonates with *h.Herm.* 120 (ἔργῳ δ' ἔργον ὄπαζε, "he was adding task to task"). The epinician text may be drawing from the Homeric Hymn (or an older precept that underlies *h.Herm.* 120), but only on the level of diction. There seems to be no meaningful intertextual engagement between *I*.6.66–67 and the Homeric Hymn.

[17] Of course, Perses is the primary but not the only addressee in the *WD*; see Clay 1993.

[18] D'Alessio 2005b: 231–32 on παραινέω in *I*.6.66–69 and *P*.6.19–22; cf. Kurke 1990: 91.

At this point, it may be illuminating to compare the reception of *WD* 412 in Pindar's *Isthmian 6* to another potential allusion to the same gnomic statement. Composed for Phylacidas' brother a few years before *I.6*, Bacchylides' *Ode* 13 praises the victor as well as his trainer, Menander from Athens:[19]

> νίκαν ἐρικυ[δέα] μέλπετ', ὦ νέοι,
> [Π]υθέα, μελέτα[ν τε] βροτω-
> φ[ε]λέα Μενάνδρου
> (Bacchylides, *Ode* 13.190–92)

Sing, young men, of the glorious victory of Pytheas and of Menander's industry, beneficial to mortals.

Pindar's *I.6* paraphrases the Hesiodic *gnome* creatively, while marking the reference to it explicitly. The Bacchylidean μελέταν βροτωφελέα, however, constitutes a much more elusive allusion that completely suppresses Hesiod's authorship. The noun (μελέταν) in 13.191 echoes directly *WD* 412 (μελέτη), but the adjective βροτωφ[ε]λέα revises the Hesiodic original through word-play (ὀφέλλειν - ὠφελεῖν).[20] While the original Hesiodic line emphasizes the beneficial effect of diligence on work, Bacchylides' rendering goes one step further and draws attention to the fact that μελέτη ultimately benefits people. The shift is well justified in the context of an epinician ode that praises, first and foremost, accomplished individuals and the social groups to which they belong. In effect, Pindar's ξυνὸς κόσμος (*I.6.69*) communicates the same idea. The engagement with the same Hesiodic passage in both *I.6* and *Ode* 13 has been taken as an indication that this gnomic statement was a popular motto in Lampon's *oikos*; along these lines, it has also been interpreted as a reflection of the close relationship between the epinician poets and their patron.[21] Compared to the close paraphrase of *WD* 412 in *I.6*, however, the allusion in the Bacchylidean ode is far more oblique, thus perhaps appealing to a smaller group within the poem's primary audience with a reference that only those close to Lampon could fully appreciate. If indeed these odes reflect a case of Hesiodic

---

[19] Menander, the Athenian trainer, is included in *N.5* and Ba. *Ode* 13, two odes composed for Pytheas, but not in *I.6*. On the treatment of Menander as indicative of the relationship between Aegina and Athens, see Pfeijffer 1995: 318 and 323–25 with bibliography. Cf. Cairns 2010: 133–34, who has voiced strong objections to proposed readings of Menander's treatment as negative in *N.5* and Ba. *Ode* 13.

[20] See Ford 2010: 149 with a sharp analysis of the passage (and of βροτωφελέα in particular). I suggest that βροτωφελέα is not just an adaptation of the Hesiodic vocabulary, as Ford suggests, but a commentary on its universal value.

[21] Cairns 2010: 324–25 and Maehler 1982: 284–85.

reception in everyday life, finally, they provide an insight into the decontextualized (oral) circulation of individual Hesiodic precepts.[22] Having been
detached from the *WD*, μελέτη δέ τοι ἔργον ὀφέλλει has gained a broader
meaning and applicability, although, as *I.6* attests, it is still identified as
Hesiodic and thus carries the authority guaranteed by Hesiod's authorship.

Assuming that these passages reflect Lampon's reception of *WD* 412 as
an independent motto detached from its original context, it is all the more
interesting that *Isthmian 6* continues to allude to other Hesiodic precepts
in the lines immediately following its complex paraphrase of *WD* 412
(*I.6.70–73*). For instance, Lampon's pursuit of and adherence to measure
(μέτρα μὲν γνώμᾳ διώκων, μέτρα δὲ καὶ κατέχων, *I.6.71*) evokes Hesiod's
admonition in *WD* 694 (μέτρα φυλάσσεσθαι, "keep in mind due measure").[23] Furthermore, the agreement between his prudent mind and his
tongue (γλῶσσα δ᾽ οὐκ ἔξω φρενῶν, *I.6.72*)[24] conforms to the *gnome*:

> γλώσσης τοι θησαυρὸς ἐν ἀνθρώποισιν ἄριστος
> φειδωλῆς, πλείστη δὲ χάρις κατὰ μέτρον ἰούσης·
> (Hesiod, *Works and Days* 719–20)

Among men, the best treasure is that of a sparing tongue, and the greatest delight
comes from a tongue that moves according to measure.

It has also been suggested that Lampon's relationship to his *xenoi* recalls
the ideal attitude towards foreigners in the following Hesiodic lines:[25]

> οἳ δὲ δίκας ξείνοισι καὶ ἐνδήμοισι διδοῦσιν
> ἰθείας καὶ μή τι παρεκβαίνουσι δικαίου,
> τοῖσι τέθηλε πόλις, λαοὶ δ᾽ ἀνθεῦσιν ἐν αὐτῇ.
> (Hesiod, *Works and Days* 225–27)

But those who give straight judgments to foreigners and fellow citizens, and do not
stray away at all from what is just, the city of these men blooms, and the people in
it flourish.

There are considerable differences, however, in meaning and scope
between *WD* 225–27 and *I.6.70*, which cast doubt on whether the

---

[22] Compare the circulation and consumption of Hesiodic poetry through collections of excerpts; see
pp. 16 and 185–87.
[23] For the allusion, see already Bury 1892: 118 and Farnell 1932: 362.
[24] Koning 2010a: 312 claims that γλῶσσα δ᾽ οὐκ ἔξω φρενῶν "is presented as a quality deriving from his
life motto, the Hesiodic line that 'industry advances work'." Koning's interpretation assumes a
logical connection between *I.6.66–69* and 72 that is not in the text; it also limits the meaning of line
72 to honesty, even though the line extolls the consistency between thoughts and words both in
content and in quality. Cf. Kirkwood 1982: 296.
[25] Koning 2010a: 175 n.65.

audience would relate the Pindaric lines to Hesiod's vision of the ideal city. Admittedly, εὐεργεσία in the context of *xenia* (including *xenia* between poet and patron) is a broad term that encompasses a multitude of material and immaterial benefactions; as such, it fails to communicate the emphasis on justice, which is at the heart of the Hesiodic lines. However, if Aeginetan *xenia* was distinct for incorporating legal arbitration, as Kowalzig has tentatively suggested, then it is possible that at least the primary audience of *Isthmian 6* would perceive *I.6.70–72* as praise for Lampon in his capacity as arbitrator for foreigners,[26] and the connection with the Hesiodic passage would be easier to establish. Even though this particular interpretative point must remain tangential, it is clear that, in its final praise for Lampon, *Isthmian 6* not only embeds a paraphrase of *WD* 412 but also clusters echoes of other precepts from the same Hesiodic source immediately after it. By expanding the reception of individual Hesiodic *gnomai* in Lampon's words and deeds beyond *WD* 412, the poem strengthens its evocation of the *WD*, thus perhaps resisting decontextualization to some extent and underscoring the value of the whole.[27]

Pindar's *I.6.66–72* present the victor's father as an embodiment of Hesiodic values, a man who has learned much more from the *Works and Days* than the single gnomic statement paraphrased in lines 66–67. Lampon appropriates both the wisdom of the *WD* and the authoritative voice of its poet. Far more than the poetic voice of the *WD*, however, Lampon is constructed as a man of deeds, who actively applies the wisdom he has acquired and teaches it with his own example, not only with words.[28] Pindar's portrait of Lampon displays Hesiodic admonition as a key element for the success of an individual and his *oikos* within the city-state but also at a Panhellenic level. At the same time, the third-person account as well as the complex paraphrase in *I.6.66–68* allows the poet to channel the Hesiodic voice through Lampon's own, thus keeping it separate from the first-person epinician voice. More on this point shortly.

---

[26] On *themixeny* see Kowalzig 2011: 151–58, who suggests that "on Aegina a form of commercial jurisdiction was in place that, though it may or may not have been formally institutionalized, was practised between parties and was part of Aeginetan self-understanding" (152). Cf. Figueira 1981: 326–32 and Hubbard 2001: 393–94.

[27] On the merits of presenting one's behavior as informed by Hesiodic precepts, cf. sch. *P.4.507*, where the ancient commentator traces Damophilus' laudable tendency not to antagonize noble men (*P.4.285*) directly to *WD* 716: τὸ χ′, ὅτι ἐκ τῶν Ἡσιόδου Ἔργων εἴληπται "(the line bears) the mark χ′ because it has been taken from Hesiod's *Works*." On the χ′, see Deas 1931: 72–76.

[28] *WD* 648–49 (cf. 661–62) imply that the didactic voice derives authority largely from personal experience; he refrains, however, from framing his admonition as his own practice.

I would like to make one final remark regarding the engagement of *Isthmian 6* with the Hesiodic corpus. While the ode draws attention to its reception of Hesiod in its final two strophes, it is possible that it subtly encourages its audience to recall Hesiod and his poetic corpus already in the preceding mythological narrative. According to the Pindaric scholia, the aetiological story of Ajax's name that dominates the ode's narrative (*I.*6.27–56) is drawn from the *Megalai Ehoiai*:

> "τὸν μὲν ἐν ῥινῷ λέοντος στάντα κελήσατο": τοῦτο ἰδίως. οὐ γὰρ ὁ Τελαμὼν ἐκέλευσε τῷ Ἡρακλεῖ ἐμβῆναι τῷ δέρματι καὶ εὔξασθαι, ἀλλ' αὐτὸς ὁ Ἡρακλῆς τοῦτο κατ' ἰδίαν ἔπραξε προαίρεσιν. εἴληπται δὲ ἐκ τῶν μεγάλων Ἠοιῶν ἡ ἱστορία· ἐκεῖ γὰρ εὑρίσκεται ἐπιξενούμενος ὁ Ἡρα-κλῆς τῷ Τελαμῶνι καὶ ἐμβαίνων τῇ δορᾷ καὶ εὐχόμενος οὕτως, καὶ ὁ διόπομπος αἰετός, ἀφ' οὗ τὴν προσωνυμίαν ἔλαβεν Αἴας.
>
> (sch. Pindar, *Isthmian* 6.53a = Hesiod fr. 250 MW)[29]

"(Telamon) bade him, who had stood in his lion-skin": this is said in a peculiar way. For Telamon did not ask Heracles to step on the lion-skin and to pray, but Heracles himself did this on his own. The story has been taken from the *Megalai Ehoiai*. For there we find Heracles being hosted by Telamon and stepping on a lion-skin and praying in this way; also found there is the god-sent eagle, from which Ajax got his name.

The scholiast takes the Pindaric phrase to mean that Heracles stepped *on* the lion-skin rather than that he approached wrapped in it, a detail he reads also in the Hesiodic account. The interpretation of this particular detail is generally dismissed as unreliable;[30] however, the scholion is valuable for preserving information about the *Megalai Ehoiai*, and in particular about the claim to a traditional alliance between the Theban hero and Telamon that was embedded in that Panhellenic poem. Also of interest is the scholiast's remark that Pindar has revised the Hesiodic account in respect to whether Heracles' prayer was invited or spontaneous; this slight revision renders Heracles even more eager to please and benefit his host.[31] Pindar's adaptation of the *ME* paves the way for the much more open and explicit references to the *WD* in the concluding strophes.[32] More

---

[29] Cf. Ps.-Apollod. *Bibl.* 3.162.      [30] See, e.g., Kirkwood 1982: 294.

[31] D'Alessio 2005b: 192–95 suggests that both the *ME* and *I.6* featured Heracles coming to Telamon's wedding as an uninvited guest. If so, the timing of the prophecy before Ajax's birth in *I.6* (as opposed to other versions of the story) would probably be Hesiodic as well. Cf. also Wüst 1967: 199–200 and Hirschberger 2004: 448–49.

[32] Bacchylides' *Ode 5* has been interpreted in similar terms. There, the mythological narrative recounts the encounter between Meleager and Heracles in the Underworld (5.56–175). There is no doubt that the text incorporates several Homeric elements; see, e.g., Lefkowitz 1969: 63–87 and 1976: 43–76,

importantly, it aligns the ode with widely circulating Hesiodic poetry that elevates the prestige of Aegina on a Panhellenic level.

## Chiron: A Hesiodic Voice in *Pythian* 6

*Pythian* 6 celebrates the victory of Xenocrates of Acragas in the chariot race of 490 BCE. Despite the explicit reference to the occasion in its opening lines (1–9), the poem never addresses the victor directly. Instead, it focuses exclusively on his son, Thrasyboulus, who receives praise throughout this ode for the values he upholds.[33] The poem represents the young man as the quintessence of aristocratic excellence: first, it draws a parallel between Thrasyboulus and two exceptional heroes of the past, Achilles and Antilochus (*P*.6.19–42), and then it extolls him as preeminent among his contemporaries (*P*.6.44–54, esp. 44–46). The encomium of Thrasyboulus encompasses many aspects of the aristocratic ideal (*P*.6.47–54), but the most prominent angle through which his excellence shines is his relationship with his father (*P*.6.19–42 and 44–45).[34]

more recently Most 2012: 265–67 and Fearn 2012: 325–29. Yet *P. Ibscher* preserves a similar dialogue between Meleager and Theseus in the Underworld in hexameters, which may belong to the Hesiodic *Katabasis of Peirithous* (Hes. frs. 280–281 MW) and could be a major intertext for *Ode* 5. If so, one could argue that the Hesiodic engagement in the mythological narrative is preparatory for the explicit reference to Hesiod in the final strophe (*Ode* 5.191–94). It is debated, however, whether the fragment in question belongs to the Hesiodic corpus in the first place (see *Minyas* fr. dub. 7 Bernabé with Cingano 2009: 126–28) and whether it provided a model for Bacchylides at all. Instead, Bacchylides may be drawing from a circulating tradition regarding Heracles' own *katabasis* rather than Theseus' (cf. Pindar, frs. 249a and 346 SM; according to Robertson 1980: 287–92, Heracles' *katabasis* was featured in the Hesiodic *Aegimius*). On the *katabasis* of Heracles, see Maehler 2004: 107–09 and Cairns 2010: 83–86. On the possibility of a Hesiodic model for the mythological narrative of *Ode* 5, see D'Alessio 2005b: 236–37. On the ode's engagement with Hesiodic poetry in lines 191–94, see Chapter 1, pp. 16–35.

[33] Pindar's choice to direct his praise towards Thrasyboulus rather than Xenocrates has invited a variety of interpretations. Sch. *P*.6.15 preserves an ancient reading according to which Thrasyboulus was directly involved in his father's victory as his charioteer, and most modern critics find this interpretation plausible; see, e.g., Burton 1962: 20, Carey 1975, Nagy 1990b: 206–14, Kurke 1991a: 156–57, Gentili et al. 1995: 184. If Thrasyboulus was indeed involved in his father's athletic victory, it is surprising that the text is not more explicit about it, given that other odes make a clear distinction between the charioteer and the victor (e.g. *I*.2.20–22, cf. *O*.6.22). On the performative context of *P*.6, see most recently Athanassaki 2012, who successfully combines the two suggested performance scenarios: a public performance at Delphi and a more private, sympotic performance (for the latter, see also Clay 1999a: 30–31). Finally, although genre classification is irrelevant to my argument, I should note here that the uncertainty regarding Thrasyboulus' role has generated a biographical reading of the poem not as an epinician ode but as an erotic encomium motivated by Pindar's personal feelings; see, e.g., Bury 1892: 28–35, Wilamowitz 1922: 139, and Burton 1962: 15–16.

[34] Notice that Thrasyboulus' favorable relationship with his uncle Theron, the future tyrant of Acragas, is linked to his filial devotion in *P*.6.46, even though it is by no means as prominent in this poem as the young man's relationship to his father.

The ode's first laudatory iteration of Thrasyboulos' exemplary attitude towards his father involves a parallel between the Acragantine youth and young Achilles under the tutelage of Chiron:

> σύ τοι σχεθών νιν ἐπὶ δεξιὰ χειρός ὀρθὰν
> ἄγεις ἐφημοσύναν,
> τά ποτ' ἐν οὔρεσι φαντὶ μεγαλοσθενεῖ
> Φιλύρας υἱὸν ὀρφανιζομένῳ
> Πηλεΐδα παραινεῖν· μάλιστα μὲν Κρονίδαν,
> βαρύοπα στεροπᾶν κεραυνῶν τε πρύτανιν,
> θεῶν σέβεσθαι· ταύτας δὲ μή ποτε τιμᾶς
> ἀμείρειν γονέων βίον πεπρωμένον.
> (Pindar, *Pythian* 6.19–27)

Indeed, keeping it at your right hand, you uphold the command which they say that once upon a time in the mountains Philyra's son gave as an admonition to the mighty son of Peleus, when he was away from his parents: on the one hand, to revere most of all gods the son of Cronus, the loud-sounding lord of lightning and thunder; on the other, never to deprive of this honor the allotted life of one's parents.[35]

The ancient scholiast finds in these Pindaric lines a reference to a didactic poem relating Chiron's teachings to young Achilles, which circulated under the name of Hesiod:[36]

> τὰς δὲ Χείρωνος ὑποθήκας Ἡσιόδῳ ἀνατιθέασιν, ὧν ἡ ἀρχή·
> "εὖ νῦν μοι τάδ' ἔκαστα μετὰ φρεσὶ πευκαλίμῃσιν
> φράζεσθαι·πρῶτον μὲν, ὅτ' ἂν δόμον εἰσαφίκηαι,
> ἔρδειν ἱερὰ καλὰ θεοῖς αἰειγενέτῃσιν." (= Hes. fr. 283 MW)
> (sch. Pindar, *Pythian* 6.22)

And they attribute to Hesiod the *Chironos Hypothekai*, the beginning of which is: "Now note well with your shrewd mind these things one by one; first, whenever you come home, perform a fine sacrifice to the eternal gods."

We know very little about the didactic poem entitled *Chironos Hypothekai*, "the Precepts of Chiron."[37] Quintilian informs us that it was considered

---

[35] In line 19 νιν is ambiguous. It refers either to the precept (ἐφημοσύναν, *P*.6.20) or to victory (νίκαν, *P*.6.17); see Gentili et al. 1995: 545–46.

[36] Cf. sch. *P*.6.16: φανερὸν ὅτι ὁ Θρασύβουλος υἱὸς Ξενοκράτους. τὰς γὰρ Χείρωνος ὑποθήκας αὐτῷ διὰ τοῦτο λέγει, ἐπειδὴ τὰς περὶ πατέρων εὐσεβείας περιέχει ("it is evident that Thrasyboulos is the son of Xenocrates. For he mentions the *Chironos Hypothekai* to him for this reason, because this work mentions acts of reverence towards fathers").

[37] See Kurke 1990: 92–95 with a discussion of the cultural value of *Chironos Hypothekai* in the context of aristocratic *paideia;* cf. Friedländer 1913: 571, Schwartz 1960: 228–44, and Lardinois 1995: 226–29. Kurke argues persuasively that the allusion to the *Hypothekai* is part of the ode's evocation of the

Hesiodic until Aristophanes of Byzantium challenged the authorship (Quint. *Inst.* 1.1.15). Thanks to the Pindaric scholia we have these three lines of the poem, and it is reasonable to assume that *P.*6.23–27 preserve two more precepts in paraphrasis, one about piety towards the gods and another about proper behavior towards one's parents. Both *P.*6.19–27 and sch. *P.*6.22 point to moral instruction, and parody of the *Chironos Hypothekai* in Old Comedy also involves practical advice.[38] In addition, evidence from lyric poetry indicates that the poem may have included a prophecy of Achilles' accomplishments and death at Troy as well.[39] Pindar's narrative of Achilles' miraculous accomplishments as a toddler in *N.*3.43–53 may be drawing from *Chironos Hypothekai* too; it is noteworthy (although inconclusive) that the passage evokes poets of the past as its source (λεγόμενον δὲ τοῦτο προτέρων ἔπος ἔχω, *N.*3.52–53).[40] Did this didactic poem have a narrative frame, as is the case for *WD*? We cannot determine based on sch. *P.*6.22 whether the beginning of the instructions coincided with the beginning of the whole poem, and one expects that the poem had at least a proem. *P.*6.21–23 may be hinting at the wider narrative in which the precepts were embedded, but there is no way to confirm this hypothesis. Along the same lines, we have no information regarding the self-representation of the didactic voice,[41] and we are left wondering whether the teachings were presented in a monologue (as in the *WD*) or in a dialogue.[42]

   Since no lines of the *Chironos Hypothekai* survive beyond the fragment preserved in sch.*P.*6.22, we have no idea how and to what extent the original precepts have been reframed and rephrased in *P.*6.23–27.[43] However, we can

---

sympotic culture of homoerotic *paideia* that permeates *P.*6 and accounts for its themes and its erotic tone. On Chiron as the traditional trainer of heroes, cf. Pfeijffer 1999: 214–15 and 228–30.

[38] See, e.g., Cratinus fr. 250 KA and 252 KA; cf. Pherecrates fr. 162 KA, as well as Aristophanes' Δαιταλῆς with Phrynichus *Eclog.* p. 91 Lobeck (=Hes. fr. 284 MW). See Chapter 5, pp. 188–92.

[39] Pi. *N.*3.56–63 with Pfeijffer 1999: 214–15 and especially Bacchylides' *Dith.* 27.34–45 (*Chiron*) with Maehler 1997: 280–82. Cf. Horace *Epode* 13.11–18.

[40] Merkelbach and West include *N.*3.43–63 in the testimonia for *Chironos Hypothekai*; cf. tentatively Most 2007: 296. However, Pfeijffer 1999: 211–13 and esp. 351–52 dismisses the reference to earlier sources as a rhetorical ploy that builds up the credibility of the narrative.

[41] There is no evidence that the poem included a Hesiodic *sphragis*; still, as Quintilian attests, *Chironos Hypothekai* was considered Hesiodic until the Hellenistic era.

[42] Friedländer 1913: 571 n.2 is in favor of a monologue. In his reconstruction of the poem, Schwartz 1960: 244 argues that the poem involved dialogue; his hypothesis, however, depends on the arbitrary attribution of fr. 301 MW to the *Chironos Hypothekai* and on the identification of the speaker with Chiron's mother or wife.

[43] Schein 1987: 242–43 points out that all the key figures in this section (Chiron, Achilles, and Zeus) are defined as sons. The Pindaric text thus establishes and reiterates subtly the centrality of the relationship between father and son.

still trace how the Pindaric text marks its engagement with the didactic poem. As Kurke has shown, the verb παραινεῖν functions as a generic marker for didactic poetry and signals the appropriation of Chiron's didactic voice. Note that the same verb was used in *I.6.68* to mark Lampon's appropriation of the didactic voice of the *WD*.[44] Moreover, the infinitive structures σέβεσθαι and ἀμείρειν aptly reflect the characteristic *infinitivum pro imperativo* of instructions. The Pindaric text thus mirrors at least a formal aspect of the poetic genre it evokes, if not the specific formulation of the precepts in question.[45]

While the ode identifies Chiron as the didactic voice, however, the source for the narrative of Achilles' tutelage remains elusive and Hesiod's poetic authority is buried under a third plural verb φαντί (*P.6.21*). It is rather unlikely that φαντί reflects doubts about the Hesiodic authorship of the *Hypothekai*, since, as far as we know, the first to deny it was Aristophanes of Byzantium (Quint. *Inst.* 1.1.15). On the contrary, assuming that one of the contexts in which the *Chironos Hypothekai* was performed and consumed was the education of aristocratic youth,[46] Pindar's primary intended audience, namely Xenocrates and his elite circle, must have immediately recognized the allusion to the Hesiodic didactic poem. Perhaps, then, we can read φαντί as an 'Alexandrian footnote' *avant la lettre*, a signpost of reflexive annotation that draws the audience's attention to the ode's intertext.[47] Why does the epinician refrain from naming Hesiod? I suggest that, since the paradigmatic function of the *Chironos Hypothekai* relies largely on the exceptional mythological figures involved, the suppression of Hesiod's poetic mediation in *P.6* allows Chiron to retain his didactic authority in its fullest degree. As for φαντί, the plural number of the verb and the absence of an explicit subject underscore the wide reception and circulation of the *Hypothekai*.[48] Φαντί encompasses the plurality of voices that perform Chiron's instructions in various contexts

---

[44] Kurke 1990: 89–91. On *I.6.66–68*, see above, pp. 106–11.

[45] Cf. the infinitives in Hes. fr. 283.2–3 MW.

[46] Kurke 1990. We have no conclusive evidence that other didactic poems featuring Chiron were circulating under different authorship.

[47] On the 'Alexandrian footnote', see Hinds 1998: 1–5, building on Ross 1975: 78. However, Horsfall 1991: 33–34 points out that the signposting is found in pre-Hellenistic literature; cf. Stinton 1976.

[48] Gentili et al. 1995: 546 offer as a parallel *N.3.52–53* (λεγόμενον δὲ τοῦτο προτέρων / ἔπος ἔχω). In both *P.6* and *N.3* the narratives concerning Chiron and Achilles are attributed to unspecified plural sources. However, since there is no firm ground for the assumption that *N.3* alludes to *Chironos Hypothekai* for Achilles' childhood deeds, the plural προτέρων may not stand for Hesiod in the same way as φαντί does in *P.6*. On Pindar's references to unspecified earlier authorities, see Pfeijffer 1999: 351–52 and below, n.49.

(including education), and thus confirms and reinforces the cultural value of the didactic poem.[49] Even though the third plural person of φαντί excludes the epinician *persona loquens*, it nonetheless acknowledges the established authority of the *Chironos Hypothekai* and communicates effectively its wide reception, of which *Pythian 6* itself is a part.

The ode connects seamlessly Chiron's instructions to Achilles and the deeds of Antilochus, the son of Nestor (*P.6.28–42*). As a young hero who sacrificed himself out of filial devotion, Antilochus embodies and exemplifies precisely the values that Chiron promotes in the preceding lines (*P.6.19–27*).[50] In *Pythian 6*, therefore, both poetic traditions, the didactic and the heroic, appear integrated within the value system of the elite, and they emerge as complementary components in the education of the aristocratic youth: Chiron lays out the theory through precepts, while Antilochus teaches by example. The ode's engagement with both didactic and heroic poetry pays tribute to the well-rounded aristocratic *paideia* that Thrasyboulus has received; the parallel drawn between Achilles and Antilochus, on the one hand, and the son of Xenocrates, on the other, underscores that Thrasyboulus has learned his lesson well.[51]

Though distinct in their reception of didactic poetry attributed to Hesiod, both *Isthmian 6* and *Pythian 6* contextualize Hesiodic wisdom within the education of young men and associate didactic poetry with the relationship between fathers and sons. In *Isthmian 6*, Lampon bequeaths to his sons a gnomic statement from the *WD* and teaches it with his own words and deeds. On the other hand, *Pythian 6* evokes Chiron in his guise as a Hesiodic sage to elucidate the ideal of filial love, and Thrasyboulus earns praise for having internalized the Chironian precepts. The two odes, then, offer complementary perspectives on the appropriation of Hesiodic

---

[49] Elsewhere in the Pindaric corpus φαντί indicates widespread traditions. *P.1.52–53*, *P.2.21–23*, *P.4.88–89*, *I.8.46–48*; cf. the use of λέγοντι in *O.2.28*, *O.9.49–53*, and *N.7.84*; λέγεται occurs in *O.6.29–30* and *N.9.39–40*; λέγονται for Peleus and Cadmus in *P.3.88–89*. A variation of this use of φαντί places the origin of the traditions explicitly in the past: *O. 7.54–55*, φαντὶ δ' ἀνθρώπων παλαιαί / ῥήσιες (on the allotment of spheres of influence among the gods); cf. *N. 3.52–53*: λεγόμενον δὲ τοῦτο προτέρων / ἔπος ἔχω (for Achilles' childhood labors). In addition, *P.4.287–89* and *P.7.19–21* use φαντί for proverbial statements that are (presumably) widely circulating. Cf. Mackie 2003: 67–71.

[50] On Thrasyboulus, Antilochus, and the chariot race of *Iliad* 23, see esp. Nagy 1990b: 206–14. Antilochus' death was narrated in the *Aethiopis* although whether he died defending his father in the epic is unknown. On Pindar and the Cyclic epic poems, see Bowra 1964: 284, Nisetich 1989: 1–23, and most recently Rutherford 2015. On the Cycle as part of the Homeric corpus during Pindar's time, see Ford 1997: 87–88; cf. Graziosi 2002: 180–200 with the earliest evidence for the distinction between poems of the epic cycle and Homeric poetry.

[51] Note that the remaining strophe continues to praise the young man for embodying the aristocratic way of living.

didactic: in *Isthmian* 6, it is the father rather than the victorious son who emerges as the embodiment of Hesiodic wisdom, while in *Pythian* 6 it is the son rather than the victorious father. Nonetheless, both poems stress that adherence to Hesiodic teachings brings distinction and success.

Another striking similarity between the two odes pertains to their poetics of reception: in both cases, the epinician *persona loquens* does not engage directly with Hesiod's didactic authority. In *Isthmian* 6, Hesiodic wisdom finds its expression exclusively through the words and deeds of Lampon. In *Pythian* 6, on the other hand, Chiron's precepts are transmitted by an unspecified multitude (φαντί) that not only remains separate from the epinician voice but also obscures Hesiod's authorship completely. Pindar's reception of Hesiodic didactic, then, tends to push Hesiod's authority to the margins; this consistent trait invites comparison to the Bacchylidean reception of the ancient poet in *Ode* 5 (191–94).[52] In Ba. *Ode* 5.191–94, the *persona loquens*, which doubtlessly encompasses the epinician poet, internalizes what is perceived and reconstructed as a Hesiodic message regarding poetics and commemoration. The speaker engages directly not only with the Hesiodic text but also with the authority of this ancient poet. By contrast, while clearly endorsing Hesiodic poetry as beneficial for individuals and cities, the Pindaric *persona loquens* explores it through the mediation of other voices. Although Pindar's lyric poetry is rich in gnomic statements and often unabashed about its Boeotian provenance,[53] his first-person speakers refrain from interacting with Hesiod's authority and wisdom.

## Hesiodic Didactic and Pindaric *Gnomai*

In the final section of this chapter, I would like to articulate a necessary distinction that emerges from the study of odes in which Hesiod's didactic poetry is explicitly evoked. In lyric poetry, gnomic statements attributed explicitly to specific poetic authorities require a different interpretative approach than *gnomai* that simply express ideas also found in other poetic corpora. There is no indication that lyric *gnomai* which overlap in content but not in language with gnomic statements found in the Hesiodic corpus would compel their audience to identify them as Hesiodic unless they were explicitly labeled as such. Unmarked overlaps indicate that the lyric *gnomai* communicate ideas consistent with a mainstream set of beliefs and values, of which Hesiodic precepts are

---

[52] Chapter 1, pp. 26–35.        [53] See, e.g., the *sphragis* in *I*.6.74–75 and the Boeotian pig of *O*.6.90.

but one authoritative formulation. The audience would most probably perceive these lyric gnomic statements as conventional or traditional, not as Hesiodic in particular. In other words, agreement with Hesiod's *gnomai* in content alone could inspire a sense of familiarity and legitimacy, but there is no good reason to assume that it would mark allusions to the Hesiodic corpus in particular.

An illuminating case study for this distinction is the lyric treatment of toil as a necessary condition for success. We have examined closely how *Isthmian 6* approaches this theme within a framework that is marked as Hesiodic; several other epinician odes, however, treat the same theme in their *gnomai* without recourse to Hesiod's authority or verbal echoes of the *WD*.[54] It is noteworthy in this connection that, whenever the ancient scholia involve Hesiodic passages in their explication of Pindaric *gnomai*, they refrain from doing so in the context of a *Quellenforschung*. At several points, the Pindaric scholia (at least in their extant form) quote *gnomai* attributed to Hesiod in order to clarify the Pindaric text rather than to trace the source of its content.[55] For example, the Pindaric scholia quote

τῆς δ' ἀρετῆς ἱδρῶτα θεοὶ προπάροιθεν ἔθηκαν
(Hesiod, *Works and Days* 289)

but the gods have placed sweat before excellence

on three separate occasions. Given that the enjambment ἀθάνατοι in *WD* 290 is consistently omitted, the Hesiodic line may have found its way into the scholia through a collection of excerpts rather than straight from its original context in the *WD*. However that may be, the scholia quote *WD* 289 not as a source but as a parallel passage that can facilitate the

---

[54] E.g. *O.*8.4–7, *O.*10.91–93, *O.*11.4–6, *P.*12.28–29 (followed by a remark about the role of the divine in the dispensation of happiness), *N.*3.17–18, *N.*5.48–49, *N.*6.23–24, *N.*8.48–50, *N.*10.24 and 29–30 (with emphasis on the dependence upon divine favor), *I.*1.41–46 (success as a combination of toil and expenditure; cf. *I.*6.10–13), *I.*5.54–58, *I.*8.1–5; contrast *P.*8.73–77 (on happiness without toil). Cf. Willcock 1995: 15 and, recently, Boeke 2007: 56–57 and 59–64.

[55] In addition to sch. *O.*5.34c, *O.*6.14f, *O.*9.161c, and *P.*3.38c, which I discuss in this section, see also sch. *I.*1.56, which explains *I.*1.40 through Alcman fr. 125 *PMGF* and *WD* 218 (in this order), and sch. *N.*7.127a and c, which quote *WD* 345 and 346 respectively as passages that reinforce Pindar's statement about good neighbors (*N.*7.86–89). Hesiodic didactic is quoted elsewhere too but not in the context of explicating Pindaric *gnomai*. For instance, the only scholion outside the commentary to *I.*6 that quotes *WD* 412 (sch. *N.*6.91b) does so to clarify a word; likewise, sch. *I.*4.81 uses *WD* 325 to clarify vocabulary, whereas sch. *P.*3.64b frames a certain element in the Pindaric narrative (*P.*3.35–36) as a fulfillment of *WD* 240. Cf. sch. *N.*3.1a that includes the general statement about poets in *Th.* 94–95 in the context of explaining the address to the Muse in *N.*3.1; on sch.*P.*6.22, see above (pp. 114–15). Other quotations from the Hesiodic corpus in the Pindaric scholia do not involve gnomic statements. It is noteworthy that two of the scholia that quote Hesiodic *gnomai* misattribute them to Homer (sch. *I.*1.56 and *N.*6.91b).

comprehension of the Pindaric text, presumably because the Hesiodic *gnome* was accessible and familiar to the intended readership of the scholia:[56]

> "πόνος δαπάνα": πονεῖν ἔφη καὶ δαπανᾶν τοὺς ὀρεγομένους ἀρετῆς· καὶ πόνον μὲν τὴν γυμνασίαν εἶπε, δαπάνην δὲ τὴν ἱπποτροφίαν. "τῆς ἀρετῆς ἱδρῶτα θε<οὶ προπάροιθεν ἔθηκαν>" (sch. Pindar, *O.5.34c*)

"pain (and) expenditure": he said that those who strive for excellence toil and spend. And by "toil" he meant the physical exercise, by "expenditure" he meant the keeping of horses. "The gods have placed sweat before excellence."

> "ἀκίνδυνοι δ' ἀρεταί": Ἡσίοδος λέγει· "τῆς δ' ἀρετῆς ἱδρῶτα θεοὶ προπά-ροιθεν ἔθηκαν." ὁ δὲ λέγει ὅτι αἱ ἀρεταὶ αἱ χωρὶς πόνων καὶ κινδύνων οὐκ εἰσὶ τίμιαι οὔτε παρὰ τοῖς ἄλλοις ἀνθρώποις οὔτε παρὰ τοῖς θαλαττεύουσιν ἁπλῶς ... (sch. Pindar *O.6.14f*)

"safe acts of excellence": Hesiod says "but the gods have placed sweat before excellence." And he (*sc.* Pindar) says that acts of excellence which do not involve toils and dangers are held in honor neither by all the other people nor by those who are, in a word, seafaring ...

> "σοφίαι μὲν αἰπυναί": ἢ οὕτως· ὑψηλόν ἐστι καὶ ἐν μετεώρῳ κείμενον τὸ ἀρετὴν ἔχειν. ὡς Ἡσίοδος· "τῆς δ' ἀρετῆς ἱδρῶτα θεοὶ προπάροιθεν ἔθηκαν." (sch. Pindar *O.9.161c*)

"the ways of wisdom are steep": or thus: to have excellence is lofty and elevated up high. As Hesiod (says): "but the gods have placed sweat before excellence."

Sch. *O.5.34c* and *O.6.14f* explicate passages in which toil and excellence are associated with the *laudandus* (*O.5.15–16* and *O.6.9–11* respectively). Sch. *O.9.161c*, on the other hand, reflects on a Pindaric *gnome* (*O.9.107–08*) that seems broad and all-encompassing but, given its context, it almost certainly refers to epinician poetics in particular.[57] In all three cases, the Hesiodic *gnome* is put forward to help the reader understand the broader gist of the Pindaric text.

Even when the scholia point out a (perceived) close affinity between Pindaric and Hesiodic *gnomai*, they still refrain from using language that would explicitly frame the latter as the source of the former. Sch. *P.3.38c*, for instance, elucidates Pindar's generic commentary on people who

---

[56] On these types of scholia, see Nünlist 2009: 11. Notice that, in sch. *O.5.34c*, the source of the poetic quotation remains unstated.

[57] Gentili et al. 2013: 552. While discussing the metaphors of steepness and loftiness, the scholiast in sch. *O.9.161c* cites *WD* 289 rather than *WD* 290, a line that actually describes the path towards virtue as steep (μακρὸς δὲ καὶ ὄρθιος οἶμος ἐς αὐτήν). This choice reinforces the hypothesis that the scholiasts are drawing Hesiodic *gnomai* from an anthology of excerpts, unless the quotation of *WD* 289 is intended to evoke *WD* 289–92 as a whole.

foolishly scorn what is available and chase what is not (*P*.3.21–23) as follows:

> ἐπιχώρια· νῦν λέγει τὰ παρόντα· ἔστι δὲ ὅμοιον τῷ:
> "νήπιος, ὃς τὰ ἑτοῖμα λιπὼν ἀνέτοιμα διώκει" (= Hes. fr. *24/61)
> <div align="right">(sch. Pindar, <i>Pythian</i> 3.38c)</div>

"familiar (things)": now he means the things that are present. This is similar to: "Foolish is he who abandons the things that are attainable and chases unattainable things."

Much like sch. *O*.5.34c, this scholion does not attribute the line to Hesiod. However, the gnomic hexameter was circulating in collections of proverbs, and at least in one such anthology (*Orionis Anthol. Gnom.* 1.25) it is clearly identified as Hesiodic.[58] It is possible, then, that readers of sch. *P*.3.38c would be familiar with Hes. fr. *24/61 and would be able to supply mentally the missing attribution. Notice that the ancient commentator defines the relationship between *P*.3.21–23 and the Hesiodic fragment in terms of similarity rather than dependence. This is particularly interesting when we consider that *P*.3.21–23 are embedded in the story of Coronis and that, in sch. *P*.3.52b, the Pindaric narrative is framed as a reception of the Hesiodic Coronis-*ehoie*.[59] In other words, the scholia preserve a discussion of Hesiodic poetry as a source with which Pindar actively engaged while shaping his ode's narrative elements. Sch. *P*.3.38c, on the other hand, points out that there is common ground between *P*3.21–23 and Hes. fr. *24/61, but does not employ the language of reception nor does it envision Pindar's active engagement with Hesiodic *gnomai*.

Admittedly, it is impossible to know what was lost in the long process of selection and abbreviation that produced the extant corpus of the Pindaric scholia. Nonetheless, the scholia that we have seem to acknowledge the qualitative difference between a direct engagement with Hesiodic poetry and parallel instantiations of common and traditional themes and ideas.[60]

---

[58] The line is attributed to Hesiod also in sch. Theocr. 11.75.

[59] This reading belongs to Artemon of Pergamum; on the reception of the *ehoie* in *P*.3, see Chapter 2, pp. 66–68.

[60] On the conventional nature of gnomic statements, cf. Stenger 2004: 10–20; cf. also 1–6 and 39–56. As I mentioned earlier, I was unable to consult Tom Phillips' *Pindar's Library* (Oxford, 2016).

CHAPTER 4

# Hesiodic Narratives and the Tragedians

No study of Hesiodic reception in Athenian drama can overlook the *Prometheus Bound* (henceforth *PV*), the play that offers the most extensive engagement with Hesiodic poetry in the extant corpus of fifth-century tragedy. Many studies of the *PV* have explored how it appropriates mythological material from the Hesiodic tradition, focusing mainly on the story of Prometheus (*Th.* 521–616 and *WD* 42–105), the Titanomachy (*Th.* 629–731), the Typhonomachy (*Th.* 820–80), as well as the narrative of succession that permeates the *Theogony*.[1] Arguably the most influential book on the play's reception of Hesiodic poetry is Solmsen's 1949 monograph.[2] Solmsen raises some excellent points, but his analysis is hampered by his limited view of what is "genuinely Hesiodic" in the extant text of the *Theogony* and by several arbitrary assumptions based on the belief that the author of the Prometheus-plays is superior to Hesiod both intellectually and morally.[3] The reading proposed in this chapter inevitably reiterates some of the observations made in earlier scholarship. Instead of approaching Hesiodic poetry as a mythological source for the tragedy, however, I examine how the *PV* integrates Hesiodic elements and gradually changes their value in the plot, how the Hesiodic tradition becomes a foil for the tragic version of the story as it is scrutinized and challenged. I suggest that, by inviting juxtaposition to Hesiodic poetry, the dramatization of Prometheus' punishment and restitution draws attention to the limitations of Hesiod's representation of the cosmos. Ultimately, Attic

---

[1] Wilamowitz 1914: 130–42, Grossmann 1970: 85–102, Conacher 1980, esp. 3–20, Lenz 1980, Saïd 1982 and 1985, esp. 115–30, 188–92, 216–17, 260–325, Griffith 1983b, esp. 1–10. See also Vandvik 1943, a rather unsatisfactory study, and Neschke-Hentschke 1983: 395–401. For the *PV*, I use the line-numbers and text (except for 354) in Griffith 1983b.

[2] Solmsen 1949, esp. 124–77. I have opted not to discuss here the reception of Hesiod in the *Oresteia*, partly because Solmsen 1949: 178–224 still offers an excellent reading; cf. now Scully 2015: 101–08.

[3] Solmsen also assumes that the *Prometheia* conforms to patterns traced in Aeschylean plays and trilogies, especially the *Oresteia* and the Danaid-trilogy; on this issue, see below.

tragedy overwrites the Hesiodic narrative of Zeus's rule with its own polyphonic and complex vision.

Ideally, one would explore the reception of the Hesiodic tradition in the entire sequence of plays that included the *PV*, but the lack of information is so great that such an endeavor would face insurmountable difficulties. The scholia to the *PV* indicate that the tragedy was immediately followed by the *Prometheus Lyomenos* (henceforth *Lyomenos*),[4] a play in which Prometheus is liberated and receives restitution (frs. 190–204 Radt). The parody of the *Lyomenos* in Cratinus' *Ploutoi* (430/29 BCE) provides a *terminus ante quem* for the performance of the Prometheus-tragedies in Athens. The *terminus post quem*, on the other hand, is much more elusive,[5] but it seems most likely that the two Prometheus plays were composed (at least in part) and performed after Aeschylus' death.[6] To make things more complicated, there is no secure evidence that these two tragedies were part of a thematically connected trilogy.[7] It is possible that the *PV* and the *Lyomenos* constituted a dilogy performed along with an unrelated third tragedy and a satyr play that may or may not have had some connection to the Prometheus-tragedies.[8] We have no evidence that

---

[4] sch. *PV* 511b and 522. Taplin 1975: 185 and Griffith 1977: 13 suggest that the scholiast's phrase τῷ ἑξῆς may not refer to the sequence of performance but to the order of plays in the scholiast's collection; see, however, West 1979: 130–31, who rejects Taplin's suggestion that the titles *Prometheus Desmotes*, *Lyomenos*, and *Pyrphoros* indicate that the plays do not belong to the same trilogy. Objecting to the sequence *PV–Lyomenos*, Podlecki 1975: 14 and 16 suggests that the trilogy may have included a play between the *PV* and the *Lyomenos* that was set in the Underworld.

[5] It is beyond the scope of this book to delve into the long-standing debate regarding the date and authorship of the Prometheus plays. For a thorough discussion of the evidence (as well as the vast scholarship on the subject), see Bees 1993; earlier studies include Schmid 1929, Méautis 1960, Herington 1970, Griffith 1977, Taplin 1977: 460–69, Saïd 1985: 27–80, Flintoff 1986, Pattoni 1987, West 1990: 51–72, Hubbard 1991b, and Zuntz 1993. For a brief survey of the relevant scholarship, see Lloyd-Jones 2003: 53–54, who nonetheless defends the Aeschylean authorship of the Prometheus plays. Bees 1993 dates the *PV* to ca. 445 BCE based on the play's engagement with Herodotus. For an earlier date (ca. 463 BCE), see, e.g., the arguments summarized by Ruffell 2012: 18. On the parody of the *Lyomenos* in Cratinus' *Ploutoi*, see Chapter 5, pp. 223–24.

[6] Sommerstein 2010a²: 231–32. On the attractive hypothesis that Euphorion, Aeschylus' son, produced the plays while claiming that they were composed by his late father, see Robertson 1938, Dodds 1973: 37–40, West 1990: 67–72 and, more recently, 2000: 339. West has suggested that Euphorion composed a trilogy of his own plays, including the *PV* and the *Lyomenos*, but capped it with the genuine Aeschylean satyr play *Prometheus Pyrkaeus* (originally produced in 472 BCE), and attributed the entire tetralogy to his father.

[7] Aeschylus' *bios* comments on the all-divine cast of the tragedies collectively referred to as his Προμηθεῖς (*Vit. Aesch.* Suppl. d), but there is no indication that these are plays which constituted a thematic trilogy or tetralogy.

[8] For a recent discussion, see Sommerstein 2010a²: 37–38 and 227–28, who follows Brown 1990: 56 in entertaining the possibility that the dilogy was performed at the Lenaea, where tragic poets competed with two tragedies (e.g. Csapo and Slater 1994: 122–24). Focke 1930: 269–70 already argued that the plays were performed as a dilogy, but he envisions a premiere in Sicily. Following Focke, Lloyd-Jones

tetralogies of this structure were staged in fifth-century Athens, but perhaps the *PV* and the *Lyomenos* warranted an exceptional arrangement if they were considered genuine Aeschylean works produced posthumously.

In the absence of evidence for the performance of thematic dilogies, scholars have been much more willing to posit that the *PV* and the *Lyomenos* were part of a trilogy that was (or was deemed to be) authored by Aeschylus. This hypothesis normalizes the plays and fosters the comforting assumption that the mutilated trilogy can be reconstructed to some extent, based on the single Aeschylean trilogy that survives intact, i.e. the *Oresteia*.[9] Assuming that there was a thematically connected Prometheus-trilogy, however, the title and content of the third play, as well as its place in the sequence, are a matter of speculation. The most plausible candidate for the third play is the *Prometheus Pyrphoros*, whose title is included in the catalogue of Aeschylean works (T78 Radt). Yet *Prometheus Pyrphoros* may be just an alternate title for *Prometheus Pyrkaeus*, a satyr play by Aeschylus that was produced in 472 BCE but is absent from the aforementioned list.[10] If the *Prometheus Pyrphoros* was, in fact, the third play of the trilogy, it may have dramatized Prometheus' offenses against Zeus, including the theft of fire and its delivery to humankind; in this case, it would have preceded the *PV–Lyomenos* sequence. On the other hand, one could envision the *Pyrphoros* as the final play of the trilogy, celebrating the end of Zeus's enmity towards mortals, the bestowal of social values upon them, and the foundation of the festival in honor of Prometheus in Athens.[11] At any rate, whether the overarching plot was developed in a dilogy or in a trilogy, its conclusion remains obscure to

1983[2]: 97–103 and 2003: 68–70 suggested that the Prometheus-plays were part of the trilogy, but that the plot of the last play (the *Aetnaeae* according to his reconstruction) was connected very loosely with the *PV–Lyomenos* sequence. For a refutation of the hypothesis that the Prometheus-plays were composed for a Sicilian premiere, see Griffith 1978 and, more recently, Poli-Palladini 2013: 21–23. Nonetheless, building on West 2000: 339, Poli-Palladini 2013: 26–28 suggests that Aeschylus may have composed the *Lyomenos* originally for a Sicilian audience and that, when Euphorion decided to stage his father's tragedy in Athens, he created a tetralogy around it by composing the *Prometheus Bound*, revising extensively Aeschylus' *Aetnaeae*, and adding a re-performance of *Prometheus Pyrkaeus*. On the *PV* as a later composition, see also Schmid 1929 and, more recently, Lefèvre 2003.

[9] See, e.g., the reconstructions proposed in Davison 1967: 98–99 and, more reasonably, Flintoff 1995. Solmsen 1949: 157–77 offers a comparative reading of the *Oresteia*, the Danaid-trilogy, and the Prometheus-trilogy; similarly, Herington 1970: 76–87, Saïd 1985: 326–40 (*PV* and the *Oresteia*). For a critical discussion of the assumptions and fallacies involved in reconstructing Aeschylean trilogies (including the Prometheus-trilogy) based on the *Oresteia*, see Podlecki 1975; cf. Gantz 1980: 144.

[10] See the arguments in Brown 1990: 52–55, who suggests that the *Pyrkaeus* and the *Pyrphoros* are one and the same satyr play, and that possibly the former *epiklesis* replaced the latter in the title by mistake. For a summary on the bibliography regarding this question, see also Radt 1985: 321.

[11] For an overview of the two reconstructions, see Gantz 1980: 142–44 and Griffith 1983b: 282–83. For the former, see extensively West 1979: 131–35; cf. Welcker 1824: 5–18, Pohlenz 1954: 1.77–8, Fitton-Brown 1959, Griffith 1983b: 283–85. For the latter, see Westphal 1869: 216–18, Wilamowitz 1914:

us. Reconstructions in which the plot concludes with the foundation of a festival for Prometheus in Athens are clearly replicating the ending of the *Oresteia*.[12] Likewise, the hypothesis that in the end Zeus granted social virtues to humankind is based on the story that Protagoras recounts about Prometheus in Plato's *Protagoras*, a narrative that closes with the distribution of αἰδώς and δίκη to all men (*Prt.* 322b1–d6).[13] Upon closer examination, however, extrapolating information about the Prometheus-plays from the *Protagoras* proves to be very problematic.[14]

Given the uncertainty regarding the overall plot, I focus my discussion on issues pertaining to the extant text of the Prometheus-tragedies, avoiding as much as possible those aspects of the Prometheus-plot that have been reconstructed based on pure speculation. I must admit that I am

---

129–30 and 142–47, Solmsen 1949: 146–68, Mette 1963: 26–29, Herington 1963a and 1963b, Stoessl 1988: 20–22. For a refutation of both reconstructions, see Brown 1990: 50–52.

[12] See, e.g., Wilamowitz 1914: 142–47, Thompson 1932: 34–35, Solmsen 1949: 153–57.

[13] Lloyd-Jones 1983[2]: 99–103, who assumes that the third play in the Prometheus-trilogy was the *Aetnaeae*, envisions that the trilogy too concluded with the introduction of Dike. He bases this reconstruction on an extensive fragment that features the arrival of Dike and her interaction with a mortal interlocutor (fr. 281a Radt); see also Corbato 1996. Yet the Aeschylean fragment may belong to a satyr drama rather than a tragedy (Wessels 1999, Poli-Palladini 2001: 313–14); furthermore, even if the fragment belongs to a tragedy, the *Aetnaeae* is only one of several potential contexts. For a summary of the relevant scholarship, see Radt 1985: 380 and Sommerstein 2008: 276–79; see also Wessels 1999 with other fragments that may belong to the same drama as fr. 281a+b Radt (most notably 451n Radt). There is no internal indication that encourages a connection with the *PV* and the *Lyomenos*. On the contrary, Dike's commemoration of Zeus's victory over his father as justified retribution (δίκη κρατήσας, fr. 281a.6 Radt; cf. 8–9) resonates to an extent with its celebration in the *Theogony* but departs significantly from Prometheus' assessment of the same event as a crime that earned Zeus his father's curse (*PV* 910–12); cf. Garabo 1986. Although probably useless for the reconstruction of the Prometheus-plot, the Dike-fragment offers an interesting case of Hesiodic reception in drama. The extant passage evokes the Hesiodic image of Dike sitting by the throne of her father Zeus (fr. 218a.10 Radt, *WD* 259–62; assuming Dike refers to Zeus as her father in πατήρ, fr. 281a.7 Radt cf. also *Th.* 902) and dramatizes her presence among mortals (fr. 218a.11–13 Radt; *WD* 220–24). While she retains the punitive function she holds in the *WD* (fr. 218a.19–23 Radt), she also dispenses rewards for just behavior (fr. 218a.16–18 Radt). The fragment dwells extensively on one punishment in particular, as Dike seems to inflict violent war upon the unjust (fr. 218a.30–41 Radt; cf. *WD* 246 vs. 227–28) while presumably granting peace and prosperity to the just (see fr. 451n Radt, if this is indeed part of the same drama, cf. *WD* 227–37). The Aeschylean fragment replaces Zeus's agency in the *WD* with Dike's, but maintains to some extent the Hesiodic idea that justice and injustice affect not only the individual but also the entire community (fr. 218a.28–29; *WD* 240–41). Finally, notice that Dike reveals her name (fr. 218a.14–15 Radt) *after* recounting the first instantiation of her cosmic function (fr. 218a.6, δίκη κρατήσας). In prefiguring an entity through a defining action, the Aeschylean text may be tapping into the same etymologizing strategy found in *Th.* 65–79 (with Pucci 2007: 102–04) and elsewhere in epic, although not exclusively in Hesiodic poetry; cf. Risch 1947, Lendle 1957: 117–21, Mazur 2004 with bibliography, Troxler 1964: 8–28, and Ercolani 2010: 31.

[14] For a brief overview of the problems involved in drawing connections between the story in the *Protagoras* and the Prometheus-plays, see Ruffell 2012: 71–77. Cf. Podlecki 1975: 14–17 on the problems involved in reconstructing a Prometheus-trilogy.

sympathetic to the view that the *PV* was the first play in the sequence of performance, since I find no compelling argument supporting the hypothesis that the *PV* was preceded by a play that dealt with the theft of fire.[15] To begin with, there are very few fragments attributed to *Prometheus Pyrphoros* (208 and 208a Radt), and none of them excludes the possibility that the *Pyrphoros* followed the *Lyomenos* or that the *Pyrphoros* may actually be the satyr drama otherwise known as *Prometheus Pyrkaeus*.[16] Furthermore, the need to insert another play before the *PV* stems largely from the need to create a three-act sequence that deals sequentially with the crime, the punishment, and the reconciliation; this pattern, obviously, does not quite work if Prometheus' release occurs in the second play of the sequence. We should not disregard the fact that the *PV* includes not only punishment but also a new offense, namely that Prometheus refuses to divulge his secret despite Zeus's extortion. More importantly, the urge to fit plays into familiar patterns should not keep us from exploring other possibilities if they allow for a more satisfactory understanding of the whole. If the audience of the *PV* has already watched a play about the theft of the fire, the gradual and prolonged revelation of the reasons for the protagonist's suffering in the *PV* would be pointless and rather tedious. Furthermore, if there was a play that concluded with Prometheus' apprehension and condemnation, the crucial background regarding Zeus's debt to Prometheus during the Titanomachy would fit better in the context of a judgment scene or perhaps in a heated debate between Prometheus and Zeus (or an agent of his). The information may be reiterated in the *PV*, but it is hard to see how Prometheus would miss the opportunity to comment on such a past interaction if he had had one. The same could be said about Prometheus' knowledge of the secret linked to Zeus's fall, since, judging by the Hermes-scene, Zeus finds out about it during the *PV*. Finally, it seems to me that West's attempt to reconstruct the *Pyrphoros* as a reception of the Hesiodic tradition regarding the theft of fire (*Th.* 562–69), complete with a chorus of Meliae (*Th.* 563), disregards the complexities of Hesiodic reception in the Prometheus-plays, which I hope to demonstrate in this chapter.[17] The most obvious problem with West's reconstruction is that Prometheus' bene-factions to humankind, as reported in the *PV*, go far beyond the theft of fire

---

[15] For this sequence, see Pohlenz 1954: 1.77–78, Fitton-Brown 1959, and, especially, West 1979: 131–35; cf. Griffith 1983b: 283–85. Notice, however, that West 2000: 339 refrains from naming the *Pyrphoros* as the third play in the trilogy. For a refutation of the assumption that *Pyrphoros* was the first play of the trilogy, see also Winnington-Ingram 1983: 188–89 and Brown 1990: 52.

[16] For the latter argument, see Brown 1990: 53.

[17] West 1979: 132–35. Griffith 1983b: 284 proposes a broader scope for *Pyrphoros*' plot; however, it is difficult, though not impossible, to see how both the Titanomachy and the theft of fire can be central to the action of one and the same play.

and the Hesiodic tradition. Given the intricate and often subversive nature of Hesiodic reception in the *PV* and in the *Lyomenos*, I am more willing to posit a thematically connected dilogy or a trilogy with a loosely related third tragedy rather than to assume a dramatization of the Hesiodic narrative preceding the *PV.*

In what follows, I examine the multifaceted reception of Hesiodic poetry in the tragic plotline that begins with Prometheus' confinement in the *PV* and ends with his release and restitution in the *Lyomenos*. I explore how the plays invite the audience to approach the tragic Prometheus through juxta-position with his Hesiodic counterpart, and, more importantly, how they engage with the Hesiodic account of Zeus's leadership as a whole. Through the story of Prometheus, the *PV* and the *Lyomenos* channel a polyphonic commentary on Zeus's leadership that underscores his gradual transform-ation from an oppressive tyrant into a champion of reconciliation, integra-tion, and justice. By dramatizing this process, the plays undermine and rewrite the unwavering celebration of Zeus in the Hesiodic tradition. Although the cosmos that the tragedies construct is not entirely consistent with the Hesiodic tradition in its details, it is nonetheless structured in a way that strongly evokes the narrative of the succession in the *Theogony.* In addition to engaging with the Hesiodic *Theogony,* however, I will show that the Prometheus-plays take a critical view of the representation of sex and desire in the Hesiodic *Catalogue of Women.*

## The *Prometheus Bound* and Hesiod's *Theogony*

Given the Panhellenic circulation of Hesiodic poetry and its authoritative status, it is reasonable to assume that fifth-century spectators of the *PV* and the *Lyomenos* would be familiar with the treatment of the conflict between Prometheus and Zeus in the Hesiodic corpus. Both the *Theogony* (521–616) and the *Works and Days* (42–105) represent Prometheus' attitude towards Zeus as antagonistic; his defiance culminates with the theft of fire, which leads to the punishment of Prometheus and the degradation of humankind with the introduction of the first woman. The two Hesiodic accounts are consistent, but, since they belong to different contexts, they emphasize different aspects of the story.[18] The *Works and Days* focuses primarily on

---

[18] For an excellent comparative reading of the two Hesiodic versions, see Clay 2003: 100–28, who is in turn influenced by the structuralist analysis by Vernant 1974: 178–94 and 1979; cf. along the same lines, Judet de la Combe 1996, esp. 269–280, in conjunction with Judet de la Combe and Lernoud 1996, esp. 306–07. See also Lendle 1957: 93–103, West 1966: 307, Duchemin 1974: 59–67, Lamberton 1988: 96–103, Most 1993: 89–91. For a defense of the episode's cohesion against earlier scholarship, see Schmidt 1988.

the consequences that the recovery of fire had for mortals, namely the fundamental change in the human condition following the introduction of Pandora and all the inescapable evils for which womankind is responsible (*WD* 54–105). As a result, the poem offers only a crude two-line summary of Prometheus' first attempt to deceive Zeus (*WD* 47–48), which led to the retraction and stealthy restoration of fire. The *WD* also ignores entirely the fate of Prometheus.[19]

The *Theogony*, on the other hand, demonstrates greater interest in Prometheus' actions, his motivation, and the fate he suffers. The poem introduces Prometheus as a member of Iapetus' troubled progeny and defines him indirectly through the nature of his brothers: Menoetius, who is blasted by Zeus's thunderbolt for his transgression (*Th.* 514–16), Atlas, whom Zeus has burdened with an arduous and confining task (*Th.* 517–20), and Epimetheus, who becomes the source of all evils for men by unwittingly accepting the first woman from Zeus (*Th.* 511–14).[20] As expected from the short genealogical profiles of his siblings, Prometheus too suffers at the hands of Zeus (*Th.* 521–34). The account of his fate follows a reverse temporal trajectory, as it begins with his punishment (*Th.* 521–25) and the partial relief he received eventually when Heracles shot down the flesh-eating eagle with the permission of Zeus (*Th.* 526–34).[21] The poem then proceeds to explain the cause of Zeus's wrath that led to the confinement of Prometheus (*Th.* 535–69), and returns to his inevitable punishment in the concluding lines of the account (*Th.* 613–16).[22]

---

[19] The brief threat that Zeus utters to Prometheus in *WD* 56 quickly shifts from his immortal antagonist to the mortals ("a great bane for you yourself and for men to come"). Compare the gnomic statement that follows the extensive account of Pandora's negative impact upon humankind and concludes the treatment of Prometheus and Pandora (*WD* 105, "thus there is no way to evade the mind of Zeus"). The *gnome* should refer to Prometheus' punishment, since he was the one who actually deceived Zeus (cf. *Th.* 613); yet it seems to be reflecting on the state of humankind instead, given that the poem explores exclusively their punishment but ignores Prometheus'. On *WD* 105 as a reflex of *Th.* 613, see West 1978: 172.

[20] On Prometheus' siblings, see Reinhardt 1960: 195, Lamberton 1988: 95, and Judet de la Combe 1996: 280–85, who is particularly interested in their engagement with the human realm; cf. already Kerényi 1963: 35–38. Taking Judet de la Combe's remarks a bit further, Clay 2003: 114–15 suggests an intriguing (albeit not entirely persuasive) reading of the Iapetid line as a projection of "the fate of men/Giants."

[21] According to the *Th.*, Zeus relaxes his anger against Prometheus and allows Heracles to shoot down the vulture only because he wants to increase the κλέος of his son (*Th.* 530–31). Notice that Heracles does not release Prometheus from his chains as well (cf. Pherecydes fr. 17 Fowler). On the unnecessary athetization of Heracles' intervention (*Th.* 526–34), see West 1966: 313–14.

[22] There is a sharp contrast between the Iapetids and the passages that frame them within the poem, in which Zeus frees gods from confinement and gains their alliance in response: (a) the liberation of the Cyclopes, who reciprocate by granting Zeus the power of the thunderbolt (*Th.* 501–06), and

The *Theogony* constructs Prometheus exclusively as a challenger of
Zeus's intelligence and authority. In the extensive account of the incident at Mecone, the narrator attributes Prometheus' action to his desire
to cheat Zeus (Διὸς νόον ἐξαπαφίσκων *Th.* 537; δολίη ἐπὶ τέχνῃ, *Th.* 540
and 555, δολοφρονέων, *Th.* 550); this assessment is later endorsed and
reiterated by Zeus himself (οὐκ ἄρα πω δολίης ἐπελήθεο τέχνης,
*Th.* 560; cf. δόλου μεμνημένος αἰεί, *Th.* 562). Similarly, the theft of fire
is presented exclusively as an act of deception (μιν ἐξαπάτησεν.../
κλέψας, *Th.* 565–66). In both incidents, the poem underscores Zeus's
anger at Prometheus' actions (*Th.* 551–55, 558, 561, 567–69), but refrains
from ascribing them to Prometheus' concern for mortals, even though
humankind is clearly affected by them (*Th.* 551–52, 563–64, 570–612). The
poem insists on a one-dimensional portrayal of Prometheus as a paradigmatic rival of Zeus; consequently, his punishment, featured prominently as
the frame of the entire account (*Th.* 521–34, 613–16), appears to be well
deserved and confirms the superiority of the divine ruler. Furthermore,
it is noteworthy that the *Theogony* treats the conflict between Zeus and
Prometheus as an independent incident, unrelated to the other challenges to Zeus's authority. The text refrains from making any explicit
connections to the other foes of Zeus but it also shows no signs of Ge's
involvement, an element shared by all other crises that punctuate Zeus's
reign in the *Theogony*: the Titanomachy (*Th.* 617–720), the Typhonomachy (*Th.* 820–80), and the threat posed by Metis' unborn son
(*Th.* 888–900). Still, Prometheus' antagonism and his successful suppression are undoubtedly part of the broader narrative of the poem, which
justifies Zeus's power and celebrates him as the ultimate ruler.[23] Along
with Cronus and the Titans, Typhoeus, and the unborn male successor,
Prometheus emerges as yet another challenger whom Zeus successfully
neutralizes in the course of the poem, thus proving that he deserves to be
the ruler of the cosmos.[24]

(b) the liberation of the Hundred-Handers (*Th.* 617–28), who join the other allies that Zeus has
secured by reciprocity (*Th.* 389–96) and eventually tilt the long battle against the Titans in his favor
(*Th.* 617–720). On the placement of the Iapetids within the *Theogony*, see Clay 2003: 105–07. On
the structure of the Prometheus-narrative in the *Theogony*, see Neschke-Hentschke 1983: 388–90;
cf. the rather superficial reading by Carter Philips 1973: 297–300.

[23] It is often assumed that this celebratory agenda is responsible for the poem's revision of an earlier
version of the events at Mecone in which Zeus was actually duped; see, e.g., von Fritz 1947: 253,
Solmsen 1949: 48–9, and Schmidt 1988: 130–31, who proceeds to debunk the idea.

[24] On the complementarity of the challenges in the Hesiodic narratives, see, e.g., Detienne and
Vernant 1978: 90–92, Saïd 1977, and Blaise 1992 in the context of defending the authenticity of
the Typhonomachy (cf. Saïd 1982: 81–85), Pellizer 1996, Clay 2003: 25.

The audience of the Prometheus-tragedies may have expected the plays to engage with the Hesiodic narratives, and their expectation was perhaps all the greater since, as I discuss below, Aeschylus' Prometheus-themed satyr play, the *Prometheus Pyrkaeus* (472 BCE), seems to have involved extensive interaction with the Hesiodic tradition. Whether there were such preexisting expectations or not, however, the text of the *PV* establishes firm connections with Hesiodic narratives, thus encouraging the spectators to interpret the unfolding plot in part through juxtaposition with the Hesiodic tradition. The prologue of the *PV* draws attention to elements that strongly recall the *Theogony* and programmatically mark the Hesiodic poem as an important intertext for the entire plot. The play has the same starting point as the account of Prometheus in the *Theogony*, namely his confinement in inescapable fetters, and the language of binding which it employs (ἀδαμαντίνων δεσμῶν ἐν ἀρρήκτοις πέδαις, *PV* 6) evokes the Hesiodic text (δῆσε [sc. Ζεύς]δ' ἀλυκτοπέδῃσι Προμηθέα ποικιλόβουλον / δεσμοῖς ἀργαλέοισι, μέσον διὰ κίον' ἐλάσσας, *Th*. 521–22). Even the wedge that Hephaestus drives through Prometheus' chest in *PV* 64–66 can be read as an interpretation and adaptation of *Th*. 522.[25] Prometheus' punishment is, of course, Zeus's will in the *PV* (*PV* 3–4, 12) as it is in the *Theogony*, even if the latter underscores Zeus's agency (*Th*. 521–23) while the former assigns the execution of Zeus's order to a cast of intermediaries (Bia, Kratos, and Hephaestus). Consistent with the Hesiodic account (e.g. *Th*. 542, 548, 571–72), the tragic script clearly situates the unfolding event sometime after Zeus's ascent to the cosmic throne, adding the important detail that Zeus has not held power for very long (*PV* 10–11 and esp. 34–35). Through the presence of Bia and Kratos, two figures marked in the Hesiodic tradition as eternal attendants of Zeus in his capacity as cosmic leader (*Th*. 383–88), the prologue reinforces the impression that the plot takes place in a post-Titanomachic era. In the *Theogony*, Kratos and Bia join Zeus as tokens of his success in securing lasting alliances during the war against his father (*Th*. 389–403).[26] The aetiological tale explaining how Kratos, Bia, and the rest of Styx's progeny became integrated in Zeus's entourage culminates with the etymological appropriation of Kratos into Zeus's own power: αὐτὸς δὲ (*sc*. Ζεύς) μέγα κρατεῖ ἠδὲ ἀνάσσει (*Th*. 403). The *PV* reiterates the connection between Kratos and Zeus's rule not only

---

[25] Griffith 1983b: 96. On ἀποτυμπανισμός, see Allen 2000: 200–01; cf. 25–35 and 293–302 on Prometheus' punishment and reform in relation to Zeus's power in the *PV* and the *Lyomenos*. On the language of magical binding in the *PV*, see Marston 2007.

[26] Unterberger 1968: 24–25.

by shaping the former into a representative and an executive agent of the latter, but also by reiterating the etymological play of *Th.* 403 in the conclusion of Hephaestus' initial address to Kratos: ἅπας δὲ τραχὺς ὅστις ἂν νέον κρατῇ (*PV* 35).[27]

Yet perhaps the most crucial element through which the prologue of the *PV* evokes the Hesiodic tradition and shapes the audience's expectations is the information it reveals regarding Prometheus' crime. When Kratos identifies the reason for Prometheus' suffering, he mentions exclusively the theft of fire (τὸ σὸν γὰρ ἄνθος, παντέχνου πυρὸς σέλας, / θνητοῖσι κλέψας ὤπασεν, *PV* 7–8; cf. *PV* 38), explicitly aligning the background story of the *PV* with the Hesiodic accounts (*Th.* 613–16; cf. *WD* 53–58). Admittedly, Prometheus' transgression is attributed to his favorable disposition towards humankind (*PV* 10–11; cf. 82–84), an element not found in the Hesiodic tradition. Yet it is also framed in terms of an unsuccessful competition of wits against Zeus. Kratos' utterance ἵνα / μάθῃ σοφιστὴς ὢν Διὸς νωθέστερος (*PV* 61–62) can be understood as an iteration of Hesiod's Prometheus, the antagonistic trickster.[28] Even after Zeus's agents depart, the text continues to encourage the assumption that the plot relies heavily on the Hesiodic account: when Prometheus ponders for the first time what led to his punishment (*PV* 107–13), he focuses exclusively on the theft of fire in a fennel stalk (cf. *Th.* 566–67). As soon as he utters his first words in the play, therefore, Prometheus reinforces the impression that his character and his story are profoundly informed by the Hesiodic tradition.

That is not to say that the prologue promises no aberrations at all from the Hesiodic account. In addition to attributing Prometheus' transgressions towards Zeus to his *philanthropia*, the play weaves a non-Hesiodic genealogy for its protagonist. In his first speech, Hephaestus addresses Prometheus as the son of Themis (τῆς ὀρθοβούλου Θέμιδος αἰπυμῆτα παῖ, *PV* 18). While the *Theogony* associates Prometheus with the troubled family of Iapetus, the *PV* defines its protagonist as the son of Themis,

---

[27] On the language of power (κράτος) and violence (βία) associated with Zeus throughout the play, see Saïd 1985: 286–87 and 289–91.

[28] On σοφιστής in the *PV,* see Bees 1993: 143–47, who rightly points out that the word is uttered exclusively by Prometheus' enemies as a negative term. On the sophistic resonances of the play's vocabulary, see Saïd 1985: 83–86. Saïd 1985: 314 also traces in *PV* 61–62 an echo of *Th.* 614–16 (esp. καὶ πολύιδριν ἐόντα, 616). Although, in my view, the assumption of a direct evocation of *Th.* 614–16 in the absence of verbal links is an exaggeration, there is no doubt that *PV* 61–62 recalls the defining characteristic of Prometheus in the *Theogony* as an (ultimately) failed challenger of Zeus's intelligence. Cf. Mousbahova 2007: 48–49, who acknowledges the Hesiodic resonance of *PV* 61–62.

whom Prometheus will later identify with Ge (*PV* 209–10). Clearly, this genealogical pedigree constructs the tragic Prometheus as a somewhat different character than his Hesiodic counterpart, but in the prologue the spectators are left with no further hints regarding the importance of this detail for the plot. Perhaps the most evident and well-developed aberration from the Hesiodic account in the first scene of the play, however, concerns the political context of Prometheus' punishment. As the enforcer of Zeus's order, Kratos expresses pitiless vindictiveness (*PV* 10–11, 36–38, 42–44, 61–62, 71, 76–77, 79–80, 82–83) and even threatens Hephaestus into compliance (*PV* 40–41, 53, 67–68, 73). Hephaestus, on the other hand, disapproves of the severity of Prometheus' punishment (*PV* 12–15, 34–35, 66, 69) and shows reluctance to inflict so much suffering on a kinsman and fellow god (*PV* 39, 45). Both figures agree that no one is free in this world besides Zeus (*PV* 50–51). The harshness of this absolute ruler is never denied, only explained as the mark of a fresh leader (ἅπας δὲ τραχὺς ὅστις ἂν νέον κρατῇ, *PV* 35). The first scene, therefore, introduces the spectators to the political landscape that the cast of the *PV* inhabits, and ushers them successfully into a play preoccupied with dissent, suppression, and the limits of Zeus's power. Both spectacle and dialogue construct Zeus as an oppressor.[29] First established in the prologue, this portrayal of Zeus's leadership contrasts sharply with Hesiod's vision of his rule in the *Theogony*. In the Hesiodic work, Zeus assumes the throne by popular demand (*Th.* 883–85) and no one, neither a character within the poem nor the narrator himself, ever questions or disapproves his decisions, be it the punishment of his many challengers (including his own father), the degradation of humankind, or the consumption of his first wife. While constructing Prometheus' story largely in accordance with the Hesiodic tradition, therefore, the prologue of the *PV* reveals a critical view of Zeus's leadership that subverts and problematizes the Hesiodic panegyric.[30]

By incorporating Hesiodic elements, the prologue programmatically invites the spectators to take into account the Hesiodic tradition in their interpretation of the play. Prometheus' plight seems to be consistent with his Hesiodic story, even though it is contextualized within a different political climate. As the plot moves forward, however, the play diverges

[29] On Prometheus' punishment as a spectacle throughout the play and on its meta-theatrical value, see Cerri 2006.

[30] Saïd 1985: 285–86 rightly points out that the *PV* does not maintain the Hesiodic connection between Zeus and Dike, who is his daughter in both *Th.* 901–02 and *WD* 256–57. Likewise, Zeus is divested of his association with Themis.

more and more drastically from the Hesiodic background it establishes in its prologue. Soon after the arrival of the chorus, Prometheus explains that the cause of his plight was his successful attempt to save humankind from Zeus's malicious plans. In the aftermath of his enthronement, Zeus took care of his fellow gods by allotting them privileges,[31] but, having no regard for the human race, he intended to annihilate it and replace it with a new one (*PV* 228–33). The contrast between Zeus's favorable treatment of his divine allies and his disregard for humankind conveys quite clearly Prometheus' disapproval: the planned annihilation of men is marked as a sign of poor, cruel, and unfair leadership – all the more since the motives behind Zeus's nefarious plans are never revealed. Prometheus' narrative in *PV* 228–41 does not conform to any known tradition. The destruction of humankind and the subsequent creation of a new race of mortals is the core narrative in the account of the three earliest races of men in the *WD* (109–55). Zeus exterminates the Heroic race as well, but no anthropogony follows; evidently, the Iron race is what remains of the mortal population when the heroes go extinct (*WD* 156–201). The divinely orchestrated attrition of the mortal population by means of killing the heroic race also features elsewhere in the Hesiodic corpus (*Catalogue* fr. 110/204.96–123; see esp. 98–99 γένος μερόπων ἀνθρώπων / πολλὸν ἀϊστῶσαι σπεῦδε with a potential echo in *PV* 232–33, ἀλλ᾽ ἀϊστώσας γένος / τὸ πᾶν) as well as outside the Hesiodic tradition (*Cypria* fr. 1).[32] None of these traditions, however, includes a salutary intervention of Prometheus. The only story of mass destruction that involves Prometheus is the Great Flood, after which the only survivors, Pyrrha and Deucalion, create a new race of men out of stones. The Flood is not found in Homeric poetry and was almost certainly not narrated in the Hesiodic *Catalogue* either, even though the genealogical poem dealt with Deucalion and his progeny.[33] The earliest attestations of the Flood story and the miraculous anthropogony that followed are found in a play by Epicharmus (*Promatheus* or *Pyrrha*, frs. 113–20 KA = 120–95

---

[31] This remark is consistent with the Hesiodic account in *Th.* 883–85. Later, Prometheus claims responsibility for Zeus's distribution of privileges as well, but no details are given regarding his (presumably advisory) role (*PV* 439–40).

[32] Scodel 1982: 36–40; cf. *Il.* 1.1–3 with Clay 1999b and Allan 2008: 209–10. On correlating the various traditions regarding past human races, and on the challenges such an endeavor entails, see, e.g., Schmitt 1975, Koenen 1994, Mayer 1996, Arrighetti 1998: 449–50 and 458–60, Cerutti 1998, Most 1998, Clay 2005, González 2010: 382–91, Scodel 1982 and 2014: 65–68.

[33] See also the anthropogony in Hes. fr. *16/234, which nonetheless does not necessarily presuppose the Flood. See Scodel 1982: 43–44, West 1985a: 50–56, esp. 55–56, West 1994: 133–34, Bremmer 1999: 44; cf. Hirschberger 2004: 171–76, who appears reluctant to exclude the Flood from the Hesiodic corpus and suggests that it may have been assumed in the *Catalogue* even if it was not narrated.

RN)[34] and in Pindar's *O.*9.41–61. Pindar's account, which situates the survivors in mainland Greece (Opous), makes no reference to Prometheus, but instead underscores Zeus's agency in terminating the flood (*O.*9.52–53) and in the creation of the new race of men (*O.*9.42–46; cf. his intervention in 57–61).[35] On the other hand, Epicharmus' play, which integrates Deucalion and Pyrrha in Sicilian territory (cf. Hyginus, *fab.* 153), attributes to Prometheus not only the theft of fire but also the instructions for the construction of the ark that saves Deucalion and Pyrrha from the Flood (fr. 113 KA).[36] It has been suggested that in *PV* 228–41 Prometheus alludes to the rescue of Deucalion and Pyrrha from the Great Flood.[37] Yet rescuing two individuals hardly counts as averting a mass destruction, which is what Prometheus claims to have done. In addition, a new race of mortals out of stone would serve rather than oppose Zeus's intention to create a new human race.

Since Prometheus' account in *PV* 231–38 is so selective in its details, the spectators remain in the dark not only about Zeus's motives for annihilating humankind, but also about the details of his plan and the specifics of Prometheus' intervention. Instead, the protagonist focuses exclusively on the pitiless divine wrath he incurred and the cruel punishment he suffers as a result (*PV* 237–41). When the chorus inquires whether he committed additional transgressions, Prometheus mentions that he curbed the ability of mortals to foresee their own death, thus instilling into them blind hope (*PV* 247–51), and finally adds that he also bestowed upon them fire and the technology it entails (*PV* 252–54). Prometheus offers no further explanation here, but he elaborates in the second episode with a detailed catalogue of his benefactions to

---

[34] For a discussion of the several titles attested for the same play, see *DTC*² 1962: 265–66 and, more recently, Rodríguez-Noriega Guillén 1996: 97; cf. Rusten 2011: 71.

[35] Cf. Hes. fr. *16/234.2–3 as well as Acusilaus fr. 35 Fowler with no mention of Zeus. On the word-play between λᾶες (stones) and λαοί (people) in the case of Deucalion's anthropogony, see Pi. *O.*9.44–46 and Epicharmus fr. 120 KA; see Rodríguez-Noriega Guillén 2012: 82.

[36] Epicharmus lived at the time of Hieron, and, since Aeschylus visited Syracuse at the time (*Vita* 8–11=T1.27–47 Radt; cf. T88–92 Radt), it is very likely that the two dramatists got acquainted with each other and their oeuvres (cf. sch. Aesch. *Eum.* 626). Whether there is any relationship between Epicharmus' play and the *PV* is a debated matter that hinges largely upon the dating of the tragedy. It is much more plausible to talk about a relationship between Epicharmus' *Promatheus* or *Pyrrha* and Aeschylus' satyr drama *Prometheus Pyrkaeus* (discussed below). On Epicharmus and Aeschylus, see *DTC*² 1962: 265–68, Griffith 1978: 116–17, Flintoff 1986, Bees 1993: 24–26 (with extensive criticism of Flintoff's arguments), and Kerkhof 2001: 136–40; cf. Rodríguez-Noriega Guillén 2012: 82 and 85–86.

[37] See Thomson 1932: 147, Caduff 1986: 101–02, and especially West 1994: 129–44, who argues that the *PV* draws the association of Prometheus with the Flood from the epic *Titanomachy*, which was itself influenced by Near Eastern literature and, in particular, the *Atraharsis* (cf. Bremmer 1999: 44).

humankind. Just as in the first episode (*PV* 247–51 and 252–54), Prometheus focuses first on the enhancement of human perception and intelligence (*PV* 442–50), and then divulges a long list of practical improvements he brought upon human life. Thanks to him, mortals took control over their natural environment and their own bodies, acquired mathematics and writing, and even gained insight into the future through various oracular techniques (*PV* 450–68, 476–506). Prometheus aptly sums up his pivotal role as the source of human civilization with the line πᾶσαι τέχναι βροτοῖσιν ἐκ Προμηθέως (*PV* 506).[38]

By the end of the second episode, the play has completed its construction of Prometheus as a civilizing figure, a πρῶτος εὑρετής and a teacher[39] of human technology.[40] As the bestowal of fire on mortals, the only transgression with which Prometheus is charged in the prologue, is contextualized within a broader tapestry of benefactions, it becomes clear that the protagonist of the *PV* exceeds the Hesiodic parameters established for his character in the opening scene. The tragic Prometheus saved humankind from annihilation and changed the way mortals perceive their present and their future; furthermore, he granted them access to the divine element of fire, but he also taught them how to use it and paved the way to technological development. The gradual expansion of Prometheus' role as a civilizer corresponds to an incremental departure from the Hesiodic tradition, which ultimately becomes a foil that casts in sharper relief the richness of Prometheus' figure as developed in the *PV*.

---

[38] Vernant 1974 and other readings based on his work (e.g. Saïd 1985: 118–22) interpret the element of fire in the two Hesiodic poems strictly as the fire of sacrifice (*Theogony*) and as the fire of alimentation and cooking (*WD*). The *PV*, therefore, shows a dramatic shift in the value of fire, since it emphasizes its application in technology. While the structuralists' approach has its heuristic merits, the Hesiodic discourse about fire is far less restricting in its formulation than they admit. A careful consideration of the language in *Th.* 563, 566, 569, *WD* 50 (which structuralists read in conjunction with *WD* 42), 55, and 57 reveals that the Hesiodic fire could be understood as all-inclusive or at least as not excluding the potential for technology.

[39] In the second episode, Prometheus makes extensive use of language that underscores his role as an inventor: ἐξηῦρον, 460, κἄζευξα πρῶτος, 462, οὔτις ἄλλος ἀντ' ἐμοῦ /... ηὗρε, 467–68, τοιαῦτα μηχανήματ' ἐξευρών, 469, οἵας τέχνας τε καὶ πόρους ἐμησάμην, 477, τρόπους δὲ πολλοὺς μαντικῆς ἐστοίχισα / κἄκρινα πρῶτος, 484–85, τίς /φήσειεν ἂν πάροιθεν ἐξευρεῖν ἐμοῦ; 502–03. He occasionally shifts the emphasis to the transmission of information: ἔδειξα, 458 and 482, ἐγνώρισ(α) 487, δυστέκμαρτον εἰς τέχνην / ὥδωσα θνητούς, 497–98 cf. ἐξωμμάτωσα, 499. Notice by contrast that Prometheus' discourse in the first episode grants humans an active role in their technological development (Χο. καὶ νῦν φλογωπὸν πῦρ ἔχουσ' ἐφήμεροι; / Πρ. ἀφ' οὗ γε πολλὰς ἐκμαθήσονται τέχνας, *PV* 253–54). On the πρῶτος εὑρετής in the *PV*, see Kleingünther 1933: 66–94.

[40] As Griffith 1983b: 167–68 and 176 points out, the *PV* refrains from crediting Prometheus with the development of social and ethical values, such as justice or piety.

The gradual displacement of the Hesiodic intertext from the center of Prometheus' story to its margins is evident in the position that fire holds in the long list of technological knowledge that Prometheus claims to have imparted to mortals. In the prologue, fire is synonymous with Prometheus' crime, and, in the first episode, it is discussed as the source of *technai* (*PV* 254). Yet Prometheus' extensive catalogue of cultural and technological advancements in the second episode does not dwell on the use of fire, not even when he mentions metallurgy (*PV* 500–04). Fire is prominent only in the context of prophecy performed during sacrifice:

> κνίσῃ τε κῶλα συγκαλυπτὰ καὶ μακρὰν
> ὀσφῦν πυρώσας δυστέκμαρτον εἰς τέχνην
> ὥδωσα θνητούς, καὶ φλογωπὰ σήματα
> ἐξωμμάτωσα πρόσθεν ὄντ' ἐπάργεμα.
> *(Prometheus Bound 496–99)*

Having burnt the thigh-bones covered in fat and the long chine, I set the mortals on the road towards a skill that is hard to figure out based on signs, and I opened their eyes to flaming-red signs that were obscure (to them) before.

Prometheus describes how he initiated a certain sacrificial ritual (πυρώσας). Even though this is not explicitly described as the first sacrifice ever performed, we can infer at the very least that Prometheus is credited here with the origins of blood sacrifice involving the incineration of animal parts (which was previously impossible without fire) and some mantic activity (φλογωπὰ σήματα / ... πρόσθεν ὄντ' ἐπάργεμα).[41] The focus on the detail of burning bones wrapped in fat (*PV* 496–97) recalls the aetiological connection established in Hesiod's *Theogony* (535–57) between Prometheus and this particular sacrificial practice. The Hesiodic poem traces the origin of this custom to Prometheus' attempt to outsmart Zeus at Mecone: Prometheus divided the meat into two different types of portions and Zeus chose bones wrapped in fat rather than the portion that contained the edible meat. The *Theogony* treats this incident primarily as a challenge to Zeus's authority, the first act of a transgressor who eventually gets the punishment he deserves (*Th.* 613–16). Nonetheless, the passage concludes with a brief aetiology that traces to this incident the practice of burning bones wrapped in fat on altars and eating the rest of the sacrificial animal (*Th.* 556–57).[42] In the *PV*, Prometheus has a more

---

[41] On the medical language in these lines, see, e.g., Garson 1984: 126.

[42] Cf. Stoddard 2004: 148–49 and 170–72, who reads this *aition* and similar proleptic statements as part of the poem's ubiquitous goal "to explain and reveal the relative positions of god and man in the cosmos as it has evolved."

direct involvement in the establishment of the ritual but also a different motive.[43] The play, then, hints at a Hesiodic aetiology right before it reconfigures it into a different *aition*, thus reiterating the idea that this tragic Prometheus is by no means a replica of his counterpart in the *Theogony*. The protagonist does not suffer for deeds driven by a desire to antagonize the cosmic ruler, even if he speaks of sacrifice not in terms of pleasing the gods, but in terms of granting mortals yet another way to access oracular insight.

Prometheus' wide-ranging list of benefactions is never questioned or viewed as a by-product of his antagonism with Zeus until the final scene. When Hermes comes to extort information from Prometheus on behalf of Zeus, his attitude towards the protagonist is strongly reminiscent of Kratos' in the prologue:[44]

> σὲ τὸν σοφιστήν, τὸν πικρῶς ὑπέρπικρον,
> τὸν ἐξαμαρτόντ᾽ εἰς θεοὺς ἐφημέροις
> πορόντα τιμάς, τὸν πυρὸς κλέπτην λέγω·
> *(Prometheus Bound* 944–46)

You, the clever one, the one who is harshly ill-tempered beyond measure, the one who committed a crime against the gods by giving privileges to those who live for a day, the thief of fire, you I address.

Hermes reiterates Kratos' minimalist view of Prometheus as the treacherous thief of fire; he also addresses Prometheus as a σοφιστής (*PV* 944), which recalls Kratos' utterance in *PV* 61–62 but lacks the competitive element implied in the comparative σοφιστὴς ... Διὸς νωθέστερος (*PV* 62). When the prologue and the final scene are considered together, there seems to be a consistent dissonance between Prometheus' account of his deeds and their reductive representation in the words of Zeus's henchmen. In the prologue, the underestimation of Prometheus contributes to the evocation of the Hesiodic tradition, but, by the time Hermes reiterates it in the final scene, the play has revised its relation to the Hesiodic narrative and has constructed its own version of the past that contrasts sharply with the Hesiodic tradition. At this late stage in the plot, therefore,

---

[43] Cf. Griffith 1983b: 176, whose discussion of *Th.* 535–61 in relation to *PV* 496–99, however, emphasizes exclusively the different outcome for humankind: an "unalloyed blessing" in the *PV* but miseries in the *Theogony*; on this point, see below. Even if one were to follow Griffith in assuming that *Th.* 535–37 implicitly represents Prometheus as the *heuretes* of burnt sacrifices, there is no doubt that in the *PV* Prometheus' engagement with humankind is much more direct. The sacrificial practice is not represented as a commemoration of a single ancient event but as knowledge that Prometheus shared with the mortals for repeated use.

[44] On the similarities between Kratos and Hermes, see, e.g., Reinhardt 1960: 218 and Griffith 1983b: 253.

the reduction of Prometheus' actions to a single act, namely the theft of fire, appears to invite a reinterpretation: rather than triggering an allusion to the Hesiodic tradition, it represents the perspective of Zeus and like-minded gods, who have no interest in humankind and thus are only concerned with the theft of fire probably because, of all the deeds of Prometheus, this alone deprived gods of an element that used to be exclusively theirs.

Finally, while departing from the Hesiodic portrayal of Prometheus as a challenger of Zeus and constructing him as a civilizing hero instead, the *PV* not only reconfigures Prometheus' relationship with Zeus but also discards the Hesiodic vision of human history. In both the *Theogony* and the *WD*, the element of fire seems to have been accessible to men before Zeus withheld it in reaction to the incident at Mecone (*Th.* 562–69, esp. 563 οὐκ ἐδίδου μελίῃσι πυρὸς μένος ἀκαμάτοιο; *WD* 47–52, esp. 50, κρύψε δὲ πῦρ). Thus both Hesiodic accounts envision a fall of humankind into an inferior state of existence. When Prometheus remedies somewhat the human plight by restoring fire,[45] Zeus retaliates with the creation of Pandora, the ultimate deception. Through Pandora, Zeus finalizes the terms of human existence and defines human nature as both separate from and inferior to that of the immortals. In the world of the *PV*, humankind follows a different trajectory.[46] Prometheus averts the scenario of successive and mutually exclusive human races that defines human history in the *WD* (109–201). Instead, informed by more recent anthropological views, the play envisions the trajectory of humankind through time as a linear progression from savagery to civilization, in which Prometheus acts as a crucial catalyst.[47]

It is evident, then, that the *PV* uses the Hesiodic tradition as a foil that ultimately highlights the play's own version of Prometheus as well as of his relationship to Zeus and to humankind. As I pointed out in my

---

[45] *Th.* 535–36 indicates a world where mortals and immortals converse and feast together; cf. the presentation of the first woman/wife to a gathering of gods and men in *Th.* 586.

[46] As Saïd 1985: 120–21 points out, in the *Theogony* and the *WD* fire is defined by ambiguity, since its restoration among mortals is both good and detrimental. This is not the case in the *PV*.

[47] For a brief overview of the intellectual context that informs the anthropology of the *PV*, see Griffith 1983b: 166–68; cf. also Kleingünther 1933, Edelstein 1967: 3–56, Dodds 1973 (see esp. 4–7 and 26–44 on the *PV*), and Podlecki 2005: 16–27. For a juxtaposition between the fate of humankind in the Hesiodic tradition and in the *PV*, see Grossmann 1970: 15–17 and Saïd 2006. On the impact of Prometheus' gifts, see also Benardete 1964: 127–135. I am not persuaded by Sommerstein 2010b: 183–84, who suggests that the *PV* does not exclude a Golden Age for humankind under Cronus, during which mortals lived a happy and blissful life devoid of intelligence. Presumably, they would still have the paralyzing anxiety of death that Prometheus removes (*PV* 248–50).

discussion of the prologue, however, even when Prometheus' story appears to be most consistent with the Hesiodic tradition, the political landscape that the play's characters inhabit is dominated by Zeus's oppressive regime and is thus at odds with the positive vision of the god's reign in the *Theogony*.[48] The *PV* (and subsequently the *Lyomenos*) uses Prometheus' plight as a gateway through which it explores Zeus's rule, its history and its values. The broad scope of the dramatic engagement with Zeus as a leader is facilitated by the fact that the plays embed Prometheus in the cosmic narrative of succession and power struggle.

In the *PV*, Prometheus is an indispensable thread in the fabric of Zeus's power. In the past, he imparted the guile (δόλῳ, *PV* 213; cf. αἱμύλας μηχανάς, *PV* 206) with which Zeus won the Titanomachy and became supreme leader;[49] currently, he holds the secret that Thetis is fated to bear the son who will overpower and overthrow Zeus. His knowledge comes from his mother Themis/Ge, and the genealogical connection hints at the fact that Prometheus has assumed in the play the role that Gaia (Ge) holds in the *Theogony* as Zeus's advisor both in his battle against the Titans (*Th.* 624–28) and with regard to the impending threat from the son fated to be born of a specific consort, Metis (*Th.* 889–93).[50] Prometheus' un-Hesiodic genealogy also means that Zeus is divested of his close Hesiodic association with Themis. In the *Theogony*, the appropriation of Themis as one of Zeus's consorts reinforces his legitimacy as a supreme ruler and links him inextricably with Eunomia, Dike, and Eirene, three fundamental social values (*Th.* 901–03). In the *PV*, however, Ge/Themis is more closely associated with Prometheus than Zeus, and, as we will see below, the legitimacy of Zeus's rule is not left unchallenged.[51] Prometheus recounts briefly to the chorus his involvement in the Titanomachy as a preamble to explaining the causes of his suffering. Acting as a proxy for his mother, he offered the secret of victory first to the Titans (*PV* 204–08, 214–15), a choice he subtly justifies by reminding his audience of their shared pedigree (*PV* 204–06). When they rejected his proposed strategy

---

[48] For a reading of Zeus's tyranny in the *PV* as a reflex of Athenian discourse about power and leadership after the Persian Wars, see, e.g., Grossmann 1970: 272–90.

[49] Saïd 1985: 88–89.

[50] The genealogy may be an innovation of the dramatist, as Reinhardt 1949: 58–59 has argued (for whom the playwright was Aeschylus), or it may have been already established in Attic cult, as Pohlenz 1954: 65–66 has suggested.

[51] See esp. νεοχμοῖς δὲ δὴ νόμοις / Ζεὺς ἀθέτως (Bentley: ἀθέσμως mss.) κρατύνει (*PV* 150–51) with Flintoff 1984; cf. Di Benedetto 1978: 59–60 n.16, Griffith 1983b: 117 and Saïd 1985: 285–86. On Themis and θέμιστες, cf. Rudhardt 1999: 15–52, who nonetheless privileges the oracular semantics of θέμιστες in the association between Ge and Themis found in the *PV* (cf. Verdenius 1976: 456).

in favor of physical violence, however, Prometheus (with Ge's agreement) offered the same advice to Zeus, who took it, thus securing his victory (*PV* 216–21).

From a rhetorical perspective, the account lends effective support to the claim that Zeus failed to reciprocate Prometheus' benefaction (*PV* 221–23). Other divine allies were rewarded when Zeus came to power (*PV* 229–30; cf. *Th.* 885), but Prometheus, the most crucial ally of them all, received merciless punishment for thwarting Zeus's plans for humankind. Prometheus uses his Titanomachic account as a vantage point to portray Zeus explicitly as an ungrateful, distrustful, and pitiless tyrant (*PV* 222–25; cf. 240–41), but he undermines Zeus's leadership in more subtle ways as well. To begin with, it does not inspire much confidence that Zeus did not enjoy the crucial support of Ge and Prometheus from the beginning, but only after the Titans failed to appreciate Ge's wise insight (*PV* 216–18).[52] Equally unflattering for Zeus is Prometheus' representation of the two sides in the long Titanomachic war:

> ἐπεὶ τάχιστ' ἤρξαντο δαίμονες χόλου
> στάσις τ' ἐν ἀλλήλοισιν ὠροθύνετο,
> οἱ μὲν θέλοντες ἐκβαλεῖν ἕδρας Κρόνον
> ὡς Ζεὺς ἀνάσσοι δῆθεν, οἱ δὲ τοὔμπαλιν
> σπεύδοντες ὡς Ζεὺς μήποτ' ἄρξειεν θεῶν
> (*Prometheus Bound* 199–203)

As soon as the gods started being angry, and mutual strife was rising up among them, one faction because they wanted to overthrow Cronus from his throne so that Zeus might be king (indeed!), and the other striving for the opposite so that Zeus might never rule over the gods ...

The Titanomachy is viewed as a power struggle between two factions. Zeus's opponents fought to prevent him from taking the throne; if they ever shared an allegiance to Cronus, Prometheus silences it and foregrounds instead the urgency to resist Zeus. What defines this faction is their rejection of Zeus as an aspiring ruler. The Olympian faction, on the other hand, is exclusively interested in usurping the throne. Prometheus offers no justification for their actions other than hunger for power. Neither Prometheus nor any other character in the play implies that Cronus was an undesirable ruler or mentions his attempt to prevent the birth of a successor by eating his children. This horrendous act of cannibalism defines Cronus

---

[52] Saïd 1985: 203 rightly underlines that the prophecy involved in the Titanomachy of the *PV* is impartial.

in the Hesiodic tradition and ultimately prompts Rhea to conspire with Gaia (Ge) in order to save Zeus (*Th.* 459–500). The play divests Cronus of the vice that precipitates his fall in the Hesiodic narrative. In Prometheus' version of the Titanomachy (*PV* 199–203), Cronus is deposed simply because Zeus and his supporters desire power.

In two subsequent passages that complement his Titanomachic account, Prometheus frames Zeus's ascent to the throne as an incident of interfamilial violence that is bound to be avenged. When Prometheus hints at Zeus's fall in *PV* 516, he claims that the future is in the hands not only of the three Fates but also of "the mindful Erinyes" (Μοῖραι τρίμορφοι μνήμονές τ᾽ Ἐρινύες). Later, while discussing the threat that looms over Zeus, Prometheus treats Cronus as an injured father, whose curse upon his usurping son will be fulfilled when Zeus begets the son that is fated to vanquish him:

> πατρὸς δ᾽ ἀρὰ
> Κρόνου τότ᾽ ἤδη παντελῶς κρανθήσεται,
> ἣν ἐκπίτνων ἠρᾶτο δηναιῶν θρόνων
> *(Prometheus Bound* 910–12)

. . . and then already the curse of his father Cronus, which he uttered as he was falling from his ancient throne, will be completely fulfilled.

The curse that Cronus is said to have released in his downfall is unparalleled in extant literature, and yet rather familiar:

> τοὺς δὲ πατὴρ Τιτῆνας ἐπίκλησιν καλέεσκε
> παῖδας νεικείων μέγας Οὐρανός, οὓς τέκεν αὐτός·
> φάσκε δὲ τιταίνοντας ἀτασθαλίῃ μέγα ῥέξαι
> ἔργον, τοῖο δ᾽ ἔπειτα τίσιν μετόπισθεν ἔσεσθαι.
> (Hesiod, *Theogony* 207–10)

And their father, great Ouranus, was calling the children whom he himself begot by the nickname "Titans," chiding them; and he was saying that, straining, they performed a grand deed in their wickedness, and that later, in the future, there would be vengeance for this deed.

In the *Theogony*, Ouranus declares that his castration is bound to be avenged in the future. His expectation that his transgressive progeny will suffer in the future for their violence towards him is not only explicit but also implicit in the perceived etymological connection between Τιτῆνες and the noun τίσις.[53] Later in the *Theogony*, when Rhea conspires with

---

[53] On the perceived etymological connection between Τιτῆνας and τίσις as well as τιταίνω, see Risch 1947: 77 and Troxler 1964: 33.

Gaia (Ge) to ensure the survival of Zeus and envisions her son as instrumental in Cronus' punishment, the text evokes Ouranus' Erinyes:

> ... ὅπως λελάθοιτο τεκοῦσα
> παῖδα φίλον, τείσαιτο δ᾽ Ἐρινὺς πατρὸς ἑοῖο
> παίδων <θ᾽> οὓς κατέπινε μέγας Κρόνος ἀγκυλομήτης.[54]
> (Hesiod, *Theogony* 471–73)

... in order that she might escape notice giving birth to her dear son, and that she
might make (Cronus) pay the Erinyes of her father and of her children whom
great crooked-counseled Cronus had swallowed.

When Zeus vanquishes the Titans and imprisons them in Tartarus (*Th.*
717–20), he inadvertently executes his mother's plan, in that he avenges
their offense against Ouranus. Unlike Cronus' crime against his father,
Zeus's victory over the Titans is followed not by yet another promise of
τίσις but by a unanimous acknowledgement of his leadership. In the *PV*,
on the contrary, the Erinyes wait to exact vengeance upon Zeus himself
(*PV* 516). When Prometheus talks about Zeus's ascent to the throne as a
transgression against his father that warrants a curse and promises to be
avenged (*PV* 910–12), he models Zeus after Hesiod's Cronus.[55]

   Through the words of Prometheus, therefore, the *PV* reconstructs the
Titanomachy in a way that departs radically from the Hesiodic tradition,
and this departure extends beyond Prometheus' enhanced role as Ge's
mouthpiece. As mentioned above, the Hesiodic Titanomachy justifies
Zeus's war against Cronus as retribution for Ouranus' castration and
removal from power. It displays Zeus's fierceness in battle (*Th.* 687–712)
and celebrates him as the sole recipient of Ge's support and unfailing
advice during his struggle to overpower the Titans.[56] Zeus emerges as an
intelligent and effective leader who can build lasting alliances based on
reciprocity even with gods of an older generation, as demonstrated in the
case of Styx and her progeny (*Th.* 386–403) but also in the liberation of the
Hundred-Handers at Ge's advice, a stratagem that ultimately wins the war
for Zeus and his army (*Th.* 617–28, 639–75, 713–17).[57] The celebration of
Zeus in the context of the Hesiodic Titanomachy culminates in his
enthronement after the defeat of the Titans (*Th.* 881–85); supreme power

---

[54] I print the text in West 1966.    [55] On this point, cf. Solmsen 1949: 162 and Saïd 1985: 217.
[56] Gaia supports Zeus over Cronus ever since the former's birth: *Th.* 468–84, 494, 626–28, 884; cf.
Gaia's insight on the inevitability of Cronus' fall at the hands of Zeus, *Th.* 463–65, 474–76.
[57] On Zeus's successful policy of alliance and integration, see Solmsen 1949: 71–75, Saïd 1985: 274–80.
On the combination of force and intelligence in the Hesiodic Titanomachy, see Detienne and
Vernant 1978: 68–92 and, more emphatically, Saïd 1985: 264–69.

comes to him by popular demand and with Ge's support, and his enthronement is immediately followed by his commendable distribution of privileges (ἐὺ διεδάσσατο τιμάς, *Th.* 885). The *PV* overwrites the Hesiodic tradition with a version of the divine conflict that not only involves Prometheus but redefines the political and moral circumstances under which Zeus emerges as the cosmic ruler. Prometheus' account, which remains unchallenged throughout the play, debunks the Hesiodic panegyric of Zeus's ascent to the cosmic throne by weaving a narrative of power struggle between factions and by portraying Zeus as a power-hungry, transgressive usurper whose *coup d'état* met with considerable resistance. Investing Zeus with features evocative of Hesiod's Cronus only highlights how un-Hesiodic the tragedy's version of the divine past is.

By granting him the role of Ge's mouthpiece, the *PV* integrates Prometheus successfully into the succession myth. His involvement frames Zeus's reign since he is instrumental in its establishment, but he is also in a position to let it end. Thanks to Ge, Prometheus knows which bride is bound to bear a son that will overthrow Zeus (*PV* 908–27). The threat of a male heir is an intrinsic part of the *Theogony*'s narrative. Metis, Zeus's first consort, is bound to bear two children (*Th.* 895–98): Athena, a daughter equal to her father in strength and counsel, and a son with an exceedingly violent spirit (ὑπέρβιον ἦτορ ἔχοντα, *Th.* 898) who will become the king of gods and men. Following the cunning admonition he receives from Gaia (Ge) and Ouranus, Zeus neutralizes the threat of his unborn son by deceiving and ultimately consuming Metis before she gives birth (*Th.* 888–93 and 899–900). In the *PV*, the threat of the overbearing heir is still not settled by the time Zeus punishes Prometheus, and it will not be settled for another thirteen human generations, when (in the course of the *Lyomenos*) Prometheus will reveal the identity of the dangerous bride in exchange for his freedom. The Prometheus-plays embed Zeus in the same succession pattern as the *Theogony*, but draw the identity of the threatening consort from a non-Hesiodic tradition. Even though she remains unnamed throughout the *PV*, the bride who is fated to bear Zeus's successor is Thetis. The earliest extant version of the story is found in Pi. *I.8.27–40*. Zeus and Poseidon competed for the hand of Thetis, but were forced to abort the wooing when Themis revealed the following prophecy:

εἶπε δ' εὔβουλος ἐν μέσοισι Θέμις,
εἵνεκεν πεπρωμένον ἦν, φέρτερον πατέρος
ἄνακτα γόνον τεκεῖν

πον τίαν θεόν, ὃς κεραυ-
        νοῦ τε κρέσσον ἄλλο βέλος
διώξει χερὶ τριόδον-
        τός τ᾽ ἀμαιμακέτου, Ζηνὶ μισγομέναν
ἢ Διὸς παρ᾽ ἀδελφεοῖσιν.

(Pindar, Isthmian 8.31–35a)

And Themis of good counsel said in their midst that it was destined for the sea-
goddess to bear a royal son stronger than his father, a son who would wield in his
hand some other weapon mightier than the thunderbolt and the unyielding
trident, if she should mingle with Zeus or Zeus's brothers.

The Prometheus-plays appropriate the same story with two major differences: there is no evidence that Poseidon was interested in Thetis at all
and, instead of Themis, it is Prometheus, the son of Themis/Ge, who
eventually reveals what kind of a son Thetis is fated to have with Zeus.[58]
Ultimately, Prometheus' insight secures both the continuation of Zeus's
reign and his own deliverance, when, in the *Lyomenos*, his timely intervention averts the union between Zeus and Thetis. Much like *I.*8, the *PV*
defines the superiority of this challenger in terms of a weapon greater
than Zeus's thunderbolt and Poseidon's trident (*PV* 920–25). Yet the
tragedy expands the language of conflict by describing this unborn son as
a wrestler (τοῖον παλαιστήν, *PV* 920) and a "monster that is extremely
hard to fight against" (δυσμαχώτατον τέρας, *PV* 921). The vague Hesiodic reference to the son's capacity for extreme violence (ὑπέρβιον ἦτορ
ἔχοντα, *Th.* 898), therefore, is not only amplified but also made more
concrete.

Prometheus in the *PV* is undeniably a figure of *metis* and foreknow-
ledge, but he also embodies resistance against oppression. He has already
thwarted Zeus's plans to annihilate humankind (*PV* 231–41) and in the
final scene he performs a second act of resistance when, despite the
promise of further punishment, he refuses to reveal which consort is
fated to bear Zeus's successor (*PV* 944–1093). In addition, in the course
of this play Prometheus associates himself with another rebellious figure
who, like him, has challenged Zeus in the past and is suffering as a result.
In the second episode, Prometheus rejects Oceanus' offer to act as a
mediator to Zeus, advising him to avoid provoking Zeus lest he too be
punished. Prometheus then expresses his sympathy for two figures, Atlas
(*PV* 347–50) and Typhos (*PV* 351–72), whom he constructs as fellow
victims of Zeus's punitive fury, thus presenting Oceanus with two

---

[58] Cf. sch. Pi. *I.*8.57b and 67.

additional cases that demonstrate the kind of divinely mandated suffering he should try hard to avoid.

Prometheus' treatment of Atlas is brief and his sympathy is justified on the grounds of their kinship.[59] The *PV* does not specify why Zeus has condemned Atlas to the arduous and confining duty of supporting the sky, a vagueness that the text shares with Atlas' presentation in the *Theogony* (*Th.* 517–20, 746–48). By contrast, Prometheus dwells at length on the plight of Typhos:

> τὸν γηγενῆ τε Κιλικίων οἰκήτορα
> ἄντρων ἰδὼν ᾤκτιρα, δάιον τέρας
> ἑκατογκάρανον, πρὸς βίαν χειρούμενον,
> Τυφῶνα θοῦρον· †πᾶσιν ὃς †ἀντέστη θεοῖς
> σμερδναῖσι γαμφηλαῖσι συρίζων φόβον,
> ἐξ ὀμμάτων δ' ἤστραπτε γοργωπὸν σέλας,
> ὡς τὴν Διὸς τυραννίδ' ἐκπέρσων βίᾳ.
> ἀλλ' ἦλθεν αὐτῷ Ζηνὸς ἄγρυπνον βέλος,
> καταιβάτης κεραυνὸς ἐκπνέων φλόγα,
> ὃς αὐτὸν ἐξέπληξε τῶν ὑψηγόρων
> κομπασμάτων· φρένας γὰρ εἰς αὐτὰς τυπεὶς
> ἐφεψαλώθη κἀξεβροντήθη σθένος.
> καὶ νῦν ἀχρεῖον καὶ παράορον δέμας
> κεῖται στενωποῦ πλησίον θαλασσίου
> ἰπούμενος ῥίζαισιν Αἰτναίαις ὕπο.
> κορυφαῖς δ' ἐν ἄκραις ἥμενος μυδροκτυπεῖ
> Ἥφαιστος, ἔνθεν ἐκραγήσονταί ποτε
> ποταμοὶ πυρὸς δάπτοντες ἀγρίαις γνάθοις
> τῆς καλλικάρπου Σικελίας λευροὺς γύας.
> τοιόνδε Τυφὼς ἐξαναζέσει χόλον
> θερμοῖς ἀπλάτου βέλεσι πυρπνόου ζάλης,
> καίπερ κεραυνῷ Ζηνὸς ἠνθρακωμένος.
>
> (*Prometheus Bound* 351–72)

And I have seen and pitied the earth-born dweller of the Cilician cave, a destructive monster with one hundred heads, being overpowered by force, furious

---

[59] *PV* 347–48: ἐπεί με καὶ κασιγνήτου τύχαι / τείρουσ'. Even though the *PV* does not follow the Hesiodic genealogy of Prometheus, it nonetheless retains the fraternal bonds between Atlas and Prometheus found in the *Theogony*. The brief mention of Atlas in *PV* 347–50 may also be looking forward to the *Prometheus Lyomenos*, in which Heracles encounters Prometheus on his way to retrieve the golden apples of the Hesperides, a labor that will require Atlas' assistance; see already Wilamowitz 1914: 122. Notice that, in the choral ode immediately following the departure of Oceanus, the Oceanides acknowledge the plight of Atlas (*PV* 425–30) but make no reference to Typhos. Cf. their conveniently vague formulation in *PV* 407–10 (esp. στένουσι τὰν σὰν ξυνομαιμόνων τε τιμάν).

Typhos, who opposed all the gods, hissing fear with his dreadful jaws, and was emitting from his eyes a fierce light, intending to destroy Zeus's tyranny by force. But the vigilant arrow of Zeus came upon him, the lightning that comes down breathing flame, which struck him out of his lofty boasts.[60] For, having been hit in his midriff, he was scorched and thundered out of his strength. And now he lies near the straits of the sea, an inert and outstretched body, crushed under the roots of Aetna. And sitting on its topmost peaks Hephaestus forges hot iron; from there rivers of fire will burst forth one day, devouring with their savage jaws the smooth plains of Sicily, a land of fine crops. Such rage will Typhos boil forth with the hot arrows of an unapproachable, fire-breathing storm, even though he has been burned to cinders by the thunderbolt of Zeus.

Prometheus seems to sympathize with Typhos primarily for ideological reasons, namely their shared opposition to Zeus (*PV* 357); consequently, he does not emphasize their kinship, even though they are both born of Ge (τὸν γηγενῆ, *PV* 351).[61] Much like Prometheus, moreover, Typhos has been immobilized, but not subdued. Even though he has been scorched by the thunderbolt (*PV* 362 and 372), he will have the opportunity to express his anger against Zeus again in the future through eruptions of destructive volcanic fire (*PV* 367–71).

It has been well established in the scholarship that Prometheus' treatment of Typhos in the *PV* has a lot in common with Pindar's account of the monster's imprisonment under Aetna in *Pythian* 1 (15–28), an ode composed in 470 BCE.[62] Like the Pindaric ode, the tragedy envisions Typhos as a hundred-headed monster, who was born in Cilicia (*P*.1.16–17 and *PV* 351–52) and is currently incarcerated under the Sicilian volcano (*P*.1.17–20 and *PV* 363–65). Both passages show interest in the local geography, although the Pindaric text is broader in its scope and more specific in its details than the tragedy (see esp. *P*.1.17–19; cf. *PV* 364–65). There are verbal correspondences between *PV* 371 (ἀπλάτου ... πυρπνόου ζάλης) and *P*.1.21 (ἀπλάτου πυρός),[63] as well as a close resemblance in the description of the lava streams (*P*.1.21–22 πυρός ... παγαί and *PV* 368 ποταμοὶ πυρός). Both passages

---

[60] Prometheus' choice of words in 360–61 should not be taken as a criticism of Typhos. Prometheus echoes and appropriates Oceanus' own language when, in an earlier attempt to persuade Prometheus to yield, he attributed Prometheus' sufferings to his "exceedingly vaunting language" (τῆς ἄγαν ὑψηγόρου γλώσσης, *PV* 318–19).

[61] The emphasis changes somewhat, however, if one adopts the text proposed by Huxley 1986 for *PV* 354: Τυφῶνα, θοῦρον κάσιν, ὃς ἀντέστη θεοῖς.

[62] On *P*.1, see Chapter 2, pp. 53–63. The verbal echoes between the *PV* and *P*.1 have long been recognized; see, e.g., Ardizzoni 1978, Di Benedetto 1995: 129–30, Gentili et al. 1995: 335–38, and the table in Debiasi 2008: 90–91.

[63] Cf. earlier *PV* 349 (κίον' οὐρανοῦ) in the context of discussing Atlas and *P*.1.19 (κίων δ' οὐρανία, i.e. Aetna).

associate the volcano with Hephaestus, although in the ode the κρουνοί Άφαίστοιο (*P*.1.25) serve as a metonymy for fire, whereas the tragedy locates the god's smithies on top of Aetna (*PV* 366–67). Most importantly, both *P*.1 and the *PV* maintain the aetiological connection between the vanquished challenger of Zeus and Aetna's eruptions, and focus intensely on the description of this catastrophic phenomenon, which, in the universe of the *PV*, lies in the future (*P*.1.21–28 and *PV* 367–72).

Nonetheless, the treatments of Typhos in *P*.1 and the *PV* are clearly distinct, and their dissimilarities reflect their different engagement with the Hesiodic tradition.[64] As I discuss in Chapter 2, *Pythian* 1 dwells extensively on Typhos' justified punishment, but does not recount the events that led to it. Instead, the ode invites its audience to recall the background story, namely the conflict between Zeus and Typhos, by alluding briefly to the Hesiodic Typhonomachy (*Th.* 820–80) in the lines that introduce the monster to the text (*P*.1.13–16). The *PV*, on the other hand, devotes an almost equal number of lines to the clash between Zeus and Typhos (*PV* 354–62) and to the predicament in which Typhos finds himself currently as a result of his attempt to overthrow Zeus (*PV* 363–72), although half of the latter passage describes Typhos' future act of defiance, the eruption of Aetna (*PV* 367–72). In this context, the Hesiodic Typhonomachy informs both Typhos' description and his clash with the Olympians. In addition to depicting Typhos as a hundred-headed monster, a Hesiodic detail (*Th.* 825) that the *PV* shares with *P*.1, the tragedy enriches the monster's form with several features drawn from the Hesiodic narrative. Prometheus introduces Typhos as the son of Ge (τὸν γηγενῆ, *PV* 351; ὁπλότατον τέκε παῖδα Τυφωέα Γαῖα πελώρη / Ταρτάρου ἐν φιλότητι διὰ χρυσέην Ἀφροδίτην, *Th.* 821–22) and describes him as a monster with snake-heads (σμερδναῖσι γαμφηλαῖσι συρίζων φόβον, *PV* 355,[65] cf. κεφαλαὶ ὄφιος, *Th.* 825) emitting fire from the eyes (ἐξ ὀμμάτων δ' ἤστραπτε γοργωπὸν σέλας, *PV* 356; ἐν δέ οἱ ὄσσων / θεσπεσίης κεφαλῆσιν ὑπ' ὀφρύσι πῦρ ἀμάρυσσεν, *Th.* 826–27). Following the *Theogony*, the *PV* communicates Typhos' monstrous nature and animalistic ferociousness through a combination of visual and auditory elements, although admittedly the sounds Typhos makes in the Hesiodic account (*Th.* 829–35) are far more varied and unnatural than his terrifying hissing in *PV* 355. Unlike

---

[64] On the differences between the two treatments of Typhos from a different angle, see Di Benedetto 1995: 133–36.

[65] Although the noun γαμφηλαί applies to several animals, the combination with the verb συρίζω evokes snakes in particular.

the vague phrase θεῶν πολέμιος in *P*.1.15, moreover, the *PV* follows the *Theogony* closely in stating that Typhos intended to overthrow Zeus's rule (*Th.* 836–37; *PV* 354–57) and in envisioning the conflict that ensues as a duel between Zeus and the monster (*Th.* 838–68; *PV* 358–62, 372). Before recounting how Zeus put an end to this threat by blasting Typhos and his mother Ge (*Th.* 853–68), the Hesiodic text dwells for several lines on the conflagration that afflicted the entire firmament when the monster and Zeus's thunderbolt clashed (*Th.* 844–52). Prometheus, on the other hand, captures only the moment of Typhos' defeat, but his narrative underscores repeatedly the scorching force of Zeus's fire.[66] In the *PV*, just as in the *Theogony*, the duel is fought exclusively with brute force, and the verbal echoes of Zeus's counterattack suggest in Prometheus' description of Typhos' future resurgence communicate that Zeus's violence is no different than Typhos'.[67] Finally, the description of the eruption as a storm in *PV* 371 (ἀπλάτου ... πυρπνόου ζάλης) reiterates imagery from Hesiod's Typhonomachy (πυρός τ' ἀπὸ τοῖο πελώρου / πρηστήρων ἀνέμων, *Th.* 845–46), thus projecting into the future a vivid reemergence of the destructive fierceness that the monster displayed in his Hesiodic clash against Zeus.[68]

Prometheus' engagement with the Hesiodic Typhonomachy in his treatment of Typhos is undeniably extensive, yet it contrasts sharply with his un-Hesiodic attitude towards Zeus's victory.[69] By emphasizing Typhos' monstrous nature (*Th.* 823–35), the Hesiodic narrative sets up Zeus's intervention as a welcome triumph of order over chaos, a victory that rescued the entire world from a hideous alternative (*Th.* 836–38) and demonstrated yet again that Zeus deserves the cosmic throne. Prometheus, on the other hand, expresses pity for Typhos (*PV* 352) and, without glossing over his violence and monstrosity, redefines him as a sympathetic figure who, like Prometheus himself, has suffered a harsh punishment for opposing Zeus but has not been completely crushed. Even in captivity, Typhos refuses to compromise and, when the time comes, he will have another chance to express his

---

[66] *Pythian* 1, by contrast, plays with the contrast between water and fire, both in 19–20 (snow-covered peaks of a volcano full of fire) and in 23–24 (lava meets the sea with a crash).

[67] ἀλλ' ἦλθεν αὐτῷ Ζηνὸς ἄγρυπνον βέλος,/ καταιβάτης κεραυνὸς ἐκπνέων φλόγα, *PV* 358–59 – τοιόνδε Τυφὼς ἐξαναζέσει χόλον / θερμοῖς ἀπλάτου βέλεσι πυρπνόου ζάλης, *PV* 370–71. Cf. *Th.* 844–47, where the conflagration imagery blurs the distinction between fire coming from Zeus's thunderbolt and fire emitted by Typhos.

[68] On the association of Typhos with destructive winds, cf. *Th.* 869–80. West 1966: 390 argues that πρηστήρων ἀνέμων in *Th.* 846 should be attributed to Zeus, but acknowledges that ancient readers (including sch. *Th.* 846) understood these winds as part of Typhos' attack.

[69] On the subversive reception of the Hesiodic Typhonomachy in Prometheus' account, see also Griffith 1978: 120, Saïd 1985: 294–97. On Typhos in the *PV* and the *Theogony*, see also Duchemin 1972, who is, however, mainly interested in Near Eastern sources.

opposition to the cosmic leader. Likewise, Prometheus too continues to resist Zeus by withholding the crucial information regarding the son who will overthrow him. The two sons of Ge, then, prove to be very similar indeed, even if Prometheus' resistance depends on his intelligence and insight, while Typhos' opposition involves flames and destructive violence. Finally, while Zeus's capacity for overpowering violence is celebrated in the *Theogony*, it may be viewed as problematic in the context of the *PV*, since, in the context of the Titanomachy, strategy was declared superior to brute force (*PV* 212–13). It is not a coincidence that Prometheus reiterates the language of violence he uses in the Typhos-passage later, when he scoffs at the futility of Zeus's violence in the face of his impending fall (. . . τινάσσων τ' ἐν χεροῖν πύρπνουν βέλος, *PV* 917).[70] In sum, Prometheus' treatment of Typhos' fight and fall evokes the Hesiodic Typhonomachy but rejects its panegyric of Zeus. While the *Theogony* (as well as *Pythian* 1)[71] celebrates the victory of Zeus over monstrous Typhos as the victory of order over chaos, Prometheus sympathizes with the defeated and shares with him the promise of further defiance. Prometheus' perspective on the Typhonomachy is thus consistent with his earlier unflattering account of the Olympian faction and their success during the Titanomachy.

I hope to have shown so far that the play's reconstruction of the divine realm develops a complex engagement with the Hesiodic tradition. The *Theogony* treats Prometheus' transgression and punishment as an independent incident, a crisis that occurs outside the interfamilial drama of succession and does not interact with it at all. In fact, since Zeus already rules over gods and men when he deals with Prometheus (*Th.* 542, 572, 580) and Athena is involved in the creation of the first woman (*Th.* 573–77), the *Theogony* situates the incident after Zeus has successfully eliminated the threat of his unborn son and secured his eternal reign by consuming his first wife Metis (*Th.* 886–900). The *PV* remythologizes Prometheus in a way that not only amplifies his importance but also pulls him from the margins of the cosmic narrative and integrates him into the core of the succession myth. In this context, it is important to note that the *PV* constructs a cosmos in which Zeus' ascent to power is defined and punctuated by the same challenges as in the *Theogony*: the Titanomachy, the Typhonomachy, Prometheus, and the threat of the unborn successor. Foes of the Olympian order that do not feature prominently in the

---

[70] Lenz 1980 rightly points out the contrast between Zeus's destructive fire and the constructive fire Prometheus grants to humankind.

[71] See Chapter 2, pp. 53–63.

Hesiodic poem, e.g. the Giants, are not in the purview of the *PV* either. Yet, while as a whole the *PV* follows the Hesiodic "plotline," so to speak, each individual episode within this cosmic narrative is distinctly un-Hesiodic in its details: for instance, Zeus' unborn heir will be the son of Thetis rather than Metis, Typhoeus has not been entirely neutralized, and Prometheus is far more complex than his Hesiodic counterpart. Likewise, the tragedy's treatment of the Titanomachy departs significantly from the Hesiodic account. It has been suggested that the *PV* may be informed by the Cyclic epic *Titanomachy* attributed to Eumelus (or Arctinus),[72] especially since an entry in Hesychius' *Lexicon*[73] has led some to believe that both Prometheus' involvement in the Titanomachy and his change of allegiance were elements of that Cyclic epic.[74] However that may be, the *PV* constructs a world that derives meaning from its juxtaposition to the Hesiodic tradition, and links Prometheus exclusively to other challenges that Zeus confronts in the *Theogony*, namely Cronus and the Titans, Typhos, and the prospect of a successor.

## The *Prometheus Bound* and the *Catalogue of Women*

The play's longest episode (*PV* 561–886) revolves around Io, a character that relates to the story of Prometheus only indirectly, given that she is the distant ancestor of Heracles, the hero who will be instrumental in ending

---

[72] See T2 Bernabé; West 2002 and 2003 considers the *Titanomachy* a work of Eumelus. The narrative of the *Titanomachy* began with a theogony (frs. 1–2 West) and included an account of the Titanomachy (frs. 3–8 West), but, judging by the extant fragments, the poem also recounted (or at least mentioned) some of Heracles' labors (frs. 9–10 West). On the *Titanomachy*, see West 2002: 110–18 and Debiasi 2004: 71–107; cf. Severyn 1928: 165–77, Dörig and Gigon 1963: XVI–XXIV, Kranz 1967, and Davies 2001²: 13–18. On the evidence for the (admittedly problematic) reconstruction of the *Titanomachy* as a cyclic epic that included a Gigantomachy and even a Centauromachy, see West 1994: 145–48 and Debiasi 2004: 90–94; contrast the more restrained reconstruction of the poem in West 2003: 27. For instance, the reference to Chiron as a civilizing figure (fr. 12–13 West) need not be part of a fully fledged account of the Centauromachy. Instead, these fragments may belong to an account of Chiron's involvement in the apotheosis of Heracles found in Ps.-Apollod. (*Bibl.* 2.5.4) and almost certainly alluded to in *PV* 1026–29; cf. Welcker 1849: 417–19 and West 1994: 146–47. Alternatively, it may have been embedded in the narrative as a proleptic digression connected to his father Cronus. Following Severyn 1928: 170–71, Debiasi 2004: 106–07 and Tsagalis 2013 examine the possibility that the *Titanomachy* encompassed a Typhonomachy as well; if so, this would have been markedly distinct from the Typhonomachy embedded in the Hesiodic tradition, as Tsagalis demonstrates. This view is refuted by D'Alessio 2013: 209 n.48.

[73] Hesych. *Lex.* 1 387 (=*Tit.* fr. 5* W): Ἴθας ὁ τῶν Τιτήνων κῆρυξ, Προμηθεύς. τινὲς Ἴθαξ. For the hypothesis that this Ithas/Prometheus was included in the cyclic *Titanomachy* as the messenger of the gods, see Welcker 1849: 415, Pohlenz 1916: 588 n.2, and, more recently, West 2002: 113–14. Bernabé refrains from including this fragment in his 1987 edition, and Davies 1988: 19–20 remains skeptical.

[74] West 2002: 114.

Prometheus' torment (*PV* 871–73). Her appearance in the *PV* is remarkable because her interaction with Prometheus is not only unprecedented (as far as we know) but also has no effect whatsoever upon Prometheus' fate.[75] Nonetheless, Io's presence fits well in the play as it reinforces several of its themes and prefigures some of the events that will unfold in the *Prometheus Lyomenos*.[76] To begin with, Io provides yet another demonstration of Olympian cruelty.[77] Her character can be read as a doublet of Prometheus in so far as she suffers unfairly on account of Zeus, and her torment, though presently horrible, will eventually come to an end with some restitution.[78] Up until her arrival, the play has explored suffering that stems from Zeus's power to punish his opponents. Io introduces a different paradigm of divinely induced distress. She is mortal and vulnerable, with no control over her physical form (*PV* 588; 673–75) and only temporary control over her wits (*PV* 566–81, 681–82, 877–86). Her wild roaming contrasts sharply with the confinement reserved for Zeus's immortal foes in the *PV*;[79] on the other hand, her isolation from her *oikos* and her *polis*, which Zeus achieved through manipulation and threats (*PV* 645–72), is familiar at least to the protagonist, who is now chained in the uninhabited wilderness (ἄβροτον εἰς ἐρημίαν, *PV* 2). With the introduction of Io, the *PV* expands the scope of Olympian cruelty beyond divine politics, and turns the attention of the play's internal and external audience to the mistreatment of humankind under Zeus. Io is undeniably a victim of the gods' whim; none of the ambiguities surrounding the harshness of Prometheus' own punishment or his sympathy for the monstrous Typhos apply to the vulnerable maiden who suffers simply because she attracted Zeus's erotic interest. Although inconsequential for Prometheus' current woes,

[75] Taplin 1977: 265–67 and Griffith 1983b: 6; cf. Sommerstein 2010a²: 216 with emphasis on how the Io-scene lays the ground for the *Lyomenos*, and Lefèvre 2003: 71–74, who argues that, much like the rest of the *PV*, the Io-scene is secondary to the *Lyomenos*, a doublet for the Heracles-scene in the following play. For the idea that the Io-scene contributes nothing but a filler for the *PV* and the opportunity to set up Heracles' arrival in the *Lyomenos*, see already Wilamowitz 1914: 125.

[76] On the thematic connections between Io and Prometheus in the *PV*, see Hughes Fowler 1957: 179–84 and Mossman 1996: 62–66; cf. Dawson 1951 with particular focus on the reiteration of this connection in the last scene of the *PV*.

[77] For an illuminating close reading of the Io-scene, see Unterberger 1968: 88–113. In the *PV* the blame for Io's sufferings falls on Zeus (578–81, 663–72, 735–41) and only secondarily on Hera (591–92, 703–04; cf. 600, where Hera's name is supplied by the editors, as well as 900, a problematic line in the stasimon that follows Io's departure).

[78] Pohlenz 1954: 74–75, Duchemin 1974: 75–76.

[79] Unterberger 1968: 89–90. On the geography of Io's wanderings, see Finkelberg 1998 with an excellent discussion of the problems involved. See also Bonnafé 1991 and 1992, Podlecki 2005: 201–09, Blasina 2006.

therefore, Io provides evidence that confirms the protagonist's accusations against the cosmic ruler and further legitimizes his firm defiance.

Io's scene also introduces an important event that will take place in the immediately following play, the *Prometheus Lyomenos*. Right before Io departs, lost in a new fit of frenzy, Prometheus reveals a prophecy he received from his mother regarding a distant descendant of hers who will liberate him:

> σπορᾶς γε μὴν ἐκ τῆσδε φύσεται θρασύς,
> τόξοισι κλεινός, ὃς πόνων ἐκ τῶνδ' ἐμὲ
> λύσει. τοιόνδε χρησμὸν ἡ παλαιγενὴς
> μήτηρ ἐμοὶ διῆλθε Τιτανὶς Θέμις·
> ὅπως δὲ χὤπη, ταῦτα δεῖ μακροῦ λόγου
> εἰπεῖν, σύ τ' οὐδὲν ἐκμαθοῦσα κερδανεῖς.
> *(Prometheus Bound* 871–76)

Well, from this sowing will be born a bold man, famous for his archery, who will release me from these pains. Such a prophecy my ancient mother, Themis the Titaness, recounted to me. But how and in what way (it will happen), these things require a long speech to explain, and you will gain nothing by finding out.

Even though Prometheus keeps the details of his release obscure, these lines prepare the audience for major parts of the plot's denouement in the *Lyomenos*. The passage facilitates the transition from the *PV* to its sequel not only by means of verbal cues but also by establishing a timeline, as Prometheus traces Io's descendants with emphasis on the most prominent ones: her son, Epaphus, the Danaids, and, finally, Heracles (*PV* 850–73).[80] By marking the remoteness of the era in which the *Lyomenos* takes place, the *PV* prepares the ground for the time-skip.

Yet the Io-scene points forward to the *Lyomenos* in more subtle ways too. While Io's frantic wanderings in the *PV* contrast with the confinement of gods within the play, her displacement prefigures the movement of major characters in the *Lyomenos*. The fragmentary evidence indicates that the construction of Heracles as an itinerant figure mirrors that of Io.[81] Prometheus draws up an itinerary for Heracles (frs. 195–99 Radt) much as he maps out for Io the rest of her journey (*PV* 707–35, 786–815); it is conceivable that the play also elaborated on Heracles' trajectory preceding his encounter with Prometheus (cf. *PV* 829–41). For the audience of the *Lyomenos*, the parallels between the two scenes serve as a reminder of the kinship that ties Io and Heracles but they also mark the

---

[80] On the temporal landscape of the *PV*, see also Conacher 1980: 17–18, who is interested in how the play maps the divine drama upon human history.

[81] Pohlenz 1954: 76, Unterberger 1968: 19 and 100, Duchemin 1974: 79, Lefèvre 2003: 71–74.

advent of Heracles as the fulfillment of the prophecy that Prometheus once shared with Io in the *PV*. Furthermore, the wanderings of the Argive maiden in the *PV* mirror another, less prominent journey in the *Lyomenos*. The play's *parodos* dramatizes the arrival of the released Titans, who draw attention to the fact that they have traveled all the way from south or southwest in Africa, presumably the location of the Isles of the Blessed. Their itinerary, which they divulged in some detail (frs. 191–92 Radt),[82] evokes Io's since it mirrors the maiden's trajectory to some extent even though the Titans travel in the opposite direction.[83]

In so far as Io's pathetic appearance in the *PV* demonstrates vividly the cruelty of Zeus's erotic desire and its consequences, it not only supports Prometheus' contentions about Zeus's ruthlessness throughout the *PV* but also prefigures Zeus's pursuit of Thetis that must have been integrated into the plot of the *Lyomenos*.[84] It is significant that, unlike all other extant treatments of Io by fifth-century tragedians,[85] the *PV* gives Zeus's female victim a voice and thus the opportunity to recount in the first person the events that led to her suffering and to express in her own words the intensity of her pain and desperation, as well as the bitterness she harbors against Zeus for her undeserved suffering.[86] As Io tells her story, the play invites its audience to pay close attention to the machinations and manipulations involved in the god's attempt to secure his prey: the dreams (*PV* 645–57), the corrupt oracles, and the threat of annihilation (*PV* 658–69, esp. κεραυνόν ὃς πᾶν ἐξαϊστώσει γένος, 668). Through extortion, which

---

[82] West 1979: 140, who includes fr. 203 Radt in the fragments pertaining to the journey of the Titans.
[83] Griffith 1983b: 291, Sommerstein 2010a²: 225.
[84] Whether a distressed Thetis appeared as a character or not in the *Lyomenos* is a matter of speculation. In favor is Fitton-Brown 1959: 57, followed by West 1979: 143–44. Cf. Sommerstein 2010a²: 226: "Enter now Thetis, fleeing from Zeus – a second Io, though a divine one." The suggestion is based on sch. *PV* 167: λέγει δὲ τὸν ἔρωτα τῆς Θέτιδος, ὃν ἔσχεν ὁ Ζεύς. οὗτος γὰρ ἐρασθεὶς αὐτῆς, ἐδίωκεν αὐτὴν ἐν τῷ Καυκάσῳ ὄρει ὅπως συγγένηται αὐτῇ.
[85] In Aeschylus' *Suppliants*, the Danaids use the memory of Io, their ancestor, to establish their connection with Argos, where they have come as suppliants. In their account of Io's plight, the girl loses her human self completely after her metamorphosis into a cow. Furthermore, even though the Danaids acknowledge Io's toil, they blame all her suffering on Hera's jealousy. Zeus emerges as a loving god, who pursued his beloved even in her animal form, and, most importantly, was instrumental in stopping her anguish and granting her a glorious son (*Supp.* 163–75, 291–315, and 531–89; cf. also 15–18, 40–55). See Murray 1958. Much like the *Suppliants*, Sophocles' *Inachus*, probably a satyr drama, envisions Io as fully turned into a cow (fr. 269a Radt). There is no evidence that Io had kept her human identity or was able to communicate during the mayhem. On the *Inachus*, see Sutton 1979, Heynen and Krumeich 1999a, and, more recently, O'Sullivan and Collard 2013: 314–35 with bibliography.
[86] Notice in particular how interested she is in the possibility of Zeus's demise (*PV* 757–70). Even though it remains unanswered, her inquiry about the identity of the fateful bride may even suggest her hope that she will be the one to ruin Zeus (*PV* 765–66).

verbally echoes Zeus' earlier plan to let all humankind die (ἀϊστώσας γένος / τὸ πᾶν, *PV* 232–33), the cosmic ruler forces the hand of a caring father (ἄκουσα ἄκων, ἀλλ' ἐπηνάγκαζέ νιν / Διὸς χαλινὸς πρὸς βίαν πράσσειν τάδε, *PV* 671–72) and gets what he wants. Io also relates in the first person her metamorphosis, a violation that, albeit non-sexual, marks a complete loss of the maiden's control over her body and mind (*PV* 673–79). With or without her monstrous custodian,[87] Io is forced into frenzied wanderings by a divine gadfly (οἰστροπλήξ ... /μάστιγι θείᾳ, *PV* 681–82). Having lost herself both in physical and at times in mental terms as well, Io suffers a pitiful state of existence demonstrated most vividly during her entrance as well as her abrupt exit. Despite Prometheus' reassurance that, after a lot of additional suffering, Io will get restitution from Zeus and a remarkable progeny (*PV* 848–73), this scene is dominated by the maiden's plight, her distorted form, and desperate words.

Scholars have examined with great care various aspects of the Io-scene but, in my view, they have missed a crucial aspect of its importance within the *PV*, namely how it furthers the play's subversive approach to the Olympian rule as it is celebrated in the Hesiodic corpus. I suggest that, while the conflict between Zeus and Prometheus challenges the Hesiodic narrative of Zeus's ascent to power in the *Theogony* and under-cuts the idealized image of him as a ruler, Io's words and actions undermine the celebration of the sexual unions between gods and mortal women in Hesiodic genealogical poetry. This is not to say that the tragedy is interested in the particulars of Io's treatment in the *Catalogue* or in any other part of the Hesiodic corpus. Just as in the case of the Titanomachy, the play draws the details of Io's story from non-Hesiodic traditions.[88] Apart from the birth of Epaphus in Egypt, which was probably recounted in the *Catalogue*,[89] most elements that define Io in the extant Hesiodic fragments are not found in the *PV*. In the *Catalogue* (Hes. fr. 44/124), Io is the daughter of Peiren, a descendant of Inachus,[90]

---

[87] Notice that she does not implicate Hera in the account of her metamorphosis; more importantly, she admits ignorance regarding the cause of Argus' sudden demise (*PV* 680–81). The text here constructs Io as a mortal being with limited awareness of the divine factors that have affected her life. Notice that the first person to bring up Hera's involvement in the Io-scene is Prometheus (*PV* 592).

[88] Possibly the epics *Danaid(s)* (Davies 1988: 141 and West 2003: 266–69) and *Aegimius*, which is attributed to Hesiod (frs. 294–301 MW) or Cercops. See Severyns 1926 and 1928: 177–82.

[89] On the gradual expansion of the myth's geographical scope, see the reconstruction by West 1985a: 149–50 (cf. already Friedländer 1905: 1–30). On whether the Hesiodic *Catalogue of Women* included an apotheosis of Io and Epaphus and/or associated them with Isis and Apis respectively, see Hirschberger 2004: 289–91 with bibliography.

[90] Acusilaus follows the Hesiodic genealogy of Io (fr. 26 Fowler = Ps.-Apollod. *Bibl.* 2.1.3). The earliest evidence for Inachus as Io's father dates to the fifth century BCE; in addition to the *PV*, see Ba.

and she serves Hera as a priestess.[91] The tragedy does not incorporate the proverbial false oath that Zeus took according to the Hesiodic narrative,[92] even though it is noteworthy that the god does manipulate the oracle. As for her physical transformation, finally, there is no evidence predating the fifth century BCE that Io retained part of her human identity while roaming the world in bovine form.[93] Her Hesiodic metamorphosis, therefore, must have been complete and Io could not have uttered a word throughout her frenzied journey in the *Catalogue*.[94]

While not a reception of the Io-*ehoie* in the strict sense, the scene of Io nonetheless explores precisely the kind of sexual interaction between gods and mortal women commemorated in Hesiodic genealogical poetry. Conceived and, presumably, performed as the continuation of Hesiod's *Theogony* (*Th.* 1021–22 = fr. 1.1–2), the *Catalogue of Women* defines as its subject those exceptional women who attracted the erotic interest of the gods, as well as the heroes that were born of these unions (Hes. fr. 1.1–5 and 14–21). Early in its programmatic proem, the *Catalogue* uses traditional language that constructs women as active participants in these relationships:

αἳ τότ' ἄρισται ἔσαγ[
μίτρας τ' ἀλλύσαντο.[
μισγόμεναι θεοῖσ[ιν
(Hesiod, fr. 1.3–5)

---

*Dith.* 19/5.18, Hdt. 1.1.3, and Soph. *Inachus*. On Io's place among the Inachids in the Hesiodic tradition, see West 1985a: 76–77 and 144–54.

[91] Cf. Aesch. *Supp.* 291–92 and Ps.-Apollod. *Bibl.* 2.1.3. Cf. also Hes. fr. 43/125 = Hesychius s.v. Ἰὼ καλλιθύεσσα; on the authorship of this fragment, see Hirschberger 2004: 288.

[92] Hes. fr. 124 MW = sch. Pl. *Smp.* 183b and Hesychius s.v. ἀφροδίσιος ὅρκος. I find no evidence suggesting that Zeus's false oath may have been criticized already in the Hesiodic poem.

[93] For a survey of the changes in Io's iconography, see Yalouris 1986 and 1990. Maehler 2000 argues that Io's representation as a βούκερως παρθένος is an indication that the *PV* was performed around 460–450 BCE. He points out that, while literary and artistic sources predating 460 BCE are consistent in representing Io as a cow, after 460 BCE vase painters begin to depict Io as part-human and part-cow. In Maehler's view, this shift in the iconography is due to the influence of the *PV*; however, Io the cow is said to retain some human features already in Aesch. *Supp.* 565–70. So far as Ps.-Apollod. *Bibl.* 2.1.3 (βοῦν ... λευκήν) is reliable testimony, the Hesiodic version of the story involved a metamorphosis into a heifer. In other instantiations of the myth, however, Io's transformation involves a gender switch. On the iconography of Io as a bull, see Moret 1990. For a survey of metamorphoses in the *Catalogue of Women*, see Hirschberger 2008, esp. 114–15 on Io.

[94] The *Catalogue* also included Argus and his death (Hes. fr. 126 MW; cf. Ps.-Apollod. *Bibl.* 2.1.6–7), an event that Io passes over very quickly in *PV* 677–81. For a reconstruction of the Hesiodic narrative regarding Hermes' killing of Argus, see Deubner 1905. There is evidence that his service as Io's guard and the cow's wanderings after his death were recounted in another poem attributed to Hesiod (or Cercops), namely the *Aegimius*: Hes. fr. 294 MW (description of Argus as a four-eyed sleepless guard) and fr. 296 MW (link between Io as cow and the origins of the toponym 'Euboea'), perhaps also fr. 295 MW. Io's trajectory has an aetiological function in the *PV* as well (see *PV* 732–34, 839–41). On the *Aegimius*, see Schwartz 1960: 261–64, Cingano 2009: 123–25.

those (women) who were the best at that time . . . and they loosened their girdles . . .
mingling with the gods.

Soon, however, the language shifts: the women become the objects of divine
desire and the means through which the gods produce eminent men:

τάων ἔσπετε Μ[οῦσαι
ὅσσ[αι]ς ἂν παρέλ[εκτο πατὴρ ἀνδρῶν τε θεῶν τε
σ‚περμαί‚νων τὰ ‚πρῶτα γένος κυδρῶν βασιλήων
.]ς τε Π̣[ο]σειδάω[ν
. . . . . .]ν τ᾽ Ἄρης [

(Hesiod fr. 1.14–18)

14 Μ[οῦσαι Lobel, West : μ[οι MW 15 αν Π : δὴ Lobel
ἂν παρέλ[εκτο πατὴρ ἀνδρῶν τε θεῶν τε Hirschberger : δὴ παρελ[έξατ᾽
Ὀλύμπιος εὐρύοπα Ζεὺς MW

Of these (women) tell, [Muses] . . . all those with whom used to lie [the father of men
and gods], sowing at first the race of glorious kings, and . . . Poseidon . . . and Ares . . .

Accordingly, extant fragments show that the *Catalogue* tends to "use
female stories as the frame within which male stories will be narrated."[95]
In the course of the poem, mortal women are pursued, abducted, and
deceived, they get married off, and they give birth, but the text
consistently suppresses their perspective on their experiences and
refrains from granting them a voice.[96] I argue that, by introducing Io
and allowing her to express her thoughts and feelings despite her
metamorphosis, the *PV* exposes the simplistic and one-sided view on
sex and desire that defines Hesiodic genealogical poetry, thus underscoring its limitations and undercutting its celebration of divine sexual
politics. In other words, the tragedy complements its subversion of
Zeus's panegyric in the *Theogony* with a critical take on the genealogical
poetry attributed to Hesiod.

Through Io's tormented words and actions, the play explores the sexual
domination of Olympian gods over inferior beings, and exposes the
horrors that such uneven relationships entail for the women who

---

[95] Tsagalis 2009: 166, following Rutherford 2000: 86. Cf. Hirschberger 2004: 74.
[96] Contrast the catalogue of women in the Odyssean *Nekuia* (*Od.* 11.225–332). Odysseus states his
intention to interview the famous women he encounters in the Underworld (*Od.* 11.229, 233–34),
but he also marks some of the stories he embeds as reported speeches (Tyro, Antiope, Iphimedeia).
See Tsagalis 2009: 169–70. By excluding the female perspective, the text can sustain more easily the
light tone that has been detected in some (though certainly not all) narratives of the *Catalogue*; see
Rutherford 2000: 86–87 and Tsagalis 2009: 167.

inadvertently become the object of divine erotic attention. However, Io is not the only female character who comments on this subject. The Oceanids of the chorus express their dismay and sympathy towards the human maiden as soon as they hear her account of Zeus's manipulations, her metamorphosis, and the frenzy that has plagued her ever since (*PV* 687–95).[97] Later, after Io departs in a new bout of physical agony and mental frenzy (*PV* 877–86), the goddesses contemplate sex and marriage in an ode that reiterates and succinctly concludes the play's commentary on the sexual politics of the Olympians celebrated in the Hesiodic genealogical poetry. The first strophe (*PV* 887–93) rejects unions between partners of unequal wealth and lineage and praises the idea that one should marry partners of equal status (ὡς τὸ κηδεῦσαι καθ᾽ ἑαυτὸν ἀριστεύει μακρῷ, *PV* 890). While this initial observation seems to apply to the mortal more than the divine world, the chorus proceeds to appropriate this message and apply it to themselves. While appalled by Io's plight, the Oceanids are even more alarmed by the idea that her fate could be theirs (*PV* 894–97).[98] Though not mortal, the Oceanids are aware of their inferiority to the Olympians and dismayed by their undeniable vulnerability. Impossible to escape (ἄφυκτον ὄμμα, *PV* 903), the erotic interest of the Olympians is framed as a war that these goddesses cannot win (ἀπόλεμος ὅδε γ᾽ ὁ πόλεμος, *PV* 904). The terror they experience at the thought of attracting Zeus's attention stems from Io's desperation in the previous scene and complements it. The ode concludes with their admission that they would be incapable of escaping Zeus's μῆτις (*PV* 906). The statement reinforces their self-representation as vulnerable prey against a predator they cannot fight. At the same time, however, their diction evokes Metis, a fellow Oceanid (*Th.* 358) and the first divine consort of Zeus who, according to the Hesiodic tradition, was destined to produce Zeus's usurper (*Th.* 886–900).[99] In the *Theogony*, Metis was the first female figure who attracted Zeus's erotic interest, only to be utterly consumed by her lover (*Th.* 889–91, 899–900). Her appropriation enhanced Zeus's

---

[97] Unterberger 1968: 97. On the chorus as a dynamic character in the *PV*, see Scott 1987.

[98] Unterberger 1968: 114–16. Note that, right before Io's unexpected appearance, the chorus were juxtaposing their current lament for Prometheus' sufferings with the happy songs they sang when Prometheus married Hesione, one of their sisters (*PV* 555–60). Obviously, Prometheus makes a much better consort than Zeus, although the point is not brought up explicitly in the choral ode that follows the Io-scene.

[99] Grossmann 1970: 92–94 argues that the Prometheus-plays dramatize the process through which Zeus gains the *metis* required to save his rule. *PV* 906–07, however, acknowledge that Zeus already has *metis*. In my view, it is his failing leadership that keeps him from acquiring the information required in order to neutralize the threat of his unborn son.

intellectual capacity and, more importantly, thwarted the birth of a male successor, but it also marked the permanent end of Metis as an individual entity, a fate even more harsh than Io's. The subtle evocation of this female figure, who is otherwise ignored in the *PV*, reminds the audience, as they are ushered into the final scene, that in this play the threat of a male successor is still looming over Zeus. In the context of the choral ode, however, the reference to Metis also evokes the Hesiodic beginnings of the sexual misconduct for which the Oceanids criticize the Olympians.

The tragedy, therefore, approaches Zeus's sexual politics from two different but congruent female perspectives. Women in the *PV* expose their vulnerability in the face of the Olympians and reject their sexual domination as detrimental and harmful. The prospect of glorious offspring that validates and glorifies sexual unions between gods and mortals in the *Catalogue* (fr. 1.16) is an ineffective consolation for the female cast of the *PV*. Prometheus informs Io about her future restitution and her progeny, yet she is robbed of the chance to react as frenzy takes over once again (*PV* 877–80). On the other hand, the chorus' vision of coupling with an Olympian never includes the prospect of offspring in the first place; all they focus on is the horror of being at the mercy of an Olympian suitor.

Finally, perhaps Io's construction as a pathetic figure whose suffering inspires sympathy in both internal and external audiences may help us explain why Pandora is absent from the *PV*.[100] Both Hesiodic accounts of Prometheus' transgressions involve the punishment of mankind by means of Pandora, a deceptive construct of Zeus that alters permanently the life of mortals. In the *Theogony*, this first woman and her kind are considered a necessary evil: they ensure reproduction but burden men by

---

[100] In connection with Pandora, we should consider Aesch. fr. **451u Radt. Radt includes the fragment among the *dubia*. However, it has been ascribed to the *Lyomenos* by Siegmann 1956: 21–22 and to the *Pyrphoros* by Reinhardt 1957: 12–17, who assumes that the *Pyrphoros* was the third tragedy of the Prometheus-trilogy and involved a chorus of Titans just like the *Lyomenos*. Their reading of the fragment involves Prometheus making a παρθένος, even though the vocabulary points to metallurgy rather than working with clay (χαλκεοτυπεῖ in line 7). Reinhardt finds a parallel for Prometheus' construction of Pandora in Sophocles' *Pandora* or *Sphyrokopoi* (on which, see below and Chapter 5). There is no evidence, however, that Sophocles' satyr-play attributed the making of Pandora to Prometheus rather than, e.g., Hephaestus (Hes. *Th.* 571–72, 580, and *WD* 70–71; cf. the iconography in *LIMC s.v.* Pandora no. 1, dated to 470/460 BCE, no. 3, ca. 460 BCE, and no. 6). There are two extant vase representations of Pandora coming out of the earth in front of a man holding a hammer, almost certainly Epimetheus rather than Prometheus (*s.v.* Pandora nos. 4–5); both paintings are probably related to the story dramatized in Sophocles' satyr play, although none of them involves satyrs. The earliest literary sources that link Prometheus with the creation of humans out of clay are Philemon (fourth–third century BCE; in fr. 92 KA, Prometheus fashions all living creatures out of clay) and Menander, whose fr. 508 KA identifies Prometheus as the creator of women in particular; cf. Aesop. 228 Hausrath.

consuming their sustenance (*Th.* 592–607). In the *WD*, Pandora is also responsible for inflicting on mankind all the evils, toils, and lethal sicknesses she let out of her infamous *pithos*, but also for keeping ἐλπίς inside it (*WD* 90–105).[101] In the *PV*, there is no mention of Pandora and, in fact, no indication that Zeus takes punitive action against humankind at all. Hope is bestowed upon mortals by Prometheus himself as an unambiguously positive gift that facilitates human progress by obscuring the paralyzing awareness of death (*PV* 248–51, esp. 250, τυφλὰς ἐν αὐτοῖς ἐλπίδας κατῴκισα). The play clearly retains and intensifies the Hesiodic association between ἐλπίς and Prometheus, but, given the obscurity of the Hesiodic passage, it is impossible to define exactly how *PV* interprets and receives the ἐλπίς of the *WD*.[102] However that may be, by leaving out Pandora, the *PV* circumvents the vilification of mortal women that features so prominently in Hes. *Th.* and *WD*. This framework leaves room for a sympathetic portrayal of a mortal maiden. Far from being a reflex of destructive Pandora, Io experiences the prospect of sexual union as a source of pain and suffering for herself. In fact, with the exception of Zeus, who may still beget his own successor, the only beings for whom sex and marriage emerge as potentially detrimental in the play are women, both mortal and immortal. The play's elimination of Pandora from the cosmic narrative prepares and facilitates its sympathetic view of female figures within an erotic context.

## The *Prometheus Lyomenos* and Hesiod's *Works and Days*

The *Prometheus Lyomenos*, the tragedy performed as the sequel of the *PV*, dramatizes Prometheus' release and restitution thirteen human generations after his encounter with Io (*PV* 774); in the meantime, the main character has undergone all the additional punishment that Hermes foresaw for his refusal to obey Zeus and reveal crucial information (*PV* 1016–25). After spending a long time buried in the earth (*PV* 1020, μακρὸν δὲ μῆκος ἐκτελευτήσας χρόνου), Prometheus has

---

[101] On the different interpretations suggested for ἐλπίς and for its confinement within the *pithos*, see the surveys in Fink 1958: 65–71, Verdenius 1971 (= 1985: 66–71), Casanova 1979a: 40–41 and 74–82, and Musäus 2004: 13–41; cf. also Vernant 1974: 193–94 and Clay 2003: 103 with emphasis on the ambiguity of ἐλπίς, Neitzel 1976, West 1978: 169–70, Leinieks 1984 with a survey of the use of ἐλπίς in archaic and classical poetry, Marg 1984²: 345–46, Lauriola 2000, and Clay 2009: 77–78 with bibliography.

[102] Saïd 1985: 122–30 with a survey of proposed arguments. Given the extensive revision of the Hesiodic tradition in the play, any attempt to illuminate the ἐλπίς of the *WD* through the τυφλαὶ ἐλπίδες of the *PV* (as does, e.g., Leinieks 1984: 5) seems to me equally precarious.

finally resurfaced, still bound by the chains Hephaestus applied in the prologue of the *PV* (fr. 193.5–6 Radt). As foretold in *PV* 1021–25, Zeus has added another element to his torture, an eagle that eats his liver regularly (fr. 193.10–21 Radt). In the *Lyomenos*, therefore, Prometheus' misfortunes have reached their final stage and, as such, they fully conform to the Hesiodic vision of his woes, according to which he is both tied in chains with wedges piercing his body (*Th.* 521–22; *PV* 52–77) and assaulted by a flesh-eating vulture (*Th.* 523–25). With the approval of Zeus, Heracles kills the bird that has been consuming Prometheus' liver (fr. 200 Radt)[103] and, eventually, Prometheus is also freed from the chains that restrain him, either by Heracles or by some other character.[104] Prometheus' deliverance from the eagle and the chains is linked to his decision to reveal that Thetis is the bride whose son is bound to overthrow Zeus, although the exact sequence of events in the plot is uncertain.[105] Also unclear is whether the revelation and the reconciliation were prompted by Ge's intervention or not.[106] After Prometheus saves Zeus from losing his power, there was probably some further settlement between Zeus and Prometheus,[107] possibly with cultic ramifications for mortals (fr. 202 Radt).[108]

---

[103] In fr. 193.10–12 Radt, Prometheus complains that the vulture attacks every other day.

[104] For arguments in favor of Heracles as the agent of Prometheus' release with Zeus's approval, see West 1979: 142–43, who assumes a consistency between the plot of the *Lyomenos* and the expectations raised by Prometheus' prophetic words regarding his future in the *PV* (esp. 770–74, 871–74); cf. Winnington-Ingram 1983: 193–94. Sommerstein 2010a²: 226, on the other hand, argues for an (admittedly exceptional) appearance of Zeus based on sch. *PV* 167. The scholion offers a crude summary of the events surrounding Prometheus' release, which involves no intermediaries between Zeus and Prometheus.

[105] For an overview of the views regarding the sequence of events, see Griffith 1983b: 295–96 and 301. In Philod. *De Pietate* (*P. Hercul.* 1088 V 4 (p. 41 Gomperz) ed. Schober) we read that, according to Aeschylus, Prometheus was released because he revealed the secret, although admittedly the relevant text is lacunose. For a reconstruction of the plot along these lines, see, e.g., Sommerstein 2010a²: 226. West 1979: 143–44, however, points out that the *PV* sets up the expectation of a different sequence, since on various occasions Prometheus insists that he will not reveal the secret until he has been released and compensated for his suffering (*PV* 172–7, 770, 989–91).

[106] Ge, along with Heracles, is included erroneously in the *hypothesis* of the *PV* among the *dramatis personae*. Since there is no doubt that Heracles appears in the *Lyomenos* (fr. 199–201 Radt), it has been assumed that Ge did too. See already Welcker 1824: 42–43 and Thompson 1932: 22; cf. Webster-Trendall III.1, 27 with an argument from the painting on an Apulian *krater* (Berlin Staat. Mus. 1969.9, ca. 350–340 BCE). For a suggested reconstruction of Ge's role in the *Lyomenos*, see Sommerstein 2010a²: 226. Adopting a more skeptical approach, West 1979: 141–42 finds the evidence for the inclusion of Ge among the characters of the *Lyomenos* unconvincing; cf. the discussion in Podlecki 1975: 14–15.

[107] On the role of Chiron in the *Lyomenos* (cf. *PV* 1026–29), see Robertson 1951 with a good overview of previous scholarship; very differently, Podlecki 1975: 16. West 1994: 146–47 suggests that Chiron's involvement was drawn from the Cyclic *Titanomachy*.

[108] Griffith 1983b: 303–04.

The shift from punishment to reconciliation and restitution in the *Lyomenos* is evident already in the play's opening lines. The chorus consists of Titans who, having been released from Tartarus, have come to see Prometheus (fr. 190 Radt).[109] Their anapaestic entrance communicates programmatically that, in this later era, reconciliation with Zeus is possible and that divinities once punished and oppressed are being reintegrated into the Olympian order. The reconciliation between the Olympians and the Titans is not foretold in the *PV* nor is it included in Hesiod's *Theogony*, which considers the Titans' imprisonment permanent (*Th.* 729–35, 813–14) and takes great pains to situate geographically their everlasting prison (*Th.* 717–819). However, evidence from two papyri, corroborated by sch. *WD* 160$^α$ Pertusi, confirms that there was a version of the *Works and Days* which included the reconciliation between Zeus and Cronus. *P. Mus. Berol.* 21107 (second century CE) and *P. Genav.* 94 (fifth century CE) preserve a passage not attested in the rest of the manuscript tradition of the *WD*, which consists of a three-line conclusion to the account of the Heroic Age (*WD* 173a–c) and a two-line introduction to the Iron Age (*WD* 173d–e). The first three lines complete the description of the life reserved for some heroes on the Isles of the Blessed (*WD* 170–73) as follows:[110]

> τοῖσιν Κρόνος ἐμβασιλεύει,
> αὐτὸς γάρ μ]ιν ἔλυσε πατ[ὴρ ἀνδρῶ]ν τε θε[ῶν τε·
> νῦν δ᾽ αἰεὶ] μετὰ τοῖς τιμὴ[ν ἔ]χει ὡς ἐ[πιεικές.
> (Hesiod, *Works and Days* 173a–c)

Among those Cronus is king, for the father [of men and gods himself] released [him. And now] he has honor among them always, as [is fitting].

Cronus' rule over the Isles of the Blessed is an apt compromise. It replicates on a smaller scale his earlier reign over the Golden Age (*WD* 109–11) but does not present any threat to Zeus's authority. The passage does not mention the liberation of the rest of the Titans, but the leap is not difficult. The Pindaric corpus, which features Cronus as the ruler of the Isles of the

---

[109] For the identity of the chorus see Arrian *Periplus Ponti Euxini* 19.2: καίτοι Αἰσχύλος ἐν Προμηθεῖ Λυομένῳ τὸν Φᾶσιν ὅρον τῆς Εὐρώπης καὶ τῆς Ἀσίας ποιεῖ. λέγουσι γοῦν <παρ'> αὐτῷ οἱ Τιτᾶνες πρὸς τὸν Προμηθέα ὅτι . . .

[110] Zenob. 3.86 provides an additional testimonium for *WD* 173a. On *WD* 173a–c, see Maehler 1967: 67–69 and West 1978: 194–96; contrast Livrea 2008: 49–51, who considers West's αὐτὸς γάρ μ]ιν ἔλυσε in 173b an aesthetically unsatisfactory supplement and proposes instead καὶ τότε δὴ μ]ιν ἔλυσε. Livrea creates a contrast between "then" and "now" by adopting West's supplement for the initial lacuna of 173c: νῦν δ᾽ ἤδη] μετὰ τοῖς τιμὴ[ν ἔ]χει ὡς ἐ[πιεικές. Given the tension between this passage and Cronus' fate in the *Theogony*, I find the emphasis on Zeus's agency that West's αὐτὸς γάρ μ]ιν (173b) entirely plausible and rather appealing.

Blessed in *Olympian* 2.77 (476 BCE), also offers the earliest datable attestation for the liberation of the Titans. Composed for the victory of Arcesilas of Cyrene in 462 BCE on behalf of an exile, *Pythian* 4 juxtaposes Atlas, who still suffers away from home (*P.*4.289–90), to the Titans, whose dire situation changed for the better over time (*P.*4.291): λῦσε δὲ Ζεὺς ἄφθιτος Τιτᾶνας ("but immortal Zeus freed the Titans"). Given the brevity of the statement and the lack of elaboration, the story of the Titans' release was probably known widely already by 462 BCE.[111] The reconciliation between Zeus and Cronus (with or without his cohort of Titans) is absent from Homeric epic as well as the rest of the Hesiodic corpus.[112] It is not impossible that the narrative of reconciliation coexisted with the more vengeful alternative favored in the epic tradition. Given the extant evidence, however, it seems more likely that *WD* 173a–c are an expansion of the Hesiodic text that reflects a relatively late reconsideration of the tradition prompted by criticisms regarding the traditional representation of the gods.[113] Unlike the *Theogony*, which justifies and celebrates the aggressive suppression of Cronus by his own son, the *WD* considers the mistreatment of parents at the hands of their children a trait of the most depraved phase of the Iron Age (*WD* 185–88). By reassessing Zeus's relationship with his father, therefore, *WD* 173a–c align this story with the values advocated in the rest of the didactic poem.[114]

It is impossible to determine how widely the version of the *WD* that included 173a–c was circulating; the Pindaric passages discussed above indicate that the release of Cronus and the Titans was well-known but offer no clues as to whether it was already associated with the Hesiodic

[111] West 1978: 196 is reluctant to see in *P.*4.291 the release of all the Titans ("[h]e may be thinking of Kronos, Rhea, and Prometheus"); it is difficult, however, to interpret Pindar's diction as anything but all-inclusive. On *P.*4.291, cf. Gentili et al. 1995: 508–09.

[112] Cronus and the Titans are situated in Tartarus in Hom. *Il.* 14.274, 278–79, and 15.224–25 (with reference to the Titans' defeat in the Titanomachy), as well as Hes. *Th.* 717–20, 729–35, 850–51. The inconsistency between the *Theogony* and *WD* 173a–c may have played a significant role in the passage's rejection; see Livrea 2008: 49, who talks about an athetesis by Alexandrian scholars based on the principle of Ἡσίοδον ἐξ Ἡσιόδου σαφηνίζειν.

[113] See, e.g., Xenoph. B 1.21–23 DK (cf. B 11 DK) and Pl. *R.* 377e–78e. On Zeus's mistreatment of Cronus, see also *Euthphr.* 5e–8b, Aesch. *Eum.* 640–41, Eur. *HF* 1317–19, Ar. *Nu.* 904–06. Pherecydes of Syrus seems to have envisioned a peaceful transition of power from Chronus to Zas, possibly involving the former's retirement; see Schibli 1990: 101.

[114] On the differences between the two poems, cf. Most 1993, who argues that autobiographical elements in the *Theogony* and the *WD* create a temporal succession between the two poems. Most argues that through this succession the text invites its reader to be attentive to the evolution of ideas from one Hesiodic poem to the other; he does not discuss, however, these particular lines.

tradition.[115] To audiences that considered it part of the Hesiodic corpus, the reconciliation between Zeus and Cronus would generate an overarching Hesiodic narrative of change as the way Zeus treats his opponents while he strives to establish and defend his rule in the *Theogony* would be markedly different from his attitude towards the defeated in the *Works and Days*, when his rule is the uncontested status quo. Assuming that *WD* 173a–c do not postdate the Prometheus-tragedies, it is conceivable that the audience of the plays would regard the pivotal shift in Zeus's politics from the harsh punitive oppression in the *PV* to the potential for reconciliation in the *Lyomenos* as a reflection and an amplification of Zeus's different attitudes towards Cronus in the *Theogony* and in the *Works and Days*.

To conclude: the *PV* and the *Lyomenos* use the punishment and eventual release of Prometheus as a frame through which they explore Zeus's leadership: his ascent to the throne, the treatment of his subjects, both human and divine, as well as his responses to challenges and crises. While adopting a critical view of Zeus's power, the plays revisit the Hesiodic tradition and challenge its vision of Zeus's rule as constructed not only in the *Theogony* but also in the *Catalogue of Women*. While the plays outline Zeus's ascent to power in accordance with Hesiod's *Theogony*, they rewrite key details of the narrative, including the genealogy of Prometheus, his role in the Titanomachy, the nature of his transgression against Zeus, as well as the circumstances of Prometheus' release. More importantly, the plays reject the Hesiodic panegyric of Zeus. The tragedies offer a polyphonic commentary on the cosmic ruler that allows – and even privileges – critical perspectives from gods and mortals that the Hesiodic corpus does not even acknowledge. Even though the overarching plot ultimately concludes with reconciliation, the plays problematize the vision of Zeus as a charismatic and popular leader presented in the *Theogony* and undermine the celebration of the sexual unions between gods and mortals in the *Catalogue*. In other words, the *PV* and the *Lyomenos* challenge the simplistic and partial view of the world in the Hesiodic tradition, and dramatize instead a more nuanced and complex cosmos that has room for a less than perfect cosmic leader.

---

[115] Cf. Sommerstein 2010a²: 223 n.9, who is much less tentative about this point. Note that fr. 202a Radt (= Philodemus, *De Pietate, P. Hercul.* 1088 III 18 (p. 39 Gomperz) ed. Schober) has been reconstructed so as to draw a distinction between the Hesiodic (Theogonic) tradition of imprisonment and the Aeschylean release of the Titans.

## The *Prometheus Pyrkaeus*

In 472 BCE, Aeschylus produced a tetralogy that consisted of the *Phineus*, the *Persae*, the *Glaukus*, and a satyr drama entitled *Prometheus Pyrkaeus*.[116] The fragments that can be attributed to the satyr drama with some confidence (**204a–**207a Radt) demonstrate a playful reworking of the Hesiodic tradition.[117] In fr. **204b Radt, the satyrs rejoice at the fire that Prometheus has brought to them, possibly having stolen it in the fennel stalk as in *Th.* 567 and *WD* 52.[118] Aeschylus' language evokes the *Theogony*, since πὰρ πυρὸς ἀκάματον αὐγὰν (fr. **204b.3 Radt) and τηλέγνωτον (fr. **204c.4 Radt) recall precisely the act of theft in *Th.* 565–7 (ἀλλά μιν ἐξαπάτησεν ἐὺς πάϊς Ἰαπετοῖο, / κλέψας ἀκαμάτοιο πυρὸς τηλέσκοπον αὐγήν / ἐν κοίλῳ νάρθηκι). At the same time, the characters repeatedly refer to fire as the gift of Prometheus to humankind,[119] a discourse not found in Hesiodic poetry.[120] Likewise, the satyr play may have featured Prometheus as the πρῶτος εὑρετής of certain τέχναι, as fr. 205 Radt seems to imply.[121]

In addition, the scholia to the *WD* indicate that the *Pyrkaeus* may have engaged not only with the theft of fire but also with the creation of Pandora and her reception by Epimetheus (*WD* 59–105; cf. *Th.* 511–14). A scholion to *WD* 89 summarizes probably in part the plot of a satyr play that may be Aeschylus' *Pyrkaeus*:[122]

---

[116] Sommerstein 2010c has argued that the four plays were thematically connected. On the satyr drama's two alternative *epikleseis* (*Pyrphoros* and *Pyrkaeus*), see Brown 1990.

[117] On the *Pyrkaeus*, see Germar, Pechstein, and Krumeich 1999.

[118] On vase paintings representing Prometheus giving fire to the satyrs, see Gisler 1994: 534–35 (nos. 4–19) and 551; see also Germar, Pechstein, and Krumeich 1999: 175–77.

[119] Προμηθέως δῶρον, fr. **204b.8=17 Radt; ἀμφὶ τὸν δόντα, fr. **204b.9 Radt; Προμηθε[ὺς βρο]τοῖς / φερέσβιος τ . [ . . . ] . [] σπευσίδωρ[ος, fr. **204b.11–12 Radt.

[120] It occurs, however, frequently in the *PV* and derives perhaps from the realm of cult (*PV* 8, 30, 251–52, 446, 612). See Saïd 1985: 115–18.

[121] For the various interpretations, see Radt 1985: 327. Cf. fr. 187a Radt, which Galen (*Hipp. Epid. Libr. VI comm.* 880) attributed to a *Prometheus* by Aeschylus. Sommerstein 2008: 218–19 reads in this fragment a reference to boiling water as a novelty and includes it among the fragments of Aeschylus' satyr play. On the play with fire in the *Pyrkaeus*, see also Yziquel 2001: 7–10.

[122] The lacuna in the beginning of the scholion is most unfortunate. Schömann 1857: 281 n.39 (followed by Dimitrijević) supplemented the name of Aeschylus, whereas Schmid proposed that perhaps the missing author was Sophocles; see Pertusi 1955: 43. There are two satyr plays attributed to Sophocles that appear to have dealt with Pandora: the *Kophoi* (frs. 362–66 Radt) and the *Pandora* or *Sphyrokopoi* (frs. 482–86 Radt). The former may be the play summarized in sch. Nic. *Ther.* 343–54 and in Ael. *NA* 6.51 (= Soph. fr. 362 Radt, cf. Scheurer and Krumeich 1999b); if so, the *Kophoi* dramatized a story about the aftermath of Prometheus' theft of fire that is nowhere to be found in the Hesiodic corpus. The *Pandora/Sphyrokopoi*, on the other hand, dealt with the creation of Pandora, who (based on vase representations) probably appeared as emerging from the earth; cf.

< *** > φησὶν ὅτι Προμηθεὺς τὸν τῶν κακῶν πίθον παρὰ τῶν Σατύρων λαβὼν
καὶ παραθέμενος τῷ Ἐπιμηθεῖ παρήγγειλε μὴ δέξασθαί τι παρὰ Διός, ὁ δὲ
παρακούσας ἐδέξατο τὴν Πανδώραν. ὅτε δὲ τὸ κακὸν ἔσχε παρ' αὐτῷ τότε
ἐνόησε τί αὐτῷ ἐπέμφθη· διὰ τοῦτο καὶ Ἐπιμηθεύς.

(sch. Hesiod, *Works and Days* 89 = Aeschylus fr. **207a Radt)

<***> says that, having received the jar of evils from the Satyrs and having left it
with Epimetheus, Prometheus ordered him not to accept anything from Zeus, but
he disobeyed and accepted Pandora. But, when he had the evil by his side, then he
realized what had been sent to him. For this reason, he is called "Epimetheus."

The play summarized here stayed close to the narrative of the *WD*. Once
Pandora has been constructed and endowed by all the gods with gifts that
make her a "sheer, intractable deception" (δόλον αἰπὺν ἀμήχανον, *WD*
83), Zeus orders Hermes to deliver her as a gift to Epimetheus (*WD* 84–85).
In this context, the narrator reveals that Prometheus had warned Epimetheus that he should not receive any gift from Zeus but he should send
it back, lest some evil might befall humankind (*WD* 85–88). Epimetheus
failed to think of his brother's advice when he received Pandora (οὐδ'
Ἐπιμηθεὺς / ἐφράσαθ', *WD* 85–86) but realized his mistake once he had
already received the evil (αὐτὰρ ὁ δεξάμενος ὅτε δὴ κακὸν εἶχ' ἐνόησεν, *WD*
89).[123] In addition to concluding the aetiological story surrounding the
introduction of womankind among men, the juxtaposition between Prometheus and Epi-metheus in relation to Zeus's deceptive gift brings into
relief a core feature of these characters and explicates their names.[124] The
satyr play summarized in sch. *WD* 89 appears to dramatize the moment of
Epimetheus' belated realization as told in the Hesiodic poem. As for the
*pithos* of evils that Pandora opens in *WD* 90–99 with lasting and almost
entirely negative repercussions for humankind, its provenance is left
unspecified in the Hesiodic poem, but the narrator points out that the
change upon the human condition that resulted from that action was part
of Zeus's plan (*WD* 105; cf. *WD* 99 on ἐλπίς). The satyr play remythologizes the *pithos* of evils as an offering of the satyrs to Prometheus; if indeed
the scholion to *WD* 89 summarizes part of the *Pyrkaeus*' plot, the *pithos*

---

Simon 1981. Pearson 1917: 136–37 has suggested that sch. *WD* 89 actually summarizes Sophocles'
*Pandora/Sphyrokopoi*, but Aesch. fr. 369 Radt indicates that it is just as likely that an Aeschylean
play (presumably the *Pyrkaeus*) involved Pandora's creation and her subsequent delivery to
Epimetheus (cf. Mette 1963: 11–12). For more on Sophocles' *Pandora/Sphyrokopoi*, see Radt 1977:
388 and Chapter 5, pp. 218–19.

[123] I print here the text in West 1978.

[124] On Prometheus' foresight, compare ὁ Προμαθεὺς ... προμαθεούμενος, Epich. fr. 113.12 KA (cf. also
fr. 113.251) and Kratos' taunt in *PV* 85–87.

may have been a token of thanks for his gift of fire.[125] Did the satyr play also mention Prometheus' punishment? Assuming Brown is right in suggesting that the *Pyrkaeus* and the *Pyrphoros* are the same play, then fr. 208a Radt could be a reference to the long sentence to which Prometheus was condemned.[126] Finally, I should point out that, in addition to the summary in sch. *WD* 89, the Hesiodic scholia have also preserved an Aeschylean fragment about a mortal woman made out of clay (ἐκ πηλοπλάστου σπέρματος θνητὴ γυνή, fr. 369 Radt = sch. *WD* 157a).[127] This fragment would fit very well in a play that featured Pandora and engaged closely with the Hesiodic account.

Aeschylus' *Prometheus Pyrkaeus* may have had some influence on Epicharmus. His *Pyrrha* or *Promatheus* constructs Prometheus as a civilizing hero, whose theft of fire entails great benefits, such as cooking and hot water (fr. 113.241–53 KA).[128] We have no direct evidence that the *Pyrkaeus* was performed in Syracuse. However, if the performance of the *Persae* in Syracuse was not a premiere but a re-performance as the Aeschylean *Vita* reports (ἀναδιδάξαι, *Vita* 18 = T1.68–69 Radt),[129] it is possible that *Prometheus Pyrkaeus* was re-performed on the same occasion, since it belonged to the same tetralogy as the *Persae*.[130] So far as we can deduce from the fragments of Epicharmus' play, however, the Sicilian poet dramatized mythical events that are supposed to have taken place after the plot of the *Pyrkaeus*, since Epicharmus' cast includes the progeny of Prometheus and Epimetheus, namely Deucalion (or Leucarion) and Pyrrha

---

[125] So Sommerstein 2008: 211.

[126] Brown 1990. On the perfect δεδέσθαι in fr. 208a Radt (cf. *alligatum*, Hyg. *astr.* 2.15), see Fitton-Brown 1959: 32–53 and Griffith 1983b: 284. The other fragment attributed to the *Pyrphoros* (fr. 208 Radt) could fit several different contexts and may even be misattributed to the *Pyrphoros*; see Griffith 1983b: 283.

[127] Schömann 1857: 303 n.85, Kraus 1957: 670; cf. Sommerstein 2008: 220–21. For bibliography regarding other ascriptions of the line, see Radt 1985: 426. Given the presence of Io in the *PV*, I find it difficult to see how the line would fit in the *Lyomenos* or the third Prometheus-tragedy, if one ever followed the *PV–Lyomenos* sequence.

[128] On Epicharmus, see Rodríguez-Noriega Guillén 1996: IX–XIII, Olson 2007: 6–11. On *Pyrrha* or *Promatheus*, see *DTC*² 1962: 266–68, Rodríguez-Noriega Guillén 1996: 97–123, Kerkhof 2001: 136–40 (with a response to Webster in *DTC*²), Willi 2008: 166–67, and above, pp. 133–34.

[129] Contrast, however, Bosher 2012, who suggests that the *Persae* may have been composed originally for performance in Syracuse as a single play and that it was embedded in a tetralogy only after Aeschylus' return to Athens. According to the *Vita* of Aeschylus, there were two versions of the *Persae*; see T56a+b Radt. Taplin 2006: 6, however, has argued that this is historically inaccurate and stems from an attempt to explain the inconsistency between *Ra.* 1028–29 and the transmitted text of the *Persae*. Taplin 2006 discusses the Panhellenic orientation of the *Persae* in relation to its performance in Syracuse, but does not exclude a first performance of the *Persae* in Athens.

[130] Shaw 2014: 67.

respectively.[131] Furthermore, Epicharmus situates the primordial couple in his home territory of Sicily, and, as I discussed earlier, features prominently the story of the Great Flood and Prometheus' role in the construction of the ark. These plot elements were probably not included in the *Pyrkaeus*, although admittedly the fragments are too few and scant to be conclusive.

It has been suggested that the *Pyrkaeus* was re-performed in Athens as part of the tetralogy that included the *PV* and the *Lyomenos*. The inclusion of a play known to be undeniably Aeschylean would strengthen the claim that the entire tetralogy was a genuine work of Aeschylus, even though at least the *PV* and the *Lyomenos* were most probably composed by a later poet, possibly Aeschylus' son Euphorion.[132] This tempting hypothesis yields a performative context in which a tetralogy would encompass multiple and diverse approaches towards the Hesiodic tradition. Like the *Pyrkaeus*, the *PV* and the *Lyomenos* feature Prometheus as a civilizing figure defined by his gift of fire and technology. Yet the tragedies dwell on the dire consequences of Prometheus' intervention in the context of Olympian politics, while the satyrs of the *Pyrkaeus* are celebrating on behalf of humankind the new element that Prometheus has delivered (fr. **204b Radt). In addition to presenting complementary perspectives on Prometheus' benefactions, the plays dramatize complementary aspects of the Hesiodic storyline. The tragedies focus exclusively on the drama of Prometheus and remythologize the early history of humankind, while forgoing the making of Pandora. The *Pyrkaeus*, on the other hand, appears to engage with the first woman and with the male character who received her with detrimental repercussions for humankind. Overall, this tetralogy would have stood out for its multiple and diverse receptions of the Hesiodic tradition.

## Rewriting the *Catalogue*: Euripides' *Ion*

Another play that boldly overwrites the Hesiodic tradition and, much like the *PV*, exposes its simplistic representation of women is Euripides' *Ion*. This play dramatizes a moment of crisis in the early days of Athens. Creousa, the only surviving descendant of Erichthonius, has been married to Xouthus, a son of Aeolus and a descendant of Zeus, who has proved his bravery in battle and his allegiance to Athens but is not himself an Athenian (*Ion* 57–64; 1296–99). The plot begins at a point where the union between Creousa and Xouthus has failed to produce children.

---

[131] Hes. frs. 2–4 MW with Casanova 1979a: 135–65, West 1985a: 50–53, and Dräger 1997: 36–42.
[132] West 2000: 339; cf. Poli-Palladini 2013: 26–28. See also above, pp. 123–27.

Athens is without an heir to the throne, and the genealogical branch of Erichthonius, who embodies both the close connection of Athens with its patron goddess Athena and the Athenian claim to autochthony (*Ion* 999–1015), is threatened with extinction. The couple and their entourage arrive at Delphi, seeking to solve the problem with an oracle from Apollo, but, from the beginning, there seems to be no perfect solution. No child of Xouthus and Creousa will be an Erechtheid through paternal filiation; thus any offspring they may have will guarantee the continuation of Creousa's royal house but will also contaminate its purely Athenian identity. If Xouthus has a son with a woman other than Creousa, on the other hand, Athens may have an heir to the throne but he will be no Erechtheid. Creousa feels so threatened and bitter at the prospect of welcoming Xouthus' bastard in her house that she turns murderous: when, in compliance with the oracle, Xouthus declares Ion, the attendant of Apollo's temple, to be his long-lost son with another woman (*Ion* 517–62), the queen plots the young man's assassination (*Ion* 774–858, 970–1047). Yet the situation is even more complicated, since, as we find out early in the play (*Ion* 8–56), Creousa is not actually childless. Having been raped by Apollo when she was a maiden, she gave birth secretly to a son, whom she subsequently abandoned. She has kept the whole affair secret – until now. Creousa thinks that her baby died, but it turns out that, thanks to Apollo's providence, the child grew up safely at Delphi and that, in her ignorance, Creousa almost murdered her own son. Mother and son are eventually reunited towards the end of the play, but while this reunion solves the problem of extinction for the Erechtheids, it does not immediately resolve the political crisis of Athens: since Ion is not Xouthus' son, his claim to the Athenian throne is bound to be highly problematic. Yet, as Hermes reveals in the prologue (*Ion* 69–75), Apollo has a plan that will fully restore his son in Athens without exposing his own past indiscretions. This divine scheme involves manipulating Xouthus with oracles and tricking him into accepting Ion as his own offspring.[133] The god expects Creousa to realize who Ion really is when he comes to Athens and thus to keep the rape secret forever.

By the play's last episode, the god's scheme succeeds but only partially: Xouthus has been duped but, at the same time, Creousa has disclosed her rape not only to her entourage but also to her son. Athena intervenes on Apollo's behalf with a revised plan of action (*Ion* 1553–1605): finally

---

[133] It is noteworthy that Creousa seems to realize the god's plan by herself before Athena arrives (*Ion* 1540–45).

reunited, Ion and Creousa must sustain Xouthus' illusion, so that Ion, the son of Apollo and a true descendant of Erichthonius, may assume the Athenian throne.[134] Athena thus mandates the deception of Xouthus even as she lifts the veil of ignorance from the eyes of Creousa and Ion.[135] In the context of arranging and, to some extent, justifying this conspiracy, the goddess divulges the future of Creousa's family (*Ion* 1575–94), starting with Ion's progeny. According to Athena, Ion will have four sons, who will give their names to the original four Athenian tribes (cf. Hdt. 5.66.2); their descendants will in turn found colonies in the Cyclades, the Hellespont, and on the coast of Asia Minor (*Ion* 1575–88; cf. the *prolepsis* in *Ion* 74). In this context, she reiterates the link between Ion and the Ionians by making the etymological connection between the tribe and its eponymous hero explicit (*Ion* 1587–88). The goddess's account of Ion's progeny embeds colonization within the history of Athens but also underscores the autochthony of the metropolis by juxtaposing it implicitly with the aggressive mobility of the colonizers.[136] Athena's speech also establishes the relationship between Athens and its colonies as one that strengthens the former (*Ion* 1584–85), thus legitimizing the Athenian appropriation of resources from allied city-states. In other words, Athena uses origins to create a hierarchy that can be read as resonating with and justifying fifth-century Athenian politics after the Persian Wars.

After recounting the glorious future of Ion's progeny, Athena reveals that the marriage of Creousa and Xouthus will not remain barren after all, since the couple will beget Dorus and Achaeus (*Ion* 1589–94). While Ion's descendants are bound to expand the glory and power of Athens to the east, the offspring born of the Erechtheid queen and the non-Athenian son of Aeolus will settle in the Peloponnese and in western Greece respectively, eventually becoming the eponymous heroes of the Dorians and the Achaeans. Here, too, genealogy entails hierarchy and conveys a political message: the eponymous heroes of the three major Greek tribes share the

---

[134] Burnett 1971: 101–02 with n.2 offers a survey of other dramas of return, both violent and non-violent. Cf. Solmsen 1934 and Strohm 1957: 75–86, who contextualize the *Ion* among other extant Euripidean plays that involve recognition.

[135] On the tension between divine will and human ignorance established already in Hermes' prologue, see, e.g., Erbse 1984: 81–82 and Rehm 1992: 134; in connection with the criticism that Apollo receives from mortal characters in the play, Strohm 1957: 153 and 161–63, Spira 1960: 77–79, Burnett 1962 with a rather idiosyncratic and thoroughly unsatisfactory reading of Creousa's plight, Imhof 1966: 15–18 and 48–53, Wolff 1965, esp. 184–85, Lloyd 1986: 36–40, and Matthiessen 2004: 59–60.

[136] On the word-play involving Ion's name in the context of colonization, see Zacharia 2003: 125–28.

same mother, and thus have strong ties to Athens. However, Ion stands out since he alone is the son of a god.

It is clear, then, that genealogy is central to the *Ion*. The play not only focuses on the reintegration of a hero born of a mortal and an immortal, but also explores what legacy figures like Ion and his half-siblings enjoy. It has been long acknowledged that, in this play, Euripides departs from the traditional genealogy of Hellen's descendants that was circulating in the Greek world under the authoritative name of Hesiod.[137] In the *Catalogue of Women*, the eponymous heroes of the Dorians and the Aeolians are siblings of Xouthus, not Ion:[138]

> Ἕλληνος δ' ἐγένοντο φιλοπτολέμου βασιλῆος
> Δῶρός τε Ξοῦθός τε καὶ Αἴολος ἱππιοχάρμης
> (Hesiod, fr. 4/9)

From Hellen the war-loving king were born Dorus and Xouthus and Aeolus who fights from battle-chariots.

Furthermore, the *Catalogue* included Ion among the legitimate children of Xouthus and Creousa along with two siblings, Achaeus and Diomede:[139]

> Ξοῦ]θος δὲ Κ[ρείουσαν ἐπή]ρατον εἶδος ἔχ[ουσαν
> κούρ]ην καλλ[ιπάρηον Ἐρε]χθῆος θείοιο
> ἀθανά]των ἰ[ότητι φίλην ποι]ήσατ' ἄκ[οι]τιν·
> ἥ οἱ Ἀ]χαιὸν ἐγ[είνατ' Ἰ]άονά τε κλυ]τότ̣π̣ωλ[ο]ν
> μιχθ]εῖσ' ἐγ [φιλότητι καὶ εὐε]ι̣δέα Διομήδην.
> (Hesiod, fr. 5/10a.20–24)

And Xouthus made [Creousa], who [had] a lovely form, [the fair-cheeked daughter] of divine Erechtheus, [his dear wife by the will of the immortals]; having mingled in [love], she bore [to him] Achaeus and [Ion] of the famous horses [and beautiful] Diomede.

There is no way of knowing to what extent the divine origins of Ion, including the rape of Creousa, are the invention of Euripides. Perhaps

---

[137] For a diachronic survey of extant genealogical arrangements involving Xouthus and his sons, as well as a study of their cultural value, see Càssola 1953.

[138] Cf. Acus. fr. 34 Fowler and Hellanic. fr. 125.1–5 Fowler. In the Hesiodic tradition, Hellen's father was almost certainly Deucalion; see Càssola 1953: 282–83 n.2, West 1985a: 50–52, and Hirschberger 2004: 173–74. Smith 2012 surveys the various genealogical traditions involving Xouthus and suggests that, by making Xouthus the descendant of Zeus, Euripides' *Ion* coopts "the western Greek, Dorian, Heraclid Xouthus" alongside the Hesiodic tradition regarding Ion. On the relationships among Greek tribes as projected upon the genealogical relationships among their eponymous heroes, see Hall 1997, esp. 42–44.

[139] On line 23, see West 1983a: 28 and 1987. The inclusion of Ion in this passage is virtually indisputable given the immediate context (fr. 5/10a).

this genealogy was already established by the mid-fifth century BCE.[140] However, it is worth noting that, when Herodotus refers to Ion as the eponymous hero of the Ionians, he considers him the son of Xouthus, not of Apollo.[141] Even Euripides himself follows Ion's traditional pedigree in his *Wise Melanippe* (fr. 481.9–11 Kannicht). If the story connecting Apollo, Creousa, and Ion came out of the world of tragedy in the first place, perhaps Sophocles was responsible for part of it at least. We know that Sophocles produced a *Creousa*, if not also an *Ion*, but the exact relationship of his work to Euripides' *Ion* remains obscure.[142]

However that may be, there is no doubt that the non-Hesiodic genealogical arrangement celebrated in Euripides' *Ion* reflects and serves contemporary Athenian ideology by integrating the ideal of autochthony with an intrinsic link between Athens and the Ionians.[143] Investing Ion with a divine father glorifies not only the hero himself but also the entire city of Athens and the Ionian tribe.[144] At the same time, Dorus no longer belongs to the generation of Ion's father, but becomes Ion's younger half-sibling, and, as the son of Creousa, acquires Athenian origins. The genealogy proposed in *Ion* situates the three eponymous heroes (Ion, Dorus, and Achaeus) within the same generation, thus inviting its audience to think of them in comparative terms. All three share the same mother, but, as the

[140]  Owen 1936: xii views the genealogical link between Ion and Apollo in the context of the cult of Apollo πατρῷος. See Plato, *Euthd.* 302d (ἀλλὰ Ἀπόλλων πατρῷος διὰ τὴν τοῦ Ἴωνος γένεσιν, "but Apollo is called 'ancestral' because of Ion's birth"); cf. Dem. 18.141, 57.54 and 67; Arist. *Ath.* 55.3. On the cult of Apollo πατρῷος, see also Hendrick 1988, esp. 200–10. Recently, however, Cromey 2006 has shown that the cult of Apollo πατρῷος was "an Athenian patriotic creation of the early fourth century, 'Ancestral Apollo', manufactured purely for home consumption" (45–46).

[141]  Hdt. 7.94 (ἐκαλέοντο Πελασγοὶ Αἰγιαλέες, ἐπὶ δὲ Ἴωνος τοῦ Ξούθου Ἴωνες) and 8.44.2 (Ἴωνος δὲ τοῦ Ξούθου στρατάρχεω γενομένου Ἀθηναίοισι ἐκλήθησαν ἀπὸ τούτου Ἴωνες).

[142]  Whether Sophocles' *Creousa* and *Ion* were one and the same play has been debated; see Pearson 1917: 23–24. On different views about how (if at all) the myth in Euripides' *Ion* relates to the plot of Sophocles' *Creousa*, see Wilamowitz 1926: 11, Grégoire and Parmentier 1923: 161–63, Owen 1939: xii–xiv, Burnett 1971: 103–04, Radt 1977: 321.

[143]  Loraux 1993b: 184–236; Hall 1997: 51–56 (p. 56 on the *Ion*); Zacharia 2003: 44–102 with some commentary on Hall 1997; Calame 2007. On Athenian autochthony and/or "Ionianism" in the fifth century, see also Connor 1993, Parker 1987: 193–95, Rosivach 1987, and Forsdyke 2012: 130–37; cf. Sourvinou-Inwood 2011: 24–134.

[144]  On Apollo in the *Ion*, see Zacharia 2003: 103–49. Some scholars have pointed out a tension between the play's pro-Athenian agenda and the unfavorable portrayal of the god who mainly promotes it; after all, Apollo comes across as indecent, inefficient and manipulative. On this issue, see Conacher 1967: 269–70 and 275–85 with a discussion of previous scholarship. Cf. Spira 1960: 77–79 and Burnett 1962, who refuse to acknowledge that Apollo's representation is actually problematic in the play; Erbse 1975a, who views gods as auxiliary figures in a play about human tragicomedy (cf. Hunter 2011); Gellie 1984, who argues that Apollo simply serves what he views as the "comic plot" of the *Ion*; and Lloyd 1986, who reads in the play a negotiation between human perspectives and the divine will. On the failure of the plan announced by Hermes in the prologue in the context of other Euripidean plays that involve prophecies in their prologues, see also Hamilton 1978.

son of a god, Ion stands out. Dorus and Aeolus are inferior in pedigree not only because their father is a mortal but also because he is portrayed as a clueless idiot who gets manipulated and deceived by immortals and mortals alike.[145] In other words, the play remythologizes the origins of the Dorian tribe, linking the Dorians with Athens, but, at the same time, signaling their inferiority to the Ionians – a bold move that would have been particularly powerful if the play was indeed performed soon after the disastrous Sicilian Expedition, as is often assumed.[146] Since all this information comes from Athena herself, the *Ion* unapologetically invests its untraditional and Athenocentric genealogical account with divine authority. More importantly, shortly after divulging this (presumably true) account of Creusa's future progeny, the goddess demands the circulation of a different, false genealogy linking Ion to Xouthus (*Ion* 1601–03). The play, thus, makes room for competing traditions regarding Ion's pedigree, only to disparage them as fabrications.

The *Ion*, therefore, confirms the ongoing symbolic value of genealogical traditions and the importance of their public performance. On the other hand, however, it adopts a competitive attitude towards the established and widely known Hesiodic tradition. I suggest that the play's competitive engagement with Hesiodic genealogy goes beyond supplanting it with a new, Athenocentric version of Ion's family tree. Euripides' *Ion* explores heroic genealogy from different evolving perspectives, including Ion's but mainly Creusa's. As the play invites juxtaposition to the Hesiodic *Catalogue*, it exposes the limitations of traditional genealogical poetry as a medium for performing genealogies.

Now, in principle, when compared to the modest genealogical entries in the Hesiodic *Catalogue*, every aspect of Euripides' intricate plot (e.g., Apollo's grand plan and Ion's identity quest) seems to accentuate the greater possibilities afforded by the dramatic genre. Yet I propose that the play uses Creusa's story in particular to explore more systematically the complexities involved in performing genealogy in tragedy as opposed to Hesiodic poetry. As mentioned earlier, the untraditional genealogical arrangement celebrated in the *Ion* entails a series of traumatic experiences that burden Creusa until the final recognition scene: her forceful rape, her clandestine pregnancy, and the painful abandonment of her baby boy.[147]

[145] Zacharia 1995: 51–57 and 2003: 72–76, Lee 1997: 29.
[146] Calame 2007: 280. On the date of the *Ion*, see Conacher 1967: 273–75, Lee 1997: 40 and Zacharia 2003: 3–5.
[147] In addition to the *Ion*, Euripides produced several plays that revolved around a god's sexual union with a mortal woman and its consequences (*Alope, Antiope, Danae, Wise Melanippe*; cf. Sophocles'

The circumstances of Ion's conception and birth are recounted several times throughout the play and in different contexts.[148] With the exception of Hermes' brief summary in the prologue (*Ion* 8–27), all other accounts are given by Creousa herself. It is worth noting that initially Creousa refrains from assuming the role of the protagonist in her own story. When she mentions the rape and the fate of the newborn for the first time to Ion and the Chorus, it is in the third person under the pretense that it happened to some other woman (*Ion* 330–91). Yet, at the news that Xouthus has discovered his long-lost bastard, the queen breaks down and sings about her past trauma in the first person (*Ion* 859–922). The impact of this heartbreaking autobiographical monody is amplified further by the details she reveals in her subsequent exchange with the Old Man who responds to her confession (*Ion* 925–69). Finally, Creousa returns to these events one last time as soon as she realizes that the young man she attempted to kill is actually the son she bore to Apollo all those years ago (*Ion* 1398–1500). Unlike her monody, this first-person account of the events is an expression of joy and relief,[149] even if Ion, her addressee, harbors a few doubts about the truthfulness of her story until Athena arrives and confirms his divine pedigree (*Ion* 1521–48).[150]

These variations on a theme demonstrate the malleability of a genealogical narrative in the context of a dramatic genre that involves

---

first *Tyro*), but these plays survive only in fragments. See extensively Huys 1995; cf. also Aélion 1983: 2.99 n.43, Seaford 1990: 160–63, Foley 2001: 85–86, Matthiessen 2004: 42–43, Scafuro 1990: 136–50, and Sommerstein 2006.

[148] Rabinowitz 1993: 198–201, following Burnett 1962: 90–91, argues that the various accounts of Creousa's past create ambiguity about whether this was actually a rape. While the accounts emphasize different aspects of Creousa's experience, I do not think there is anything in the text of the *Ion* that supports this rather cynical reading. Equally unconvincing is Wassermann's attempt to downplay rape in the *Ion* by pointing out that coercive sex was the only way gods mated with mortal women in the Greek imagination (Wassermann 1940: 588–90; cf. Spira 1960: 80). This reading does not do justice to Creousa's voice in the play but also ignores the fact that other representations of sexual unions between mortals and immortals do not dwell on the trauma they entail for the women involved; see, e.g., Hesiodic genealogical poetry and Pindar's *Pythian* 9. For a balanced reassessment of the value of Creousa's rape in relation to her marriage to Xouthus, see Dunn 1990, esp. 131–35, although the parallels between Creousa and Pandora that he traces are less convincing, given that the archetypical γηγενής in Creousa's family is Erichthonius, a male rather than a female.

[149] On Euripidean duets, see Cyrino 1998, esp. 95–97 on the recognition duet in *Ion*. On the preoccupation with issues of legitimacy and citizenship in contemporary Athens, see Saxonhouse 1986: 252–73, Loraux 1993: 188–95 and, especially, 199–220, Zeitlin 1996: 288, 294–300, 322–26; cf. also Walsh 1978 and Parker 1987: 205–07.

[150] For the doubts that Ion harbors regarding the veracity of his mother's claim (*Ion* 1521–27; cf. 340), cf. *Ba.* 26–31 and perhaps also *Danae* frs. 320, 324–26 Kannicht with Seaford 1990: 161. On the skepticism, see also Huys 1995: 99–100. On the various instantiations of this narrative in the *Ion*, cf. Scafuro 1990: 140–49.

different characters interacting in ever-evolving circumstances. For instance, viewed together as a sequence, Creousa's revelatory monody (*Ion* 859–922) and her exchange with the Old Man (*Ion* 925–69) draw attention to how different and yet complementary these two dramatic modes are. Constructed as a subversive hymn to Apollo, Creousa's song communicates raw agony, bitterness, and suffering, thus adding depth to her character and inspiring sympathy.[151] The song does not move the action forward, yet it contextualizes the upcoming conspiracy against Ion's life, sheds additional light upon Creousa's motivations, and prevents her from becoming an unsympathetic villain.[152] The dialogue between the Old Man and Creousa, on the other hand, complements Creousa's emotional retelling of her past and offers a new perspective on her story from the point of view of a supportive paternal figure (*Ion* 942–45). Through the Old Man, the play suggests to its audience a particular emotional reaction towards Creousa's trauma, a combination of sympathy, pity, and indignation (e.g. *Ion* 925–30, 940, 967). By the time Creousa responds to the Old Man's call for vengeance (*Ion* 970), the play has solidified her portrayal as a victim.[153]

Euripides' play, then, does not simply grant the female figure involved in the birth of a hero a voice of her own. Through Creousa's multiple and diverse performances of the story of Ion's conception and birth, the play draws attention to the dynamic aspect that the genealogical narrative acquires in drama. Furthermore, each performance of the story generates a different commentary from its internal audience. I have already discussed the response of the Old Man to Creousa's monody, but, in this context, Ion's reactions are perhaps much more important. Creousa's initial, third-person account remains vague about the exact nature of the sexual encounter between Apollo and the woman Creousa supposedly represents (*Ion* 330–91), yet Ion infers correctly from her words that Apollo raped the maiden in question (*Ion* 436–39). Despite his devotion to Apollo, when the young man contemplates the story he heard from Creousa, he chastises the god; in fact, he goes beyond that and criticizes

---

[151] On Creousa's song as a subversive hymn, see Larue 1963; cf. Schadewaldt 1966²: 181–82, Gauger 1977: 34–39, and Furley 1999–2000: 189–190. On the song's representation of Apollo, see also Barlow 1986: 15–16; cf. Chong-Gossard 2008: 49 on the sensory language involved in Creousa's recollection of her rape.

[152] Lee 1997: 257–58; see already Wilamowitz 1926: 11–12.

[153] On the role of the Old Man and the chorus in setting in motion Creousa's vengeance drama, see Burnett 1971: 112–15 and Chong-Gossard 2008: 174–76, who focuses on the chorus.

the sexual domination of the Olympian gods over mortal women as a whole (*Ion* 440–51).[154] However, this condemnation of divine sexual politics comes from a male character who, by the end of the play, realizes that he is the product of such a union and, more importantly, that much glory awaits him and his legacy on account of it (*Ion* 1485, 1488). In other words, the *Ion* problematizes the celebration of the unions between mortals and immortals that defines the Hesiodic genealogical tradition, but it does not reject it. On the contrary, the play's final scene acknowledges that these unions, no matter how traumatic, can have great benefits for the families and the communities to which these heroes belong. The play, therefore, uses Creousa's story to explore both the negative and the positive aspects of this core narrative of traditional genealogical poetry, and revises it so that it acknowledges and accommodates at the same time celebration and trauma. Even the rift between Creousa and Apollo is mended by the end of play. Yet, as Buxton points out, her praise of the god in her final few lines (1609–13) does not mean that her feelings about her rape have changed or that she instantly forgot the pain she experienced for years when she thought that her child was dead.[155]

One could argue that Creousa's accounts of her past invite juxtaposition with the Hesiodic tradition simply by virtue of deviation from that other, widely known version of Ion's origins. Yet I suggest that there may a more compelling factor that encourages this reading. The audience of the play is first introduced to Creousa's rape and the fate of her baby by Hermes in the prologue (*Ion* 8–27).[156] Hermes' account is replete with Athenian references that programmatically introduce the central issue of autochthony.[157] When it comes to the actual rape, however, the god lays out the facts without much elaboration:

> οὗ παῖδ᾽ Ἐρεχθέως Φοῖβος ἔζευξεν γάμοις
> βίᾳ Κρέουσαν
>                          (Euripides, *Ion* 10–11)

---

[154] Cf. Scafuro 1990: 142 on Ion's response. On this passage, see also Spira 1960: 53–59, Saxonhouse 1986: 262–63, Yunis 1988: 129–33, who goes on to point out that Ion remains loyal to Apollo throughout the play.

[155] Buxton 2013: 138. Cf. Lloyd 1986: 37, Saxonhouse 1986: 260 with n.17.

[156] On the language of this passage, see Rehm 1992: 134.

[157] Hermes dwells on the geography of the Athenian acropolis when he pinpoints the place where the rape happened (*Ion* 11–13). Furthermore, in connection with the tokens Creousa leaves with the child, he recounts the aetiological story that goes back to Erichthonius (*Ion* 20–26). On the negotiation between Delphic and Athenian space in the play, see, e.g., Kuntz 1993: 43–55.

In this place Phoebus yoked forcefully in sexual union the daughter of Erechtheus, Creousa

> ἀγνῶς δὲ πατρί (τῷ θεῷ γὰρ ἦν φίλον)
> γαστρὸς διήνεγκ᾽ ὄγκον. ὡς δ᾽ ἦλθεν χρόνος,
> τεκοῦσ᾽ ἐν οἴκοις παῖδ᾽ ἀπήνεγκεν βρέφος
> ἐς ταὐτὸν ἄντρον οὗπερ ηὐνάσθη θεῷ
> Κρέουσα, κἀκτίθησιν ὡς θανούμενον
> κοίλης ἐν ἀντίπηγος εὐτρόχῳ κύκλῳ
>
> (Euripides, *Ion* 14–19)

Unbeknownst to her father (for the god wished it so) she carried to term the burden of her belly. And when the time came, having given birth in her home, Creousa carried the infant to the same cave where she had slept with the god, and she exposed him, to die, in the well-rounded hollow of a cradle

> ἀλλ᾽ ἦν εἶχε παρθένος χλιδὴν
> τέκνῳ προσάψασ᾽ ἔλιπεν ὡς θανουμένῳ.
>
> (Euripides, *Ion* 26–27)

So, having put on the child the finery that she had, the maiden left him to die.

Hermes' third-person account of the events is brief, succinct, and straight-forward. As such, his report contrasts sharply not only with the extensive and emotional first-person narrative in Creousa's monody (esp. *Ion* 887–904), but also with her third-person account (*Ion* 338–60), which is moving enough to elicit a strong emotional reaction from Ion (e.g. *Ion* 355, 436–51). Even though he acknowledges that the union between Creousa and Apollo was forced (βίᾳ, in line 11), Hermes as a narrator has no interest in the maiden's emotions during or after the rape. He displays the same detach-ment towards her plight again later, when he summarizes her marriage to Xouthus and her lack of children (*Ion* 57–67).[158] Furthermore, Creousa's voice is completely suppressed in Hermes' narrative, yet Apollo gets seven lines of direct speech (*Ion* 29–36).[159]

---

[158]  The only emotion that Hermes mentions, namely the desire for children (ἔρωτι παίδων, *Ion* 67), does not belong to Creousa alone but is shared by the couple.

[159]  Direct speech is rare in Hesiodic genealogical poetry: Hes. fr. 24/31 (Poseidon addresses Tyro after he deceives and sleeps with her), fr. 72/165 (a male god addresses the king Teuthras ), fr. *3/75 (Schoeneus proclaims the footrace for the hand of Atalanta), fr. *4/76 (Hippomenes addresses Atalanta in order to deceive her). Cf. fr. 100/211.7–13 (a μακαρισμός of Peleus by a male collective). The only female voices granted direct speech in the extant fragments of the *Catalogue* belong to goddesses and do not involve an erotic context: Athena settles a dispute between Sisyphus and Aethon in fr. 37/43a.41–43, and an unidentified goddess (probably Athena or Artemis) addresses Chiron in fr. 103.5–13H. In the *ME*, on the other hand, we find Alcmene lamenting the toilsome fate of her son Heracles (frs. 10–11/248–49).

I propose that, in the prologue, Hermes offers a narrative of Creousa's rape and Ion's birth that evokes Hesiodic genealogical poetry not only due to its content but also due to its style. Just like the narrator of the Hesiodic *Catalogue*, Hermes offers a third-person male perspective on the birth of a hero from a god and a mortal woman, which privileges the male main figure and ignores the perspective of his female counterpart. He also relates information about the past that is either completely unknown or only partially known to the mortal cast of the *Ion*; in this sense, he recalls the Hesiodic narrator who, thanks to the Muses, possesses otherwise inaccessible knowledge about the heroic age and its interaction with the divine world.[160]

Far from being the mute two-dimensional character that Hermes constructs and Apollo presumes (*Ion* 71–73), Euripides' Creousa turns out to be both vocal and proactive. Even though she cannot undo her traumatic past, she dares to take the future in her own hands when she plots the assassination of Ion. By telling her story and taking action, Creousa thus inadvertently derails Apollo's initial scheme (*Ion* 71–73) and forces the god to ensure her compliance with the revised version of his plot to make Ion the next king of Athens (*Ion* 1563–68).

Much like the *PV*, therefore, the *Ion* offers a critical commentary on traditional genealogical poems such as the *Catalogue of Women* and the *ME*, as it exposes their inadequate treatment of female characters and of their perspectives. The unions between gods and mortal women produced a race of glorious heroes whose political and social significance was still upheld and celebrated in the fifth century. As acts of control and domination of male divinities over mortal women, however, these unions entail the potential of trauma and pain, which poems like the *Catalogue of Women* and the *ME* systematically elide in the interest of celebrating the Olympians.[161] While the *PV* focuses exclusively on female trauma, Euripides' play dwells also on the positive legacy of these unions and attempts to integrate these two aspects. In the end, Apollo and Creousa reach some sort of reconciliation, and, even though this takes place through the mediation of Athena, the catalyst is Ion

---

Still, in the few preserved lines, the mother's pathetic speech seems to reflect on her son's experiences rather than her own. For a comparison between the *Catalogue* and the *Theogony* in the distribution of direct speech, see Rengakos 2009: 216; cf. 169–70 and Rutherford 2000: 87–88 for a comparison between the Hesiodic *Catalogue* and the catalogue of women in the Homeric *Nekuia* (Hom. *Od.* 11.225–332).

[160] Imhof 1966: 13 briefly views the prologue's narrative of the past in relation to epic poetry, but does not talk about genealogical poetry in particular.

[161] See above, pp. 88–89 and 153–59. Hermes' explicit mention of sexual violence (βίᾳ, *Ion* 11) in his summary of Apollo's union with Creousa already gives a hint about the play's critical take on traditional genealogical poetry.

himself, the product of Creousa's rape, for whom Apollo has planned a glorious future, thus benefiting both Creousa's *oikos* and the entire city of Athens.[162] In other words, while celebrating a new, Athenocentric version of Ion's family tree, the play not only lets Creousa tell her story but also allows her and other characters (including Ion) to express their disillusionment and disapproval regarding Apollo's conduct. By offering this complex treatment of Ion's story, Euripides' *Ion* exposes the shortcomings of traditional genealogical poetry and perhaps goes so far as to suggest itself (or dramatic poetry in general) as a better alternative for the public performance of genealogy.

---

[162] Contrast Prometheus' prophecy in *PV* 844–76, which places Io's deliverance in the future and seems to have no immediate consolatory effect (*PV* 877–86).

# CHAPTER 5

# *Hesiod and Old Comedy*

Much like tragedy, Old Comedy interacts boldly with Hesiodic poetry and appropriates it in various degrees and contexts. In this chapter, I focus mainly on the extensive engagement of Aristophanes' *Birds* with Hesiodic narratives as well as with their rich reception. Ultimately, I argue, the *Birds* offers a bold revision of the Hesiodic vision of the cosmos but, while doing so, it situates itself within the reception of the Hesiodic corpus. Before turning to the *Birds*, however, I discuss some comic receptions of Hesiodic didactic poetry and authority; I also investigate how some comedies appropriate the biographical fiction of Hesiod's victory over Homer at the funerary games of Amphidamas. The final section of this chapter probes the comic reception of the Hesiodic Golden Age by way of one case study. Although some points remain speculative, I hope that my discussion demonstrates the richness and variety of Hesiodic reception in Old Comedy.

## Hesiod as a Comic Character

Among the earliest plays for which there is some (admittedly slim) evidence hinting at Hesiod's appearance as a comic character is Cratinus' *Archilochoi*, a play that, in all likelihood, dramatized an *agon* between Homer and Archilochus.[1] For Cratinus, Archilochus' immediate and caustic responses to contemporary events represented a type of poetic intervention that could

---

[1] Geissler 1925: 18–19 dates the *Archilochoi* to shortly after 449 BCE, whereas Luppe 1973 dates the play to 435–423 BCE. For the *agon* between Homer and Archilochus, see fr. 6 KA with Baker 1904: 138, Pieters 1946: 132–35, Rosen 1988: 42–48, Pretagostini 1982, esp. 45–47 and 50–51, Conti Bizzarro 1999: 45–50, and Bakola 2010: 71–72. Kugelmeier 1996: 181–85 suggests a different reading, according to which Archilochus' opponent was a fifth-century proponent of New Music (e.g. Gnesippus, who appears in Cratinus fr. 276 KA), while Homer and Hesiod appeared in support of Archilochus. If Archilochus' opponent was blind, however, as one can infer from fr. 6.3 KA (ὁ τυφλός), Homer emerges as a more likely contestant.

potentially benefit the *polis* greatly. Thus Cratinus appropriated elements of Archilochean poetics in his own *persona* as a comic poet and situated his comedy within the iambic tradition of blame-poetry (ψόγος).[2] In the case of the *Archilochoi*, it is conceivable that the *agon* between Homer and Archilochus highlighted the benefits of ψόγος by contrasting it to the inherent disinterest of traditional epic towards contemporary politics.[3] In this context, then, Archilochus' victory would emerge as a vindication of his reception and appropriation by Cratinus' comic poetics.

Cratinus' play included other poetic figures besides Homer and Archilochus. The chorus, for instance, seems to have consisted of poets. This assumption arises from fr. 2 KA (οἷον σοφιστῶν σμῆνος ἀνεδιφήσατε, "what a swarm of sophists you sought"), which Clement of Alexandria cites as evidence that poets could be referred to as σοφισταί (*Strom.* 1.3.24.1–2). It is possible that during the *agon* the poets of the chorus were split into two semi-choruses, each in support of a contestant,[4] and that they were united as supporters of Archilochus after his victory.[5] There is also evidence that Hesiod may have appeared in the play. While almost certainly alluding to fr. 2 KA, Diogenes Laertius (1.12) reports that, in his *Archilochoi*, Cratinus uses the word σοφισταί as praise for τοὺς περὶ Ὅμηρον καὶ Ἡσίοδον. The phrase may indicate simply that the chorus of the *Archilochoi* was composed of poets summoned to defend hexameter poetry or, at least, what hexameter poetry stood for in this comedy. Nonetheless, Diogenes' comment allows for the possibility that Hesiod appeared as a character in this play alongside Homer. What could Hesiod's role be in the *Archilochoi*? One may extrapolate from Diogenes' phrase that Hesiod and Homer belonged to the same camp and that the former came in support of the latter. However, it is also conceivable that Hesiod's role was – or turned out to be – that of a buffoon (βωμολόχος).[6] While

---

[2] On Cratinus' Archilochean poetics, see Pieters 1946: 133–35, Rosen 1988: 37–58 (now with consideration of Rosen 2013), Conti Bizzarro 1999: 47, Biles 2002: 175–76, and Bakola 2010: 70–80.

[3] In her excellent discussion, Bakola 2010: 70–79 explores the possibility that the *agon* may also have involved a relative assessment of Archilochus and Homer in terms of piety, solemnity, and cultic relevance. For a different reading, see Ornaghi 2004: 224–28, who suggests that in the *agon* the *Archilochoi* may have privileged a representation of Homer as the poet of the *Margites*, thus constructing a history of comedy as a genre.

[4] On the split chorus, see already Baker (1904) 140 and, more recently, Pretagostini 1982: 45 n.9 and Ornaghi 2004: 218–23. On Cratinus' fr. 2 KA, see Conti Bizzarro 1999: 39–45.

[5] The plural title *Archilochoi* probably stands for "Archilochus and his supporters." On this type of title, see already Baker 1904: 138–40 and, more recently, Pretagostini 1982: 45 n.9 and Bagordo 2013: 117 n.117. Cf. Teleclides' *Hesiodoi* (see below).

[6] Whittaker 1935: 185 envisions Hesiod as a *tertius gaudens*. On the βωμολόχος, see Kidd 2012.

any discussion of Hesiod's contribution(s) to the poetic *agon* of the *Archilochoi* is bound to remain speculative, it is worth considering the possibility that Hesiod's presence facilitated the evocation of another well-known poetic competition, namely that between Homer and Hesiod.

The contest between Homer and Hesiod is a fictional narrative based on the "autobiographical" digression in the *Works and Days* (650–59), in which the poetic voice recounts his victory "with a poem" (ὕμνῳ, *WD* 657) against unidentified competition at the funerary games for Amphidamas in Chalcis.[7] The most extensive version of the story survives in the second-century CE biographical compilation known as the *Certamen Homeri et Hesiodi*; there is good evidence, however, that the *Certamen* reiterates to a considerable extent the account of the *agon* included in the *Mouseion* of Alcidamas, a fourth-century BCE sophist.[8] In all likelihood, Alcidamas produced a version of the contest that fit his own agenda, but it is highly unlikely that he invented the story altogether. Rather, he must have worked with a preexisting narrative that was circulating in the fifth century and perhaps as early as the sixth century BCE.[9]

It has been suggested that such a pre-Alcidamean version of the *agon* between Homer and Hesiod informs thematically and structurally the competition between Aeschylus and Euripides that Aristophanes stages in his *Frogs*, a play produced in 405 BCE.[10] Just like the *Certamen*, the *Frogs* puts the poets' skill to the test but ultimately foregrounds the contribution of their poetry to the community as a prime measure of their value. The formative effect of poetry as a measure of its quality is discussed early on in the contest between Aeschylus and Euripides (*Ra.* 954–1088) and recurs in the end as the criterion that ultimately determines the outcome of the contest (*Ra.* 1419–66; cf. 1500–03). As the similarities encourage the play's audience to evoke the *agon* at Chalcis as part of the play's rich intertext, however, the differences throw into sharp

---

[7] See Introduction, pp. 1–6.

[8] Stobaeus (4.52b.22 Wachsmuth) explicitly attributes to Alcidamas' *Mouseion* the first response that Homer gives in the poetic contest of the *Certamen* (*Cert.* 78–79 = Thgn. 425, 427). The same two lines are found in *P. Flinders-Petrie* 25, a third-century century BCE papyrus that preserves a section of the contest that corresponds closely to *Cert.* 68–101 and is thus most probably a fragment of Alcidamas' *Mouseion*. See, e.g., Winter 1925, esp. 120–25, Vogt 1959, Avezzù 1982: 84–87. The *Certamen* mentions the *Mouseion* only as a source regarding the fate of Hesiod's murderers (238–40); *P. Mich.* 2754, however, indicates that it was also the source for the narrative of Homer's death in *Cert.* 324–38. On the papyrological evidence related to the *Certamen*, see Bassino 2012 and 2013: 61–89.

[9] See Introduction, pp. 4–5 with n.19.

[10] Extensively Cavalli 1999: 91–105; cf. Richardson 1981: 1–3 and Rosen 2004. For another case study of the *Certamen*'s reception by Aristophanes, see Telò 2013 on Ar. *Pax* 1298–1301.

relief the play's engagement with literary criticism. In the *Certamen*, king Panedes rewards Hesiod for exhorting his audience towards peaceful agriculture rather than war (*Cert.* 207–10); in the end of the *Frogs*, on the other hand, Dionysus chooses to resurrect Aeschylus, the poet who claims to have shaped his audience into valiant warriors (*Ra.* 1013–44; cf. 1463–65). This outcome can be interpreted, of course, as a response to the status of Athenian affairs at the time of the play's production, but the juxtaposition between this *agon* and the one at Chalcis draws further attention to the implications of Dionysus' decision. Along the same lines, the comedy's near-aporetic representation of literary criticism as a complex and constantly frustrated process becomes even sharper when compared with the *agon* between Homer and Hesiod.[11] In the *Certamen*, king Panedes privileges only one criterion in his assessment, namely the poet's contribution to the common good. He does not waver; rather, he makes his decision immediately and bestows the reward accordingly even though his judgment clashes with the popular opinion.[12] In the *Frogs*, by contrast, Dionysus constantly alters his criteria and repeatedly fails to make a choice. The text raises the expectation that the contest will be judged based on poetic τέχνη (*Ra.* 761–70, 780, 785–86, 793–94, etc.), and eventually the contestants themselves agree that a poet's value is determined by both δεξιότης (skill) and νουθεσία (counsel) of the sort that makes people better citizens (*Ra.* 1008–10).[13] Yet the focus of the *agon* shifts quickly from issues of νουθεσία (*Ra.* 1009–88) to technical skill and the use of language (*Ra.* 1119–1410), only to reach an impasse because Dionysus cannot choose (*Ra.* 1411–13). Ultimately, it appears that Dionysus will judge the contest based on each poet's potential to save Athens (*Ra.* 1419–23 and 1435–36), but he fails to make up his mind yet again (*Ra.* 1433–34). The final verdict is postponed for a few more lines, until Dionysus decides to follow his ψυχή (*Ra.* 1468) and picks Aeschylus (*Ra.* 1471).[14] This long and tortuous process exposes the complexity and

---

[11] Rosen 2004: 304–22, Ford 2002: 281–82 and 292–93.

[12] On the different responses that the two poets elicit in the *Certamen*, see Graziosi 2001: 71 and Koning 2010a: 248–54, 258–59, and 267–68. Rosen 2004: 309–13 suggests that the Athenian audience of the *Frogs* would consider Panedes' choice poor. Although in later sources Panedes' verdict appears to be proverbial for unsuccessful judgments (Apostolius, *Coll. Paroem.* 14.11: Πανίδου ψῆφος· ἐπὶ τῶν ἀμαθῶς ψηφιζομένων), there is no evidence that this assessment dates as far back as the classical era. See also below, n.17.

[13] Woodbury 1986: 244.

[14] See Hunter 2009: 10–38, esp. 36–38; cf. also Woodbury 1986: 244–46 and Wright 2012: 66. On the overarching disparity between Dionysus' intense desire for Euripides in the beginning of the play (*Ra.* 52–105) and his decision to resurrect Aeschylus in the end, see Erbse 1975b with a critical discussion of earlier scholarship, Lada-Richards 1999, esp. 216–325, Silk 2000: 258–60 with

elusiveness of literary criticism;[15] inevitably, any comparison to the relatively straightforward *agon* at Chalcis draws attention to the comedy's nuanced and complicated take on the assessment of poetry.

It is possible that Cratinus' *Archilochoi* also evoked the competition between Homer and Hesiod in the context of the *agon* between Homer and Archilochus.[16] Here too, the final judgment almost certainly took into serious consideration the poet's contribution to the common good, and, just as in the *Certamen*, the outcome was not in Homer's favor. I suggest that the presence of Hesiod as a character in the *agon* of the *Archilochoi* would solidify the link between the two poetic contests. If present, Hesiod would be a living, breathing, and perhaps rather vocal reminder of Homer's other failure at the Games of Amphidamas. From this perspective, Whittaker's suggestion that Hesiod held the role of the βωμολόχος in the *Archilochoi* is particularly attractive: one can imagine a scenario in which Hesiod undermined Homer by reminding the audience of the outcome at Chalcis, while at the same time comically undercutting himself too with his ridiculous buffoonery.[17] Such a role would enhance Archilochus' superiority to both Homer and Hesiod, the two embodiments of authoritative hexameter poetry.[18]

Finally, while Cratinus' *Archilochoi* explored issues pertaining to poetics and literary criticism mainly through the interaction of Homer, Archilochus, and perhaps Hesiod, the chorus must have contributed to this intellectual exercise as well. Although the identities of the poets in the play's chorus are unknown,[19] we should entertain the possibility that they were chosen at least partly for their own poetic engagements with the competing genres, hexameter poetry and Archilochean ψόγος. Through its

---

bibliography, and Bakola 2010: 67–70 with emphasis on a self-reflexive meta-literary reading of the *Frogs*. For a different view, see Biles 2011: 250–51.

[15] Rosen 2004: 315: "Aristophanes seems to have understood the near futility of articulating exactly what it meant to say that an artistic phenomenon as complex as poetry could 'teach,' especially, at least, when one starts with the assumption that the subject of poetic teaching must be that which is 'morally beneficial.'" See also Hunter 2009: 10–52 and Halliwell 2011: 93–154.

[16] Ornaghi 2004: 219–20 and Bakola 2010: 73.

[17] There is no reason to assume that a comic subversion of Hesiod in this play reflects a negative reaction to his victory at Chalcis. Some scholars have read an anti-Hesiodic bias in the *Certamen* ever since Nietzsche 1870: 539; cf. Heldmann 1982: 21–31, Rosen 1997: 476 and 2004: 304. Contrast, however, West 1967: 443 and Koning 2010a: 255–56.

[18] On the satiric potential of Hesiod's *persona* in the *Works and Days*, see Hunt 1981 and, more recently, Telò 2013: 135. In his reading of Ar. *Pax* 1298–1301, Telò 2013 proposes that Archilochus' *iambos* and Hesiod's didactic *persona* complement each other as generic forefathers of Aristophanes' comic self.

[19] Wilson 1977: 279 argues that the chorus of Cratinus' *Archilochoi* was individualized; cf. Harvey 2000: 107–08 on Phrinychus' *Musae*.

chorus, therefore, the play may have reflected upon poetic reception in its various forms, including generic affiliation, appropriation of themes and attitudes, quotations, allusions, and references to the earlier and established poets. The play's self-consciousness on these matters would be consistent with its effort to defend and promote Cratinus' appropriation of Archilochean poetics.[20]

While Hesiod's appearance in the *Archilochoi* must remain hypothetical, his inclusion in Teleclides' *Hesiodoi* seems inevitable.[21] The *Hesiodoi* is tentatively dated to the 420s and, judging by the title of Cratinus' *Archilochoi*, it must have featured Hesiod and his supporters.[22] This play too was concerned, to some extent at least, with literary criticism: fr. 17 KA attests that the comedy dealt with Nothippos the tragedian,[23] while in fr. 15 KA a female figure (a personification of Tragedy or Poetry, or perhaps Aeschylus' Muse) laments her sufferings at the hands of the tragedian Philocles, a grandson of Aeschylus.

Unfortunately, these fragments tell us nothing about the involvement of Hesiod in the plot. It is possible that the play encompassed an *agon* between Hesiod and a tragedian; such a confrontation, however, would have broken several known conventions, since literary competitions usually involve poets who were considered more or less contemporaries and representatives of the same genre.[24] One could argue that the contest between Homer and Archilochus in Cratinus' *Archilochoi* already diverges from this pattern, but these contestants share two important characteristics that level the plain somewhat: their antiquity and their established Panhellenic status.[25] A contest between Hesiod, an authoritative poet of the

---

[20] In fr. 7 KA, the *Archilochoi* draws attention to Διὸς ψῆφος, a pivotal, monumental part of the Athenian landscape, thus underscoring the distinctly Athenian context in which the comedy receives three authoritative poets of Panhellenic caliber and defends Cratinus' Archilochean poetics (cf. Quaglia 1998: 51–52). On the performance of Homer, Hesiod, and Archilochus at Panhellenic festivals, see Pl. *Ion* 531a–532a. These are also the only poets whom Pindar mentions by name in his (extant) victory odes, a choice possibly informed by the fact that these three poetic corpora were already circulating widely throughout the Greek world (Homer: *P.* 4.277–78, *N.*7.20–21, *I.* 4.37–39; Hesiod: *I.*6.66–68; Archilochus: *O.* 9.1–2, *P.* 2.54–56).

[21] Bagordo 2013: 117. Nicostratus, a fourth-century poet, wrote a comedy entitled *Hesiodos*, but the only extant fragment (fr. 11 KA) is a short list of dishes involving fish and thus reveals nothing about the plot.

[22] See Bagordo 2013: 117–18; cf. also Ornaghi 2007: 38 and 2012: 390.

[23] On Nothippus and Gnesippus, see Bagordo 2013: 127–28. Storey 2014: 107 offers a brief survey of Teleclides' engagement with poetry in the extant fragments.

[24] Homer and Hesiod compete in hexameter poetry in the *Certamen*; Aeschylus and Euripides in Ar. *Frogs* are both tragedians. Cf. the competition between the two seers Calchas and Mopsus (Hes. fr. 278 and 279 MW).

[25] Pl. *Ion* 531a–532a; see also above, n.20.

distant past, and a late fifth-century tragedian has comic potential but
seems rather implausible, given how disparate these two literary figures
are.[26] Perhaps we should consider the possibility that Hesiod was invited
(by the female figure speaking in fr. 15?) to be a judge in a literary *agon*
between fifth-century tragedians. He may have been summoned to advise
the new generation of tragedians (if not the entire city of Athens) or to
offer his commentary on their art with an emphasis perhaps on the moral
depravity and other failures of contemporary poetry; one could even
imagine the ancient poet commenting on his own reception. However
that may be, it is most likely that Teleclides' *Hesiodoi* represented Hesiod
primarily as an authoritative didactic figure whose poetry contributed to
the preservation and proliferation of traditional values. In this context, the
play may have constructed Hesiod as the quintessential poet who benefits
the *polis* with his work, an ideal against which the poets criticized in the
play presumably failed to measure up. Just as Cratinus appropriated
Archilochus in his poetics, Teleclides may have aligned his comic *persona*
with Hesiod, the didactic poet par excellence.

## Hesiodic Didactic and Old Comedy

Of course, reception of Hesiodic didactic in Old Comedy can take place
without the inclusion of Hesiod among the characters. In Aristophanes'
*Frogs* we find Hesiod embedded in a list of authoritative poets of the past
whose poetry is beneficial for the community. After Euripides claims that
the Athenians have learned to think critically and express themselves with
subtlety thanks to his tragedies (*Ra.* 954, 956–58, 971–79), Aeschylus
prepares his defense by inviting Euripides to define what makes a poet
admirable (*Ra.* 1008). Euripides responds that it is skill, sound advice, and
a positive formative effect upon the members of the *polis* (*Ra.* 1009–10).
Aeschylus proceeds to demonstrate that his tragedies benefited Athens
by inspiring bravery in its citizens, while Euripides' art had a negative
effect upon the people of his *polis* (*Ra.* 1013–88). In this context, Aeschylus
offers a catalogue of ancient poetic authorities and their contributions to
the education of the citizens:

Αι.                      σκέψαι γὰρ ἀπ' ἀρχῆς
ὡς ὠφέλιμοι τῶν ποιητῶν οἱ γενναῖοι γεγένηνται.

[26] Cf. Bagordo 2013: 120. Ornaghi 2012: 401–05 discusses extensively the scenario of an *agon* between
Hesiod and a tragedian but makes no comment about the unusual pairing.

Ὀρφεὺς μὲν γὰρ τελετάς θ' ἡμῖν κατέδειξε φόνων τ' ἀπέχεσθαι,
Μουσαῖος δ' ἐξακέσεις τε νόσων καὶ χρησμούς, Ἡσίοδος δὲ
γῆς ἐργασίας, καρπῶν ὥρας, ἀρότους· ὁ δὲ θεῖος Ὅμηρος
ἀπὸ τοῦ τιμὴν καὶ κλέος ἔσχεν πλὴν τοῦδ', ὅτι χρήστ' ἐδίδαξεν,
τάξεις, ἀρετάς, ὁπλίσεις ἀνδρῶν;

(Aristophanes, *Frogs* 1030–36)

Aeschylus: Consider how beneficial the noble poets have been from the beginning. Orpheus taught us mystic rites and to abstain from killing; Musaeus (taught
us) cures for diseases and oracles; Hesiod (taught us) agricultural activities, the
seasons for crops, and ploughing. And from where did divine Homer acquire
honor and fame if not from this, namely that he instructed useful things: battle-
formations, acts of valor, and armings of men?

Aristophanes' Aeschylus adopts a reductive reading of ancient poets,
approaching their corpora in a highly selective manner. Orpheus and
Musaeus are constructed as authorities in different aspects of cult and
ritual; Hesiod and Homer, on the other hand, emerge as experts in
agriculture and war respectively. We have already encountered the association of Hesiod with (peacetime) farming and of Homer with warfare in
the context of their contest in the *Certamen*.[27] The *Frogs* follows the same
comparative approach towards the two poetic authorities but does not
adopt an agonistic frame: here Homer and Hesiod are regarded as complementary.[28] The chronological arrangement of the four poets in Aeschylus'
list,[29] as well as the selective reading of their corpora with an emphasis
on their educational value, may be evocative of the excerpting practices
of fifth-century anthologies. These were works produced to optimize
education by extracting useful quotes from all sorts of sources, including
poets, and by arranging these decontextualized passages according to
specific criteria, such as chronology and subject matter.[30] Hippias' anthology is of particular interest here. In the proem of this work (B 6 DK),
Hippias claims that he has collected material from a broad pool of sources
(prose and poetry, Greek and non-Greek); however, he only mentions by
name the four poets included in *Ra.* 1030–36 and he lists them in the same
chronological order.[31] Thus *Ra.* 1030–36 not only situates Hesiodic poetry
within a literary canon but also evokes its reception in anthologies that

---

[27] See above, pp. 181–83.     [28] Cf. Koning 2010a: 276–84.
[29] On *Ra.* 1030–36 as a chronological list of πρῶτοι εὑρεταί, see Ford 2002: 144–45; cf. Kleingünther
    1933: 142–43.
[30] On the culture of excerpting in classical Athens, see Ford 2002: 194–97.
[31] On Hippias' doxography, see Classen 1965: 175–78, Kerferd 1981: 48–49, Mansfeld 1986, Patzer 1986,
    and Balaudé 2006. On the proem of his anthology (B 6 DK), see Koning 2010b: 101 and esp. Patzer
    1986: 15–32.

aimed at the preservation, proliferation, and consumption of wisdom through excerpts.[32]

As suggested in the previous section, it is probable that the audience of the *Frogs* would evoke the *agon* at Chalcis and interpret the contest between Aeschylus and Euripides partly in juxtaposition to that between Homer and Hesiod. The *Frogs* shares with the *Certamen* the emphasis on the formative power of poetry as a cardinal criterion in literary criticism, even though, admittedly, the evaluation of poetry in the play is much more complicated than in the *Certamen* (176–210). In *Ra.* 1030–36 Aristophanes' Aeschylus constructs Orpheus, Musaeus, Hesiod, and Homer not only as didactic authorities but also as positive paradigms for other poets. In this context, the tragic poet clearly aligns himself exclusively with Homer, since his poetry had an impact on the military aspect of Athenian life (*Ra.* 1013–42). Rosen has suggested that the correspondence between Aeschylus and Homer is complemented by an alignment between Euripides and Hesiod in *Ra.* 976–78.[33] In this passage, Euripides boasts that he has taught the Athenians how to run their households better (καὶ τὰς οἰκίας / οἰκεῖν ἄμεινον ἢ πρὸ τοῦ / κἀνασκοπεῖν), which *prima facie* appears to iterate in part the didactic agenda of the *Works and Days*. If there is a Hesiodic resonance at all, it is certainly not as central to Euripides' definition of his didactic function in the *polis* as Homeric poetry is for Aristophanes' Aeschylus. Euripides mentions improved οἰκονομία as evidence for the intellectual training that Athenians have received through his tragedies, but he makes this point only briefly as he concludes the account of his benefaction to his city (*Ra.* 954–75). More importantly, any Hesiodic resonance in *Ra.* 976–78 is quickly diffused in the immediately following lines, in which the house-management skills that one supposedly acquires from Euripidean tragedies are explained only in the non-Hesiodic terms of safeguarding one's property through observation and interrogation (Euripides in *Ra.* 978–79; Dionysus in *Ra.* 980–91).

Even without a firm correspondence between the contestants of the two poetic competitions, the association of war with Homer and of agriculture

---

[32] On the consumption of Hesiodic poetry through the para-literature of anthologies, see Ford 2010, esp. 136–38 and 146–54 on the *WD*. Regarding Hippias in particular, we do not know how he dealt with the *WD* in his anthology but he seems to have included *Th.* 116–20; see Mansfeld 1986: 23–24. Judging by sch. Hes. *WD* 633b, *Cert.* 45–53, and Proclus *Vit. Hom.* 4 West, the biographical tradition reframed the canon embedded in *Ra.* 1030–36 in terms of kinship by implicating Orpheus, Hesiod, and Homer in the same genealogical tree. Cf. the testimony in Proclus *Vit. Hom.* 4 West that Gorgias from Leontini took Homer's (and presumably Hesiod's?) genealogy all the way back to Musaeus.

[33] Rosen 2004: 306.

with Hesiod in *Ra.* 1030–36 could still prompt members of the audience to involve the *agon* at Chalcis in their interpretation of the play. At the same time, however, we should not overlook that the passage suggests an alternative to the agonistic framework. Aeschylus' catalogue reflects an inclusive attitude towards diverse poetic corpora: the *Iliad* and the *WD* are considered complementary rather than competing, and the two poets are integrated in a broader literary canon. While enriching the current competition with an allusion to an ancient one, therefore, *Ra.* 1030–36 also undermines the agonistic setting altogether and hints at the potential of a similar inclusive approach towards Aeschylean and Euripidean tragedy.

Reception of Hesiodic didactic in Old Comedy is not limited to the *Works and Days*; rather, there is evidence of comic engagement with the *Chironos Hypothekai* as well.[34] For instance, Chiron featured prominently as a didactic figure in Cratinus' *Chirones*. Judging by the title, the chorus of this play consisted of Chiron and other centaurs or, alternatively, of multiple Chirons.[35] That the chorus draws its identity at least partly from the Hesiodic instantiation of the centaur is evident in a line from the *parodos*:[36]

σκῆψιν μὲν Χείρωνες ἐλήλυμεν ὡς ὑποθήκας (Cratinus fr. 253 KA)

As for our excuse, we have come as Chirones in order that . . . precepts

The chorus' self-identification with Chiron and their mention of *hypothe-kai*, all expressed in dactylic hexameter, invite the audience to recall *Chironos Hypothekai*, the didactic epic that was circulating under Hesiod's authorship and was used in the education of young Athenian men at least as early as the early fifth century.[37] As embodiments of Chiron the Hesiodic educator, the members of Cratinus' chorus may have deplored the moral decline of contemporary Athens and perhaps offered updated precepts to rectify the problems they criticized. It is very likely that at least

---

[34] On the *Chironos Hypothekai*, see pp. 8–9 and 114–16.

[35] See Goossens 1935: 413–14 and, more recently, Quaglia 1998: 42–43; cf. Kassel-Austin 4.245 with bibliography. We know of a few other comedies that involved Centaurs: Aristophanes' *Centaurs* or *Dramata* (426 BCE?), Apollophanes' *Centaurs*, and Nicochares' *Centaur*. Given that Aristophanes' *Centaurs* featured Euripides, it is more likely that it engaged with tragedy rather than Hesiod's didactic poem (see Kassel-Austin 3.2.158–59); about the other two we know virtually nothing. Bowie 2000: 320 speculates that Centaurs may have been favored by comic poets because they could be represented as agents of violence as well as civilization.

[36] Quaglia 1998: 42–43. My translation of fr. 253 KA is tentative.

[37] See already Norwood 1931: 126–27 and Picard 1951: 14. An Athenian *kyathos* (Berol. 2322) that dates to ca. 500 BCE and represents a scene from the education of boys appears to identify a scroll as ΧΙΡΟΝΕΙΑ, most probably an alternative title for (some version of) the Hesiodic *Chironos Hypothekai*. See Kurke 1990: 92–93 and Ford 2010: 147. On *Chironos Hypothekai* in the context of aristocratic education, see also Chapter 3.

some of the *hypothekai* formulated in this play engaged playfully with the didactic poetry of Hesiod. We find an example of such a creative and humorous reception of Hesiodic precepts in Cratinus fr. 349 KA,[38] which may or may not belong to the *Chirones*.[39] The two lines

ἔσθιε καὶ σῇ γαστρὶ δίδου χάριν, ὄφρα σε λιμὸς
ἐχθαίρῃ, Κοννᾶς δὲ πολυστέφανός σε φιλήσῃ
(Cratinus fr. 349 KA)

Keep eating and indulging your belly, so that hunger may despise you, but Connas of the many garlands may love you.

reformulate a piece of advice that Hesiod gives his brother in the *WD*

ἐργάζευ, Πέρση, δῖον γένος, ὄφρα σε λιμὸς
ἐχθαίρῃ, φιλέῃ δέ σ᾽ ἐυστέφανος Δημήτηρ
(Hesiod, *Works and Days* 299–300)

Keep working, Perses, offspring of Zeus, so that hunger may despise you, but Demeter of the beautiful garlands may love you.

Cratinus' speaker transforms a quintessentially Hesiodic exhortation towards labor into a call for feasting, admittedly a much more immediate and enjoyable way to thwart hunger. Hesiod's precept presupposes a harsh world where resources are scarce and survival depends on work, but the comedy reshapes it so as to fit a setting of ease and abundance. The comic subversion of Hesiod's somber advice is amplified by the substitution of the goddess Demeter with Connas, a drunkard flute-player who frequented the symposia and managed to remain poor despite his many victories (sch. Ar. *Eq.* 534a). As an invitation to indulgence, Cratinus' paraphrase of *WD* 299–300 derives its comic effect largely from being egregiously un-Hesiodic in spirit.

The few known details of the plot of the *Chirones* open the possibility for other kinds of engagement with Hesiodic didactic. For instance, there is evidence that the comedy involved critical remarks about μουσικὴ τέχνη and its contemporary decline (frs. 247, 248, 254 KA). This perceived crisis was associated with the corruption of the youth and the collapse of traditional education, in which Hesiodic poetry (including the *Chironos Hypothekai*) featured prominently. Furthermore, it is noteworthy that the

---

[38] Cf. Phryn. *ecl.* 64 = Hes. fr. 284 MW (*Chironos Hypothekai*): ἀκεστὴς λέγουσιν οἱ παλαιοί, οὐκ ἠπητής, ἠπήσασθαι ἔστι μὲν ἅπαξ παρ᾽ Ἀριστοφάνει ἐν Δαιταλεῦσι, παίζοντι τὰς Ἡσιόδου Ὑποθήκας· καὶ κόσκινον ἠπήσασθαι (=Ar. fr. 239 KA). It is impossible to tell if this Aristophanic fragment quotes verbatim the end of a Hesiodic hexameter line or not (cf. Most 2007: 297 n.18).

[39] Crusius 1889: 40 assigns the fragment to the *Chirones*; for other opinions, see Kassel-Austin 4.292.

cast of Cratinus' *Chirones* included Solon (fr. 246 KA), an important figure in Athenian history whose poetry often engages with the Hesiodic corpus, and especially with the *Works and Days*.[40] Unfortunately, the extant fragments do not provide insight as to whether Cratinus' Solon or any other character of the *Chirones* discussed Solonian poetry in terms of Hesiodic reception.

Much remains speculative regarding the engagement with the Hesiodic corpus in the *Chirones*; on the other hand, it is important to keep in mind that what looks like Hesiodic reception at first glance does not necessarily yield a satisfactory reading. Frs. 258–59 of the *Chirones* offer a variation on a rather common joke, namely the conflation of Pericles with Zeus.[41] The fragments contain genealogies for Zeus/Pericles and Hera/Aspasia that define these two figures through the negative qualities of their immediate ancestors: Civil Strife (Στάσις) and Time (Χρόνος) beget Zeus/Pericles (fr. 258 KA), Slutty Lustfulness (Καταπυγοσύνη) bears Aspasia (fr. 259 KA). Based on these genealogies, one may be tempted to argue that the *Chirones* responds not only to the didactic part of the Hesiodic corpus but also to its theogonic narrative. There is no reason to assume, however, that the text evokes the birth of Zeus as recounted in Hesiod's *Theogony*. On the contrary, the derivation of Zeus and Hera from different mothers and the involvement of Chronos discourage any Hesiodic association.[42]

The wise Centaur probably featured also in Pherecrates' *Chiron*.[43] This play includes a long dialogue between the personifications of Μουσική and Δικαιοσύνη, in which the former is complaining about the sufferings

[40] On Solon and Hesiodic poetry, see Solmsen 1949: 107–23, Irwin 2005: 155–98 with bibliography, and Scully 2015: 86–89; cf. Noussia-Fantuzzi 2010 on Solon 4, 6, 11, 12, 13, 22a, 27, 29, and 36W². On Solon's appearance in Cratinus' *Chirones*, see Quaglia 1998: 43; on his appropriation in Old Comedy, see Telò 2007: 82–92 and Bakola 2008: 4–7.

[41] Variations of this joke are found in plays by Cratinus (*Thrattai*, fr. 73.1–2 KA and *Nemesis*, fr. 118 KA), as well as Aristophanes' *Ach.* (530–31), Teleclides' *Hesiodoi* (fr. 18 KA), and Hermippus' *Moirai* (fr. 42 KA). See Schwarze 1971.

[42] For a thorough discussion of fr. 258 KA, including the textual problem surrounding Κρόνος/Χρόνος in line 2, see Noussia 2003. On the para-epic tone in frs. 255, 258, and *259 KA, see Revermann 2013: 114–16 and 124.

[43] There is a pseudo-Epicharmian work entitled *Chiron* (frs. 289–95 KA) that constructs Chiron as a didactic figure with medical expertise; see Kassel-Austin 1.168 and Rodríguez-Noriega 1996: 34, 209–11. According to the Suda (4.803.3), Chiron was the author of a *Hippiatricon*. His medical expertise is mentioned already in *Il.* 4.219; see also Pi. *P*.3.5–7 and 45–46, *N*. 3.53–55, and Pfeiffer 1999: 354 with more references. It is unknown whether medical instruction was part of the Hesiodic *Chironos Hypothekai* and, given the fragmentary state of both the didactic poem and Ps.-Epich. *Chiron*, we cannot trace any intertextual connections.

inflicted upon her by four proponents of New Music (fr. 155 KA);[44]
like Cratinus' *Chirones*, therefore, Pherecrates' *Chiron* offered critical
remarks about new trends in music and their moral implications. Given
the parody of *Il.* 9.270–71 in fr. 159 KA (cf. fr. 161), it is very likely that
Achilles was a character in the play. Any comic representation of the
relationship between Achilles and the legendary centaur could have
engaged to some extent with the *Chironos Hypothekai*, given that the
Hesiodic didactic poem related precepts addressed by Chiron to young
Achilles. The education of the youth is brought up in fr. 156 KA, when an
unidentified character, now an old man (line 6), speaks to his former
teacher and reflects on the futility of the instruction he received from him
when he was young. The fragment contrasts the rashness of the young
with the more mature and methodical approach one has in older age. By
admitting his inability to internalize instruction in his youth, the speaker
comically exposes the futility of teaching wisdom to the young and
immature. The audience, however, could also interpret the speaker's
comments as a jibe at the ineffective use of didactic literature such as
the *Chironos Hypothekai* in education – all the more, if the addressee in
this scene is Chiron himself.

Finally, evidence from Athenaeus may indicate further engagement with
Hesiodic didactic in Pherecrates' *Chiron*. The *Deipnosophistae* (8.364a–b)
preserves three hexameter lines with instructions about how to be a good
host even to unwanted guests. The lines belong to a composition entitled
*Chiron*, which may be Pherecrates' comedy although the attribution
remains uncertain:

> μηδὲ σύ γ' ἄνδρα φίλον καλέσας ἐπὶ δαῖτα θάλειαν
> ἄχθου ὁρῶν παρεόντα· κακὸς γὰρ ἀνὴρ τόδε ῥέζει.
> ἀλλὰ μάλ' εὔκηλος τέρπου φρένα τέρπε τ' ἐκεῖνον.
> (Pherecrates fr. 162.1–3 KA)

And, if you invite a friend to a luscious feast, you should not be grieved when you
see him present, for that's what a base man does. But, being very much at ease,
keep yourself cheerful and keep delighting that man as well.

A longer set of lines follows immediately (*Deipn.* 8. 364b–c), marked as the
continuation of the previous lines (τὰ δὲ ἑξῆς αὐτῶν). In this fragment
(Pherecr. fr. 162.4–13 KA), the speaker describes how he and his peers
(ἡμῶν ... τις in line 4, perhaps Centaurs?) get rid of unwanted guests when

---

[44] On Pherecr. fr. 155 KA, see Dobrov and Urios-Aparisi 1995, Olson 2007: 182–86, and Henderson
2000: 143.

they host feasts. Thus he undermines irreverently the sound advice given earlier in fr. 162.1–3 KA, bolstering his mockery with verbal echoes.[45] According to Athenaeus, however, the second fragment also parodies the Hesiodic *Great Works*:[46]

νῦν δὲ τούτων μὲν οὐδ' ὅλως μέμνηνται, τὰ δὲ ἑξῆς αὐτῶν ἐκμανθάνουσιν, ἅπερ πάντα ἐκ τῶν εἰς Ἡσίοδον ἀναφερομένων [μεγάλων Ἡοίων καὶ][47] μεγάλων Ἔργων πεπαρῴδηται.

(Athenaeus, *Deipnosophistae* 8.364b)

Nowadays, however, they don't keep in mind these admonitions (*sc.* fr. 162.1–3) at all, but they learn by heart the ones following them (*sc.* fr. 162.4–13), which are all a parody of the *Great Works* attributed to Hesiod.

If lines 4–13 parody both the instructions formulated in lines 1–3 and some admonition given in the *Megala Erga*, it is possible that these two texts coincide at least partially. In other words, lines 1–3 may paraphrase closely a Hesiodic precept about hosting, which lines 4–13 then proceed to subvert.[48] If fr. 162 KA does indeed belong to Pherecrates' *Chiron*, it complements the aforementioned fr. 156 KA, which also undercuts the value of didactic literature (including Hesiod's didactic) albeit from a different angle.

### Rewriting the Hesiodic Cosmos: Aristophanes' *Birds*

So far, I have explored how Old Comedy appropriates and responds to Hesiodic didactic; I now turn from precepts to narratives that circulated as part of the Hesiodic corpus. I am particularly interested in Old Comedy's reception of Hesiodic narratives about the creation of the cosmos, the negotiation of boundaries between mortals and immortals, and the history of the human race. For this endeavor, I focus primarily on the bold and extensive engagement of Aristophanes' *Birds* with the Hesiodic tradition.

---

[45] καλέσας, 1 ~ ἢν ... καλέσῃ, 4; ἄχθου, 2 ~ ἀχθόμεθ', 5 and ἄχθεται, 9; ὁρῶν παρεόντα, 2 ~ ὑποβλέπομεν παρεόντα, 5.

[46] On the *Megala Erga*, see Schwartz 1960: 245–46 and Cingano 2009: 129. For the hypothesis that the *Megala Erga* was a collection of all Hesiodic didactic poems, including the *Chironos Hypothekai*, see Marckscheffel 1840: 89 and 187–89.

[47] Merkelbach and West 1967: 146 are justified in proposing the deletion of μεγάλων Ἡοίων καί; cf. Schwartz 1960: 84–85.

[48] Cf. Olson 2007: 319: "it is tempting to think that Athenaeus (or the textual tradition of the *Deipnosophistae*) has somehow got things backwards and that the first three verses rather than the final ten are adapted from a passage in Hesiod." Olson rightly points out that lines 1–3 involve epic diction, while lines 4–13 do not.

Aristophanes' *Birds* was produced by Callistratus at the City Dionysia of 414 BCE.[49] The play features two insolent Athenians, Peisetairus and his sidekick Euelpides, who, in their attempt to escape the constraints of Athenian life and law, persuade the birds to found a city in the air and usurp the power of the Olympians. The plan is ultimately successful and the utopian plot comes to a closure with the celebration of Peisetairus as the new ruler of the cosmos.[50] Here, I examine closely how Peisetairus' ascent to power appropriates creatively several core elements from the Hesiodic corpus. As the play rewrites Hesiod's narrative and pushes it to the breaking point, I argue, it demonstrates a keen interest not only in the Hesiodic tradition but also in its reception.

The *Birds* aligns Peisetairus' actions with the most significant power struggles in the history of the cosmos: the Gigantomachy and the inter-generational conflicts that constitute the Succession Myth. Some scholars have privileged the Gigantomachy as the primary mythological paradigm for Peisetairus' endeavor.[51] This view has been encouraged by an ancient *hypothesis* of the play, which mentions briefly an ancient interpretation of the plot as a reaction to the Gigantomachic myth:

τινὲς δέ φασι τὸν ποιητὴν τὰς ἐν ταῖς τραγῳδίαις τερατολογίας ἐν μὲν ἄλλοις διελέγχειν, ἐν δὲ τοῖς νῦν τὴν τῆς Γιγαντομαχίας συμπλοκὴν ἔωλον ἀποφαίνων, ὄρνισιν ἔδωκε διαφέρεσθαι πρὸς θεοὺς περὶ τῆς ἀρχῆς.

*(hypothesis* to Aristophanes, *Birds* 2.33–37)

And some say that in other plays the poet criticizes the marvelous tales found in tragedies, but in these present verses, proclaiming the conflict of the Gigantomachy to be trite, he made birds fight against gods over the rule (of the cosmos).

There are certainly occasional references to the Gigantomachy in the *Birds*. When Peisetairus first proposes to the chorus that they found a city which would enclose the space between earth and heaven within walls[52] and would deny the Olympians access to earth *(Av.* 550–52), the chorus (or, according to a different distribution of speakers, Euelpides)[53] reacts by evoking

---

[49] On the historical context of the play's performance and the degree to which it interacts with contemporary events, see Hubbard 1991c: 158–60 with a summary of the various positions.

[50] On the utopia constructed in the *Birds*, e.g., Zimmerman 1983, esp. 66–72 as well as Konstan 1995: 29–44 and 1997 with a keen interest in the typology of utopias; cf. Hubbard 1997 on the utopia of the *Birds* as a reflection upon sophistic ideas.

[51] Especially Hofmann 1976: 79–90 (on the assimilation of the Titanomachy to the Gigantomachy in the play, see 85–88) and Zannini-Quirini 1987: 47–87; cf. Bowie 1993: 161.

[52] *Av.* 551–52 with Dunbar 1995: 374. Inhabiting and barricading the elevated space between earth and sky bears some resemblance to the Giants' attempt to reach the heights of Olympus by piling up mountains.

[53] For arguments in favor of the attribution of line 553 to the chorus, see Dunbar 1995: 374–75.

Cebriones and Porphyrion, two of the Giants (*Av.* 553). This evocation invites the audience to think of Peisetairus' unfolding plan in terms of the Giants' challenge to Zeus's power.[54] It also introduces the jocular contrast between Porphyrion, whom Pindar identifies as the king of the Giants (*P.*8.12–17), and the tiny bird that bears the same name (Purple Gallinule).[55] The joke is reiterated in *Av.* 1249–52, when Peisetairus threatens to send against Zeus an army of six hundred porphyrions, presumably a greater menace than the single Porphyrion of the Gigantomachy.[56]

Another explicit invitation to consider Peisetairus' coup in terms of the Gigantomachy is found in a passage which identifies the bird-city as the field of Phlegra, the site of the battle between the Olympians and the Giants:

> Ευ. ἆρ' ἐστὶν αὕτη γ' ἡ Νεφελοκοκκυγία,
> ἵνα καὶ τὰ Θεογένους τὰ πολλὰ χρήματα
> τά τ' Αἰσχίνου γ' ἅπαντα;
> Πε. καὶ λῷον μὲν οὖν·
> τὸ Φλέγρας πεδίον, ἵν' οἱ θεοὶ τοὺς γηγενεῖς
> ἀλαζονευόμενοι καθυπερηκόντισαν.
>
> (Aristophanes, *Birds* 822–25)[57]

Eu.: So, is this the Nephelokokkygia where most possessions of Theogenes and all of Aeschines are?
Pe.: Even better: it is the plain of Phlegra, where the gods outshot the earth-borns at bragging.

Peisetairus' utterance radically redefines the conflict between the Olympians and the Giants as a competition in empty boasts. His reinterpretation of the Gigantomachy is irreverent and provocative, especially if one considers that the Gigantomachy was culturally significant primarily as a story celebrating the victory of order and civilized power over the crude and insolent. By drawing our attention to the Giants' failure, the text underscores how grand and unprecedented Peisetairus' eventual success is. Yet the play hints at Peisetairus' upcoming victory also by comically attributing the triumph of the Olympians to their superior ἀλαζονεία, since the Athenian will soon demonstrate his competence in overpowering

---

[54] Sch. *Av.* 553 already points out the connection; cf. sch. *Av.* 1252.
[55] Zannini Quirini 1987: 60–61. On the bird πορφυρίων, see Thompson 1895: 150. Cebriones is potentially problematic, since no source other than sch. *Av.* 553 identifies him as a Giant. For a discussion of proposed emendations, see Dunbar 1995: 375–76.
[56] Not all references to the bird porphyrion in play are found in a Gigantomachic context; see *Av.* 707 and 881.
[57] On Bentley's λῷον for the transmitted λῷστον in *Av.* 823, see Dunbar 1995: 493–94.

the ἀλαζόνες.[58] First, he will outsmart an oracle-monger explicitly identified as ἄνθρωπος ἀλαζών (*Av.* 983), and later, when he chases away Meton, he will evoke a decree calling for violence against all the ἀλαζόνες (*Av.* 1015–16).[59] While reiterating the Giants' challenge to the Olympians as a paradigm for Peisetairus' coup, therefore, lines 822–25 establish the failure of the Giants as a foil for Peisetairus' success.

Ultimately, the assumption that the Gigantomachy is the dominant mythological framework of the *Birds* proves to be unsatisfactory and even misleading. For instance, in the following passage Zannini Quirini interprets the "sacred war" mentioned in *Av.* 556 as part of the Gigantomachic theme that is introduced in *Av.* 553:[60]

> Χο. ὦ Κεβριόνη καὶ Πορφυρίων, ὡς σμερδαλέον τὸ πόλισμα.
> Πε. κἀπειδὰν τοῦτ᾽ ἐπανεστήκῃ, τὴν ἀρχὴν τὸν Δί᾽ ἀπαιτεῖν·
> κἂν μὲν μὴ φῇ μηδ᾽ ἐθελήσῃ μηδ᾽ εὐθὺς γνωσιμαχήσῃ,
> ἱερὸν πόλεμον πρωὐδᾶν αὐτῷ, καὶ τοῖσι θεοῖσιν ἀπειπεῖν
> διὰ τῆς χώρας τῆς ὑμετέρας ἐστυκόσι μὴ διαφοιτᾶν,
> ὥσπερ πρότερον μοιχεύσοντες τὰς Ἀλκμήνας κατέβαινον
> καὶ τὰς Ἀλόπας καὶ τὰς Σεμέλας· ἥνπερ δ᾽ ἐπίωσ᾽, ἐπιβάλλειν
> σφραγῖδ᾽ αὐτοῖς ἐπὶ τὴν ψωλήν, ἵνα μὴ βινῶσ᾽ ἔτ᾽ ἐκείνας.

(Aristophanes, *Birds* 553–60)

Ch.: O Cebriones and Porphyrion, how formidable this city is!
Pe.: And once it has been established, demand from Zeus his rule! And if he refuses and is unwilling and doesn't submit immediately, declare a Sacred War against him, and forbid the gods from passing through your land while erect, the way they used to descend in the past in order to debauch the Alcmenes and the Alopes and the Semeles. And, in case they approach, put a seal upon their erect penises, so that they may no longer fuck those women.

Yet there are no parallels for the use of ἱερὸς πόλεμος in reference to the Gigantomachy. More importantly, by insisting on a sustained Gigantomachic reference, one overlooks that for Aristophanes' Athenian audience the phrase had different connotations. Ἱερὸς πόλεμος recalled conflicts for

---

[58] On ἀλαζών in Greek comedy, see MacDowell 1990 and Major 2006: 135–38. The ἀλαζών claims to be what he is not or to be more than he really is. In Xenophon (*Mem.* 1.7.1–2; *Cyr.* 2.2.11–13) ἀλαζονεία is treated as a source of laughter; cf. Pl. *Phlb.* 48c–49e on the lack of self-awareness and Arist. *EN* 1127a13–b32 on ἀλαζονεία as the opposite of εἰρωνεία.

[59] On the treatment of Meton and Kinesias in the *Birds*, see Zimmermann 1993: 267–75.

[60] Zannini Quirini 1987: 49, who also suggests that the reference to Zeus's thunder in lines 570 and 576 is another Gigantomachic element. However, the thunderbolt is Zeus's weapon of choice against all his enemies; for instance, he uses it against the Titans and Typhos in Hesiod's *Theogony* (689–94 and 853–56 respectively). Furthermore, *Av.* 570 is a rather generic comment regarding Zeus's prospective anger, while *Av.* 576 focuses exclusively on the representation of the thunderbolt as winged.

control over Delphi, the most recent of which took place around 448 BCE and involved an Athenian intervention that overturned the outcome of a Spartan expedition.[61] In other words, *Av.* 556 alludes to a struggle for access, not for cosmic power. This interpretation makes much better sense in context, since Peisetairus proceeds to reveal his plan to hinder the gods' access to sex with mortal women (*Av.* 556–59).

Peisetairus' interest in controlling divine sexuality in this passage is a further indication that his attempt to usurp Zeus's power surpasses the Gigantomachy in complexity. Peisetairus isolates three women who exemplify the type of divine rapes he intends to prevent.[62] The female figures in this short list are carefully chosen: in addition to Alope, whose son with Poseidon was the eponymous hero of an Athenian tribe, we find Alcmene, mother of Heracles, and Semele, mother of Dionysus (*Av.* 558–59). The list confers prestige on the local heroine since Semele and Alcmene are the most famous and significant of Zeus's mortal lovers.[63] More importantly, however, this mini-catalogue of women as well as the plural number of their names (τὰς Ἀλκμήνας ... καὶ τὰς Ἀλόπας καὶ τὰς Σεμέλας) allude summarily to the entire corpus of circulating stories about unions between gods and mortals that led to the birth of heroes. The Aristophanic text here highlights the plurality and variety that emerges as these narratives are developed in the context of diverse genres, including tragedy but also poetic genealogies such as the Hesiodic *Catalogue* and the *ME*.[64] Peisetairus intends to control the sexual activity of the male Olympians not only to kill their fun but also to divest them of the power celebrated in these genealogical traditions. The partial castration of the gods imposed by Peisetairus ends their sexual domination over mortals and thus undercuts the possibility of creating another hybrid race of men comparable to the heroes. Instead, the play yields hybrids of human and avian elements that are generated not by the will or the seed of the Olympians but of men's own volition. As strategies for usurping and maintaining cosmic rule, castration and control over procreation have nothing to do with the story

---

[61] Cf. sch. *Av.* 556. On the "sacred war" of the mid-fifth century BCE, see Thucydides 1.112.

[62] For this use of proper names in Aristophanes, cf. Ornaghi 2007: 26–30.

[63] Heracles and Dionysus are exceptional among the heroes in that they were deified. Both unions as well as the apotheoses of Heracles and Dionysus can be found already in the brief catalogue of women embedded in Hesiod's *Theogony* (940–42 on the apotheosis of both Semele and Dionysus; 943–44 on the birth of Heracles from Alcmene, 950–55 on Heracles' apotheosis). Cf. the Hesiodic *Catalogue of Women*, where Alcmene's impregnation is treated extensively (fr. 91/195.8–63 = *Sc.*1–56); regarding Dionysus' birth from Semele, on the other hand, only the prophecy in fr. 103.5-7H survives.

[64] Dunbar 1995: 378 points out that Alcmene and Semele were featured in Athenian tragedy, but it does not necessarily follow that Aristophanes evokes exclusively their treatment in Attic drama.

of the Gigantomachy, but are integral to a different mythological narrative, namely the Succession Myth.

There is no good reason to study the play's appropriation of elements from the Succession Myth as part of its engagement with the Gigantomachy as Hofmann does in his seminal work on the mythological frame of the *Birds*.[65] Hofmann's approach stems not only from the aforementioned *hypothesis* of the play (2.33–37) but also from Vian's influential thesis that by the end of the fifth century BCE the Titanomachy and the Gigantomachy had been conflated.[66] Vian's reading of such a conflation in Euripides, however, is far from indisputable,[67] and the interpretation of the *Birds* through this lens is even less satisfactory. The Aristophanic comedy engages both with the Gigantomachy and the Titanomachy, but these two remain distinct paradigms and contribute different elements to the characters and the plot. We have already seen that the failed challenge of the Giants provides a foil for the victory of Peisetairus. The Titanomachic elements, on the other hand, should be studied as part of the play's broader appropriation of the Succession Myth, through which Peisetairus and his birds legitimize and bring to pass their coup against the Olympians. Despite the prevalence of the Gigantomachy in the interpretation attested in the second *hypothesis*, it is the Succession Myth that provides the fundamental template for the plot of the *Birds*. In what follows, I examine in detail how Peisetairus revisits the Succession Myth to justify his proposed war against the Olympians, and how the hero eventually succeeds in grafting himself and his coup onto this long sequence of strife over cosmic rule.

Peisetairus' attempt to persuade the birds that they should colonize the sky begins with the claim that they are the primordial beings of this universe and that, in fact, they once ruled over the cosmos; therefore, they have every right to reclaim their long-lost reign. Evidence that the birds used to rule over men once upon a time is comically extrapolated from contemporary experience and customs in Greece and elsewhere (*Av.* 481–507), from the Heroic Age and its representation in tragedy

---

[65] Hofmann 1976: 79–90 (on the assimilation of the Titanomachy to the Gigantomachy in the play, see 85–88).

[66] Vian 1952: 173 with the claim that Euripides is the first to abandon the distinction between Giants and Titans (*Hec.* 466–74 and *IT* 218–24). Regarding the *Birds*, Vian 1952: 173 and 184–85 points out that Aristophanes draws indiscriminately from the Gigantomachy and the Titanomachy.

[67] Stamatopoulou 2012 with an emphasis on characterization. Vian's theory remains influential; see, e.g., D'Alessio 2015: 208, who, nonetheless, interprets rather generously Vian's argument about Euripides and completely ignores the *Birds*.

(*Av.* 508–13), from the iconography of the gods and from religious practices (*Av.* 514–21). First, however, Peisetairus uses an Aesopic tale to support his assertion that the birds preceded all other entities in the cosmos:

Πε.                                 . . . οὕτως ὑμῶν ὑπεραλγῶ,
οἵτινες ὄντες πρότερον βασιλῆς—
Χο.                     ἡμεῖς βασιλῆς; τίνος;
Πε.                               ὑμεῖς
πάντων ὁπόσ' ἔστιν, ἐμοῦ πρῶτον, τουδί, καὶ τοῦ Διὸς αὐτοῦ,
ἀρχαιότεροι πρότεροί τε Κρόνου καὶ Τιτάνων ἐγένεσθε,
καὶ Γῆς.
Χο.      καὶ Γῆς;
Πε.           νὴ τὸν Ἀπόλλω.
Χο.                            τουτὶ μὰ Δί' οὐκ ἐπεπύσμην.
Πε. ἀμαθὴς γὰρ ἔφυς κοὐ πολυπράγμων, οὐδ' Αἴσωπον πεπάτηκας,
ὃς ἔφασκε λέγων κορυδὸν πάντων πρώτην ὄρνιθα γενέσθαι,
προτέραν τῆς γῆς, κἄπειτα νόσῳ τὸν πατέρ' αὐτῆς ἀποθνῄσκειν·
γῆν δ' οὐκ εἶναι, τὸν δὲ προκεῖσθαι πεμπταῖον· τὴν δ' ἀποροῦσαν
ὑπ' ἀμηχανίας τὸν πατέρ' αὐτῆς ἐν τῇ κεφαλῇ κατορύξαι.
Ευ. ὁ πατὴρ ἄρα τῆς κορυδοῦ νυνὶ κεῖται τεθνεὼς Κεφαλῆσιν.
Πε. οὔκουν δῆτ', εἰ πρότεροι μὲν γῆς, πρότεροι δὲ θεῶν ἐγένοντο,
ὡς πρεσβυτάτων ὄντων αὐτῶν ὀρθῶς ἐσθ' ἡ βασιλεία;

(Aristophanes, *Birds* 466–78)

Pe.: I ache so much for you, who, being kings before . . .
Ch.: We (were) kings? Of what?
Pe.: Yes, you, of all that is, first of all, of me, and of this guy here, and of Zeus himself; you came to being during an older and earlier era than Cronus and the Titans, and Gaia.
Ch.: Gaia too?
Pe.: Yes, by Apollo.
Ch.: By Zeus I had not heard about that.
Pe.: That's because you were born ignorant and not meddlesome, and you haven't thumbed through Aesop, who said in his fable that the lark was the first bird of all, predating the earth, and then her father died of a disease; but the earth did not exist, and he was laid out for four days; and, being at a loss, she buried her father in her own head out of desperation.
Eu.: Thus to this day the father of the lark lies dead in Cephale.
Pe.: So, if they came to being before the earth and before the gods, isn't kingship rightly their own since they are the eldest?

In lines 466–70, Peisetairus traces the history of the cosmos in reverse. His account is a highly selective outline that shifts quickly from the present to the past, and strings together the wannabe king of the world (ἐμοῦ πρῶτον) and his companion (τουδί) with the current ruler of the universe (καὶ τοῦ Διὸς αὐτοῦ) as well as the preceding one (Κρόνου καὶ Τιτάνων). While the two most recent eras in the history of the cosmos are represented by their male rulers, the oldest phase in this reverse timeline is represented by Gaia, not Ouranus. The culmination of the catalogue with Gaia in 470 paves the way for the tale of the lark, but it also aligns the summary of cosmic history with the Hesiodic tradition, since Gaia's role as a primeval being and the origin of rulers seems to have been a trademark feature of the cosmogonic narrative in Hesiod's *Theogony.*[68]

In the Hesiodic poem, Gaia emerges in the universe following Chaos, the first entity (*Th.* 116–18). Immediately, the text draws attention to the fact that she is the first solid body, a mass destined to be the universal "ever-unfailing seat" (ἕδος ἀσφαλὲς αἰεί, *Th.* 117).[69] In this tradition Gaia is the source of all cosmic rulers: she produces Ouranus (*Th.* 126–28) and the genealogical branch that includes Cronus and the Titans, as well as Zeus and the Olympians. In fact, according to the Hesiodic narrative, she is not only the origin of cosmic rulers, but also the driving force behind the repeated cycles of usurpation in the Succession Myth (*Th.* 159–75, 459–80,

---

[68] It is not fortuitous that theogonies rivaling the Hesiodic tradition undermine Gaia's role. The Orphic literature provides ample (albeit indirect) indications that Gaia's dominant role in the cosmic power struggle was considered distinctly Hesiodic. Already in the Derveni papyrus, the Night is not only a source of oracles (fr. 6 Bernabé) but also the mother of Ouranus (fr. 10 Bernabé), and thus the source of the male succession line Ouranus–Cronus–Zeus; see esp. Brisson 1997. Similarly, in the Orphic cosmogony attested by Eudemus (fr. 150 Wehrli), Night is the first cosmic entity and the source of everything else, including the Earth and Sky. Gaia is denied a spot among the primordial beings in the *Rhapsodies* and the Hieronymus–Hellanicus theogony as well. Night, on the other hand, still plays a central role as the child of Phanes, a cosmic ruler, the mother of Gaia and Ouranus, and a source of oracles. On the importance of Night in the Orphic traditions, see the discussion in Betegh 2004: 153–54; cf. Ramnoux 1986: 177–31, Tortorelli Ghidini 1991, Ricciardelli Apicella 1993: 51, Bernabé 2008: 1220, Christopoulos 2010: 208. Notice that other theogonic accounts too distinguish themselves from the Hesiodic tradition by deliberately changing the role of Gaia; see, e.g., Pherecydes of Syrus fr. 14, 60, 65–66 Schibli, Epim. fr. 6a+b Fowler.

[69] Although Peisetairus does not allude verbally to *Th.* 117, perhaps the tale of the lark would trigger a recall of the Hesiodic description of Gaia as she emerges into the cosmos (Γαῖ' εὐρύστερνος, πάντων ἕδος ἀσφαλὲς αἰεί, *Th.* 117). The connection would be even more poignant if the spectators had in mind a version of the *Theogony* that did not include line 118, since it limits the meaning of πάντων in 117 to the gods (ἀθανάτων οἳ ἔχουσι κάρη νιφόεντος Ὀλύμπου). Such a version of the Hesiodic text is attested as early as Plato's *Smp.* 178b5–7 and Arist. *Metaph.* 984b26–29 (cf. Ps.-Arist. *de Melisso* 975a11–14), where *Th.* 116–20 are quoted (with some paraphrasis) without lines 118 and 119. On the transmission of *Th.* 117, see Rzach (1902) 21–25; cf. West (1966) 193–94. The omission of *Th.* 118–19 in the Platonic and Aristotelian passages can be read as the result of deliberate selective quotation (e.g. Ford 2010: 140–42). Yet it is also possible that it reflects a different version of the Hesiodic text (e.g. KRS 1983²: 35) or an excerpt derived from an anthology (e.g. Mansfield 1986: 24). Cf. Montanari 2009: 328–31. The formula ἕδος ἀσφαλὲς αἰεί is applied to Gaia only in *Th.* 117; all its other occurrences in poetry involve the abode of gods, whether it is the Sky (*Th.* 128) or Olympus (*Od.* 6.42–43).

493–96, 626–28, 820–22, 888–91).[70] I suggest that Gaia's inclusion in Peisetairus' speech evokes both aspects of her character in the *Theogony*: her extreme antiquity, which is relevant to the immediate context of *Av.* 470–76, and her pivotal role in instigating a series of successful usurpations, which Zeus halts in the *Theogony* (853–68; cf. 899–900) but Peisetairus ultimately manages to revive and expand.

Peisetairus proceeds to establish that the birds not only predate Gaia and her progeny of cosmic rulers, but also that they used to rule the world during this glorious primordial era (*Av.* 477–522) – a far cry from the mistreatments the birds suffer in the present (*Av.* 523–38). The wily Athenian introduces a version of cosmic history that adopts and asserts the traditional Hesiodic timeline yet, at the same time, extends it by adding a pre-Gaia era of avian rule. This partial revision of the Hesiodic timeline transforms and redefines the power structure that the *Theogony* constructs and explains.[71] In the Hesiodic tradition, sons usurp the power of their fathers; according to Peisetairus' account, on the other hand, the entire dynasty of Gaia's progeny presupposes the dethronement of the birds. In other words, the succession of Ouranus, Cronus, and Zeus stems from an original act of usurpation that Peisetairus has appended to the Hesiodic timeline.

Peisetairus ingeniously reinvents the traditional history of the cosmos to accommodate an era of avian rule predating Gaia, but it is not until its endorsement by the birds that this new version of the past acquires legitimacy as part of their 'reality' and becomes the ideological foundation of their co(s)mic *coup d'état*. The swiftness with which Peisetairus convinces the birds is no doubt comical: no sooner has the Athenian finished his *epideixis* than the chorus laments the reign they have lost:

> πολὺ δὴ πολὺ δὴ χαλεπωτάτους λόγους
> ἤνεγκας, ἄνθρωφ'· ὡς ἐδάκρυσά γ' ἐμῶν πατέρων
> κάκην, οἳ τάσδε τὰς τιμὰς προγόνων παραδόν-
> των ἐπ' ἐμοῦ κατέλυσαν.
>
>        (Aristophanes, *Birds* 539–43)

O human, you have delivered very, very painful words. How I wept for the cowardice of my fathers, who destroyed in my time these privileges that they received from my forefathers!

---

[70] On Gaia and the Succession Myth in Hesiod's *Theogony*, see Detienne and Vernant 1978: 57–105; Arthur 1982: 70–74; Lamberton 1988: 75–76; Clay 2003: 17–18, 26–28; Felson 2011: 257–61.

[71] Epstein 1981: 9 attributes Peisetairus' transformation of the Hesiodic narrative to his inability to understand its logic. I find this reading rather unsatisfactory.

As the birds reconceptualize their past on the basis of Peisetairus' speech, they lay claim to an inherited right to cosmic power that the previous generation failed to pass on to them successfully. Dunbar suggests that the link between power and the succession of generations resonates with contemporary political discourse in Athens.[72] Yet the birds' tripartite division of their past based on successive generations also mirrors the paradigm of the Succession Myth that Peisetairus implicated in the preceding *epideixis*. Not only do the birds organize their history in three male-dominated sequential eras (the forefathers, their fathers, and the current generation), but they also attribute their plight to a disruption in an established (albeit non-violent) pattern of succession.

Having accepted their newly discovered glorious history, the birds proceed to elaborate it in the *parabasis* (*Av.* 676–800). Peisetairus' earlier *epideixis* demonstrated the birds' antiquity mainly through evidence of their now-lost reign; the *parabasis*, on the other hand, supports the same point with an account of origins. The birds develop a systematic cosmogony that pinpoints the emergence of their species within the cosmic timeline and defines their pedigree (*Av.* 693–703). The performance of this cosmogony, therefore, is central to the birds' self-legitimizing act.[73]

In the opening of the cosmogony, the chorus, who remain in character throughout the *parabasis*, contrast emphatically their own divine existence with the inferior nature of their mortal audience (*Av.* 685–92). These introductory lines thus evoke an epiphany and, as such, suggest programmatically that the *parabasis* will reiterate and further advance the birds' claim to divinity. By affirming the vast gap between human and divine nature, the birds enhance and reinforce the authority of the cosmogony they are about to reveal, a rhetorical strategy that can be traced back to Hesiod's encounter with the Muses (*Th.* 22–34).[74] The Hesiodic Muses address Hesiod not as an individual but as a collective, and their tone is unambiguously contemptuous: "Field-dwelling shepherds, base disgraces, mere bellies" (ποιμένες ἄγραυλοι, κάκ' ἐλέγχεα, γαστέρες οἶον, *Th.* 26). Likewise, the birds address the audience as representatives of the entire human species, emphasizing their inferiority, even as they comically go overboard with a bloated list of attributes and dense poetic allusions

---

[72] Dunbar 1995: 369.

[73] Cf. Hermes' poetic celebration of his own birth as an act of self-legitimization in *h.Herm.* 57–59; cf. Clay 2006²: 109–11 and Vergados 2011: 4–6 and 271–73. For the connection between the cosmogony and the foundation of Nephelokokkygia, see Bowie 1993: 158–59.

[74] Cf. Bernabé 1995: 199, who nonetheless foregrounds the generic aspects of *Av.* 685–92. On *Th.* 22–34, see the discussion in Chapter 1, pp. 18–21.

(*Av.* 685–87).[75] Furthermore, much like Hesiod's Muses, the birds draw attention to the defining quality of their discourse. Yet, while in the *Theogony* the Muses lay claim to two types of discourse, one that is true and one that is false albeit verisimilar (ψεύδεα ... ἐτύμοισιν ὁμοῖα, *Th.* 27; ἀληθέα, *Th.* 28), Aristophanes' birds advertise the accuracy of their upcoming account (ὀρθῶς, *Av.* 690; εἰδότες ὀρθῶς, *Av.* 692). Their insistence on accuracy is, of course, funny because they have been duped by Peisetairus' manipulative and utterly fictitious reconstruction of the remote past. At the same time, the text mocks Prodicus (*Av.* 692), who is put on the spot for his linguistic ideas about ὀρθότης ὀνομάτων ("correctness of names") but also for his theory regarding the origin of religion, according to which the gods originate in the worship of those natural elements that proved most beneficial to men (esp. *Av.* 691).[76]

As promised in the programmatic opening, the birds perform a novel cosmogony in which they establish their claim to cosmic rule by inscribing their own primordial emergence and divine nature. The birds reinvent the origins of the universe as follows:

> Χάος ἦν καὶ Νὺξ Ἔρεβός τε μέλαν πρῶτον καὶ Τάρταρος εὐρύς,
> Γῆ δ' οὐδ' Ἀὴρ οὐδ' Οὐρανὸς ἦν· Ἐρέβους δ' ἐν ἀπείροσι κόλποις
> τίκτει πρώτιστον ὑπηνέμιον Νὺξ ἡ μελανόπτερος ᾠόν,
> ἐξ οὗ περιτελλομέναις ὥραις ἔβλαστεν Ἔρως ὁ ποθεινός,
> στίλβων νῶτον πτερύγοιν χρυσαῖν, εἰκὼς ἀνεμώκεσι δίναις.
> οὗτος δὲ Χάει πτερόεντι μιγεὶς μύχιος κατὰ Τάρταρον εὐρὺν
> ἐνεόττευσεν γένος ἡμέτερον, καὶ πρῶτον ἀνήγαγεν εἰς φῶς.
> πρότερον δ' οὐκ ἦν γένος ἀθανάτων, πρὶν Ἔρως ξυνέμειξεν ἅπαντα·
> ξυμμειγνυμένων δ' ἑτέρων ἑτέροις γένετ' Οὐρανὸς Ὠκεανός τε
> καὶ Γῆ πάντων τε θεῶν μακάρων γένος ἄφθιτον. ὧδε μέν ἐσμεν
> πολὺ πρεσβύτατοι πάντων μακάρων ἡμεῖς.
>
> (Aristophanes, *Birds* 693–703)

In the beginning, there was Chaos and Night and dark Erebos and broad Tartarus, and there was no Earth (Ge) or Air or Sky. And in the infinite recesses of Erebos black-winged Night bore first of all a wind-egg, from which, as the

---

[75] On the rich allusions to Homeric poetry, lyric poetry, and tragedy, especially the *PV*, see Herington 1963b: 238 and Dunbar 1995: 429–32; cf. Rau 1967: 177 and Bernabé 1995: 199–203.

[76] On the mockery of Prodicus in the *parabasis* of the *Birds*, see, e.g., Nestle 1936: 162, De Carli 1971: 52, Zanetto 1987: 239, Sommerstein 1991: 241, Dunbar 1995: 433–34 and 436–37, Hubbard 1997: 32. Prodicus may also be ridiculed as an investigator of the μετέωρα, see Dunbar 1995: 436; cf. Ar. *Nu.* 360–62. On Prodicus' radical theory on the origins of gods, see, e.g., Untersteiner 1954, Guthrie 1969: 238–42, Kerferd 1981: 168–69, Mayhew 2011: xxi–xxiii and 172–74. On his ὀρθότης ὀνομάτων, see Mayer 1913, Untersteiner 1954: 212–16, Classen 1976: 230–38, Kerferd 1981: 70–74, O'Sullivan 1992: 75–79, and, more recently, Koning 2010b with a particular interest in the reception of Hesiod in the context of Prodicus' linguistic theory.

seasons came round, sprung forth Eros who inspires longing, shining on his back with his golden wings, looking like swift whirlwinds. And, having mingled with winged Chaos in broad Tartarus, he hatched our species, and he brought it first to light. And there was no race of immortals before Eros mixed everything; and after different elements mixed with each other, Sky (Ouranus) came to being and Ocean and Earth and the entire immortal race of the blessed gods. Thus, we are by far the oldest of all the blessed (gods).

According to the chorus, in its initial state the cosmos consisted of four entities: Chaos, Night, dark Erebos, and Tartarus (*Av.* 693). Within Erebos, Night laid an egg that, despite being described as infertile (ὑπη-νέμιον, *Av.* 695),[77] paradoxically produced Eros, the cosmic generative force envisioned by the avian chorus as a bird-like being with golden wings (*Av.* 694–97). Eros eventually caused elements to combine into the components of the known physical world; first, however, he mingled with Chaos and, through this seemingly infertile union with another male divinity, he begot the species of the birds (*Av.* 698–99).[78] Developing Peisetairus' earlier claim regarding their antiquity (*Av.* 467–69), the birds draw attention to the fact that the emergence of their progenitor from Night's unhatched egg as well as the comically unorthodox birth of their own kind date to a time prior to the birth of the gods (*Av.* 700 and 702–03). In fact, the birds envision their creation as an event that not only predates the appearance of the immortals but also results from a different process: birds are direct descendants of Eros, while the rest of the world formed from disparate elements united by Eros.[79] The narrative constructs the cosmogonic process that postdates the hatching of the birds exclusively

---

[77] Sch. Ar. *Av.* 695. For alternative interpretations of ὑπηνέμιον, see Pardini 1993: 64–65, Bernabé 1995: 205–06, and Dunbar 1995: 441–42; cf. Jouanna 2006 and Christopoulos 2010: 209. Birth from an infertile egg is a funny paradox, but the polysemy of the adjective ὑπηνέμιον may add a second layer to the joke if juxtaposed to the birds' preceding promise to speak with Prodicean precision (ὀρθῶς, *Av.* 690, cf. 692). On non-Greek cosmogonies involving a cosmic egg, see West 1994, esp. 290–303; cf. Luján 2011, who nonetheless misreads *Av.* 695.

[78] Given Eros' mingling with another male entity, it is hardly surprising that, when his feathered descendants advertise their contribution to human courtship later in the *parabasis* (*Av.* 703–08), they focus exclusively on the wooing of young ἐρώμενοι; cf. Calame 1991: 231. Based on this passage and on Hes. *Th.* 123, where Χάος gives birth by parthenogenesis to Erebos and Night, West 1966: 193 argues that Χάος was treated as a female element even though the word is grammatically neuter. There is no basis for this assumption, however, since (at least in the *Theogony*) parthenogenesis is not limited to female entities: in *Th.* 233 Pontus gives birth to Nereus. Note also that Ἔρεβος, another grammatically neuter element, is clearly treated as a male element in Hes. *Th.* 124–25.

[79] My discussion focuses on Eros in the context of theogonic and cosmogonic narratives. On the play's engagement with the contemporary political connotations of Eros, see, e.g., Arrowsmith 1973, Newiger 1983: 54–57, and, in response, Henderson 1997: 142–43. See also Reckford 1987: 341–43, who reads *eros* in the *Birds* as encompassing both politics and creativity.

through the emergence of Ouranus, Ocean, Ge, and the immortals (*Av.* 701–02).

The birds' cosmogony fills with cosmic activity the primordial era that extends from the very beginning to the appearance of Gaia. A veritable tour de force, this Aristophanic passage has been shown to be a creative composite of elements drawn from a variety of circulating cosmogonic narratives.[80] My discussion of these lines will not contribute much new material to the long list of intertextual references that scholars have already identified in *Av.* 693–703; it will offer, however, a careful reassessment of the embedded Hesiodic elements. I am particularly interested in how these Hesiodic elements are contextualized in relation to non-Hesiodic features, and what that may tell us about the play's reception of the theogonic tradition attributed to Hesiod.

The avian cosmogony begins by unambiguously evoking the Hesiodic tradition. Chaos, the first of four primordial entities mentioned by the chorus of the *Birds* (*Av.* 693), is also the first of the four beings that emerge initially in the *Theogony* (*Th.* 116). Evidence from Plato and the Aristotelian corpus leaves little doubt that Chaos was considered a distinctly Hesiodic primordial being.[81] By including Chaos in the avian cosmogony, the Aristophanic text programmatically defines the Hesiodic tradition as an important intertext and invites the audience to expect further engagement with it. Indeed, the earliest cosmic era according to the *Birds* includes three additional entities (Night, Erebos, and Tartarus, *Av.* 693) that also populate the cosmos of the *Theogony* in its initial stage. Tartarus is one of four primordial beings in the *Theogony* (*Th.* 119),[82] while Night and Erebos, born of Chaos through parthenogenesis in *Th.* 123, are the first set of offspring in the entire *Theogony*.[83] The overlap between the avian cosmogony and the *Theogony* also includes Eros (*Av.* 696–700) and Ge (*Av.* 694 and 702), both of which are primordial entities in the Hesiodic tradition (*Th.* 116–17, 120–22), as well as Ouranus

---

[80] For a line-by-line analysis of the allusions to literary and philosophical works in *Av.* 693–703, see esp. Bernabé 1995 and Dunbar 1995: 437–47; cf. Hubbard 1991c: 165–66 and 1997: 32.

[81] Pl. *Smp.* 178b2–9, Arist. *Ph.* 208b30–31; cf. Ps.-Arist. *De Melisso* 976b 15–17. See Koning 2010a: 195–98. There is a comic debate about the primordiality of Chaos in (Ps.-?)Epich. fr. 275 KA = 248 RN (with Kerkhof 2001: 65–68 and 78).

[82] Note, however, this was probably not true in all versions of the *Theogony* circulating in the classical era. *Th.* 119 is consistently present in the manuscript tradition of the poem, including *P. Achmîn* 3 (fourth or fifth century CE). Yet it is missing from fourth-century BCE texts that quote *Th.* 116–17 +120 (Pl. *Smp.* 178b5–7, Arist. *Metaph.* 984b26–29, Ps.-Arist. *De Melisso* 975a11–14). See above (note 81).

[83] Notice the rearrangement of the epithet μέλας from ἐκ Χάεος δ' Ἔρεβός τε μέλαινά τε Νὺξ ἐγένοντο in *Th.* 123 to Νὺξ Ἔρεβός τε μέλαν in *Av.* 693; cf. Dunbar 1995: 439.

(*Av.* 694, 701) and Oceanus (*Av.* 701), both born of Gaia early on in the *Theogony* (*Th.* 126–27 and 133 respectively). At its earliest stages, therefore, the world according to the avian cosmogony of the *Birds* consists of the same entities that populate the Hesiodic universe in its infancy. There seems to be only one exception to this pattern. *Av.* 694 defines the earliest stage of the cosmos as the absence of three elements: "and there was no Earth or Air or Ouranos" (Γῆ δ' οὐδ' Ἀὴρ οὐδ' Οὐρανὸς ἦν).[84] Unlike Ge and Ouranus, Ἀὴρ is not part of the *Theogony*'s genealogical tree.[85] The emergence of Ge and Ouranus becomes explicit in *Av.* 701–02, but Ἀὴρ remains an absence in the Aristophanic cosmogony. This exceptional case is best understood, I suggest, if we read Ἀὴρ as a foil: by acknowledging an element featured in non-Hesiodic visions of the cosmos[86] only to exclude it, the text underscores its intent to construct a cosmogony with elements familiar from the Hesiodic tradition.

The fact that the entities included in the avian cosmogony are also found in the *Theogony*, however, does not mean that they are identical to their Hesiodic counterparts. On the contrary, their places in the cosmic genealogical system have been reshuffled and their characteristics have been redefined. Night and Erebos follow Chaos not as its offspring (*Th.* 123) but as beings that emerge spontaneously.[87] Night retains her Hesiodic ability to reproduce by parthenogenesis, but, unlike the impressive crowd of children she bears in the *Theogony* (211–25), the outcome of her generative power in the *Birds* is a single egg that hatches Eros. On the other hand, Erebos and Tartarus do not have offspring of their own, as they do in the *Theogony*, but provide the space that harbors new beings:[88] they are the dark regions in which Eros and the birds respectively are

---

[84] In favor of the capitalization, see Dunbar 1995: 439; not all editors, however, assume a personification of Earth, Air, and Ouranus here. See, e.g., the text in Sommerstein 1991 and in Wilson 2007.

[85] Still, as Dunbar 1995: 440 points out, Τάρταρα are ἠερόεντα as early as *Th.* 119.

[86] Epimenides (B 5 DK), Anaximenes (A 1 and 4–10 DK), Anaximander (A 10 DK with KRS 1983²: 131–33), Empedocles (A 30 and B 6 DK with an allegorical connection between ἀήρ and Ἥρα). Diogenes of Apollonia considered Ἀήρ the divine source of intelligence and life; KRS 1983²: 441–45. On Archelaus, see KRS 1983²: 388.

[87] Note that the use of the verb ἦν to describe the initial state of the cosmos (*Av.* 693) is in sharp contrast to the Hesiodic γένετ' (*Th.* 116) that describes a dynamic emergence of the four primordial beings. The distinction between the two verbs was of interest to Prodicus, if Plato is a reliable witness (*Prt.* 340b3-d6); see already Mayer 1913: 34. On the use of εἰμί already in Pherecydes, see Ricciardelli Apicella 1993: 34.

[88] In the *Theogony*, Erebos fathers Aether and Day with Night (124–25), while the offspring of Tartarus and Gaia is Typhos (820–22).

produced (*Av.* 694 and 698). Even Chaos, an entity capable only of parthenogenesis in the *Theogony* (*Th.* 123), demonstrates non-Hesiodic qualities in his comically fertile mingling with Eros. Finally, while further supporting the claim about the birds' extreme antiquity made by Peisetairus earlier in his *epideixis*, the sequence Ouranus–Oceanus–Ge (*Av.* 701–02) undermines the priority that defines Gaia in the Hesiodic tradition.[89] The text not only defers the creation of Earth and her progeny of immortal gods as much as possible, but also dissociates Gaia from the creation of Ouranus and Oceanus.[90]

Far from being random, the configurations into which the birds have rearranged elements found in the *Theogony* evoke other theogonic and cosmogonic accounts. The line-up of primordial beings in *Av.* 693, for instance, deviates from Hesiod's *Theogony* in a manner that parallels Acusilaus' version of cosmic beginnings. According to the extant testimonia (fr. 6a–d Fowler), Acusilaus postulated that Chaos emerged first, followed by Erebos and Night, a male and a female element respectively, whose union produced Eros and two other entities, Aether and Metis.[91] Likewise, the birth of Eros from an egg is evocative of non-Hesiodic traditions. While Night's spontaneous generation of an egg recalls her propensity towards parthenogenesis in the *Theogony* (211–25), the egg is a mode of reproduction foreign to the Hesiodic poem. A cosmic egg is attested in the theogony attributed to Epimenides (fr. 6a Fowler), yet it is unlikely that the audience of the play would call to mind this Epimenidean account since that egg seems to have had a different origin and a different product.[92] It is far more likely that the birth of Eros in the Aristophanic

---

[89] Notice that the sequence Ouranus–Oceanus–Ge is consistent with the perspective of creatures that allegedly do not need firm ground to exist (cf. *Av.* 470–75).

[90] In the *Theogony*, Gaia produces Ouranus spontaneously (*Th.* 126–28) and then mingles with him to bear Oceanus (*Th.* 132–33). Oceanus is mentioned as the source of everything in the *Iliad* (Ὠκεανόν τε, θεῶν γένεσιν, καὶ μητέρα Τηθύν, *Il.* 14.201=302; καὶ ἂν ποταμοῖο ῥέεθρα / Ὠκεανοῦ, ὅς περ γένεσις πάντεσσι τέτυκται, *Il.* 14.245–46). The sequence Ouranus–Oceanus, however, is not entirely consistent with what the Homeric tradition appears to envision as the beginnings of the cosmos.

[91] Cf. Fowler 2013: 5–7. Contrast the theogony attributed to Epimenides, according to which Night pairs with Aer and they produce Tartarus (fr. 6a+b Fowler with Fowler 2013:7–8); cf. Musaeus fr. 81 Bernabé, in which the primordial beings are Tartarus and Night, while Aer emerges last, probably out of the union of the former two. It is possible that this unusual inclusion of Aer among the primordial entities was a reaction to Anaximander's theory. On this point see Leclerc 1992: 223, Bernabé 2001: 200–01, and Fowler 2013: 7; for a skeptical view, however, see Mele 2001: 247.

[92] In this account, the egg is produced from the union of two Titans, the children of Night and Aer, although Τιτᾶνας is an emendation suggested by Kroll (1894) 425–26; on the Titans, see Bernabé (2001) 202–07. Furthermore, what emerges from this egg is described as "another generation," presumably of gods (West 1994: 290): ᾠόν...ἐξ οὗ πάλιν ἄλλην γενεὰν προελθεῖν (Damasc. *De princ.* 124 = Eudemus fr. 150 Wehrli). Nothing in Damascius' language compels us to assume with Bernabé 2001: 208 that this egg produces an Eros-like figure; cf. Mele 2001: 249–50.

passage evokes Orphic literature.[93] Some theogonic narratives attributed to Orpheus envision a cosmic egg in the early stages of the cosmos; from this egg emerges Phanes, a splendid being that engenders the world and is identified with Eros.[94] It is certainly tempting to think that Aristophanes ingeniously adapts the Orphic egg for the purposes of a made-up cosmogony fashioned by birds. We should keep in mind, however, that our information about Orphic literature comes from sources that postdate the *Birds* and that any identification of Orphic elements in *Av.* 695–97 relies purely on assumptions regarding the state of Orphic literature at the end of the fifth century BCE.[95] Besides, in addition to any Orphic associations, the distinct capacity of Aristophanes' Eros to unite disparate elements into coherent masses also evokes Empedocles' concept of φιλότης (*Av.* 700–02).[96]

Finally, in reconstructing gods after their own image, the birds not only support their claim to a divine status but are also in dialogue with Xenophanes, who famously criticized Homer and Hesiod for their

---

[93] For a brief overview, see Bernabé 2008: 1220–2. For a survey of Eros in Greek cosmogonies, see Calame 1991.

[94] For the Orphic fragments on the cosmic egg and Phanes, see Bernabé's edition (vol. 2.1, frs. 114–67); cf. Pardini 1993: 54–58. Not all extant Orphic theogonies in the extensive and diverse corpus of Orphic literature include a cosmic egg. It was included in the Rhapsodic narrative, in the Hieronymus–Hellanicus tradition, and the Orphic *Argonautica*. On the other hand, there seems to have been no cosmic egg in the Eudemian and the cyclic theogonies. The Orphic literature transmitted by the Derveni Papyrus does not appear to have involved an egg, and it is debated whether it included Protogonus at all. For the assumption that it did, see West 1983b: 84–88, Rusten 1984 and 1985: 123–26, Brisson 1997 and 2003, Lebedev 1989: 40–41 (esp. on the identification of Protogonus with the Sun), and Calame 1997: 66–70; for the opposite view, see Bernabé 2002: 105–11 and 2007: 128, Betegh 2004: 154–58, Torjussen 2005: 13–14. When included in Orphic theogonies, the cosmic egg is the product of Chronus rather than Night (frs. 120–37, esp. 120–1). See frs. 141 and 144 Bernabé, as well as *Arg.* 14–16 for the identification of Phanes with Eros, which Rudhardt 1986: 12–13 considers an Orphic reception of the Hesiodic Eros of the *Theogony*. On the splendor of the winged Orphic Phanes/Protogonus/Eros, see frs. 123.4, 125, 127, and especially 136 Bernabé (χρυσείαις πτερύγεσσι φορεύμενος ἔνθα καὶ ἔνθα) as well as fr. 143.3–8 Bernabé = *Oph.H.* 6.3–8 (esp. ὠογενῆ, χρυσέαισιν ἀγαλλόμενον πτερύγεσσι, line 3). Dunbar 1995: 444 entertains the possibility that the Aristophanic *parabasis* influenced the Orphic traditions regarding Phanes rather than the other way around, but I find this scenario rather implausible (cf. Bernabé 2004: 74–75). Also unsatisfactory is the reading in Zannini Quirini 1987: 134–45, who focuses exclusively on the Orphic elements in the *parabasis* while ignoring the other components of this complex text.

[95] Eur. *Hyps.* fr. 758a.1103–08 Kannicht is possibly an allusion to a (presumably Orphic) theogony involving Protogonus and the Night, but there is no extant trace of a cosmic egg. See the discussion in Cockle 1987: 170–71.

[96] On Empedocles' φιλότης/φιλία, see KRS 1983²: 286–94. Bernabé 1995: 208 points out that the whirlpools to which Eros is compared in the avian cosmogony in *Av.* 697 recall the cosmic rotation found in Empedocles B 35 DK (esp. lines 3–4; cf. KRS 1983²: 296–99) as well as other pre-Socratic philosophers. Cf. Dover 1968: 150 on Aristophanes' jocular take on the philosophical δῖνος/δίνη in *Nub.* 380–82.

anthropomorphic representation of the gods.[97] The birds talk about creation in terms that reflect their own procreative process (τίκτει ... ᾠόν, *Av.* 695; οὗτος ... ἐνεόττευσεν γένος ἡμέτερον, *Av.* 699). In addition, they shape key entities in the universe after their own avian image, since their cosmogony combines the Orphic figure of shiny golden-feathered Phanes (*Av.* 697) with black-winged Night (*Av.* 695) and feathered Chaos (*Av.* 698).[98] Thus in the *parabasis* the birds exhibit precisely the type of behavior that animals would adopt according to Xenophanes if they could ever envision the divine (B 15 DK).[99]

There is no doubt that Aristophanes' complex and highly allusive cosmogony engages with Hesiod's *Theogony*, but the nature and extent of this engagement should be considered carefully. While the claim that Hesiod's *Theogony* is the "main model" of the avian cosmogony is reasonable,[100] I suggest that the birds' account also draws attention to the plasticity of the Hesiodic material and to the amplitude of its reception. To the extent that it adopts, adapts, and rearranges entities found in the *Theogony* (Chaos, Night, Erebos, Tartarus, and Eros), the birds' cosmogony offers a commentary on narratives that recount the cosmic beginnings largely by revising, modifying, and enriching aspects of the Hesiodic tradition. Although neglected in the scholarship, the allusion to Acusilaus' cosmogony early on in the avian account (*Av.* 693) underscores precisely this point, since we find evidence in Plato's *Symposium* that Acusilaus' vision of the primordial cosmos was read in conjunction with Hesiod's *Theogony* and as a reception of it.[101] Even the radically non-Hesiodic elements, such as the cosmic egg, are used to remythologize a set of entities that, with the exception of the birds themselves, does not expand to encompass non-Hesiodic beings. The Aristophanic text, therefore, casts

---

[97] Xenophanes, B 11 DK; see also B 14 and 16 DK on people fashioning their gods according to their own image. Cf. (Ps.?-)Epich. fr. 279 KA = 251 RN with Kerkhof 2001: 76–78. On the criticism against Hesiod, see Koning 2010a: 82–84 and 206.

[98] For a description of Night as winged, however, see Eur. *Or.* 174–77 (Νύξ ... κατάπτερος); cf. Pardini 1993: 59. All extant art depicting Night as winged dates to the Roman period; see Papastavrou 1992.

[99] Kanavou 2011: 393 suggests that Aristophanes here parodies the myth of the "first man" exemplified by the Deucalion of the Hesiodic *Catalogue*. However, there is no indication that the first creatures represented with avian characteristics in the *Birds* (Night, Chaos, and especially Eros) are considered identical in nature to the birds. Deucalion, on the other hand, was considered a mortal like any other.

[100] Dunbar 1995: 428, who nonetheless acknowledges the additional influences of Empedoclean poetry as well as Orphic hexameter poetry. Cf. KRS 1983²: 28 and MacDowell 1995: 207–08.

[101] Pl. *Smp.* 178b8–11. On the crucial textual corruption in the passage, see Dover 1980: 90–91 and Fowler 2000: 6.

this and other non-Hesiodic cosmogonies as post-Hesiodic constructs that do not simply circulate parallel to the Panhellenic Hesiodic tradition but, in fact, have been conceptualized in response to it.

The birds reinvent the primordial stages of the cosmos until the emergence of Gaia in order to introduce their own origins and thus construct an identity that defines them as both ancient and divine. Once established, the birds' close association with Eros paves the way for a catalogue of their contribution in several aspects of human life: they help in erotic pursuits, they indicate the seasons, thus allowing for timeliness and success in agriculture and seafaring, and through augury they offer humans insight into the future (*Av.* 703–22).[102] There is little doubt that the use of birds for determining the seasons was common knowledge, especially among farmers and sailors.[103] Although we find information of this type gathered and arranged in Hesiod's *Works and Days*, there are no substantial allusions to the Hesiodic text in the birds' catalogue of benefactions.[104] The chorus may still be evoking the Hesiodic corpus in broader terms, as the choice to mention augury and oracles (*Av.* 716–22) immediately after the use of birds as markers of seasons (*Av.* 709–15) mirrors the transition from the *Works and Days* to the (now lost) *Ornithomanteia*.[105] If there is any Hesiodic allusion here, it is not as prominent as the birds' engagement with the hymnic genre. Aristophanes' birds not only demonstrate awareness of their contributions in different areas of human life, but they also

---

[102]  Note the tension between the birds' emphasis on the polysemy of ὄρνις (*Av.* 720–21) and Prodicus' theory of ὀρθότης ὀνομάτων alluded to earlier in the *parabasis* (*Av.* 690–92); cf. Mayhew 2011: 173–74.

[103]  Contrast *Av.* 1088–1101, where the birds are portrayed not as marking the seasons but as experiencing them. Their experience is distinctly more pleasant and safe than the human experience. Nestle 1936: 162 already suggested that the Aristophanic text (ὥρας, *Av.* 709; ὥραν, *Av.* 713) evokes the Ὧραι by Prodicus, who is mentioned by name earlier in the *parabasis* (*Av.* 692). In the Ὧραι, Prodicus developed his ideas about the cultural development of humankind; the work included a praise of agriculture as well as the theory that religion originates in the worship of the natural elements that proved most beneficial to humankind. See Mayhew 2011: xxi–xxiii and 173–74. On sophistic ideas regarding the evolution of human culture in Aristophanes' *Birds*, see also De Carli 1971: 50–52.

[104]  Shearing the sheep at the appearance of the kite (*Av.* 713–14) is not part of the Hesiodic calendar. Furthermore, while the swallow is a sign of spring both in the *Birds* (*Av.* 714–15) and in the *WD* (568–69), the activities associated with it are very different. Only the birds' comments about winter bear some similarities to Hesiod's poem. In *Av.* 709–12, the crane is said to herald the time to sow and to give up sailing as it marks the advent of the winter. In Hes. *WD* 448–51, the migration of the cranes marks the season for ploughing and sowing, as well as the beginning of winter. Even though there are no distinct verbal echoes of the Hesiodic text, Gigante 1948: 21–23 has suggested that the joke about Orestes weaving a χλαῖνα (*Av.* 712) invokes Hesiod's advice to put on a χλαῖνα and a χιτών in order to survive the winter cold (WD 536–40). MacDowell 1995: 208 takes a more moderate stance when he talks about "comic variation on themes of Hesiod."

[105]  On the *Ornithomanteia*, see Introduction, p. 8.

celebrate them as their special prerogatives, their *timai*. In defining and praising their powers along with their origins, the birds perform a song that approximates a self-referential hymn.[106] These hymnic elements support the self-celebratory function of the *parabasis* and, in combination with the subsequent promise of a new Golden Age (*Av.* 723–36),[107] they reinforce the birds' claim to divinity.[108]

Having redefined the history of the cosmos before the emergence of Gaia's progeny of rulers, the play now promises to move the Succession Myth forward beyond its Hesiodic boundaries, as Peisetairus proceeds with his ambitious plan to usurp Zeus's power. After the *parabasis*, the foundation of the new city is finalized and the name Νεφελοκοκκυγία is concocted. Furthermore, sacrifices are performed in a manner that both confirms the beginning of a new era in which the birds have replaced the Olympian gods, and underscores the dearth of offerings that the Olympians are about to experience thanks to Peisetairus' plan (*Av.* 848–904).[109] After considerable interruptions by a poet (*Av.* 905–58), an oracle-monger (*Av.* 959–91), Meton the geometer and urban-planner (*Av.* 992–1020), an inspector (*Av.* 1021–34), and a decree-seller (*Av.* 1035–55), Peisetairus eventually completes the sacrifices alone (*Av.* 1056–57; 1118) and away from the birds who, in the meantime, perform the play's second *parabasis* (*Av.* 1058–1117).[110] As soon as the first messenger confirms that the building of the city-walls has been completed, a second messenger appears with Iris, who has been apprehended as a trespasser.

This scene captures the first confrontation between the aspiring usurper and an Olympian agent (*Av.* 1202–61).[111] The conversation confirms that

---

[106] Generic features of hymns include the praise of divine births as well as a celebration of divine attributes. See, e.g., Furley 2007: 129–30, Richardson 2010: 4–9, and Clay 2011: 241–43.

[107] Here the birds develop further Peisetairus' earlier suggestions about how they could persuade mortals to worship them as gods (e.g. the protection of crops in *Av.* 587–91; cf. *Av.* 1058–71). It is noteworthy that, in that context, Peisetairus evoked the extended lifespan of the crow: "don't you know that the screaming crow lives for five generations of men?" (οὐκ οἶσθ' ὅτι πέντ' ἀνδρῶν γενεὰς ζώει λακέρυζα κορώνη; *Av.* 609), thus comically deflating Hes. fr. 304.1–2MW (ἐννέα τοι ζώει γενεὰς λακέρυζα κορώνη / ἀνδρῶν ἡβώντων); see Cusset 2003: 55–58. On the Golden Age and utopias of abundance in Old Comedy, see below.

[108] Compare the *Homeric Hymn to Hermes* in which Hermes' first song is a self-legitimating celebration of his own lineage (*hHerm* 57–59); note that, later in the hymn, the god sings an inclusive theogony (*hHerm* 427–33).

[109] On the word-play involved in *Av.* 864–83 and the ingenious blending between bird-species and divinities who had a cult in Athens, see Dunbar 1995: 510–14. On the sacrifices, cf. Bowie 1993: 160–61.

[110] On ritual parodied here, see Furley 2007: 120–21.

[111] Herington 1963b: 238 traces in Iris' threats a parody of Hermes' interaction with Prometheus in the final scene of the *PV* (944–1093). He also suggests that the description of Iris' approach in

Peisetairus' plan to starve the Olympians is working; furthermore, it offers a demonstration of the challenger's aggression towards the established regime. Even though Peisetairus' violence remains verbal, the mortal clearly prevails over Iris: he not only counters the prospect of Zeus's punishing thunderbolt with a Gigantomachic clash (*Av.* 1247–52), but he also dismisses the winged goddess with the threat of rape framed in terms of punishing a troublesome slave (*Av.* 1253–56). The harassment of Iris may be a *topos* drawn from satyr drama,[112] and the punishment of a slave by rape is an erotic fantasy found elsewhere in the Aristophanic corpus (*Ach.* 271–75). In this particular scene, however, Peisetairus' self-fashioning as Iris' master conveys vividly his unilateral reconfiguration of his relationship with the Olympians. Read in the context of a cosmic *coup d'état*, the scene marks Peisetairus' trajectory towards appropriating not only Zeus's rule but also his sexual politics, which include the unchecked license to rape whomever he wishes. Earlier in the play, Peisetairus mentioned the rape of mortal women among the aspects of Olympian domination that he would inhibit with his embargo plans (*Av.* 557–60). The threat of sexual assault against Iris, therefore, can be viewed as part of Peisetairus' gradual transformation into a Zeus-like cosmic ruler, which will be completed with another act of sexual politics, namely his marriage to Basileia in the end of the play.[113]

After Iris retreats, Peisetairus' clash with the gods remains dormant for a while as the protagonist deals with different types of disruptive humans who come to join Nephelokokkygia. The arrival of Prometheus in line 1494, however, brings our attention back to the pending question of Peisetairus' ascent to the cosmic throne. Prometheus arrives in comic disguise, terrified that he may be spotted by the Olympians while helping Zeus's challenger. He delivers crucial information about the famine that has plagued the gods on Olympus ever since the mortals discontinued their sacrifices to them, and has stirred foreign gods to threaten Zeus (*Av.* 1515–24). Prometheus not only provides Peisetairus with special insight regarding the divine realm (including the existence of foreign gods), but also advises him about the appropriate course of action: when the joint embassy of Greek and non-Greek gods arrives, Peisetairus must not come

---

*Av.* 1182–83 echoes the arrival of the Oceanids as perceived by Prometheus in the *PV* 125–26; on this point, however, see the objections raised by Rau 1967: 165 and 177.

[112] See Dunbar 1995: 612–13, Scharffenberger 1995, and, more recently, Bakola 2010: 107–08.

[113] Peisetairus threatens rape as a punitive measure. When he comments on Iris' attractiveness, he limits her power of seduction exclusively to younger men (*Av.* 1260–61). On this age distinction, see Dunbar 1995: 630.

to an agreement until Zeus has yielded his scepter and has agreed to give Basileia to Peisetairus in marriage (*Av.* 1532–36). After clarifying the identity of Basileia, Prometheus departs swiftly, but not before he draws attention to his comically feminine disguise (*Av.* 1549–51).

The scene constructs Prometheus as a comic version of his character in the *Prometheus Bound* and the other play(s) that complemented it.[114] His parting exchange with Peisetairus renders the reception of the *PV* in this scene explicit: his declaration of benevolence towards humans in *Av.* 1545 (ἀεί ποτ' ἀνθρώποις γὰρ εὔνους εἴμ' ἐγώ, "for I am perpetually well disposed towards men") recalls the philanthropy for which he is penalized in the *PV*, as Kratos and Hephaestus point out already in the prologue (lines 11 and 28). Furthermore, the proclamation of Prometheus' hatred towards the gods (μισῶ δ' ἅπαντας τοὺς θεούς, *Av.* 1547) echoes a similar utterance in *PV* 975 (ἁπλῷ λόγῳ τοὺς πάντας ἐχθαίρω θεούς). More importantly, the comic scene duplicates Prometheus' crucial contribution to Zeus's victory over the Titans. In the tragedy, Prometheus recounts to the Oceanids that Zeus owes his triumph against the Titans to him. During the Titanomachy, Prometheus revealed first to his fellow Titans the secret to victory, but the Titans shunned him. Prometheus then approached Zeus, who took his advice and won (*PV* 199–221). Much like the tragic Prometheus, his comic version holds the secret to victory, but, while the tragic Prometheus claims that he changed sides only after his advice was rejected by the Titans, the Prometheus of the *Birds* rushes to betray Zeus and help the new challenger. His willingness to facilitate Peisetairus' victory appears at first to be an extension of his *philanthropia*, even though the humans he has come to aid now bear avian features. Very soon, however, Prometheus spontaneously reveals his aversion towards the gods, and thus raises the suspicion that complementing (or even underlying) the noble cause of *philanthropia* is a burning hatred that stems from the mistreatment he has suffered in tragedy.[115]

The Aristophanic text evokes unambiguously the *PV*, and yet, of the long list of benefactions to humankind that defines Prometheus in tragedy

---

[114] On the allusions to the Prometheus-plays in this scene, see Herington 1963b: 237–38, Griffith 1977: 11–12 and 1983b: 284; cf. West 1979: 132 with n.13. West suggests that Prometheus' furtive arrival in the *Birds* mirrors a scene from the *Prometheus Pyrphoros*, the play which, in his opinion, was the first installment of the Prometheus-trilogy and dramatized the theft of fire. West also formulates the hypothesis that ἀπόλωλεν ὁ Ζεύς in *Av.* 1514 may have been drawn from the *Prometheus Lyomenos*. For a much more skeptical approach on this issue, see Rau 1967: 175–77. On the Prometheus-plays, see also Chapter 4, pp. 122–67.

[115] On Prometheus' recommendation of Basileia and the *PV*, see below.

(*PV* 248–54, 436–506), the only one mentioned explicitly during his encounter with Peisetairus is the gift of fire and, in particular, its culinary application in barbecues (Πε. μόνον θεῶν γὰρ διὰ σ' ἀπανθρακίζομεν, *Av.* 1546).[116] In expressing his appreciation for the gift of broiling, Peisetairus gives an idiosyncratic spin on the tradition that resonates with comedy's fixation on food. Yet the line also prepares us for the next scene, in which Peisetairus takes full advantage of Prometheus' benefaction by throwing a few dissident birds to the grill (*Av.* 1579–693; see esp. πυρπόλει τοὺς ἄνθρακας, *Av.* 1580). Romer has suggested that these grilled birds, with which Peisetairus baits the starved gods of the embassy, are part of a sacrifice, but there is no good reason to view Peisetairus' barbecue in this scene as sacrificial. To begin with, these birds are killed in the name of politics, not ritual (*Av.* 1583–85); furthermore, unlike the earlier scene of sacrifice for the foundation of Nephelokokkygia, there is no sign here of a priest or a prayer. Instead, there is a cook (*Av.* 1637), and great attention is drawn to culinary preparation (*Av.* 1579–80, 1582, 1589, 1637). In this scene, then, cooking appears to be an act of self-indulgence. In addition, as the text recalls the references to the consumption of birds that framed Peisetairus' initial plea in *Av.* 462–66 and 524–38,[117] cooking emerges as emblematic of Peisetairus' deceptive and manipulative plan that has now come to a successful fruition. I suggest that the Prometheus-scene marks the collapse of sacrifice. Up until the arrival of Prometheus, Peisetairus has worked hard to disrupt the communication between gods and men by obstructing the sacrificial smoke with the walls of Nephelokokkygia and, subsequently, by convincing the mortals not to sacrifice to the Olympians any more. The sacrifices for the foundation of Nephelokokkygia were offered to none other than the birds themselves, the new gods.[118] Iris already confirmed that the lack of sacrifices has proved effective, and, since she was apprehended by the birds and never managed to convey to the mortals Zeus's request for sacrifices, the famine on Olympus has only gotten worse. The subplot of the embargo culminates when Prometheus, the immortal credited in the *PV* with establishing sacrifice among humans,[119] revels in its failure (*Av.* 1515–24). As Prometheus announces enthusiastically the defeat of Zeus (ἀπόλωλεν ὁ Ζεύς, *Av.* 1514), therefore,

[116] On ἀπανθρακίζω as a culinary term, see Dunbar 1995: 707.
[117] Peisetairus warms up for his first address to the birds with references to dining (*Av.* 462–66), and he ends his *epideixis* with a lament for the treatment birds suffer at the hands of cooks (*Av.* 524–38). See Auger 1979: 83.
[118] Differently Wilkins 2000: 344, who suggests that the sacrifices were offered to the old gods after all.
[119] *PV* 496–99; see also Chapter 4, pp. 136–38.

he also marks the collapse of a fundamental mode of communication between mortals and immortals and, with it, the breakdown of the distinction among gods, humans, and animals.[120]

Peisetairus' exclusive focus on roasting in *Av.* 1546 not only marginalizes sacrifice by foregrounding the culinary, i.e. the secular, aspect of burning killed animals but it also probes the relationship between the tragic Prometheus, with whom the comedy engages extensively in this scene, and his Hesiodic counterpart. We have already seen that the *Birds* constructs its Prometheus by appropriating features of his character in the Prometheus-tragedies, including ostensibly non-Hesiodic elements such as his involvement in the cosmic power struggle. Given the long list of Prometheus' many and varied benefactions to humankind in the *PV* (248–54, 436–506), the exclusive focus on a single one (fire) in *Av.* 1546 is surprisingly reductive. It is consistent, though, with the Hesiodic tradition, according to which Prometheus' sole benefaction to the mortals is the restoration of fire (*Th.* 558–69 and *WD* 49–52). By recalling a common denominator between the Hesiodic and the tragic treatment of Prometheus, the *Birds* reflects upon the legacy of the Hesiodic tradition, which, having been rewritten already in the *PV*, is now transformed once again through the lens of Aristophanic comedy. Much like the play's *parabasis*, then, the Prometheus-scene demonstrates awareness of Hesiodic poetry as well as its reception.

Overall, the Prometheus-scene establishes that Peisetairus' attempt to take over Zeus's throne must entail appropriating and rewriting the traditional Succession Myth narrative. Prometheus talks about the return of the cosmic scepter to the birds (ἐὰν μὴ παραδιδῷ / τὸ σκῆπτρον ὁ Ζεὺς τοῖσιν ὄρνισιν πάλιν, *Av.* 1534–35), thus validating the reinvention of the cosmic past that Peisetairus initiated earlier in the play. Furthermore, in so far as it recalls Prometheus' crucial intervention during the Titanomachy (as recounted in the *PV*), the scene solidifies the play's representation of the clash between the birds and

---

[120] On this point, see Auger 1979: 85 and Romer 1997: 59–62. Following a structuralist approach to the reception of the *Theogony* in the *Birds*, Romer argues that Peisetairus's barbecue returns the world to the state it was in at Mecone (*Th.* 535–57 with Vernant: 1979). Romer is right to point out that Peisetairus' plan throughout the *Birds* relies on breaking all boundaries among human, subhuman, and superhuman entities. Yet I do not view this as a return to an earlier stage but as a deliberate reconfiguration orchestrated by Peisetairus and a demonstration that the cosmos is entering a new era under his control; cf. Wilkins 2000: 345, who nonetheless sees similarities between the new and the old status quo in terms of sacrificial practices and of the way gods, humans, and domesticated animals interrelate.

Zeus as an extension of the Succession Myth, a new conflict in this series of power struggles. Unlike all previous usurpations of power, however, this comic crisis promises no violence at all (*Av.* 1532–36). Instead, Prometheus' advice emphasizes strategy (cf. *PV* 212–13): in the upcoming negotiations, Peisetairus should demand not only the scepter of power but also the hand of Basileia in marriage. Prometheus' voluntary recommendation of a specific bride who will secure Peisetairus' reign reverses his staunch refusal to reveal the identity of the bride destined to produce Zeus's challenger in the *PV.* In addition, the positive association of a bride with cosmic power marks Peisetairus' reign as a genuinely new era for the cosmos: unlike Ouranus, Cronus, and Zeus, the Athenian appears not to be facing the menacing prospect of an overpowering son. In the comic utopia of the *Birds*, the divine bride secures the cosmic reign with no threats attached.

The marriage to Basileia brings the comedy to its climactic conclusion. Given its metrical position in lines 1537 and 1753, the name of this silent female figure is Βασίλεια ("Princess"), as attested in the tenth-century Ravenna manuscript (*Ravennas* 429), rather than Βασιλεία ("Kingship") as in the rest of the manuscript tradition.[121] Scholars have attempted to identify Basileia with an actual cultic divinity, often interpreting Peisetairus' betrothal as a *hieros gamos.*[122] Given that Peisetairus asks Prometheus to explain who Basileia is, however, this female figure is most likely an Aristophanic invention.[123] Prometheus describes Basileia as the character who manages not only the thunderbolt (*Av.* 1538) but also "everything else" (καὶ τἄλλ' ἁπαξάπαντα, *Av.* 1539) – at least everything that pertains to politics and administrative authority, as the list in lines 1540–41 indicates. Regardless of the accentuation

---

[121] On female personifications in Old Comedy, see Hall 2000, Henderson 2000: 142–43; cf. the survey in Newiger 1957: 104–22 and 155–65, who nonetheless considers Basileia of the *Birds* exceptional (121) because he thinks she represents an actual goddess (92–103). On personifications as *dramatis personae*, see also Stafford 2000: 12–13.

[122] For a concise discussion of suggested identifications, see Newiger 1957: 92–103; on the *hieros gamos* and Basileia as the new Hera, see esp. Hofmann (1976) 138–60. The identification of Basileia with Hera has been encouraged by *Av.* 1633–35, but I agree with the objections raised by Dunbar 1995: 728. The argument that Basileia is modelled after Athena, on the other hand, has been based largely on *Eum.* 827–28; in addition to Newiger, see West 1979: 132 n.13 and, more recently, Anderson and Dix 2007 with bibliography and a supplementary discussion of several other figures that the audience may have associated with Aristophanes' Basileia (Basile, Basilinna, and Peisistratus' Phye). Athena, however, is not a goddess the Athenian audience would associate with marriage, and *Eum.* 827–28 may be referring to a single event rather than a permanent attribute of Athena; see also MacDowell 1995: 218 on the mention of Athena in *Av.* 1653. On the association of leaders (e.g. Peisistratus) with women embodying politically powerful concepts, see Bowie 1993: 164–65.

[123] See Sommerstein 1991: 298, MacDowell 1995: 218, and Dunbar 1995: 703–05.

of Basileia's name, therefore, the text encourages the audience to perceive her as the embodiment of cosmic rule.[124]

Peisetairus' marriage to Basileia changes permanently the protagonist's place in the cosmos and the way he relates to the Olympians. The involvement of Prometheus in the betrothal between Peisetairus and a female figure sent by Zeus, as well as the cosmic impact of this union, has led to a reading of Basileia as a new Pandora. Bowie views Pandora and Basileia as functionally equal because in both cases the transfer of a female figure from gods to men reconfigures both realms.[125] While endorsing Bowie's argument, Romer also argues that Basileia is at once the new Hera (for marrying the new Zeus) and the new Pandora "because she literally bestows on her husband all the bounty of the universe." For the latter point, Romer does not rely on Prometheus' description of the desired bride in *Av.* 1537–42, but on the reference to Earth as Pandora in *Av.* 971 (πρῶτον Πανδώρᾳ θῦσαι λευκότριχα κριόν, "first sacrifice a white-haired ram to Pandora"), in which he readily assumes a resonance of Hesiod's Pandora.[126] Holzhauser, on the other hand, offers a careful reading of *Av.* 1537–42, looking for hints that prompt Basileia's identification with Hesiod's Pandora, whom he supposes that Aristophanes is parodying here.[127] Holzhauser argues that the verb ταμιεύω in *Av.* 1538 and 1542 evokes the storage jar (πίθος) that defines the Hesiodic figure of Pandora. More importantly, he reads an etymological play on Pandora's name in *Av.* 1539 (ἀπαξάπαντα), 1542 (ἅπαντα), and 1543 (ἤν γ' ἤν σὺ παρ' ἐκείνου παραλάβῃς, πάντ' ἔχεις, "if you receive her [*sc.* Basileia] from him [*sc.* Zeus], you have everything").[128] Although this etymology is not among those suggested in *WD* 80–82 and the ancient scholia to the Hesiodic

[124] See Dunbar 1995: 703–04, MacDowell 1995: 217–18, Romer 1997: 63 and 72 n.39. Peisetairus requests the betrothal to Basileia after the embassy has agreed to return the scepter to the birds. Poseidon finds the prospect of surrendering Basileia so outrageous that he wants to walk out of the negotiations (*Av.* 1635–36). When Heracles refuses to follow him, Poseidon summarizes the concession to Peisetairus' demands as "giving up the monarchy" (ὁ Ζεὺς παραδοὺς τούτοισι τὴν τυραννίδα, *Av.* 1643). The word-choice (τυραννίς) implies the integration of kingship (βασιλεία) in the figure of Βασίλεια. Cf. sch. *Av.* 1536 (with the reading Βασιλεία).
[125] Bowie 1993: 163.
[126] Romer 1997: 63. Cf. also Auger 1979: 75 and 81–82, who suggests that the sequence sacrifices–banquet–marriage reiterates Hesiod's early Iron Age; such a reading, however, presupposes complete decontextualization and disregards the details. In fact, Auger himself abandons the Iron Age for the Golden Age in the rest of his piece.
[127] Holzhauser 2002: 37–41; cf. 42 on *Av.* 1753–54.
[128] Cf. already Bowie 1993: 163. Less convincingly, Holzhauser 2002: 38 also finds evocations of Pandora's name in the repeated use of the verb διδόναι and its compounds in the context of betrothal (e.g., καὶ τὴν Βασιλείαν σοι γυναῖκ' ἔχειν διδῷ, *Av.* 1536; τὴν δὲ Βασιλείαν τὴν κόρην γυναῖκ' ἐμοὶ / ἐκδοτέον ἐστίν, *Av.* 1634–35).

poem,[129] Holzhauser argues that it is "the correct etymology" that underlies Pandora's identification with Gaia.[130]

Basileia is indeed a female figure who brings about change for the entire
universe: her marriage to Peisetairus marks his ascent to the cosmic throne
and thus completes the unraveling of the boundaries between gods,
humans, and animals that already began with the assimilation of Peisetairus and Euelpides to birds (*Av.* 801–07).[131] I suspect, however, that
scholars may have been too eager to see her representation in the *Birds*
as evocative of Hesiod's Pandora. Upon close examination, there are more
differences between Basileia and Pandora than there are similarities. The
text states repeatedly that Basileia can give access to "everything" (*Av.*
1539–43); when Prometheus specifies what he means (*Av.* 1537–41), however, he associates Basileia exclusively with elements of power and politics
that she administers for Zeus (αὐτῷ, *Av.* 1542), not with fertility, reproduction, or sustenance, the kinds of gifts that underlie Holzhauser's
"correct etymology" of Pandora/Gaia. Furthermore, even though the
aspects of civic life included in Prometheus' list are a mix of positive
(*Av.* 1538–40) and negative elements (*Av.* 1541), the former outweigh the
latter by far; Hesiod's Pandora, on the other hand, is created to burden
humankind with her predominantly negative presence.[132] Zeus orders
Hephaestus to create Pandora so that she can be given over to men and
be a bane to them, and she is eventually delivered to humankind by

---

[129]  *WD* 80–82: ὀνόμηνε δὲ τήνδε γυναῖκα / Πανδώρην, ὅτι πάντες Ὀλύμπια δώματ᾽ ἔχοντες / δῶρον
ἐδώρησαν, πῆμ᾽ ἀνδράσιν ἀλφηστῇσιν ("and he named this woman Pandora because all those who
inhabit Olympus gave her (as?) a gift, a bane to bread-eating men"); *sch.* Hes. *WD* 81: Πανδώρην: ἢ
ὅτι πάντων δῶρα ἔλαβεν ἢ ὅτι δῶρον πάντων τῶν θεῶν ("Pandora: either because she received
gifts from all (the gods) or because she is a gift from all the gods"). Cf. Lendle 1957: 51–54, and West
1978: 166–67.

[130]  Holzhauser 2002: 37–38. Cf. *sch. Av.* 971: Πανδώρᾳ· τῇ γῇ. ἐπειδὴ πάντα τὰ πρὸς τὸ ζῆν δωρεῖται.
ἀφ᾽ οὗ καὶ ζείδωρος καὶ ἀνησιδώρα ("to Pandora: (namely) to the earth because it offers all things
required for living. That's why (the earth is called) also 'life-giving' and 'the one who sends up
gifts'") with Hsch. *s.v.* ζείδωρος. Tzetzes on *WD* 79 identifies Pandora with agriculture using
similar language.

[131]  Tereus' involuntary metamorphosis offers a blueprint for the merging of humans and birds.

[132]  Contrast the reception of Hesiod's Pandora by Euripides in his first *Hippolytus* (fr. 429 Kannicht):
ἀντὶ πυρὸς γὰρ ἄλλο πῦρ / μεῖζον ἐβλάστομεν γυναῖκες πολὺ δυσμαχώτερον ("for, in exchange for
fire, we, women, came to being, a different, greater fire that is much harder to fight"). The speaker,
whom Kannicht identifies as the women of the chorus, acknowledges in the first person the birth of
their kind as retaliation for the recovery of fire. The Euripidean fragment evokes the Hesiodic
accounts of Pandora's creation through verbal echoes (esp. τοῖς δ᾽ ἐγὼ ἀντὶ πυρὸς δώσω κακόν, "in
exchange for fire I will give them an evil," *WD* 57; cf. *Th.* 570), and was, in fact, read as a paraphrase
of Hes. *WD* 57–58 already by Clement of Alexandria (*Strom.* 6.2.12.1–2). It is noteworthy, however,
that this Euripidean reception of Hesiod's Pandora combines the positive value of the literal fire
found in Hesiodic poetry with the negative metaphor of consuming erotic desire.

Hermes (*WD* 84–85). On the other hand, Basileia is a divinity that resides with the gods on Olympus and her duty focuses on Zeus's resources;[133] in order to get "Basileia and everything," Peisetairus must ascend to the sky (*Av.* 1686–87), and their betrothal, which Poseidon considered an outrageous demand in the first place (*Av.* 1635–36), seals Zeus's permanent surrender. Finally, there is no reason to assume that the union of Peisetairus and Basileia, which guarantees the former's apotheosis and marks a new era for the cosmos under his rule,[134] is a prototype, a relationship that is supposed to be replicated like the union between Pandora and Epimetheus. In my view, therefore, there is little in the play's portrayal of Basileia that encourages the audience to think of her as a new Pandora. As for the explicit reference to Gaia as Πανδώρα earlier in the play (*Av.* 971), it presents great interest for the study of Pandora as a chthonic figure in Athens.[135] Thanks to iconographic evidence, we know of at least one Athenian play, a satyr drama by Sophocles entitled *Pandora* or *Sphyrokopoi*, that combined the Hesiodic narrative of Pandora's introduction to Epimetheus by Hermes at Zeus's

---

[133] In the context of the play's final celebration, *Av.* 1753 (καὶ πάρεδρον Βασίλειαν ἔχει Διός [*sc.* Πεισέταιρος]) draws attention one more time to the close connection that Peisetairus' bride has with Zeus. It is ambiguous whether Basileia is said to be the daughter of Zeus (Βασίλειαν Διός), who is now sitting by Peisetairus' side (πάρεδρον ἔχει), or a figure who used to be at the side of Zeus (πάρεδρον Βασίλειαν Διός). If understood as the πάρεδρος of Zeus, Basileia would be in the same league as Themis (Pi. *O.*8.21–22, Διὸς ξενίου / πάρεδρος ... Θέμις) as well as Dike (*WD* 256–62, esp. 259, αὐτίκα πὰρ Διὶ πατρὶ καθεζομένη Κρονίωνι, "immediately sitting next to her father Zeus, the son of Cronus"). On πάρεδρος applied to a divine consort, cf. Ba. *Ode* 11.51–52, where Hera is Zeus's πάρεδρος. Either way, Basileia is defined in a manner that does not evoke Pandora at all.

[134] On marriage to a goddess in the context of a man's apotheosis, cf. Heracles' union with Hebe, the daughter of Zeus and Hera already in Hes. *Th.* 950–55. According to sch. *Av.* 1536, Euphronius considered Basileia to be a daughter of Zeus and interpreted her betrothal to Peisetairus as his immortalization. Cf. Hofmann 1976: 140–41.

[135] In his influential structuralist reading of the Prometheus story in the *Theogony* and the *WD*, Vernant 1974: 189–90 draws attention to the parallel between Pandora/Ge and Pandora the woman as fecund bodies. His argument seems to presuppose that Pandora was originally an attribute of Gaia that the *WD* appropriates as the name of the first woman/wife – although, admittedly, his prose remains conveniently vague on the issue. Cf. also Casanova 1979a: 62–89, who traces the origins of Hesiod's Pandora to a deity such as "all-giving Ge" despite the fact that all his evidence dates to the classical period or later; he does, nonetheless, acknowledge that the audience of Hesiodic poetry would not confound the Hesiodic first woman with the divine figure of the "original" Pandora. For a recent survey of πανδώρη as an attribute of Earth, see Musäus 2004: 56–57, who also rightly points out that Gaia/Ge is never described as "all-giving" in the Hesiodic corpus. In my view, if one were to read (or retroject) a connection between Pandora and "all-giving Ge" in the Hesiodic text, one should also explore its limitations. As a figure made of earth (*WD* 61, 70; cf. *Th.* 571), Pandora shares Ge's all-giving fecundity; however, thanks to the Olympians, Pandora also brings misery, painful toil, and lethal sickness (*WD* 90–104; note that, in *Th.* 211–32, Κῆραι and Πόνος belong to Night's progeny, not Gaia's). By contrast, what Hesiod's Earth offers to the Iron Race seems to be unambiguously beneficial even if access to her "gifts" is not easy or even guaranteed. For a different argument against the association of Hesiod's Pandora with Earth, see Loraux 1993b: 83–84.

orders with an ascent from the earth.[136] Despite Romer and Holzhausen, however, I do not see how this Pandora/Gaia of *Av.* 971 contributes anything to the character of Basileia, the steward of Zeus's thunderbolt.

Ending a comedy with the union between the main protagonist and the incarnation of what he desires is not unique to the *Birds*.[137] Yet Peisetairus' betrothal to Basileia is more than just the fulfilment of fantasy; as it marks the dethronement of Zeus and the dawn of a new era, the marriage can also be read as the challenger's appropriation of his predecessor's sexual politics. Unlike Cronus and Ouranus who only couple with one consort, Zeus engages in a series of unions with female divinities; both his divine lovers and the offspring produced from these unions support Zeus's reign. The importance of sex as a strategy for creating alliances and securing stability is evident in Hesiod's *Theogony*. The poetic celebration of Zeus does not end with his ascent to the cosmic throne (*Th.* 881–85) or with his success in preventing the birth of a usurper by swallowing his first wife, Metis (*Th.* 886–900). Instead, the Hesiodic poem offers a long catalogue of marriages that follow the cooption of Metis. First, Zeus bonds with personified concepts such as Themis (*Th.* 901–06) and Eurynome (*Th.* 907–11) who – together with their offspring – define and exemplify characteristic features of his reign. Themis gives birth to the civic values of Lawfulness, Justice, and Peace (collectively identified as the Horae),[138] as well as the three Fates that dispense good and evil to humans. Eurynome, on the other hand, produces the three Graces who personify merriment in social settings (Aglaia, Euphrosyne, and Thalia). Once these fundamental concepts have emerged in the cosmos, the *Theogony* turns to other unions that contribute different types of offspring to the world.[139] The marriage of

---

[136] Harrison 1900: 106–08 and more thoroughly Robert 1914; cf. also Pearson 1917: 137 and, much more recently, Olson 1998: xxxvi–xxxviii, Heynen and Krumeich 1999b.

[137] Cf. the *Peace*, where Hermes gives Ὀπώρα to Trygaeus as a bride in lines 706–07; the rest of the comedy looks forward to the wedding feast with which the play ends. Perhaps also comparable are the happy reunions that conclude the *Lysistrata* (1182–1321). On gender and marriage in Aristophanic comedy, see Loraux 1993a: 204–15.

[138] The genealogical connection of these three personifications to Themis and their grouping as Ὧραι (justified through etymology in *Th.* 903, αἵ τ' ἔργ' ὠρεύουσι καταθνητοῖσι βροτοῖσι) is specific to the *Theogony*. The Horae of the *Theogony* appear in Pi. *O.*13-6–8, *O.*9.15–16, *Pa.*1/52a.6, fr. 30 SM, as well as Ba. *Dith.* 15/1.54–55 (with no explicit reference to their genealogical connection); contrast, however, Pi. fr. 75.14–15 SM. In the *WD*, on the other hand, the Horae remain unidentified, but their association with spring and attraction in the context of adorning Pandora (*WD* 74–75) point to seasons and to timeliness rather than civic virtues; cf. *h.Ap.* 194–96. In Homeric poetry the Horae stand for the seasons (*Il.* 5.749–51 and 8.393–95).

[139] After Themis and Eurynome, Zeus beds with Demeter to produce Persephone, whom Zeus will offer as a bride to Hades (*Th.* 912–14); he then produces the Muses with Mnemosyne (*Th.* 915–17), thus giving birth to his own panegyrists (cf. *Th.* 1–115). After Mnemosyne, Zeus beds Leto, who

Peisetairus and Basileia, therefore, is more than the iteration of a comic *topos*; in the context of cosmic usurpation, it draws additional meaning from the cooption of personified concepts, a strategy which, according to the Hesiodic tradition, markedly defined and solidified Zeus's rule in its beginnings.[140]

In the *Birds*, we find a similar appropriation of the succession narrative already in the scene of the divine embassy. The confrontation between Peisetairus and the embassy of gods (*Av.* 1565–1693) has been read as an evocation of the Gigantomachy, mainly because Heracles is involved.[141] It is certainly true that Heracles is recruited to help the gods in this embassy just as he was to fight for the Olympians in the Gigantomachy, but we should not forget that, in the post-heroic era of the *Birds*, he has become an Olympian himself. Heracles enters the stage in a state of hunger-induced anger, ready to strangle Zeus's new challenger (*Av.* 1574–78). The prospect of partaking in Peisetairus' barbecue, however, changes his attitude and he insists that the gods should agree to Peisetairus' terms even when Poseidon threatens to walk away from the negotiations (*Av.* 1635–40). Poseidon attempts to persuade Heracles that giving in to Peisetairus would deprive him of his inheritance, i.e. the rule of the cosmos, when Zeus dies (*Av.* 1641–45). Peisetairus matches the absurdity of Poseidon's argument: he evokes Athenian law to counter-argue that Heracles has no right to the inheritance anyway, since he is a bastard who has never been introduced to the phratry, while Zeus has a legitimate heiress, Athena Ἐπίκληρος, with a genuine paternal uncle, Poseidon (*Av.* 1646–70).[142] At this point, Peisetairus manages to turn Heracles into an ally by promising him a place of power in the new era (*Av.* 1672–73, esp. καταστήσας σ' ἐγώ / τύραννον). I suggest that Peisetairus here follows a strategy that comes straight from Zeus's playbook in the *Theogony*. According to the Hesiodic account of Zeus's ascent to the cosmic throne, his victory against the Titans was largely due to alliances he formed

bears Apollo and Artemis (*Th.* 918–20), and with Hera, who produces Hebe, Ares, and Eileithuia with Zeus, but also Hephaestus by herself (*Th.* 921–23 and 927–29). The catalogue continues with the union of gods other than Zeus, but it includes three more offspring of Zeus: Hermes born of Maia (*Th.* 938–40), Dionysus born of Semele (*Th.* 940–43), and Heracles son of Alcmene (*Th.* 943–44). On the marriages of Zeus in *Th.* 886–929 and 938–44, and their relevance to his reign, see Detienne and Vernant 1978: 107–09, Bonnafé 1985: 79–102, Rudhardt 1986: 31–32, Ramnoux 1987: 157–59, Miralles 1993, and, more recently, Clay 2003: 29–30.

[140] For a different reading of Basileia in the context of the sophistic history of civilization found in Pl. *Prt.* 320c–323a, see De Carli 1971: 51.

[141] Hofmann 1976: 127–37; cf. Zannini Quirini 1987: 73.

[142] For the legal background of the passage, see MacDowell 1995: 220 and Dunbar 1995: 730–34. On the connection between Heracles and bastards, see Humphreys 1974: 91–95.

by promising honors to divinities who had none under Cronus' rule (*Th.* 383–403, esp. 389–96; cf. the restoration of the Hundred-Handers, *Th.* 639–63). Similarly, Peisetairus' offer earns him a crucial ally who ultimately tilts the negotiation in his favor. While coopting Zeus's strategy, however, Peisetairus also eliminates a potential male challenger, since he persuades – or rather dupes[143] – Heracles to give up the prospect of inheriting Zeus's rule in exchange for a powerful position in Peisetairus' regime.[144]

To sum up, the usurpation of cosmic rule by an Athenian in the *Birds* entails the extensive appropriation of the cosmogonic narrative developed in and proliferated by the Hesiodic *Theogony*. The *coup d'état* requires the revision of the Hesiodic timeline of the cosmos on both ends, as it rewrites the primeval beginnings of the world and successfully renews the crisis of succession. Moreover, as a challenger, Peisetairus adopts some of the strategies that define Zeus's success in the *Theogony*. While appropriating, subverting, and rewriting the Hesiodic narrative, however, Aristophanes' *Birds* also acknowledges the rich and varied reception of Hesiodic poetry, and situates itself within it.[145]

## Hesiod's Golden Age and Comic Utopias of Abundance

In Aristophanes' *Birds*, Peisetairus and Euelpides are initially attracted to the life of the birds because they enjoy abundant natural resources and have no need of money (*Av.* 156–60). Later, the worship of the birds is

---

[143] The proverbial "birds' milk" in *Av.* 1673 (ὀρνίθων γάλα, cf. 734) is, of course, an impossible offer.

[144] Compare Hermes' voluntary defection in Aristophanes' *Wealth* (1107–70). When Chremylus successfully restores the eyesight of Wealth, he benefits only the just. Since all irrationality, absurdity, and uncertainty regarding wealth distribution disappears, people no longer feel the need to seek divine aid through sacrifice. A famine ensues on Olympus. Hermes comes seemingly to restore sacrifices for the gods (*Pl.*1107–09), but very quickly reveals that he is only interested in saving his own skin (*Pl.* 1118–19). He defects to the human world (*Pl.* 1151) and reinvents himself as part of Chremylus' new status quo (*Pl.* 1152–70). In the *Wealth*, Aristophanes reworks creatively the old motif of the blind Wealth (e.g. Hippon. fr. 36 W²): here Zeus is responsible for blinding Wealth in the first place out of spite of human beings, and, in particular, out of envy towards good men (*Pl.* 87–92). Zeus's actions, as well as the marginalization of the gods once Wealth regains his eyesight, negate the close link between just behavior and god-given abundance that Hesiod's *WD* promotes (e.g. *WD* 225–37). On the end of the play, see Sommerstein 1996: 269–70 with n.67.

[145] Carrière 1983: 52–54 suggests an evolutionary scheme, according to which the second generation of Old Comedy poets inherited from the first generation the assimilation of the Olympians with political leadership in Athens and pushed it to its limits, challenging what Carrière terms "l'orthodoxie hésiodique" to the point of challenging the entire rule of Zeus (e.g. Cratinus' *Ploutoi*, Aristophanes' *Birds*).

promoted as the avenue towards a world of easy and safe labor on land and
at sea (*Av.* 588–609, 704–36). The play, therefore, envisions animal life as a
utopia of natural abundance and constructs human life under avian gods
as a variation on this utopia, in which work is still required but has lost its
negative aspects.[146] Far from being Aristophanes' own invention, the
utopia of abundance is at least as old as Hesiod's Golden Age and Homer's
Phaeacians. The *Odyssey* situates natural fecundity and abundance exclusively on the geographic margins of the world (Libya in *Od.* 4.85–89 and
Scheria in *Od.* 7.114–28).[147] In the Hesiodic tradition, on the other hand,
we find several instantiations of this utopic ideal. The most elaborate
variation on this theme is the Golden race of mortals, who lived under
Cronus without old age and without cares, and experienced a spontaneous
abundance of natural resources that rendered labor unnecessary (*WD*
116–19). A similar kind of blissful existence is reserved for a select group
of heroes who inhabit the Isles of the Blessed after death (*WD* 167–73).
Finally, although those living in the Iron Age cannot enjoy such a com-
fortable existence permanently, they can experience an approximation of it
as Zeus rewards communities that behave justly with a state of natural
fecundity and prosperity that maximizes agricultural production and keeps
them away from the perils of seafaring (*WD* 230–37).

The ideal of a carefree life and spontaneous abundance is widespread in
comic utopias of the fifth century, but, of course, not every instantiation of
it involves a reception of Hesiod's Golden Age in particular. In the *Birds*,
for instance, the worship of birds promises facilitation of labor but not
complete relief from it, while access to natural abundance is available only
to those who acquire wings and are thus no longer entirely human. More
importantly, the easy life that the birds enjoy involves behavior that the
Hesiodic text does not associate with its idealized vision of the Golden Age
(*Av.* 753–68, cf. 793–97). As studies of utopias in fragmentary comedies
demonstrate,[148] Old Comedy encompasses a varied multitude of utopic
worlds, only some of which involve natural abundance and relief from toil,
and even those do not necessarily evoke the theme in a manner that invites
the audience to recall the Hesiodic tradition.

---

[146] A theoretical study of utopia in Old Comedy is beyond the scope of this book. On the subject, see
Schwinge 1977, Heberlein 1980, Bertelli 1983, Zimmermann 1983 and 1991 with bibliography,
Konstan 1995: 33–44 and 1997, Hubbard 1997, Pellegrino 2000 on gastronomic utopias, and Farioli
2001.

[147] For a succinct survey of the theme of natural abundance in archaic poetry, see Farioli 2001: 15–26.

[148] See Ceccarelli 1996 and, especially, Ruffell 2000; cf. already Carrière 1983: 85–118.

It is not my intention here to produce yet another survey of the theme of natural abundance in Old Comedy. Instead, I want to examine one play in particular, whose fragments show evidence of a complex engagement with the Hesiodic tradition.[149] Cratinus' *Ploutoi* dramatizes the return of Cronus' Golden Age after the fall of Zeus's tyranny (fr. 171.22–23 KA). The chorus consists of Titans who claim that they were called Πλοῦτοι when Cronus used to rule (Τιτᾶνες μὲν γενεὰν ἐσμ[εν] / Πλοῦτοι δ᾽ ἐκαλούμεθ᾽ ὅτ᾽ [ἦρχε Κρόνος, fr. 171.11–12 KA). Upon their arrival, these Titans announce that they have come to visit a chained brother now that Zeus's tyranny has finally collapsed (fr. 171.24–26 KA). The self-identification of the chorus has been rightly associated with the description of the Golden Race in the *WD* since the members of that race, the only one that lived under Cronus according to the Hesiodic tradition, became "wealth-giving spirits" (δαίμονες πλουτοδόται) under Zeus (*WD* 121–26). The Hesiodic function of these figures as supervisors of the distribution of wealth is particularly apt in the *Ploutoi* given that its plot involves a trial concerning the unjust acquisition of riches.[150] In addition, Cratinus' play appropriates the Hesiodic vision of Cronus' era as one of natural abundance (*WD* 116–19; Cratin. fr. 172 and 176 KA). Unlike the *Birds*, which situates the culmination of an unprecedented utopia in a brand-new era of the cosmos, then, the arrival of the Titans in the *Ploutoi* marks the reemergence of utopian elements from a past era.[151]

It is important to keep in mind, however, that the comedy recontextualizes Hesiod's Golden Age in a plot that depends on a profoundly un-Hesiodic view of the cosmos. In the *Works and Days*, the post-mortem immortalization of the Golden Race and their function as wealth-giving spirits are part of Zeus's preoccupation with justice. Cratinus' *Ploutoi*, on the other hand, presupposes the unfair, tyrannical Zeus of the Prometheus-tragedies, plays

[149] Reading fr. 171.22–23 KA as a reference to Pericles' removal from office in late summer or autumn of 430 BCE, Bakola 2010: 213–19 adopts 429 BCE as the comedy's date and discusses extensively the immediate historical and political context that such a date entails. For a more reserved attitude towards the play's allusion to contemporary historical events and for an alternative date, see Storey 2011: 347 (cf. Austin 1973: 39 on Cratinus fr. 73). In Athenaeus *Deipn.* 6.267e, Cratinus' *Ploutoi* is considered the oldest of the plays cited in the passage as examples of abundance utopias.

[150] On the Titans of the *Ploutoi* and Hesiod's δαίμονες πλουτοδόται, see already Mazon 1934: 607–08 and Goossens 1935: 406; cf. Bakola 2010: 208–13 and 2013: 231–33 on the *Ploutoi* in the context of Hagnon's trial (fr. 171.57–76, cf. line 46). On the tension between just wealth acquisition and the comic fantasy of utopian abundance, see Ruffell 2000: 477–81.

[151] Fr. 175 KA indicates that the play juxtaposed Cronus' era of abundance with another utopia that exists in the present but somewhere far from Athens, possibly in Sparta. See Ceccarelli 1996: 115, although in 141–42 she suggests that the fragment may allude to a piece of Athenian history, namely the banquets given by Cimon. See also Farioli 2001: 42–45.

with which the comedy must have engaged intensely, given that the addressee of the chorus in fr. 171 KA is most probably Prometheus[152] and the extant *parodos* evokes the entrance of Titans in the *parodos* of the *Prometheus Lyomenos* (fr. 190 Radt).[153] In other words, the *Ploutoi* here appropriate the Hesiodic tradition through its reception in tragedy. As the chorus views Zeus's regime – possibly a metaphor for Pericles' political power[154] – in a negative light and celebrates its collapse, Cronus' era emerges as a much better alternative. Yet we should not overlook that, at the same time, the comic text subverts this idyllic image of the past. When the Titans recall that Cronus feasted on his children, they inadvertently point out how inherently contradictory the vision of a utopic euphoria under his reign is (fr. 171.13–15 KA, τότε δ᾽ ἦν φωνῆνθ᾽ ὅτε ... / κατέπιν᾽ ἀκόναις / κλωγμὸν πολὺν αἰνετὸς ὑ[μῖν].[155] Cratinus' diction recalls the Hesiodic treatment of the dysfunctional relationship between Cronus and his children in the *Theogony* (*Th.* 459–500, esp. 459 καὶ τοὺς μὲν κατέπινε μέγας Κρόνος), although most probably the lines engage primarily with the reception and dramatization of this mythological episode in some non-extant drama.[156]

While there is little doubt that Cratinus' *Ploutoi* evokes to some extent Hesiod's Golden Age, then, its approach to the Hesiodic corpus is complex. The extant fragments indicate that the play receives the Hesiodic tradition largely through the mediation of contemporary drama and not without subversion. The comedy appropriates the δαίμονες πλουτο-δόται of the *Works and Days* but dissociates them from the Hesiodic vision of Zeus's justice. Furthermore, it draws attention to a glaring inconsistency in the Hesiodic tradition as it problematizes the close connection between Cronus, whom the *Theogony* constructs as the ruthless, gruesome cannibal, and the carefree existence of the golden race under his reign in the *WD*.

---

[152] For a discussion of the debate surrounding the identity of the chorus' interlocutor in the *parodos*, see Bakola 2010: 129–34 with a strong case in favor of Prometheus.

[153] Farioli 2001: 37 with n.14, Bakola 2010: 123–25 (cf. 2013: 231). If the upgrade of the Golden Race of men (Χρύσεον μὲν πρώτιστα γένος μερόπων ἀνθρώπων, *WD* 109) to Titans is Cratinus' idea in the first place, it can be attributed to his simultaneous engagement with the *parodos* of the *Prometheus Lyomenos*. After all, the Prometheus-plays also upgrade Hesiod's Prometheus from a Titan's son to a Titan.

[154] Bakola 2010: 213–19; cf. Schwarze 1971 and n.41 above.

[155] I take φωνῆνθ᾽ of line 13 as referring to the shouts of Cronus' children, not to the existence of speaking animals (cf. Crates' *Theria*). On the textual and interpretative problems in lines 13–15, see Farioli 2001: 36–37 with n.11 and Bakola 2010: 51–53.

[156] On line 15 as a metadramatic reference to the staging of this episode in some earlier play, see Quaglia 1998: 45, Ruffell 2010: 478, and Bakola 2010: 52–53. Cf. adesp. fr. 1062 KA (perhaps from Philiscus' *Birth of Zeus*) with Olson 2007: 116 and 125.

# Conclusion

This study has explored the rich and complex reception of the Hesiodic tradition in fifth-century lyric poetry and drama. Before I consider the project as a whole, I would like to summarize the main arguments of each chapter.

The first chapter explores lyric engagements with Hesiodic poetics. After an overview of Hesiodic poetics, I revisit the argument that Pindar and Bacchylides associate Hesiodic poetry with the poetics of truth while rejecting the Homeric tradition for its poetics of falsehood. I demonstrate that this view does not take into consideration the meaning of *aletheia* in the context of lyric performance; in addition, it misrepresents the reception of the Homeric and the Hesiodic traditions by reading isolated passages out of context. Having rejected the simplistic opposition between Hesiod/truth and Homer/lies, I turn to some case studies that highlight different lyric responses to the Hesiodic tradition in the context of poetics. In Bacchylides' *Ode* 5.191–95, I trace a complex allusion to the programmatic connections between divine favor and human speech in *Th.* 81–97 and *WD* 1–8. The ode reframes and integrates these Hesiodic ideas into its laudatory agenda. The final triad of Bacchylides *Ode* 3, on the other hand, evokes the Hesiodic *ainos* of the hawk and the nightingale (*WD* 202–12) as a foil for the harmonious relationship between the praise poet and Hieron, his powerful addressee. *Ode* 5, therefore, situates its epinician poetics in alignment with the Hesiodic tradition, whereas *Ode* 3 defines them in opposition to it. The chapter concludes with a poem that does not simply invite juxtaposition with the Hesiodic tradition but distances itself from it: Pindar's *Paean* 7b/52h constructs a discourse of poetic creativity that is marked as non-Homeric but gradually reveals itself to be non-Hesiodic as well.

The second chapter focuses on the appropriation of Hesiodic narratives in lyric poetry. We begin with Pindar's *Pythian* 1, which casts the Sicilian connection between Typhos and Aetna's volcano as the direct consequence of the Hesiodic Typhonomachy. In my view, there is no good reason to emend the extant text of the Typhonomachy so as to include Aetna, as Debiasi suggests. One cannot exclude the possibility, however, that rhapsodes performing in Sicily may have tailored the Hesiodic text along these lines in order to appeal to local audiences. The Pindaric text remains vague enough to accommodate both the extant (presumably Panhellenic) version and any local variations that tied Aetna to Typhos' defeat. After *Pythian* 1, I examine Pindar's creative reception of two women that featured in Hesiodic genealogical poetry: Coronis (*Pythian* 3) and Cyrene (*Pythian* 9). Pindaric poetry grants both female figures a stronger presence in their own stories than the Hesiodic tradition does, and constructs them as characters who defy gender-bound expectations. While both Pindaric odes transform the Hesiodic maidens into remarkable figures, the effect in each case is different: *Pythian* 9 celebrates Cyrene while *Pythian* 3 vilifies Coronis. The chapter ends with the complex reception of the Hesiodic tradition in Pindar's account of Ixion and his progeny (*Pythian* 2). The ode associates the cloud-simulacrum of Hera with the nefarious figure of Hesiod's Pandora but it also casts Ixion's progeny as a perversion of the heroic race in terms that evoke the genealogical poetry attributed to Hesiod.

The third chapter explores the (admittedly limited) reception of Hesiodic didactic poetry in fifth-century lyric. I take a close look at *Isthmian* 6 and *Pythian* 6, two poems that evoke the *WD* and the *Chironos Hypothekai* respectively in the context of education. In both odes, the value of following Hesiodic precepts is uncontested: in *Isthmian* 6 they bring success for the individual, his *oikos*, and his community, while in *Pythian* 6 they guarantee proper aristocratic behavior. The final section of the chapter draws attention to a methodological issue as it underscores the crucial distinction between lyric *gnomai* that are explicitly attributed to Hesiod and thus constitute a form of Hesiodic reception, and lyric *gnomai* that overlap in content with Hesiodic utterances but are not explicitly identified as Hesiodic.

The last two chapters of this book are dedicated to the reception of the Hesiodic tradition in drama. Chapter 4 studies Hesiodic reception in tragedy, although I have included some observations that pertain to satyr drama as well as the works of Epicharmus. The chapter begins with an extensive analysis of Hesiodic reception in the Prometheus-plays attributed to Aeschylus (*Prometheus Bound, Prometheus Lyomenos, Prometheus Pyrkaeus/Pyrphoros*). Building on previous scholarship, I argue that the *Prometheus Bound* undercuts systematically the panegyric of Zeus in the

*Theogony*; with the inclusion of Io, however, the play also undermines the celebration of the Olympians' sexual politics in Hesiodic genealogical poetry. Furthermore, I propose that the *Lyomenos* involves a revision of the relationship between Zeus and Cronus that, by the second half of the fifth century BCE, may already have become part of the *WD*. Finally, I inquire to what extent the *Pyrkaeus* receives the Hesiodic version of the Prometheus-myth and how it compares in this respect to Epicharmus' *Pyrrha*. Overall, my reading of the Prometheus-plays reveals a combination of several diverse responses to the Hesiodic corpus. The fourth chapter also explores the complex reception of Hesiodic genealogical poetry in Euripides' *Ion*. The play acknowledges the symbolic importance of genealogies as it appropriates and reconfigures the traditional pedigrees of Ion, Dorus, and Achaeus into a distinctly Athenocentric arrangement. On the other hand, much like the *Prometheus Bound*, the *Ion* exposes the limitations of genealogical poetry by allowing Creousa to tell her own story of rape and misery. Ultimately, the play upholds the value of genealogies but undermines the genre of genealogical poetry as simplistic and inadequate.

The fifth and final chapter of this study explores the gamut of Hesiodic receptions in Old Comedy. The first section examines Hesiod as a comic character in Cratinus' *Archilochoi* and Teleclides' *Hesiodoi*. It is likely that, in these plays, Hesiod featured primarily as a didactic poet and that his character was informed largely by the biographical tradition of the *agon* between Homer and Hesiod in Chalcis. Similarly, Aristophanes' *Frogs*, Cratinus' *Chirones*, and Pherecrates' *Chiron* seem to approach the Hesiodic tradition through a reductive frame that focuses exclusively on the didactic poems. After considering the reception of Hesiodic didactic voices and verses in Old Comedy, I turn to the extensive and complex appropriation of the *Theogony* in Aristophanes' *Birds*. In my close reading of the play, I track the comic subversion, usurpation, and complete revision of the Hesiodic narrative; I also show that the play acknowledges the rich reception of Hesiod's *Theogony* and situates itself within it. The final section of this chapter discusses Hesiodic reception in the context of comic utopias, with a particular focus on Cratinus' *Ploutoi*, a play that coopts the Hesiodic vision of the Golden Age in the *Works and Days* but, at the same time, subverts it by evoking the menacing figure of Cronus from the *Theogony*.

Through all these case studies, therefore, this book surveys the landscape of Hesiodic reception across diverse poetic genres of the fifth century BCE and captures its complexity. If there is an overarching argument in this project, it is precisely that the reception of the Hesiodic tradition is rich and multifaceted. Any further categorization of these case studies could be misleading, since the modes of reception seem to be intrinsically connected to the peculiarities of the receiving genres. For instance, tragedy does not lend itself to the same kind of discourse about poetics as epinician poetry nor does it resurrect ancient poetic figures in the fashion of Old Comedy. Nevertheless, it is possible to talk about emerging trends. Perhaps the most evident one concerns the reception of Hesiodic genealogical poetry as both lyric and drama show interest in developing the female characters they draw from the *Catalogue of Women* and the *ME*. Pindar's Cyrene and Coronis, just like Io in the *Prometheus Bound* and Creousa in the *Ion*, are more striking and far more active in their own narratives than their Hesiodic counterparts. The enhancement of the Hesiodic women is particularly impressive in tragedy, where they can be transformed into fully fledged individuals with a physical presence, a voice, and the space to express their own perspectives on the trauma of divine *eros* and its tragic consequences.

Another trend emerges when one considers the overall attitudes of the receiving texts towards the Hesiodic tradition. Hesiodic reception in drama tends to be far more subversive than it is in Pindaric and Bacchylidean lyric. In the lyric poems I have examined, for instance, the appropriation of Hesiod seems to be generally positive: Hesiodic poetics are appropriated by epinician poetics, Hesiodic didactic is endorsed without hesitation, and Hesiodic genealogical poetry is an important intertext in lyric mythological narratives. Even when *Paean* 7b/52h moves past Hesiodic poetics, it does so subtly and discreetly; by contrast, the poem's negative engagement with the Homeric tradition seems to be far more explicit. Fifth-century drama, on the other hand, engages with Hesiodic narratives boldly and rewrites them radically: the *Prometheus*-tragedies completely undermine the idealized image of Zeus in the Hesiodic corpus, Aristophanes' *Birds* rewrites the cosmic narrative of the *Theogony* and ends with an Athenian ruling the universe, and Euripides' *Ion* replaces the Hesiodic genealogy of Ion with a distinctly Athenocentric one. One factor that may inform this discrepancy pertains to intended audiences. While composed for a specific primary audience and occasion, lyric, and especially praise-poetry, maintains a Panhellenic orientation that could facilitate circulation and re-performance around the Greek world.[1] It is perhaps relevant to this point that the only poets mentioned by name in Pindar's extant epinicians are Homer, Hesiod, and Archilochus, i.e. poets whose

---

1 On re-performances of fifth-century lyric poetry, see Currie 2004, Hubbard 2004 and 2011.

works were performed at Panhellenic festivals.[2] Given the authority and broad circulation of the Hesiodic tradition, its relatively conservative reception and smooth appropriation by Pindar and Bacchylides may be part of their effort to appeal to Panhellenic audiences and pave the way for a positive reception of their songs in all corners of the Greek world. Attic drama, on the other hand, has a more irreverent approach towards the Hesiodic tradition. As I discuss in the pertinent chapters, this attitude is partly a response to contemporary intellectual trends and discourses. Yet it can also be viewed as the reflex of a distinctly Athenocentric perspective; hence, Ion acquires a divine father and Peisetairus the wily Athenian becomes the ruler of the universe.[3] Even the boldest attempt to undermine or rewrite the Hesiodic tradition, however, invites the audience to recall it and to reconsider their understanding of it, thus ultimately confirming its lasting cultural value.

2 Homer: *P.* 4.277–78, *N.*7.20–21, *I.*4.37–39, cf. *Pa.*7b/52h.9-13; Hesiod: *I.*6.66–68; Archilochus: *O.* 9.1–2, *P.*2.54–56. On the reception of Homeric poetry in the Pindaric corpus, see Chapter 1, pp. 23–26. On the performance of Homer, Hesiod, and Archilochus at Panhellenic festivals, see Chapter 5, p. 184, as well as Introduction, pp. 13–16.

3 This is not to say that the audience of Attic drama was not diverse; see Roselli 2012. I focus here on Attic drama because there is enough material for an assessment. By contrast, it is very difficult to tell from the extant fragments how irreverent Epicharmus' engagement with the Hesiodic tradition was (see Chapter 4). Regarding intended audiences, however, it is noteworthy that Epicharmus situates his *Promatheus* or *Pyrrha* in Sicily, thus catering to his local audience (fr. 113 KA).

# References

Aélion, R. (1983). *Euripide héritier d'Eschyle*, 2 vols. Paris.

Aguirre Castro, M. (2005). "Expressions of love and sexual union in Hesiod's *Catalogue of Women*." *Cuadernos de filología clásica: Estudios griegos e indoeuropeos* 15: 19–25.

Ahlert, P. (1942). *Mädchen und Frauen in Pindars Dichtung*. Philologus Suppl. 34. Leipzig.

Allan, W. (2008). "Performing the will of Zeus: the Διὸς βουλή and the scope of early Greek epic." In *Performance, Iconography, Reception. Studies in Honour of Oliver Taplin*, ed. M. Revermann and P. Wilson. Oxford: 204–16.

Allen, D. S. (2000). *The World of Prometheus. The Politics of Punishing in Democratic Athens*. Princeton.

Allen, T. W. (1924). *Homer. The Origins and the Transmission*. Oxford.

Aloni, A. (2008). "La performance di Esiodo." In *Atti del convegno nazionale di studi 'Arma virumque cano …': l'epica dei Greci e dei Romani*, ed. R. Uglione. Alexandria: 57–76.

    (2010). "Esiodo a simposio. La performance delle *Opere e Giorni*." In *Tra panellenismo e tradizioni locali: generi poetici e storiografia*, ed. E. Cingano. Alexandria: 115–50.

Anderson, C. and Dix, T. K. (2007). "Prometheus and the Basileia in Aristophanes' *Birds*." *CJ* 102: 321–27.

Anemoyiannis-Sinanidis, S. (1991). "Le symbolisme de l'œuf dans les cosmogonies orphiques." *Kernos* 4: 83–90.

Ardizzoni, A. (1978). "Tifone e l'eruzione dell'Etna in Eschilo e in Pindaro (Riflessioni sulla priorità)." *GIF* 9: 233–44.

Arrighetti, G. (1987). *Poeti, eruditi e biografi. Momenti della riflessione dei Greci sulla litteratura*. Pisa.

    (1996). "Hésiode et les Muses: le don de la vérité et la conquête de la parole." In *Le métier du mythe: Lectures d'Hésiode*, ed. F. Blaise, P. Judet de la Combe, and P. Rousseau. Lille: 53–70.

    (1998). *Esiodo. Opere*. Turin.

Arrowsmith, W. (1973). "Aristophanes' *Birds*: the fantasy politics of Eros." *Arion* 1: 119–67.

Arthur, M. B. (1982). "Cultural strategies in Hesiod's *Theogony*: law, family, society." *Arethusa* 15: 63–82.

(1983). "The dream of a world without women: poetics and the circles of order in the *Theogony* prooemium." *Arethusa* 16: 97–115.

Athanassaki, L. (2003). "Transformations of colonial disruption into narrative continuity in Pindar's epinician odes." *HSCP* 101: 93–128.

(2011). "Giving wings to the Aeginetan sculptures: the Panhellenic aspirations of Pindar's *Eighth Olympian*." In *Aegina: Contexts for Choral Lyric Poetry. Myth, History, and Identity in the Fifth Century BC*, ed. D. Fearn. Oxford: 257–93.

(2012). "Performance and re-performance. The Siphnian treasury evoked (Pindar's *Pythian 6, Olympian 2* and *Isthmian 2*)." In *Reading the Victory Ode*, ed. P. Agócs, C. Carey, and R. Rawles. Cambridge: 134–57.

Auger, D. (1979). "Le théâtre d'Aristophane: le mythe, l'utopie et les femmes." *Aristophane: Les femmes et la cité. Les Cahiers de Fontenay* 17: 71–101.

Austin, N. (1973). *Comicorum Graecorum Fragmenta in Papyris Reperta*. Berlin.

(1994). *Helen of Troy and her Shameless Phantom*. Ithaca, N.Y. and London.

Avezzù, G. (1982). *Alcidamante. Orazioni e Frammenti*. Rome.

Bagordo, A. (2013). *Telekleides. Einleitung, Übersetzung, Kommentar*. Heidelberg.

Baker, G. W. (1904). "De comicis Graecis litterarum iudicibus." *HSCP* 15: 121–240.

Bakker, E. J. (2002). "Remembering the god's arrival." *Arethusa* 35: 63–81.

Bakola, E. (2008). "The drunk, the reformer and the teacher: agonistic poetics and the construction of the persona in the comic poets of the fifth century." *CCJ* 54: 1–29.

(2010). *Cratinus and the Art of Comedy*. Oxford.

(2013). "Crime and punishment. Cratinus, Aeschylus' *Oresteia*, and the metaphysics and politics of wealth." In *Greek Comedy and the Discourse of Genres*, ed. E. Bakola, L. Prauscello, and M. Telò. Cambridge: 226–55.

Balaudé, J.-F. (2006). "Hippias le passeur." In *La costruzione del discorso filosofico nell'età dei Presocratici* (= The Construction of Philosophical Discourse in the Age of the Presocratics), ed. M. Sassi. Pisa: 287–304.

Ballabriga, A. (1990). "Le dernier adversaire de Zeus. Le mythe de Typhon dans l'épopée grecque archaïque." *RHR* 207: 3–30.

Barlow, S. A. (1986). "The language of Euripides' monodies." In *Studies in Honour of T. B. L. Webster*. Vol. I, ed. J. H. Betts, J. H. Hooker, and J. R. Green. Bristol: 10–22.

Barron, J. P. (1969). "Ibycus: to Polycrates." *BICS* 16: 119–49.

Bassino, P. (2012). "*Certamen Homeri et Hesiodi*: nuovi spunti per una riconsiderazione delle testimonianze papiracee." *ZPE* 180: 38–42.

(2013). "Certamen Homeri et Hesiodi: introduction, critical edition, and commentary." Ph.D. dissertation, Durham University.

Battisti, D. (2011). "Συνετός as aristocratic self-description." *GRBS* 31: 5–25.

Beasley, J. D. (1948). "Hymn to Hermes." *AJA* 52: 336–40.

Bees, R. (1993). *Zur Datierung des Prometheus Desmotes*. Stuttgart.

Benedetto, V. Di (1978). *L'ideologia del potere e la tragedia greca*. Turin.

(1991). "Pindaro, *Pae.* 7b, 11–14." *RFIC* 119: 164–76.

(1995). "Tifone in Pindaro e in Eschilo." *RFIC* 123: 129–39.

Bernabé, A. (1987). *Poetarum Epicorum Graecorum. Testimonia et Fragmenta. Pars I.* Leipzig.

(1995). "Una cosmogonía cómica: Aristófanes, *Aves* 685 ss.." In *De Homero a Libanio*, ed. J. A. López Férez. Madrid: 195–211.

(2001). "La *Teogonia* di Epimenide. Saggio di ricostruzione." In *Epimenide cretese*, ed. E. Federico and A. Visconti. Naples: 195–216.

(2002). "La théogonie orphique du papyrus de Derveni." *Kernos* 15: 91–129.

(2004). *Poetae Epici Graeci. Pars II. Fasc. 1.* Munich and Leipzig.

(2007). "The Derveni theogony: many questions and some answers." *HSCP* 103: 99–133.

(2008). "Orfeo y l'orfismo en la comedia griega." In *Orfeo y la tradición órfica: un reencuentro*, ed. A. Bernabé and F. Casadesús. Madrid: 1217–38.

Bernadete, R. (1964). "The crimes and arts of Prometheus." *RhM* 107: 126–39.

Bernardini, P. A. (1983). *Mito e attualità nelle ode di Pindaro. La Nemea 4, l'Olimpica 9, l'Olimpica 7.* Rome.

Bertelli, L. (1983). "L'utopia sulla scena: Aristofane e la parodia della città." *Civiltà classica e cristiana* 4: 215–61.

(2001). "Hecataeus: from genealogy to historiography." In *The Historian's Craft in the Age of Herodotus*, ed. N. Luraghi. Oxford: 67–94.

Betegh, G. (2004). *The Derveni Papyrus. Cosmology, Theology and Interpretation.* Cambridge.

Biles, Z. P. (2002). "Intertextual biography in the rivalry of Cratinus and Aristophanes." *AJP* 123: 169–204.

(2011). *Aristophanes and the Poetics of Competition.* Cambridge.

Bing, P. (2012). "A proto-epyllion? The pseudo-Hesiodic *Shield* and the poetics of deferral." In *Brill's Companion to Greek and Roman Epyllion*, ed. M. Baumbach and S. Bär. Leiden: 177–97.

Birt, T. (1907). *Die Buchrolle in der Kunst.* Leipzig.

Blaise, F. (1992). "L'épisode de Typhée dans la Théogonie d'Hésiode (v. 820–885): la stabilisation du monde." *REG* 105: 349–70.

Blasina, A. (2006). "Geografie africane in Eschilo." In *L'Africa romana: le ricchezze dell'Africa: risorse, produzioni, scambi.* Vol. III, ed. J. González and P. Ruggeri. Rome: 1949–59.

Blößner, N. (2005). "Hesiod und die 'Könige'. Zu *Theogonie* 79–103." *Mnemosyne* 58: 23–45.

Blumenthal, A. von (1914). "Hesiod fr. 219." *Hermes* 49: 319–20.

Boeke, H. (2007). *The Value of Victory in Pindar's Odes. Gnomai, Cosmology and the Role of the Poet.* Leiden.

Bonifazi, A. (2004). "Communication in Pindar's deictic acts." *Arethusa* 37: 391–414.

Bonnafé, A. M. (1985). *Eros et Eris. Mariages divins et mythe de succession chez Hésiode.* Lyon.

(1991). "Texte, carte et territoire: autour de l'itinéraire d'Io dans le *Prométhée* (1ère partie)." *Journal des Savants* 3: 133–93.

(1992). "Texte, carte et territoire: autour de l'itinéraire d'Io dans le *Prométhée* (2e partie)." *Journal des Savants* 4: 3–34.

Bosher, K. (2012). "Hieron's Aeschylus." In *Theater Outside Athens. Drama in Greek Sicily and South Italy*, ed. K. Bosher. Cambridge: 97–111.

Bowie, A. (2000). "Myth and ritual in the rivals of Aristophanes." In *The Rivals of Aristophanes*, ed. D. Harvey and J. Wilkins. London: 317–39.

Bowie, E. L. (1993). "Lies, fiction and slander in early Greek poetry." In *Lies and Fiction in the Ancient World*, ed. C. Gill and T. P. Wiseman. Austin: 1–37.

Bowra, C. M. (1952). *Heroic Poetry*. London.

(1964). *Pindar*. Oxford.

Boys-Stones, G. R. and Haubold, J., eds. (2010). *Plato and Hesiod*. Oxford.

Brelich, A. (1958). *Gli eroi greci. Un problema storico-religioso*. Rome.

Bremmer, J. N. (1999). "Near Eastern and native traditions in Apollodorus' account of the Flood." In *Interpretations of the Flood*, ed. F. G. Martínez and G. P. Luttikhuizen. Leiden: 39–55.

Brisson, L. (1997). "Chronos in column XII of the Derveni Papyrus." In *Studies on the Derveni Papyrus*, ed. A. Laks and G. W. Most. Oxford: 149–65.

(2003). "Sky, sex and sun. The meanings of αἰδοῖος/αἰδοῖον in the Derveni Papyrus." *ZPE* 144: 119–29.

Brown, A. L. (1990). "Prometheus Pyrphoros." *BICS* 37: 50–56.

Brown, C. G. (2006). "Pindar on Archilochus and the gluttony of blame (*Pyth.* 2.52–6)." *JHS* 126: 36–46.

Buchholz, E. (1898)[4]. *Anthologie aus den Lyrikern der Griechen*, 4th edn. Vol. II. Leipzig.

Bundy, E. L. (1962). *Studia Pindarica*, repr. 1986. Berkeley.

Burgess, J. S. (2001). "Coronis aflame: the gender of mortality." *CPh* 96: 214–27.

Burnett, A. P. (1962). "Human resistance and divine persuasion in Euripides' *Ion*." *CPh* 57: 89–103.

(1971). *Catastrophe Survived. Euripides' Plays of Mixed Reversal*. Oxford.

(1985). *The Art of Bacchylides*. Cambridge, Mass. and London.

(2005). *Pindar's Songs for Young Athletes of Aigina*. Oxford.

Burton, R. W. B. (1962). *Pindar's Pythian Odes. Essays in Interpretation*. Oxford.

Bury, J. B. (1892). *The Isthmian Odes of Pindar*. London and New York.

Buxton, R. (2007). "Tragedy and Greek myth." In *The Cambridge Companion to Greek Mythology*, ed. R. D. Woodard. Cambridge: 166–89.

(2013). *Myths and Tragedies in Their Ancient Greek Contexts*. Oxford.

Buzio, C. (1938). *Esiodo nel mondo greco sino alla fine dell'età classica*. Milan.

Cairns, D. L. (1997). "Form and meaning in Bacchylides' fifth ode." *Scholia* n.s. 6: 34–48.

(2007). "Dating 'Nemean' 5 and Bacchylides 13: criteria and conclusions." *Nikephoros* 20: 33–47.

(2010). *Five Epinician Odes (3, 5, 9, 11, 13): Text, Introductory Essays, and Interpretative Commentary*. Cambridge.

Calame, C. (1990). "Narrating the foundation of a city. The symbolic birth of Cyrene." In *Approaches to Greek Myth*, ed. L. Edmunds. Baltimore and London: 277–341.

(1991). "Eros initiatique et la cosmogonie orphique." In *Orphisme et Orphée en l'honneur de Jean Rudhardt*, ed. P. Borgeaud. Geneva: 227–47.

(1995). *The Craft of Poetic Speech in Ancient Greece*, transl. J. Orion. Ithaca, N.Y.

(1996). "Le proème des *Travaux* d'Hésiode, prelude à une poésie d'action." In *Le métier du mythe: Lectures d'Hésiode*, ed. F. Blaise, P. Judet de la Combe, and P. Rousseau. Lille: 169–89.

(1997). "Figures of sexuality and initiatory transition in the Derveni theogony and its commentary." In *Studies on the Derveni Papyrus*, ed. A. Laks and G. W. Most. Oxford: 65–80.

(1999). *The Poetics of Eros in Ancient Greece*. Princeton.

(2007). "Greek myth and Greek religion." In *The Cambridge Companion to Greek Mythology*, ed. R. D. Woodard. Cambridge: 259–85.

Cameron, A. (2004). *Greek Mythography in the Roman World*. Oxford.

Canevaro, L. F. (2015). *Hesiod's Works and Days: How to Teach Self-Sufficiency*. Oxford.

Capra, A. and Gilardi, V. (1999). "Immortalità, letizia o gloria poetica? *L'epinicio III* di Bacchilide." *SCO* 47: 159–74.

(2002). "Quattro note alla 'Pitica Nona' di Pindaro (vv. 5–25; 87–92)." *Acme* 55: 125–32.

Carduff, G. A. (1986). *Antike Sintflutsagen*. Göttingen.

Carey, C. (1975). "Pindar, *Pythian* 6, 19–20." *Maia* 27: 289–90.

(1977/78). "Bacchylides 3.85–90." *Maia* 29/30: 69–72.

(1978). "Pindarica." In *Dionysiaca. Nine Studies in Greek Poetry by Former Pupils Presented to Sir Denys Page on His Seventieth Birthday*, ed. R. D. Dawe, J. Diggle, and P. E. Easterling. Cambridge: 21–44.

(1981). *A Commentary on Five Odes of Pindar: Pythian 2, Pythian 9, Nemean 1, Nemean 7, Isthmian 8*. New York.

(1990). *Pindar's Homer. The Lyric Possession of an Epic Past*. Baltimore.

Carpenter, T. H. (1991). *Art and Myth in Ancient Greece. A Handbook*. London and New York.

Carrière, J. C. (1983)². *Le carnaval et la politique. Une introduction à la comédie grecque suivie d'un choix de fragments*, 2nd edn. Paris.

Carson, A. (1982). "Wedding at noon in Pindar's ninth *Pythian*." *GRBS* 23: 121–28.

(1984). "The burners: a reading of Bacchylides' third epinician ode." *Phoenix* 38: 111–19.

Carter Philips, F., Jr. (1973). "Narrative compression and the myths of Prometheus in Hesiod." *CJ* 68: 289–305.

Casanova, A. (1969). "Il mito di Atteone nel catalogo esiodeo." *RFIC* 97: 31–46.

(1979a). *La famiglia di Pandora: analisi filologica dei miti di Pandora e Prometeo nella tradizione esiodea*. Florence.

(1979b). "Catalogo, Eèe, e i Grandi Eèe nella tradizione ellenistica." *Prometheus* 5: 217–40.

Casevitz, M. (1978). *Commentaire des "Oiseaux" d'Aristophane*. Lyon.

Càssola, F. (1953). "Le genealogie mitiche e la coscienza nazionale greca." *Rendiconti della reale Accademia di archeologia, lettere e belle arti* 28: 279–304.

Cavalli, M. (1999). "Le Rane di Aristofane: modelli tradizionali dell'agone fra Eschilo ed Euripide." *Quaderni di acme* 36: 83–105.

Ceccarelli, P. (1996). "L'Athènes de Périclès: Un 'Pays de cocagne'? L'idéologie démocratique et l'αὐτόματος βίος dans la comédie ancienne." *QUCC* 54: 109–59.

Cerri, G. (2006). "Il dio incatenato come spettacolo, il coro come pubblico: tragedia e rapsodia nella dimensione metateatrale del Prometeo." *Lexis* 24: 265–82.

Cerutti, M. V. (1998). "Mito di distruzione, mito di fondazione: Hes. fr. 204, 95–103 MW." *Aevum antiquum* 11: 127–78.

Chamoux, F. (1953). *Cyrene sous la monarchie des Battiades*. Paris.

Chong-Gossard, J. H. K. O. (2008). *Gender and Communication in Euripides' Plays: Between Song and Silence*. Leiden.

Christopoulos, M. (2010). "Dark-winged *Nyx* and the bright-winged *Eros* in Aristophanes' 'Orphic' cosmogony." In *Light and Darkness in Ancient Greek Myth and Religion*, ed. M. Christopoulos, E. D. Karakantza, and O. Levaniouk. Lanham: 207–20.

Cingano, E. (1991). "L'epinicio 4 di Bacchilide e la data della 'Pitica' 3 di Pindaro." *QUCC* 3: 97–104.

(2005). "A catalogue within a catalogue: Helen's suitors in the Hesiodic *Catalogue of Women*." In *The Hesiodic Catalogue of Women: Constructions and Reconstructions*, ed. R. Hunter. Cambridge: 118–52.

(2009). "The Hesiodic corpus." In *Brill's Companion to Hesiod*, ed. F. Montanari, A. Rengakos, and C. Tsagalis. Leiden: 91–130.

Classen, C. J. (1959). "The study of language amongst Socrates' contemporaries." *The Proceedings of the African Classical Associations* 2: 33–49, reprinted in C. J. Classen, ed., (1976). *Sophistik*. Darmstadt: 215–47.

(1965). "Bemerkungen zu zwei griechischen 'Philosophiehistorikern'." *Philologus* 109: 175–81.

(1976). "The study of language amongst Socrates' contemporaries." In C. J. Classen, ed., *Sophistik*. Darmstadt: 215–47.

Clay, J. S. (1989). "What the Muses sang: *Theogony* 1–115." *GRBS* 29: 323–33.

(1993). "The education of Perses: from 'Mega Nepios' to 'Dion Genos' and back." *MD* 31: 23–33.

(1999a). "Pindar's sympotic epinicia." *QUCC* 62: 25–34.

(1999b). "The will and whip of Zeus." *Literary Imagination* 1: 40–60.

(2003). *Hesiod's Cosmos*. Cambridge.

(2005). "The beginning and end of the *Catalogue of Women* and its relation to Hesiod." In *The Hesiodic Catalogue of Women: Constructions and Reconstructions*, ed. R. Hunter. Cambridge: 25–34.

(2006)[2]. *The Politics of Olympus. Form and Meaning in the Major Homeric Hymns*, 2nd edn. London.

(2009). "*Works and Days*: tracing the path to *Arete*." In *Brill's Companion to Hesiod*, ed. F. Montanari, A. Rengakos, and C. Tsagalis. Leiden: 71–90.

(2011). "The Homeric Hymns as genre." In *The Homeric Hymns. Interpretative Essays*, ed. A. Faulkner. Oxford: 232–53.

Cockle, W. E. H. (1987). *Euripides. Hypsipyle. Text and Annotation Based on a Re-examination of the Papyri*. Rome.

Cohen, I. M. (1983). "The Hesiodic *Catalogue of Women*: studies on the fragments of an early Greek epic." Ph.D. dissertation, University of Toronto.

(1986). "The Hesiodic *Catalogue of Women* and the *Megalai Ehoiai*." *Phoenix* 40: 127–42.

Cole, T. (1983). "Archaic truth." *QUCC* 13: 7–28.

Collins, D. (2004). *Master of the Game: Competition and Performance in Greek Poetry*. Washington, DC.

Colonna, A. (1953). "I Prolegomeni ad Esiodo e la vita esiodea di Giovanni Tzetzes." *Accademia nazionale di Lincei: Bollettino del Comitato per la preparazione della edizione nazionale dei classici greci e latini* 2: 27–39.

(1977). *Opere di Esiodo*. Turin.

Conacher, D. J. (1967). *Euripidean Drama. Myth, Theme, and Structure*. Toronto.

(1980). *Aeschylus' Prometheus Bound: A Literary Commentary*. Toronto.

Connor, W. R. (1993). "The Ionian era of Athenian civic identity." *TAPA* 137: 194–206.

Conti Bizzarro, F. (1999). *Poetica e critica letteraria nei frammenti dei poeti comici greci*. Naples.

Cook, B. F. (1984). "Aristaeus I." *LIMC* 2: 603–07.

Corbato, C. (1996). "Le *Etnee* di Eschilo." In *Catania antica. Atti del Convegno della SISAC*, ed. B. Gentili. Pisa: 61–72.

Crane, G. (1996). "The prosperity of tyrants: Bacchylides, Herodotus, and the contest for legitimacy." *Arethusa* 29: 57–85.

Cromey, R. D. (2006). "Apollo Patroos and the phratries." *AntCl* 75: 41–69.

Crusius, O. (1889). "Coniectanea ad comoediae antiquae fragmenta." *Philologus* 47: 33–44.

Csapo, E. and Slater, W. J. (1994). *The Context of Ancient Drama*. Ann Arbor.

Currie, B. (2004). "Reperformance scenarios for Pindar's odes." In *Oral Performance and Its Context*, ed. C. J. Mackie. Leiden: 49–69.

(2005). *Pindar and the Cult of Heroes*. Oxford and New York.

(2011). "Epinician *Choregia*: funding a Pindaric chorus." In *Archaic and Classical Choral Song. Performance, Politics, and Dissemination*, ed. L. Athanassaki and E. Bowie. Berlin: 269–310.

Cusset, C. (2003). "ΛΑΚΕΡΥΖΑ ΚΟΡΩΝΗ: quand la corneille baye sur l'intertexte." *Métis* 1: 47–68.

Cyrino, M. (1998). "Sex, status and song: locating the lyric singer in the actors' duets of Euripides." *QUCC* 60: 81–101.

D'Alessio, G. B. (1992). "Pindaro *Paeana* VIIb (fr.52 h Sn.-M.)." In *Proceedings of the XIXth International Congress of Papyrology, Cairo, 2–9 September 1989*. Vol. I, ed. A. H. S. El-Mosalamy. Cairo: 353–73.

(1994). "First-person problems in Pindar." *BICS* 39: 117–39.

(1995). "Una via lontana dal cammino degli uomini (Parm. frr. 1+6 DK; Pind. Ol. VI 22–27; Pae. VIIB 10–20)." *SIFC* 13: 143–81.

(2004). "Past future and present past: temporal deixis in Greek archaic lyric." *Arethusa* 37: 267–94.

(2005a). "The *Megalai Ehoiai*: a survey of the fragments." In *The Hesiodic Catalogue of Women: Constructions and Reconstructions*, ed. R. Hunter. Cambridge: 176–216.

(2005b). "Ordered from the Catalogue: Pindar, Bacchylides, and Hesiodic genealogical poetry." In *The Hesiodic Catalogue of Women: Constructions and Reconstructions*, ed. R. Hunter. Cambridge: 217–38.

(2005c). Review of Hirschberger (2004). *BMCR* 2005.02.31.

(2015). "Theogony and Titanomachy." In *The Greek Epic Cycle and Its Ancient Reception: A Companion*, ed. M. Fantuzzi and C. Tsagalis. Cambridge: 199–212.

Dalfen, J. (1994). "Die ὕβρις der Nachtigall: Zu der Fabel bei Hesiod (Erga 202–218) und zur griechischen Fabel im allgemeinen." *WS* 107/108: 157–77.

Danielewicz, J. (1990). "*Deixis* in Greek lyric poetry." *QUCC* 34: 7–17.

Davies, D. R. (1992). "Genealogy and catalogue: thematic relevance and narrative elaboration in Homer and Hesiod." Ph.D. dissertation, University of Michigan.

Davies, M. (1986). *Prolegomena and Paralegomena to a New Edition (with Commentary) of the Fragments of Early Greek Epic*. Nachrichten der Akademie der Wissenschaften in Göttingen (Philologisch-Historische Klasse) 2. Göttingen.

(1988). *Epicorum Graecorum Fragmenta*. Göttingen.

(1989). *The Greek Epic Cycle*. Bristol.

(2001)². *The Greek Epic Cycle*, 2nd edn. Bristol.

Davison, A. J. (1967). "Aeschylus and Athenian politics, 472–456 B.C.." In *Ancient Society and Institutions: Studies Presented to Victor Ehrenberg on His 75th Birthday*, ed. E. Badian. Oxford: 93–107.

Dawson, C. M. (1951) "Notes on the final scene of *Prometheus Vinctus*." *CPh* 46: 237–39.

De Carli, E. (1971). *Aristofane e la sofistica*. Florence.

Deas, H. T. (1931). "The Scholia vetera to Pindar." *HSCP* 42: 1–78.

Debiasi, A. (2004). *L'epica perduta*. Rome.

(2008). *Esiodo e l'occidente*. Rome.

(2013). "Dioniso e i cani di Atteone in Eumelo di Corinto (Una nuova ipotesi su *P. Oxy.* xxx 2509 e Apollod. 3.4.4.)." In *Redefining Dionysos*, ed. A. Bernabé, M. Herrero de Jáuregui, A. I. Jiménez San Cristóbal, and R. M. Hernández. Berlin: 200–14.

Demarque, M. C. (1966). "Traditional and individual ideas in Bacchylides." Ph.D. dissertation, University of Illinois.

Detienne, M. (1973)². *Les maîtres de vérité dans la grèce archaïque*, 2nd edn. Paris.

Detienne, M. and Vernant, J.-P. (1978). *Cunning Intelligence in Greek Culture and Society*, transl. J. Lloyd. Hassocks, Sussex.

Deubner, L. (1905). "Zur Io-Sage." *Philologus* 64: 481–93.

Dickey, E. (2007). *Ancient Greek Scholarship: A Guide to Finding, Reading, and Understanding Scholia, Commentaries, Lexica, and Grammatical Treatises, from Their Beginnings to the Byzantine Period.* Oxford.

Dobrov, G. W. and Urios-Aparisi, A. (1995). "The maculate music: gender, genre, and the *Chiron* of Pherecrates." In *Beyond Aristophanes: Transition and Diversity in Greek Comedy,* ed. G. W. Dobrov. Atlanta: 139–74.

Dodds, E. R. (1973). *The Ancient Concept of Progress and Other Essays on Greek Literature and Belief.* Oxford.

Doherty, L. (2006). "Putting the women back into the Hesiodic *Catalogue of Women*." In *Laughing with Medusa: Classical Myth and Feminist Thought,* ed. M. Leonard and V. Zajko. Oxford: 297–326.

Dolin, E. F., Jr. (1962). "Parmenides and Hesiod." *HSCP* 66: 93–98.

Dörig, J. and Gigon, O. (1963). *Der Kampf der Götter und Titanen.* Olten.

Dougherty, C. (1993). *The Poetics of Colonization. From City to Text in Archaic Greece.* Oxford and New York.

Dover, K. (1968). *Aristophanes: Clouds.* Oxford.

(1980). *Plato: Symposium.* Cambridge.

(1993). *Aristophanes: Frogs.* Oxford.

Dräger, P. (1993). *Argo Pasimelousa. Der Argonautenmythos in der griechischen und römischen Literatur. Teil I: Theos Aitios.* Stuttgart.

(1997). *Untersuchungen zu den Frauenkatalogen Hesiods.* Stuttgart.

Drexler, H. (1931). "Nachträge zur Kyrenesage." *Hermes* 66: 455–64.

Duban, J. M. (1980). "Poets and kings in the Theogony invocation." *QUCC* 4: 7–21.

Duchemin, J. (1955). *Pindare poète et prophète.* Paris.

(1967). *Pindare. Pythiques (III, IX, IV, V).* Paris.

(1972). "Le captif de l'Etna: Typhée «frère» de Prométhée." *Studi Classici in onore di Quintino Cataudella.* Vol. I: 149–72.

(1974). *Prométhée. Histoire du mythe, de ses origines orientales à ses incarnations modernes.* Paris.

Dunbar, N. (1995). *Aristophanes. Birds.* Oxford.

Dunn, F. M. (1990). "The battle of the sexes in Euripides' *Ion*." *Ramus* 19: 130–42.

Edelstein, L. (1967). *The Idea of Progress in Classical Antiquity.* Baltimore.

Edelstein, E. J. and Edelstein, L. (1945). *Asclepius: Collection and Interpretation of the Testimonies.* Vol. I. Baltimore (repr. 1998, New York).

Effe, B. (1977). *Dichtung und Lehre. Untersuchung zur Typologie des antiken Lehrgedichts.* Munich.

Else, G. F. (1957). "The origin of ΤΡΑΓΩΙΔΙΑ." *Hermes* 85: 17–46.

Epstein, P. D. (1981). "The marriage of Peisthetairos to *Basileia* in the *Birds* of Aristophanes." *Dionysius* 5: 5–28.

Erbse, H. (1975a). "Der Gott von Delphi im *Ion* des Euripides." In *Teilnahme und Spiegelung: Festschrift für Horst Rüdiger,* ed. D. Gutzen, B. Allemann, and E. Koppen. Berlin: 40–54.

(1975b). "Dionysos' Schiedsspruch in den 'Fröschen' des Aristophanes." In *Dōrēma Hans Diller zum 70. Geburtstag: Dauer und Überleben des antiken Geistes*, ed. K. I. Vourveris and A. D. Skiadas. Athens: 45–60.

(1984). *Studien zum Prolog der euripideischen Tragödie*. Berlin.

(1999). "Über Pindars Umgang mit dem Mythos." *Hermes* 127: 13–32.

Ercolani, A. (2001). "Per una storia del testo esiodeo. Hes. fr. 343 MW." *Seminari romani di cultura greca*. 4: 181–215.

(2010). *Esiodo. Opere e giorni*. Rome.

Evelyn White, H. G. (1924). "A Peisistratean edition of the Hesiodic poems." *CQ* 18: 142–50.

Farioli, M. (2001). *Mundus alter. Utopie e distopie nella commedia greca antica*. Milan.

Farnell, L. R. (1932). *Critical Commentary to the Works of Pindar*. London (repr. 1961, Amsterdam).

Fearn, D. (2007). *Bacchylides. Poetics, Performance, Poetic Tradition*. Oxford.

(2011). "Aeginetan epinician culture: naming, ritual, and politics." In *Aegina: Contexts for Choral Lyric Poetry. Myth, History, and Identity in the Fifth Century BC*, ed. D. Fearn. Oxford: 175–226.

(2012). "Bacchylidean myths." In *Reading the Victory Ode*, ed. P. Agócs, C. Carey, and R. Rawles. Cambridge: 321–43.

Felson, N. (2004). "The poetic effects of deixis in Pindar's *Ninth Pythian Ode*." *Arethusa* 37: 365–89.

(2011). "Children of Zeus in the *Homeric Hymns*. Generational successions." In *The Homeric Hymns. Interpretative Essays*, ed. A. Faulkner. Oxford: 254–79.

Fenno, J. (2005). "Setting aright the house of Themistius in Pindar's *Nemean* 5 and *Isthmian* 6." *Hermes* 133: 294–311.

Ferrari, G. R. F. (1988). "Hesiod's mimetic Muses and the strategies of deconstruction." In *Post-Structuralist Classics*, ed. A. E. Benjamin. London and New York: 45–78.

Figueira, T. J. (1981). *Aegina, Society and Politics*. New York.

Fink, G. (1958). "Pandora und Epimetheus. Mythologische Studien." Ph.D. dissertation, Friedrich-Alexander-Universität zu Erlangen.

Finkelberg, M. (1998). "The geography of the *Prometheus Vinctus*." *RhM* 141: 119–41.

(2005). *Greeks and Pre-Greeks. Aegean Prehistory and Greek Heroic Tradition*. Cambridge.

Fitton-Brown, A. D. (1959). "Prometheia." *AJP* 79: 52–60.

Flintoff, E. (1984). "Athetos at *Prometheus Vinctus* 150." *Hermes* 112: 367–72.

(1986). "The date of the Prometheus Bound." *Mnemosyne* 39: 82–91.

(1995). "Prometheus Pyrphoros." In *Studia classica Johanni Tarditi oblata*, ed. A. Porro, G. F. Milanese, and L. Belloni. Milan: 857–68.

Floyd, E. D. (1968). "The première of Pindar's Third and Ninth Pythian Odes." *TAPA* 99: 181–202.

Focke, F. (1930). "Aischylos' Prometheus." *Hermes* 65: 259–304.

Foley, H. P. (2001). *Female Acts in Greek Tragedy*. Princeton.

Fontenrose, J. (1959). *Python. A Study of Delphic Myth and Its Origins*. Berkeley and Los Angeles.

Ford, A. (1996). "Epic as genre." In *A New Companion to Homer*, ed. I. Morris and B. B. Powell. Leiden: 396–414.

(1997). "The inland ship: problems in the performance and reception of Homeric epic." In *Written Voices, Spoken Signs. Tradition, Performance, and the Epic Text*, ed. E. Bakker and A. Kahane. Cambridge, Mass.: 83–109.

(2002). *The Origins of Criticism. Literary Culture and Poetic Theory in Classical Greece*. Princeton.

(2010). "Plato's two Hesiods." In *Plato and Hesiod*, ed. G. R. Boys-Stones and J. H. Haubold. Oxford: 133–54.

Forsdyke, S. L. (2012). "'Born from the earth': the political uses of an Athenian myth." *Journal of Ancient Near Eastern Religions* 12: 119–41.

Fowler, D. (2000). "The didactic plot." In *Matrices of Genre. Authors, Canons, and Society*, ed. M. Depew and D. Obbink. Cambridge, Mass.: 205–19.

Fowler, R. L. (1998). "Genealogical thinking, Hesiod's *Catalogue*, and the creation of the Hellenes." *PCPhS* 44: 1–19.

(2000). *Early Greek Mythography. I: Texts*. Oxford.

(2013). *Early Greek Mythography. II: Commentary*. Oxford.

Fränkel, H. (1951). *Dichtung und Philosophie des frühen Griechentums: Eine Geschichte der griechischen Literatur von Homer bis Pindar*. New York.

Friedländer, P. (1905). "Argolica. Quaestiones ad Graecorum historiam fabularem pertinentes." Ph.D. dissertation, Friedrich-Wilhelms-Universität Berlin.

(1913). "ΥΠΟΘΗΚΑΙ." *Hermes* 48: 558–616.

Fritz, K. von (1947). "Pandora, Prometheus und der Mythos von den Weltaltern." *Review of Religion* 11: 227–60.

Furley, W. D. (1999–2000). "Hymns in Euripidean tragedy." *ICS* 24/25: 183–97.

(2007). "Prayers and hymns." In *A Companion to Greek Religion*, ed. D. Ogden. Malden and Oxford: 115–31.

Gantz, T. N. (1974). "Pindar's first *Pythian*. The fire within." *Ramus* 3: 143–51.

(1980). "The Aischylean tetralogy: attested and conjectured groups." *AJP* 101: 133–64.

(1978). "Pindar's second *Pythian*: the myth of Ixion." *Hermes* 106: 14–26.

Garabo, M. L. (1986). "Eschilo, fr. 281 A, 5–13 Radt." *Giornale Filologico Ferrarese* 9: 51–57.

Garson, R. W. (1984). "Recurrent metaphors in Aeschylus' *Prometheus Bound*." *Acta Classica* 27: 124–26.

Gärtner, H. A. (1978). "Die Siegeslieder Pindars für die Söhne des Lampon." *WJA* 4: 27–46.

Garzya, A. (1958). *Teognide. Elegie I–II*. Florence.

Gaspar, C. (1900). *Essai de chronologie pindarique*. Brussels.

Gauger, B. (1977). *Gott und Mensch im Ion des Euripides. Untersuchungen zum Dritten Epeisodion des Dramas*. Bonn.

Geissler, P. (1925). *Chronologie der altattischen Komödie.* Berlin.

Gellie, G. (1984). "Apollo in the Ion." *Ramus* 13: 93–101.

Gentili, B. (1958). *Bacchilide. Studi.* Urbino.

Gentili, B., Angeli Bernardini, P., Cingano, E., and Giannini, P. (1995). *Pindaro. Le Pitiche.* Milan and Rome.

Gentili, B., Catenacci, C., Giannini, P., and Lomiento, L. (2013). *Pindaro. Le Olimpiche.* Milan and Rome.

Germar, R., Pechstein, N., and Krumeich, R. (1999). "Prometheus Pyrkaeus." In *Das griechische Satyrspiel*, ed. R. Krumeich, N. Pechstein, B. Seidensticker, and R. Bielfeldt. Darmstadt: 169–78.

Gianotti, G. F. (1975). *Per una poetica pindarica.* Turin.

Gigante, M. (1948). "La città dei giusti in Esiodo e gli «Uccelli» di Aristofane." *Dioniso* 11: 17–25.

Gildersleeve, B. L. (1885). *Pindar. The Olympian and the Pythian Odes.* New York.

Gisler, J.-R. (1994). "Prometheus." *LIMC* 7.1: 531–53.

Goldhill, S. (1983). "Narrative structure in Bacchylides 5." *Eranos* 81: 63–81.

 (1991). *The Poet's Voice: Essays on Poetics and Greek Literature.* Cambridge and New York.

González, J. M. (2010). "The *Catalogue of Women* and the end of the Heroic Age (Hesiod fr. 204.94–103 MW)." *TAPA* 140: 375–422.

Goossens, R. (1935). "Les 'Ploutoi' de Kratinos." *REA* 37: 405–34.

Graziosi, B. (2001). "Competition in wisdom." In *Homer, Tragedy and Beyond: Essays in Honour of P. E. Easterling*, ed. F. Budelmann and P. Michelakis. London: 57–74.

 (2002). *Inventing Homer. The Early Reception of Epic.* Cambridge.

Graziosi, B. and Haubold, J. (2005). *Homer: The Resonance of Epic.* London.

Grégoire, H. and Parmentier, L. (1923). *Euripide. Héraclès, Les Suppliantes, Ion*, repr. 2002. Paris.

Griffith, M. (1977). *The Authenticity of Prometheus Bound.* Cambridge.

 (1978). "Aeschylus, Sicily and Prometheus." In *Dionysiaca: Nine Studies in Greek Poetry Presented to Sir Denys Page on His 70th Birthday*, ed. R. D. Dawe, J. Diggle, and P. E. Easterling. Cambridge: 105–39.

 (1983a). "Personality in Hesiod." *CA* 2: 37–65.

 (1983b). *Aeschylus: Prometheus Bound.* Cambridge.

Grimm, R. E. (1962). "Pindar and the beast." *CPh* 57: 1–9.

Groningen, B. A. van (1966). *Theognis. Le premier livre.* Amsterdam.

Grossmann, G. (1970). *Promethie und Orestie: attischer Geist in der attischen Tragödie.* Heidelberg.

Guglielmino, F. (1928). *La parodia nella commedia greca antica.* Catania.

Guthrie, W. K. (1969). *A History of Greek Philosophy. Volume Three. The Fifth-Century Enlightenment.* Cambridge.

Hall, E. (2000). "Female figures and metapoetry in Old Comedy." In *The Rivals of Aristophanes*, ed. D. Harvey and J. Wilkins. London: 407–18.

Hall, J. M. (1997). *Ethnic Identity in Greek Antiquity.* Cambridge.

Halliwell, S. (2011). *Between Ecstasy and Truth: Interpretations of Greek Poetics from Homer to Longinus*. Oxford.

Hamilton, R. (1978). "Prologue, prophecy and plot in four plays of Euripides." *AJP* 99: 277–302.

(1989). *The Architecture of Hesiodic Poetry*. Baltimore and London.

Hardie, A. (2013) "Ibycus and the Muses of Helicon." *MD* 70: 9–36.

Harriott, R. M. (1969). *Poetry and Criticism before Plato*. London.

Harrison, E. (1902). *Studies in Theognis*. Cambridge.

Harrison, J. (1900). "Pandora's box." *JHS* 20: 99–114.

Harvey, D. (2000). "Phrynichos and his Muses." In *The Rivals of Aristophanes*, ed. D. Harvey and J. Wilkins. London: 91–134.

Haubold, J. (2005). "Heracles in the Hesiodic *Catalogue of Women*." In *The Hesiodic Catalogue of Women: Constructions and Reconstructions*, ed. R. Hunter. Cambridge: 85–98.

Heath, M. (1985). "Hesiod's didactic poetry." *CQ* 35: 245–63.

Heberlein, F. (1980). *Pluthygieia: Zur Gegenwelt bei Aristophanes*. Frankfurt.

Hedreen, G. (2011). "The Trojan War, Theoxenia, and Aegina in Pindar's *Paean* 6 and the Aphaia Sculptures." In *Aegina: Contexts for Choral Lyric Poetry. Myth, History, and Identity in the Fifth Century BC*, ed. D. Fearn. Oxford: 323–69.

Heilinger, K. (1983). "Der Freierkatalog der Helena im hesiodeischen Frauenkatalog I." *MH* 40: 19–34.

Heitsch, E. (1962). "Die Nicht-Philosophische ΑΛΗΘΕΙΑ." *Hermes* 90: 24–33.

(1963). "Das Prometheus-Gedicht bei Hesiod." *RhM* 106: 1–15.

Heldmann, K. (1982). *Die Niederlage Homers im Dichterwettstreit mit Hesiod*. Göttingen: Vandenhoeck & Ruprecht.

Henderson, J. (1997). "Mass versus elite and the comic heroism of Peisetairos." In *The City As Comedy. Society and Representation in Athenian Drama*, ed. G. W. Dobrov. Chapel Hill, N.C.: 135–48.

(2000). "Pherecrates and the women of Old Comedy." In *The Rivals of Aristophanes*, ed. D. Harvey and J. Wilkins. London: 135–50.

Hendrick, C. W., Jr. (1988). "The temple and cult of Apollo Patroos in Athens." *AJA* 92: 185–210.

Herington, C. J. (1963a). "A study in the *Prometheia*, Part I. The elements in the trilogy." *Phoenix* 17: 180–97.

(1963b). "A study in the *Prometheia*, Part II: *Birds* and *Prometheia*." *Phoenix* 17: 236–43.

(1970). *The Author of the Prometheus Bound*. Austin.

(1972). *The Older Scholia on the Prometheus Bound*. Leiden.

Heynen, C. and Krumeich, R. (1999a). "*Inachos*." In *Das griechische Satyrspiel*, ed. R. Krumeich, N. Pechstein, B. Seidensticker, and R. Bielfeldt. Darmstadt: 313–43.

(1999b). "*Pandora oder Sphyrokopoi*." In *Das griechische Satyrspiel*, ed. R. Krumeich, N. Pechstein, B. Seidensticker, and R. Bielfeldt. Darmstadt: 375–80.

Hinds, S. (1998). *Allusion and Intertext: Dynamics of Appropriation in Roman Poetry*. Cambridge.

Hirschberger, M. (2004). *Gynaikōn Katalogos und Megalai Ēhoiai. Ein Kommentar zu den Fragmenten zweier Hesiodeischer Epen*. Munich and Leipzig.

  (2008). "Il tema della metamorfosi nel *Catalogo* esiodeo delle donne." In *Esiodo: cent'anni di papiri. Atti del convegno internazionale di studi, Firenze, 7–8 giugno 2007*, ed. G. Bastianini and A. Casanova. Florence: 113–27.

Hofmann, H. (1976). *Mythos und Komödie. Untersuchung zu den Vögeln des Aristophanes*. Hildesheim.

Holzhausen, J. (2002). "Pandora und Basileia. Hesiod-Rezeption in Aristophanes' 'Vögeln'." *Philologus* 146: 34–45.

Hopfner, T. (1913). *Thomas Magister, Demetrios Triklinios, Manuel Moschopulos: eine Studie über ihren Sprachgebrauch in den Scholien zu Aischylos, Sophokles, Euripides, Aristophanes, Hesiod, Pindar und Theokrit*. Vienna.

Hornblower, S. (2007). "'Dolphins in the sea' (*Isthmian* 9. 7): Pindar and the Aeginetans." In *Pindar's Poetry, Patrons, and Festivals: From Archaic Greece to the Roman Empire*, ed. S. Hornblower and C. Morgan. Oxford: 287–308.

Horsfall, N. (1991). "Virgil, Parthenius and the art of mythological reference." *Vergilius* 37: 31–36.

Hubbard, T. K. (1985). *The Pindaric Mind: A Study of Logical Structure in Early Greek Poetry*. Brill.

  (1991a). "Theban nationalism and poetic apology in Pindar, *Pythian* 9.76–96." *RhM* 134: 22–38.

  (1991b). "Recitative anapests and the authenticity of *Prometheus Bound*." *AJP* 112: 439–60.

  (1991c). *The Mask of Comedy. Aristophanes and the Intertextual Parabasis*. Ithaca, N.Y.

  (1995). "Hesiod's fable of the hawk and the nightingale reconsidered." *GRBS* 36: 161–71.

  (1997). "Utopianism and the sophistic city in Aristophanes." In *The City As Comedy. Society and Representation in Athenian Drama*, ed. G. W. Dobrov. Chapel Hill, N.C.: 23–50.

  (2001). "Pindar and Athens after the Persian Wars." In *Gab es das Griechische Wunder? Griechenland zwischen dem Ende des 6. und der Mitte des 5. Jahrhunderts v. Chr.*, ed. D. Papenfuss and V. M. Strocka. Mainz: 387–97.

  (2004). "The dissemination of epinician lyric: Pan-Hellenism, reperformance, written texts." In *Oral Performance and Its Context*, ed. C. J. Mackie. Leiden: 71–93.

  (2011). "The dissemination of Pindar's non-epinician choral lyric." In *Archaic and Classical Choral Song: Performance, Politics and Dissemination*, ed. L. Athanassaki and E. L. Bowie. Berlin: 347–64.

Hughes Fowler, B. (1957). "The imagery of the *Prometheus Bound*." *AJP* 78: 173–84.

Hummel, P. (1997). *Philologica Lyrica. La poésie lyrique grecque au miroir de l'érudition philologique de l'antiquité à la Renaissance.* Leuven.

Humphreys, S. C. (1974). "The Nothoi of Kynosarges." *JHS* 94: 88–95.

Hunt, R. (1981). "Satiric elements in Hesiod's Works and Days." *Helios* 8: 29–40.

Hunter, R. (2009). *Critical Moments in Classical Literature. Studies in the Ancient View of Literature and Its Uses.* Cambridge.

   (2011). "Apollo and the *Ion* of Euripides: nothing to do with Nietzsche?" *Trends in Classics* 3: 18–37.

   (2014). *Hesiodic Voices: Studies in the Ancient Reception of Hesiod's Works and Days.* Cambridge.

Hutchinson, G. O. (2001). *Greek Lyric Poetry: A Commentary on Selected Larger Pieces: Alcman, Stesichorus, Sappho, Alcaeus, Ibycus, Anacreon, Simonides, Bacchylides, Pindar, Sophocles, Euripides.* Oxford.

Huxley, G. (1986). "*Prometheus Desmotes*, 354." *JHS* 106: 190–91.

Huys, M. (1995). *The Tale of the Hero Who Was Exposed at Birth in Euripidean Tragedy: A Study of Motifs.* Leuven.

Illig, L. (1932). *Zur Form der pindarischen Erzählung: Interpretationen und Untersuchungen.* Berlin.

Imhof, M. (1966). *Euripides' Ion. Eine literarische Studie.* Bern and Munich.

Indergaard, H. (2011). "Thebes, Aegina, and the temple of Aphaia: a reading of Pindar's *Isthmian* 6." In *Aegina: Contexts for Choral Lyric Poetry. Myth, History, and Identity in the Fifth Century BC*, ed. D. Fearn. Oxford: 294–322.

Irigoin, J. (1952). *Histoire du texte de Pindare.* Paris.

Irwin, E. (2005). "Gods among men? The social and political dynamics of the Hesiodic *Catalogue of Women*." In *The Hesiodic Catalogue of Women: Constructions and Reconstructions*, ed. R. Hunter. Cambridge: 35–84.

   (2011). "Herodotus on Aeginetan identity." In *Aegina: Contexts for Choral Lyric Poetry. Myth, History, and Identity in the Fifth Century BC*, ed. D. Fearn. Oxford: 373–425.

Jaeger, W. (1947). *The Theology of Early Greek Philosophers.* Oxford.

Janko, R. (1982). *Homer, Hesiod and the Hymns. Diachronic Development in Epic Diction.* Cambridge.

   (1984). "*P. Oxy. 2509*: Hesiod's *Catalogue* on the death of Actaion." *Phoenix* 38: 299–307.

   (1986). "The *Shield of Heracles* and the legend of Cycnus." *CQ* 36: 38–59.

   (2012). "πρῶτόν τε καὶ ὕστατον αἰὲν ἀείδειν. Relative chronology and the literary history of the early Greek epos." In *Relative Chronology in Early Greek Poetry*, ed. Ø. Andersen and D. T. T. Haug. Cambridge: 20–43.

Jebb, R. C. (1905). *Bacchylides. The Poems and Fragments.* Cambridge.

Jensen, M. S. (1966). "Tradition and individuality in Hesiod's *Works and Days*." *CM* 27: 1–27.

Jouanna, J. (2006). "L'œuf, le vent et éros." In *Philologia: mélanges offerts à Michel Casevitz*, ed. P. Brillet-Dubois and E. Parmentier. Lyon: 99–108.

Judet de la Combe, P. (1993). "L'autobiographie comme mode d'universalisation. Hésiode et l'Hélicon." In *La componente autobiografica nella poesia greca e latina fra realtà e artificio letterario*, ed. G. Arrighetti and F. Montanari. Pisa: 25–39.

(1996). "La dernière ruse: «Pandore» dans la *Théogonie*." In *Le métier du mythe. Lectures d'Hésiode*, ed. F. Blaise, P. Judet de la Combe, and P. Rousseau. Lille: 263–313.

Judet de la Combe, P. and Lernould, A. (1996). "Sur la Pandora des *Travaux. Esquisses*." In *Le métier du mythe. Lectures d'Hésiode*, ed. F. Blaise, P. Judet de la Combe, and P. Rousseau. Lille: 301–13.

Kanavou, N. (2011). "Political myth in Aristophanes: another form of political satire?" *GBRS* 51: 382–400.

Käppel, L. (1992). *Paian: Studien zur Geschichte einer Gattung*. Berlin.

Kenyon, F. G. (1897). *The Poems of Bacchylides from a Papyrus in the British Museum*. London.

Kerényi, C. (1963). *Prometheus. Archetypal Image of Human Existence*, transl. R. Manheim. New York.

Kerferd, G. B. (1981). *The Sophistic Movement*. Cambridge.

Kerkhof, R. (2001). *Dorische Posse, Epicharm und Attische Komödie*. Munich and Leipzig.

Kidd, S. (2012). "The meaning of *bōmolokhos* in classical Attic." *TAPA* 142: 239–55.

Kirkwood, G. M. (1982). *Selections from Pindar: Edited with an Introduction and Commentary*. Chico, Calif.

(1984). "Blame and envy in the Pindaric epinician." In *Greek Poetry and Philosophy: Studies in Honour of Leonard Woodbury*, ed. D. E. Gerber. Chico, Calif.: 169–83.

Kirsten, E. (1941). "Ein politisches Programm in Pindars erstem pythischen Gedicht." *RhM* 90: 58–71.

Kivilo, M. (2010). *Early Greek Poets' Lives: The Shaping of the Tradition*. Leiden.

Kleingünther, A. (1933). "ΠΡΩΤΟΣ ΕΥΡΕΤΗΣ. Untersuchungen zur Geschichte einer Fragestellung." Ph.D. dissertation, Georg-August-Universität Göttingen (publ. Leipzig).

Koenen, L. (1994). "Greece, the Near East, and Egypt: cyclic destruction in Hesiod and the *Catalogue of Women*." *TAPA* 124: 1–34.

Köhnken, A. (1971). *Die Funktion des Mythos bei Pindar. Interpretationen zu sechs Pindargedichten*. Berlin and New York.

(1985). "'Melichos Orga.' Liebesthematik und aktueller Sieg in der neunten Pythischen Ode Pindars." In *Pindare*, ed. A. Hurst. Geneva and Vandoeuvres: 71–111.

Kolde, A. (2003). *Politique et religion chez Isyllos d'Épidaure*. Basel.

Kolf, M. C. van der (1923). "Quaeritur quomodo Pindarus fabulas tractaverit quidque in eis mutarit." Ph.D. dissertation Universiteit Leiden (publ. Rotterdam).

Kollmann, O. (1989). *Das Prooimion der ersten Pythischen Ode Pindars. Ein sprachlich-poetischer Kommentar*. Vienna and Berlin.

Komornicka, A. M. (1972). "Quelques remarques sur la notion d'ΑΛΑΘΕΙΑ et de ΨΕΥΔΟΣ chez Pindare." *Eos* 70: 235–53.

(1981). "Termes déterminants le vrai et le faux chez Pindare." In *Aischylos und Pindar. Studien zu Werk und Nachwirkung*, ed. E. G. Schmidt. Berlin: 81–89.

Koning, H. H. (2010a). *Hesiod: The Other Poet. Ancient Reception of a Cultural Icon*. Leiden.

(2010b). "Plato's Hesiod: not Plato's alone." In *Plato and Hesiod*, ed. G. R. Boys-Stones and J. H. Haubold. Oxford: 89–110.

Konstan, D. (1995). *Greek Comedy and Ideology*. New York and Oxford.

(1997). "The Greek polis and its negotiations: versions of utopia in Aristophanes' *Birds*." In *The City As Comedy. Society and Representation in Athenian Drama*, ed. G. W. Dobrov. Chapel Hill, N.C.: 3–22.

Kowalzig, B. (2011). "Musical merchandise 'on every vessel': religion and trade on Aegina." In *Aegina: Contexts for Choral Lyric Poetry. Myth, History, and Identity in the Fifth Century BC*, ed. D. Fearn. Oxford: 129–71.

Kranz, W. (1967). "Titanomachia." In *Studien zur Antiken Literatur und ihrem Fortwirken. Kleine Schriften*, ed. E. Vogt. Heidelberg: 89–96 (orig. 1960 in *Studi in onore di Luigi Castiglioni*. Vol. I. Florence: 475–86).

Kraus, W. (1957). "Prometheus." *RE* 23: 653–730.

Krischer, T. (1965). "ΕΤΥΜΟΣ and ΑΛΗΘΗΣ." *Philologus* 109: 161–74.

Kroll, W. (1894). "Adversaria Graeca." *Philologus* 53: 416–28.

Krummen, E. (1990). *Pyrsos Hymnon: Festliche Gegenwart und mythisch-rituelle Tradition bei Pindar*. Berlin and New York.

Kugelmeier, C. (1996). *Reflexe früher und zeitgenössischer Lyrik in der Alten attischen Komödie*. Stuttgart and Leipzig.

Kuntz, M. (1993). *Narrative Setting and Dramatic Poetry*. Leiden.

Kurke, L. (1990). "Pindar's sixth *Pythian* and the tradition of advice poetry." *TAPA* 120: 85–107.

(1991a). *The Traffic in Praise: Pindar and the Poetics of Social Economy*. Ithaca, N.Y.

(1991b). "Fathers and sons: a note on Pindaric ambiguity." *AJP* 112: 287–300.

Kyriakou, P. (1994). "Images of women in Pindar." *MD* 32: 31–54.

Lada-Richards, I. (1999). *Initiating Dionysus: Ritual and Theatre in Aristophanes' Frogs*. Oxford.

(2002). "Reinscribing the Muse: Greek drama and the discourse of inspired creativity." In *Cultivating the Muse: Struggles for Power and Inspiration in Classical Literature*, ed. E. Spentzou and D. Fowler. Oxford: 69–91.

Lamberton, R. (1988). *Hesiod*. New Haven and London.

Lardinois, A. P. (1995). "Wisdom in context: the use of gnomic statements in archaic Greek poetry." Ph.D. dissertation, Princeton University.

Larson, J. (1995). *Greek Heroine Cults*. Madison.

Larson, S. (2007). *Tales of Epic Ancestry. Boiotian Collective Identity in the Late Archaic and Early Classical Periods*. Stuttgart.

Larue, J. (1963). "Creusa's monody: *Ion* 859–922." *TAPA* 94: 126–36.

Latte, K. (1946). "Hesiods Dichterweihe." *A&A* 2: 152–63.

Lauriola, R. (2000). "Ἐλπίς e la giara di Pandora (Hes. *Op*.90–104): il bene e il male sulla vita dell'uomo." *Maia* 52: 9–18.

Lavecchia, S. (2000). "Pindaro ἑρμανεὺς σοφός. Considerazioni su Ol. 2, 85–86." *Hermes* 128: 369–72.

Lebedev, A. V. (1989). "Heraclitus in P. Derveni." *ZPE* 79: 39–47.

Leclerc, C. (1992). "Epiménide sans paradoxe." *Kernos* 5: 221–33.

Ledbetter, G. M. (2003). *Poetics before Plato: Interpretation and Authority in Early Greek Theories of Poetry*. Princeton.

Lee, K. H. (1997). *Euripides. Ion*. Warminster.

Lefèvre, E. (2003). *Studien zu den Quellen und zum Verständnis des Prometheus Desmotes*. Göttingen.

Lefkowitz, M. R. (1969). "Bacchylides' *Ode* 5: Imitation and Originality." *HSCP* 73: 45–96.

    (1975). "The influential fictions in the scholia to Pindar's *Pythian* 8." *CPh* 70: 173–85.

    (1976). *The Victory Ode: An Introduction*. Park Ridge, N.J.

    (1985). "The Pindar scholia." *AJP* 3: 269–82.

    (1991). *First-Person Fictions: Pindar's Poetic "I"*. Oxford.

    (2012)². *The Lives of the Greek Poets*, 2nd edn. Baltimore.

Leinieks, V. (1984). "ΕΛΠΙΣ in Hesiod, *Works and Days* 96." *Philologus* 128: 1–8.

Lendle, O. (1957). *Die 'Pandorasage' bei Hesiod. Textkritische und motivgeschichtliche Untersuchungen*. Würzburg.

Lenz, L. (1980). "Feuer in der Promethie." *GB* 9: 23–56.

Leo, F. (1894). *Hesiodea*. Göttingen.

Levet, J. P. (1976). *Le vrai et le faux dans la pensée grecque archaïque*. Paris.

Livrea, E. (2008). "I versi 'vaganti' nel logos esiodeo delle razze (*Erga* 173 a–e West)." In *Esiodo: cent'anni di papiri. Atti del convegno internazionale di studi, Firenze, 7–8 giugno 2007*, ed. G. Bastianini and A. Casanova. Florence: 43–53.

Lloyd, M. (1986). "Divine and human action in Euripides' *Ion*." *A&A* 32: 33–45.

Lloyd-Jones, H. (1973). "Modern interpretations of Pindar: the second *Pythian* and the seventh *Nemean Odes*." *JHS* 93: 109–37.

    (1983)². *The Justice of Zeus*, 2nd edn. Berkeley and Los Angeles.

    (1990). "Pindar and the aftermath." In *Greek Epic, Lyric, and Tragedy. The Academic Papers of Sir Hugh Lloyd-Jones*, ed. H. Lloyd-Jones. Oxford: 80–109.

    (2003). "Zeus, Prometheus, and Greek ethics." *HSCP* 101: 49–72.

Lobel, E. (1962). *The Oxyrhynchus Papyri XXVIII*. London.

Lochin, C. (1990). "Ixion." *LIMC* 5.1: 857–62.

Löffler, I. (1963). *Die Melampodie: Versuch einer Rekonstruktion des Inhalts*. Meisenheim am Glan.

Loraux, N. (1993a). "Aristophane, les femmes d'Athènes et le théâtre." In *Aristophane*, ed. E. Degani, J. M. Bremer, and E. W. Handley. Geneva and Vandoeuvres: 203–53.

    (1993b). *The Children of Athena. Athenian Ideas about Citizenship and the Division between the Sexes*, transl. C. Levine. Princeton.

Ludwig, P. W. (2002). *Eros and Polis*. Cambridge.

Luján, E. R. (2011). "The cosmic egg (*OF* 64, 79, 114)." In *Tracing Orpheus. Studies of Orphic Fragments*, ed. M. Herrero de Jáuregui, A. I. Jiménez San

Cristóbal, E. R. Luján Martínez, R. M. Hernández, M. A. Santamaría Álvarez, and S. Torallas Tovar. Berlin and New York: 85–92.

Luppe, W. (1973). "Das Aufführungsdatum der 'Archilochoi' des Kratinos." *Philologus* 117: 124–27.

Luppino, A. (1959). "Divagazioni e precisazioni sulla Pitica III di Pindaro." *RFIC* 37: 225–36.

Luraghi, N. (1994). *Tirannidi arcaiche in Sicilia e Magna Grecia da Panezio di Leontini alla caduta dei Deinomenidi.* Florence.

Luther, W. (1935). *Wahrheit und Lüge im ältesten Griechentum.* Leipzig.

MacDowell, D. M. (1990). "The meaning of ἀλαζών." In *'Owls to Athens'. Essays on Classical Subjects Presented to Sir Kenneth Dover,* ed. E. M. Craik. Oxford: 287–92.

(1995). *Aristophanes and Athens. An Introduction to the Plays.* Oxford.

Mace, S. T. (1992). "Pindarus Hesiodicus." Ph.D. dissertation, Yale University.

Mackie, H. S. (2003). *Graceful Errors: Pindar and the Performance of Praise.* Ann Arbor.

Maehler, H. (1963). *Die Auffassung des Dichterberufs im frühen Griechentum bis zur Zeit Pindars.* Göttingen.

(1967). "Griechische literarische Papyri." *MH* 24: 61–78.

(1982). *Die Lieder des Bakchylides. Erster Teil. Die Siegeslieder. II. Kommentar.* Leiden.

(1989). *Pindari Carmina cum Fragmentis.* Pars II. Leipzig.

(1997). *Die Lieder des Bakchylides. Zweiter Teil. Die Dithyramben und Fragmente. Text, Übersetzung, und Kommentar.* Leiden.

(2000). "Io auf der Bühne: Bemerkungen zum Aufführungsdatum des 'Gefesselten Prometheus'." *Acta Ant. Hung.* 40: 321–29.

(2004). *Bacchylides: A Selection.* Cambridge.

Major, W. E. (2006). "Aristophanes and Alazoneia: laughing at the parabasis of the *Clouds.*" *CW* 99: 131–44.

Malkin, I. (1994). *Myth and Territory in the Spartan Mediterranean.* Cambridge.

Malten, L. (1911). *Kyrene: sagengeschichtliche und historische Untersuchungen.* Berlin.

Mancini, M. (1986). "Semantica di ρητός e ἄρρητος nel prologo agli Ἔργα di Esiodo." *Aion* 8: 175–92.

Mann, C. (2001). *Athlet und Polis im archaischen und frühklassischen Griechenland.* Göttingen.

Mansfeld, J. (1986). "Aristotle, Plato, and the Preplatonic doxography and chronology." In *Storiografia e dossografia nella filosofia antica,* ed. G. Cambiano. Turin: 1–59.

Marckscheffel, G. (1840). *Hesiodi, Eumeli, Cinaethonis, Asii et Carminis Naupactii fragmenta.* Leipzig.

Marg, W. (1970). "Mensch und Technik: Der Prometheusmythos bei Hesiod und Aeschylos." In *Proceedings of the 1st International Humanistic Symposium at Delphi, Sept. 25–Oct. 4, 1969.* Athens: 361–76.

(1970). *Hesiod. Sämtliche Gedichte.* Zurich and Munich.

(1984)[2]. *Hesiod. Sämtliche Gedichte,* 2nd edn. Zurich and Munich.

Márquez Guerrero, M. A. (1992). *Las Gnomai de Baquílides*. Sevilla.

Marshall, E. (1998). "Sex and paternity: gendering the foundation of Kyrene." In *When Men Were Men: Masculinity, Power, and Identity in Classical Antiquity*, ed. L. Foxhall and J. Salmon. London and New York: 98–110.

Marston, J. M. (2007). "Language of ritual cursing in the binding of Prometheus." *GRBS* 47: 121–33.

Martin, R. P. (1992). "Hesiod's metanastic poetics." *Ramus* 21: 11–33.

(2000). "Synchronic aspects of Homeric performance: the evidence of the Hymn to Apollo." In *Una nueva visión de la cultura griega antigua hacia el fin del milenio*, ed. A. M. González de Tobia. La Plata: 403–32.

(2005). "Pulp epic: the *Catalogue* and the *Shield*." In *The Hesiodic Catalogue of Women. Constructions and Reconstructions*, ed. R. Hunter. Cambridge: 153–75.

Massimilla, G. (1996). *Aitia. Libri Primo e Secondo*. Pisa.

Matthiessen, K. (2004). *Euripides und sein Jahrhundert*. Munich.

Mayer, H. (1913). *Prodikos von Keos und die Anfänge der Synonymik bei den Griechen*. Paderborn.

Mayer, K. (1996). "Helen and the ΒΟΥΛΗ ΔΙΟΣ." *AJP* 117: 1–15.

Mayer, M. (1933). "Mousai." *RE* 16: 680–757.

Mayhew, R. (2011). *Prodicus the Sophist. Texts, Translations, and Commentary*. Oxford.

Mazon, P. (1934). "De nouveaux fragments de Cratinos." *Mélanges Bidez* 2: 603–12.

Mazur, P. S. (2004). "Paronomasia in Hesiod *Works and Days* 80–85." *CP* 99: 243–46.

Méautis, G. (1960). *L'authenticité et la date du Prométhée enchaîné d'Eschyle*. Neuchâtel and Geneva.

Mele, A. (2001). "Il corpus epimenideo." In *Epimenide cretese*, ed. E. Federico and A. Visconti. Naples: 227–78.

Merkelbach, R. (1952). "Die pisistratische Redaktion der homerischen Gedichte." *RhM* 95: 23–47.

Merkelbach, R. and West, M. L. (1967). *Fragmenta Hesiodea*. Oxford.

Mess, A. von (1901). "Der Typhonmythos bei Aischylos." *RhM* 56: 167–74.

Mette, H. J. (1963). *Der Verlorene Aischylos*. Berlin.

Miller, T. (1997). *Die griechische Kolonisation im Spiegel literarischer Zeugnisse*. Tübingen.

Miralles, C. (1993). "Le spose di Zeus e l'ordine del mondo nella 'Teogonia' di Esiodo." In *Maschile/Femminile: Genere e ruoli nelle culture antiche*, ed. M. Bettini. Rome: 17–44.

Montanari, F. (2009). "Ancient scholarship on Hesiod." In *Brill's Companion to Hesiod*, ed. F. Montanari, A. Rengakos, and C. Tsagalis. Leiden: 313–42.

Mordine, M. J. (2006). "Speaking to kings: Hesiod's ΑΙΝΟΣ and the rhetoric of allusion in the *Works and Days*." *CQ* 56: 363–73.

Moret, J.-M. (1990). "'Ἰώ ἀποταυρουμένη.'" *RA* 1: 3–26.

Morgan, K. A. (2015). *Pindar and the Construction of Syracusan Monarchy in the Fifth Century B.C.* Oxford and New York.

Morrison, A. D. (2007). *Performances and Audiences in Pindar's Sicilian Victory Odes*. London.

(2011). "Pindar and the Aeginetan *patrai*: Pindar's intersecting audiences." In *Archaic and Classical Choral Song. Performance, Politics, and Dissemination*, ed. L. Athanassaki and E. Bowie. Berlin: 311–35.

Mossman, J. M. (1996). "Chains of imagery in *Prometheus Bound.*" *CQ* 46: 58–67.

Most, G. W. (1985). *The Measures of Praise: Structure and Function in Pindar's Second Pythian and Seventh Nemean Odes*. Göttingen.

(1986). "Pindar, *O.* 2.83–90." *CQ* 36: 304–16.

(1993). "Hesiod and the textualization of personal temporality." In *La componente autobiografica nella poesia greca e latina fra realta e artificio letterario*, ed. G. Arrighetti and F. Montanari. Pisa: 73–92.

(1998). "Hesiod's myth of the five (or three or four) races." *PCPS* 43: 104–27.

(2003). "Epinician envies." In *Envy, Spite and Jealousy: The Rivalrous Emotions in Ancient Greece*, ed. D. Konstan and N. K. Rutter. Edinburgh: 123–42.

(2006). *Hesiod: Theogony, Works and Days, Testimonia*. Cambridge, Mass.

(2007). *Hesiod. The Shield, Catalogue of Women, Other Fragments*. Cambridge, Mass. and London.

(2012). "Poet and public. Communicative strategies in Pindar and Bacchylides." In *Reading the Victory Ode*, ed. P. Agócs, C. Carey, and R. Rawles. Cambridge: 249–76.

Mousbahova, V. (2007). "The meaning of the terms σοφιστής and σόφισμα in the *Prometheus Bound.*" *Hyperion* 13: 31–50.

Mühll, P. von der (1968). "Weitere pindarische Notizen." *MH* 25: 226–30.

Murray, P. (1981). "Poetic inspiration in early Greece." *JHS* 101: 87–100.

Murray, R. D. (1958). *The Motif of Io in Aeschylus' Suppliants*. Princeton.

Musäus, I. (2004). *Der Pandoramythos bei Hesiod und seine Rezeption bis Erasmus von Rotterdam*. Göttingen.

Nagy, G. (1979). *The Best of the Achaeans*. Baltimore.

(1982). "Hesiod." In *Ancient Writers. Greece and Rome. Volume I: Homer to Caesar*, ed. T. J. Luce. New York: 43–73.

(1990a). *Greek Mythology and Poetics*. Ithaca, N.Y.

(1990b). *Pindar's Homer: The Lyric Possession of an Epic Past*. Baltimore.

(1999)². *The Best of the Achaeans. Concepts of the Hero in Archaic Greek Poetry*, 2nd edn. Baltimore.

(2009). "Hesiod and the ancient biographical traditions." In *Brill's Companion to Hesiod*, ed. F. Montanari, A. Rengakos, and C. Tsagalis. Leiden: 271–311.

(2010). *Homer the Preclassic*. Berkeley.

(2011). "Asopos and his multiple daughters: traces of preclassical epic in the Aeginetan odes of Pindar." In *Aegina: Contexts for Choral Lyric Poetry. Myth, History, and Identity in the Fifth Century BC*, ed. D. Fearn. Oxford: 41–78.

Nasta, M. (2006). "La typologie des catalogues d'*Éhées*: un réseaux généalogique thématisé." *Kernos* 19: 59–78.

Neitzel, H. (1976). "Pandora und das Fass: Zur Interpretation von Hesiod, *Erga* 42–105." *Hermes* 104: 387–419.

(1980). "Hesiod und die Lügenden Musen: Zur Interpretation von Theogonie 27f." *Hermes* 108: 387–401.

Nelson, S. (1997). "The justice of Zeus in Hesiod's fable of the hawk and the nightingale." *CJ* 92: 235–47.

Neschke-Hentschke, A. (1983). "Geschichten und Geschichte: Zum Beispiel Prometheus bei Hesiod und Aischylos." *Hermes* 111: 385–402.

Nestle, W. (1936). "Die Horen des Prodikos." *Hermes* 71: 151–70.

Newiger, H. J. (1957). *Metapher und Allegorie. Studien zu Aristophanes*. Munich.

(1983). "Gedanken zu Aristophanes' Vögeln." In *Aretēs mnēmē: aphierōma eis mnēmēn tou Kōnstantinou I. Vourverē*, ed. C. Soile. Athens: 47–57.

Nicolai, W. (1964). *Hesiods Erga, Beobachtungen zum Aufbau*. Heidelberg.

Nietzsche, F. (1870). "Der florentinische Traktat über Homer und Hesiod, ihr Geschlecht und ihren Wettkampf." *RhM* 25: 529–40.

(1873). "Der florentinische Traktat über Homer und Hesiod, ihr Geschlecht und ihren Wettkampf (Schluss von Bd. XXV S. 528–540)." *RhM* 28: 211–49.

Nisetich, F. J. (1989). *Pindar and Homer*. Baltimore.

Noorden, H. van (2015). *Playing Hesiod. The 'Myth of the Races' in Classical Antiquity*. Cambridge.

Northrup, M. D. (1980). "Hesiodic personifications in Parmenides A 37." *TAPA* 110: 223–32.

Norwood, G. (1931). *Greek Comedy*. London.

Noussia, M. (2003). "The language of tyranny in Cratinus, *PCG* 258." *PCPS* 49: 74–88.

Noussia-Fantuzzi, M. (2010). *Solon the Athenian: The Poetic Fragments*. Leiden.

Nünlist, R. (1998). *Poetologische Bildersprache in der frühgriechischen Dichtung*. Stuttgart.

(2009). *The Ancient Critic at Work. Terms and Concepts of Literary Criticism in Greek Scholia*. Cambridge.

O'Sullivan, N. (1992). *Alcidamas, Aristophanes, and the Beginnings of Greek Stylistic Theory*. Stuttgart: Steiner.

O'Sullivan, P. and Collard, C. (2013). *Euripides, Cyclops, and Major Fragments of Greek Satyric Drama*. Oxford.

Ogden, D. (2013). *Drakōn. Dragon Myth and Serpent Cult in the Greek and Roman Worlds*. Oxford.

Olson, S. D. (1998). *Aristophanes. Peace*. Oxford.

(2007). *Broken Laughter: Select Fragments of Greek Comedy*. Oxford and New York.

Oost, S. I. (1976). "The tyrant kings of Syracuse." *CPh* 71: 224–36.

Ormand, K. (2004). "Marriage, identity, and the tale of Mestra in the Hesiodic *Catalogue of Women*." *AJP* 125: 303–38.

(2014). *The Hesiodic Catalogue of Women and Archaic Greece*. Cambridge and New York.

Ornaghi, M. (2004). "Omero sulla scena. Spunti per una ricostruzione degli *Odissei* e degli *Archilochi* di Cratino." In *Momenti della ricezione Omerica*.

*Poesia arcaica e teatro*, ed. G. Zanetto, D. Canavero, A. Capra, and A. Sgobbi. Milan: 197–228.

(2007). "Note di onomastica comica (II): Aristofane e i poeti comici del V secolo." *Quaderni del Dipartimento di filologia linguistica e tradizione classica «Augusto Rostagni»* 6: 23–60.

(2012). "Gli *Esiodi* di Teleclide e le variazione comiche del modello agonale." In *Poesia, musica e agoni nella Grecia antica*. Vol. I, ed. D. Castaldo, F. G. Giannachi, and A. Manieri. Lecce: 385–414.

Osborne, R. (2005). "Ordering women in Hesiod's *Catalogue*." In *The Hesiodic Catalogue of Women: Constructions and Reconstructions*, ed. R. Hunter. Cambridge: 5–24.

Owen, A. S. (1939). *Euripides. Ion*. Oxford.

Paley, F. A. (1889). *The Epics of Hesiod*. London.

Papastavrou, H. (1992). "Nyx." *LIMC* 6.1: 939–41.

Pardini, A. (1993). "L'*Ornitogonia* (Ar. *Av.* 693 sgg.) tra serio e faceto: premessa letteraria al suo studio storico-religioso." In *Orfeo e l'Orfismo*, ed. A. Masaracchia. Rome: 53–65.

Park, A. (2013). "Truth and gender in Pindar." *CQ* 63: 17–36.

Parker, R. (1987) "Myths of early Athens." In *Interpretations of Greek Mythology*, ed. J. N. Bremmer. New York.

Parsons, P. (1974). *The Oxyrhynchus Papyri*. Vol. XLII. London.

Pattoni, M. P. (1987). *L'autenticità del Prometeo incatenato di Eschilo*. Pisa.

Patzer, A. (1986). *Der Sophist Hippias als Philosophiehistoriker*. Freiburg and Munich.

Pavese, C. O. (1998). "The rhapsodic epic poems as oral and independent poems." *HSCP* 98: 63–90.

Pavlou, M. (2008). "Metapoetics, poetic tradition, and praise in Pindar *Olympian* 9." *Mnemosyne* 61: 533–67.

Pearson, A. C. (1917). *The Fragments of Sophocles*. Vol. II. Cambridge (repr. 1963, Amsterdam).

Pellegrino, M. (2000). *Utopie e immagini gastronomiche nei frammenti dell'Archaia*. Bologna.

Pelliccia, H. (1987). "Pindarus Homericus: *Pythian* 3.1–80." *HSCP* 91: 39–63.

Pellikaan-Engel, M. E. (1978). *Hesiod and Parmenides*. Amsterdam.

Pellizer, E. (1996). "Réflexions sur les combats de la *Théogonie*." In *Le métier du mythe. Lectures d'Hésiode*, ed. F. Blaise, P. Judet de la Combe, and P. Rousseau. Lille: 236–49.

Péron, J. (1974). "Pindare et Hiéron dans la IIe Pythique (vv. 56 et 72)." *REG* 87: 1–32.

(1976). "Pindare et la victoire de Télésicrate dans la IXe Pythique (v. 76–96)." *RPh* 50: 58–78.

(1982). "Le poème à Polycrate: une 'palinodie' d'Ibycus?" *RPh* 56: 33–56.

Pertusi, A. (1955). *Scholia vetera in Hesiodi Opera et Dies*. Milan.

Pfeijffer, I. L. (1995). "The date of Pindar's Fifth Nemean and Bacchylides' Thirteenth Ode." *CQ* 45: 318–32.

(1999). *Three Aeginetan Odes of Pindar: A Commentary on Nemean V, Nemean III & Pythian VIII*. Leiden.

Philippson, P. von (1936). *Untersuchungen über den griechischen Mythos*. Zurich.

Picard, C. (1951), "Le culte et la légende du Centaure Chiron dans l'Occident méditerranéen." *RÉA* 53: 5–25.

Piccirilli, L. (1975). Μεγαρικά: *Testimonianze e Frammenti*. Pisa.

Pieters, Th. M. F. (1946). *Cratinus: bijdrage tot de geschiedenis der vroeg-attische comedie*. Leiden.

Podlecki, A. J. (1975). "Reconstructing an Aeschylean trilogy." *BICS* 22: 1–19.

(2005). *Aeschylus. Prometheus Bound*. Oxford.

Pohlenz, M. (1916). "Kronos und die Titanen." *Neue Jahrbücher für das klassische Altertum* 37: 549–94.

(1954). *Die griechische Tragödie*. Göttingen.

Poli-Palladini, L. (2001). "Some reflections on Aeschylus' *Aetnae(ae)*." *RhM* 144: 287–325.

(2013). *Aeschylus at Gela: An Integrated Approach*. Alexandria.

Pratt, L. H. (1993). *Lying and Poetry from Homer to Pindar: Falsehood and Deception in Archaic Greek Poetics*. Ann Arbor.

Pretagostini, R. (1982). "Archiloco 'Salsa di Taso' negli *Archilochi* di Cratino (fr. 6 K.)." *QUCC* 11: 43–52.

Privitera, G. A. (1980). "Politica religiosa dei Dinomenidi e ideologia dell'*optimus rex*." In *Perennitas: Studi in onore di Angelo Brelich*. Rome: 393–411.

(1982). *Pindaro. Le Istmiche*. Milan.

Pucci, P. (1977). *Hesiod and the Language of Poetry*. Baltimore.

(1996). "Auteur et destinataires dans les *Travaux* d'Hésiode." In *Le métier du mythe: Lectures d'Hésiode*, ed. F. Blaise, P. Judet de la Combe, and P. Rousseau. Lille: 191–210.

(2007). *Inno alle Muse (Esiodo, Teogonia, 1–115), Testo, Introduzione, Traduzione e Commento*. Pisa and Rome.

(2009). "The poetry of the *Theogony*." In *Brill's Companion to Hesiod*, ed. F. Montanari, A. Rengakos, and C. Tsagalis. Leiden: 37–70.

Puelma, M. (1972). "Sänger und König: zum Verständnis von Hesiods Tierfabel." *MH* 29: 86–109.

(1989). "Der Dichter und die Wahrheit in der griechischen Poetik von Homer bis Aristoteles." *MH* 46: 65–100.

Quaglia, R. (1998). "Elementi strutturali nelle comedie di Cratino." *Acme* 51: 23–71.

Rabinowitz, N. S. (1993). *Anxiety Veiled. Euripides and the Traffic in Women*. Ithaca, N.Y.

Race, W. H. (1981). "The end of Olympia 2: Pindar and the Vulgus." *CA* 12: 251–67.

(1982). *The Classical Priamel from Homer to Boethius*. Leiden.

(1997a). *Pindar. Olympic Odes. Pythian Odes*. Cambridge, Mass.

(1997b). *Pindar. Nemean Odes. Isthmian Odes. Fragments*. Cambridge, Mass.

Radermacher, L. (1938). "Zu griechischen Texten." *WS* 56: 1–10.

Radt, S. (1977). *Tragicorum Graecorum Fragmenta. Vol. 4*. Göttingen.

(1985). *Tragicorum Graecorum Fragmenta*. Göttingen.

Ramnoux, C. (1986). *La nuit et les enfants de la nuit dans la tradition grecque.* Paris.

  (1987). "Les femmes de Zeus: Hésiode, *Théogonie*, vers 885 à 955." In *Poikilia: Etudes offertes à Jean-Pierre Vernant.* Paris: 155–64.

Rau, P. (1967). *Paratragodia. Untersuchung einer komischen Form des Aristophanes.* Munich.

Reckford, K. J. (1987). *Aristophanes' Old-and-New Comedy.* Chapel Hill, N.C.

Rehm, R. (1992). *Greek Tragic Theatre.* London and New York.

Reinhardt, K. (1949). *Aischylos als Regisseur und Theologe.* Bern.

  (1957). "Vorschläge zum neuen Aischylos." *Hermes* 85: 1–17.

  (1960). *Tradition und Geist. Gesammelte Essays zur Dichtung.* Göttingen.

Reinsch-Werner, H. (1976). *Callimachus Hesiodicus. Die Rezeption der hesiodischen Dichtung durch Kallimachos von Kyrene.* Berlin.

Rengakos, A. (2009). "Hesiod's narrative." In *Brill's Companion to Hesiod*, ed. F. Montanari, A. Rengakos, and C. Tsagalis. Leiden: 203–21.

Revermann, M. (2013). "Paraepic comedy: point(s) and practices." In *Greek Comedy and the Discourse of Genres*, ed. E. Bakola, L. Prauscello, and M. Telò. Cambridge: 101–28.

Ricciardelli Apicella, G. (1993). "Le teogonie orfiche nell'ambito delle teogonie greche." In *Orfeo e l'Orfismo*, ed. A. Masaracchia. Rome: 27–51.

Richardson, N. J. (1981). "The contest of Homer and Hesiod and Alcidamas' *Mouseion*." *CQ* 31: 1–10.

  (2010). *Three Homeric Hymns. To Apollo, Hermes, and Aphrodite.* Cambridge.

Rigoglioso, M. (2009). *The Cult of Divine Birth in Ancient Greece.* New York.

Rijksbaron, A. (2009). "Discourse cohesion in the proem of Hesiod's *Theogony*." In *Discourse Cohesion in Ancient Greek*, ed. S. J. Bakker and G. C. Wakker. Leiden: 241–65.

Risch, E. (1947). "Namensbedeutungen und Worterklärungen bei den ältesten griechischen Dichtern." In *Eumusia: Festgabe für Ernst Howald zum sechzigsten Geburtstag.* Zurich: 72–91.

Robbins, E. (1978). "Cyrene and Cheiron: the myth of Pindar's ninth Pythian." *Phoenix* 32: 91–104.

  (1990). "The gifts of the gods: Pindar's third *Pythian*." *CQ* 40: 307–18.

Robert, C. (1914). "Pandora." *Hermes* 49: 17–38.

Robertson, D. S. (1938). "On the chronology of Aeschylus." *PCPhS* 169–71: 9–10.

  (1951). "Prometheus and Chiron." *JHS* 71: 150–55.

Robertson, N. (1980). "Heracles' 'catabasis'." *Hermes* 108: 274–300.

Rodríguez-Noriega Guillén, L. (1996). *Epicarmo de Siracusa. Testimonios y Fragmentos. Edición crítica bilingüe.* Oviedo.

  (2012). "On Epicharmus' literary and philosophical background." In *Theater outside Athens. Drama in Greek Sicily and South Italy*, ed. K. Bosher. Cambridge: 76–96.

Romer, F. E. (1997). "Good intentions and the ὁδὸς ἡ ἐς κόρακας." In *The City As Comedy. Society and Representation in Athenian Drama*, ed. G. W. Dobrov. Chapel Hill, N.C.: 51–74.

Roscher, W. H. (1890–94). *Ausführliches Lexikon der Griechischen und Römischen Mythologie. Zweiter Band, erste Abteilung.* Leipzig.

Roselli, D. K. (2012). *Theater of the People: Spectators and Society in Ancient Athens.* Austin.

Rosen, R. M. (1988). *Old Comedy and the Iambographic Tradition.* Atlanta.

(1990). "Poetry and sailing in Hesiod's *Works and Days.*" *CA* 9: 99–113.

(1997). "Homer and Hesiod." In *A New Companion to Homer,* ed. I. Morris and B. Powell. Leiden: 463–88.

(2004). "Aristophanes' *Frogs* and the *Contest of Homer and Hesiod.*" *TAPA* 134: 295–322.

(2013). "*Iambos,* comedy and the question of generic affiliation." In *Greek Comedy and the Discourse of Genres,* ed. E. Bakola, L. Prauscello, and M. Telò. Cambridge: 81–97.

Rosivach, V. J. (1987). "Autochthony and the Athenians." *CQ* 37: 294–306.

Ross, D. O. (1975). *Backgrounds to Augustan Poetry: Gallus, Elegy and Rome.* Cambridge.

Rossi, L. E. (1997). "Esiodo, *le Opere e i Giorgni*: un nuovo tentativo di analisi." In *Posthomerica: tradizione omeriche dell'Antiquità al Rinascimento,* ed. F. Montanari and S. Pittaluga. Genoa: 7–22.

Rousseau, P. (1996). "Instruire Persès. Notes sur l'ouverture des *Travaux* d'Hésiode." In *Le métier du mythe: Lectures d'Hésiode,* ed. F. Blaise, P. Judet de la Combe, and P. Rousseau. Lille: 93–167.

Rudhardt, J. (1986). *Le rôle d'Éros et d'Aphrodite dans les cosmogonies grecques.* Paris.

(1999). *Thémis et les Hôrai. Recherche sur les divinités grecques de la justice et de la paix.* Geneva.

Ruffell, I. (2000). "The world turned upside down: utopia and utopianism in the fragments of Old Comedy." In *The Rivals of Aristophanes,* ed. D. Harvey and J. Wilkins. London: 473–506.

(2012). *Aeschylus: Prometheus Bound.* London.

Russo, C. F. (1965)². *Hesiodi Scutum.* Florence.

Rusten, J. S. (1984). "Phanes-Eros in the theogony of 'Orpheus' (PDerveni col. IX 4)." In *Atti del XVII Congresso Internazionale di Papirologia.* Naples: 333–35.

(1985). "Interim notes on the papyrus from Derveni." *HSCP* 89: 121–40.

(2011). *The Birth of Comedy. Texts, Documents, and Art from Athenian Comic Competitions, 486–280.* Baltimore.

Rutherford, I. (1988). "Pindar on the birth of Apollo." *CQ* 38: 65–75.

(2000). "Formulas, voice, and death in *Ehoie-Poetry,* the Hesiodic *Gunaikon Katalogos,* and the Odysseian *Nekuia.*" In *Matrices of Genre. Authors, Canons, and Society,* ed. M. Depew and D. Obbink. Cambridge, Mass.: 81–96.

(2001). *Pindar's Paeans: A Reading of the Fragments with a Survey of the Genre.* Oxford.

(2005). "Mestra at Athens: Hesiod fr. 43 and the poetics of Panhellenism." In *The Hesiodic Catalogue of Women: Constructions and Reconstructions,* ed. R. Hunter. Cambridge: 99–117.

(2015). "Pindar's Cycle." In *The Greek Epic Cycle and Its Ancient Reception: A Companion*, ed. M. Fantuzzi and C. Tsagalis. Cambridge: 450–60.

Rzach, A. (1913). *Hesiodi Carmina*, repr. 1958. Stuttgart.

Saïd, S. (1977). "Les Combats de Zeus et le problème des interpolations dans la *Théogonie* d'Hésiode." *REG* 90: 183–210.

(1982). "Eschyle, Hésiode et les combats de Zeus ou comment se réécrit le mythe." *Etudes de littérature ancienne. Questions de sens* 2: 81–91.

(1985). *Sophiste et tyran, ou le problème du Prométhée Enchaîné*. Paris.

(2006). "Les dons de Prométhée et leur valeur dans le *Prométhée enchaîné* à la lumière d'une comparaison avec Hèsiode, Platon et Aelius Aristide." *Lexis: Poética, retórica e comunicaciones nella tradizione classica* 24: 247–64.

Saxonhouse, A. W. (1986). "Myths and the origins of cities: reflections on the autochthony theme in Euripides' *Ion*." In *Greek Tragedy and Political Theory*, ed. J. P. Euben. Berkeley and Los Angeles: 252–73.

Scafuro, A. (1990). "Discourses of sexual violation in mythic accounts and dramatic versions of 'The Girl's Tragedy'." *Differences* 2: 126–59.

Schade, G. (2006). "Die Oden von Pindar und Bakchylides auf Hieron." *Hermes* 134: 373–78.

Schadewaldt, W. (1928). *Der Aufbau des Pindarischen Epinikion*. Darmstadt.

(1966)². *Monolog und Selbstgespräch. Untersuchungen zur Formgeschichte der griechischen Tragödie*, 2nd edn. Berlin.

Scharffenberger, E. W. (1995). "Peisetaerus' 'satyric' treatment of Iris: Aristophanes' *Birds* 1253–6." *JHS* 115: 172–73.

Schein, S. (1987). "Unity and meaning in Pindar's sixth *Pythian Ode*." *Mètis* 2: 235–47.

Scheurer, S. and Krumeich, R. (1999). "*Kophoi*." In *Das griechische Satyrspiel*, ed. R. Krumeich, N. Pechstein, B. Seidensticker, and R. Bielfeldt. Darmstadt: 349–55.

Schibli, H. S. (1990). *Pherekydes of Syros*. Oxford.

Schmid, W. (1929). *Untersuchungen zum gefesselten Prometheus*. Tübingen.

Schmidt, D. A. (1987). "The performance of Bacchylides *Ode* 5." *CQ* 37: 20–23.

Schmidt, J.-U. (1988). "Die Einheit des Prometheus-Mythos in der 'Theogonie' des Hesiod." *Hermes* 116: 129–56.

Schmitt, A. (1975). "Zum Prooimion des hesiodischen Frauenkatalogs." *WJA* 1: 19–31.

Schömann, G. F. (1857). *Opuscula Academica. II: Mythologica et Hesiodea*. Berlin.

Schroeder, O. (1922). *Pindars Pythien*. Leipzig.

Schwabl, H. (1963). "Hesiod und Parmenides: Zur Formung des parmenideischen Prooimions (28 B 1)." *RhM* 106: 134–42.

Schwartz, J. (1960). *Pseudo-Hesiodeia; recherches sur la composition, la diffusion et la disparition ancienne d'œuvres attribuées à Hésiode*. Leiden.

Schwarze, J. (1971). *Die Beurteilung des Perikles durch die attische Komödie und ihre historische und historiographische Bedeutung*. Munich.

Schwenn, F. (1934). *Die Theogonie des Hesiodos*. Heidelberg.

Schwinge, E.-R. (1977). "Aristophanes und die Utopie." *WJA* 3: 43–67.

Scodel, R. (1982). "The Achaean Wall and the myth of destruction." *HSCP* 86: 33–50.

(2014). "Prophetic Hesiod." In *Between Orality and Literacy: Communication and Adaptation in Antiquity*, ed. R. Scodel. Leiden: 56–76.

Scott, W. C. (1987). "The development of the chorus in *Prometheus Bound*." *TAPA* 117: 85–96.

Scully, S (2015). *Hesiod's Theogony from Near Eastern Creation Myth to Paradise Lost*. Oxford.

Seaford, R. (1990). "The structural problems of marriage in Euripides." In *Euripides, Women, and Sexuality*, ed. A. Powell. London and New York: 151–76.

Segal, C. (1967). "Pindar's seventh *Nemean*." *TAPA* 98: 431–80.

(1976). "Bacchylides reconsidered: epithets and the dynamics of lyric narrative." *QUCC* 22: 99–130.

Sellschopp, J. (1934). *Stilistische Untersuchungen zu Hesiod*. Gerlingen.

Severyns, A. (1926). "Le cycle épique et l'épisode d'Io (Eschyle, Prométhée, 771 et s.)." *Musée Belge* 30: 119–30.

(1928). *Le cycle épique dans l'école d'Aristarque*. Liège and Paris.

Shaw, C. A. (2014). *Satyric Play. The Evolution of Greek Comedy and Satyr Drama*. Oxford.

Siegmann, E. (1956). *Literarische Griechische Texte der Heidelberger Papyrussammlung*. Heidelberg.

Silk, M. S. (1998). "Pindar's poetry and the obligatory crux: *Isthmian* 5.56–63, text and interpretation." *TAPA* 128: 25–88.

(2000). *Aristophanes and the Definition of Comedy*. Oxford.

Simon, E. (1981). "Anesidora." *LIMC* 1.1: 790–91.

(1992). "Coronis." *LIMC* 6.1: 103–06.

Sinclair, T. A. (1927). "The so-called Peisistratean edition of Hesiod." *CQ* 21: 195–98.

Sissa, G. (1990). "Maidenhood without maidenhead: the female body in ancient Greece." In *Before Sexuality: The Construction of Erotic Experience in the Ancient Greek World*, ed. F. I. Zeitlin, J. J. Winkler and D. M. Halperin. Princeton: 339–64.

Skempis, M. (2011). "Ironic genre demarcation: Bacchylides 17 and the epic tradition." *Trends in Classics* 3: 254–300.

Slater, W. J. (1988). "Pindar's *Pythian* 3: structure and purpose." *QUCC* 29: 51–61.

Smith, D. G. (2012). "Sicily and the identities of Xuthus. Stesichorus, Aeschylus' *Aenaeae*, and Euripides' *Ion*." In *Theater outside Athens. Drama in Greek Sicily and South Italy*, ed. K. Bosher. Cambridge: 112–36.

Snell, B. and Maehler, H. (1970). *Bacchylidis carmina cum fragmentis*. Leipzig.

(1987). *Pindari carmina cum fragmentis. I: Epinicia*. Leipzig.

Solmsen, F. (1934). "Euripides' *Ion* im Vergleich mit anderen Tragödien." *Hermes* 69: 390–419.

(1949). *Hesiod and Aeschylus*. Ithaca, N.Y.

(1982). "The earliest stages in the history of Hesiod's text." *HSCP* 86: 1–31.

Sommerstein, A. H. (1991)². *Aristophanes: Birds*. Oxford.

(1996). "Aristophanes and the demon Poverty." In *Oxford Readings in Aristophanes*, ed. E. Segal. Oxford: 252–81.

(2006). "Rape and consent in Athenian tragedy." In *Dionysalexandros. Essays on Aeschylus and His Fellow Tragedians in Honour of Alexander F. Garvie*, ed. D. Cairns and V. Liapis. Swansea: 233–51.

(2008). *Aeschlylus. Fragments*. Cambridge, Mass.

(2010a)². *Aeschylean Trilogy*, 2nd edn. London.

(2010b). *The Tangled Ways of Zeus and Other Studies in and around Greek Tragedy*. Oxford.

(2010c). "La tetralogia di Eschilo sulla guerra persiana." *Dionysus ex machina* 1: 4–20

Sourvinou-Inwood, C. (2011). *Athenian Myths and Festivals. Aglauros, Erechtheus, Plynteria, Panathenaia, Dionysia*, ed. R. Parker. Oxford.

Sperduti, A. (1950). "The divine nature of poetry in antiquity." *TAPA* 81: 209–40.

Spira, A. (1960). *Untersuchungen zum Deus ex machina bei Sophokles und Euripides*. Kallmünz.

Stafford, E. (2000). *Worshipping Virtues. Personification and the Divine in Ancient Greece*. London.

Stamatopoulou, Z. (2012). "Weaving Titans for Athena: Euripides and the Panathenaic *peplos* (*Hec.* 466–74 and *IT* 218–24)." *CQ* 62: 72–80.

(2013). "Reading the *Aspis* as a Hesiodic poem." *CPh* 108: 273–85.

(2014). "The reception of Hesiod in Plutarch's *Symposium of the Seven Sages*." *AJP* 135: 533–58.

(2016). "The quarrel with Perses and Hesiod's biographical tradition." *GRBS* 51: 1–17.

(in press). "Wounding the gods: the mortal *theomachos* in the *Iliad* and the Hesiodic *Aspis*." *Mnemosyne*.

Steffen, W. (1961). "Bacchylides' fifth ode." *Eos* 51: 11–20.

Stéfos, A. (1975). *Apollon dans Pindare*. Athens.

Steiner, D. (2005). "Nautical matters: Hesiod's *nautilia* and Ibycus fragment 282 *PMG*." *CPh* 100: 347–55.

(2007). "Feathers flying: avian poetics in Hesiod, Pindar, and Callimachus." *AJP* 128: 177–208.

(2011). "Pindar's bestiary: the 'coda' of *Pythian* 2." *Phoenix* 65: 238–67.

(2012). "Fables and frames: the poetics and politics of animal fables in Hesiod, Archilochus, and the *Aesopica*." *Arethusa* 45: 1–41.

Stenger, J. (2004). *Poetische Argumentation: die Funktion der Gnomik in den Epinikien des Bakchylides*. Berlin.

Stiewe, K. (1962). "Die Entstehungszeit der hesiodischen Frauenkataloge." *Philologus* 106: 291–99.

(1963). "Die Entstehungszeit der hesiodischen Frauenkataloge (Fortsetzung von Band 106, 1962, 291–299)." *Philologus* 107: 1–29.

Stinton, T. C. W. (1976). "*Si credere dignum est*: some expressions of disbelief in Euripides and others." *PCPS* 22: 60–89.

Stoddard, K. B. (2003). "The programmatic message of the 'kings and singers' passage: Hesiod, *Theogony* 80–103." *TAPA* 133: 1–16.

(2004). *The Narrative Voice in the Theogony of Hesiod*. Leiden.

Stoessl, F. (1988). *Der Prometheus des Aischylos als geistesgeschichtliches und theatergeschichtliches Phänomen*. Wiesbaden.

Storey, I. C. (2011). *Fragments of Old Comedy. Volume I. Alcaeus to Diocles.* Cambridge, Mass.

(2014). "The first poets of Old Comedy." In *The Oxford Handbook of Greek and Roman Comedy*, ed. M. Fontaine and A. C. Scafuro. Oxford: 95–112.

Stroh, W. (1976). "Hesiods lügende Musen." In *Studien zum antiken Epos*, ed. H. Görgemanns and E. Schmidt. Meisenheim am Glan: 85–112.

Strohm, H. (1957). *Euripides. Interpretationen zur dramatischen Form*. Munich.

Studniczka, F. (1890). *Kyrene, eine altgriechische Göttin. Archäologische und mythologische Untersuchungen*. Leipzig.

Sutton, D. F. (1979). *Sophocles' Inachus*. Meisenheim am Glan.

Svenbro, J. (1976). *La parole et le marbre: Aux origines de la poétique grecque*. Lund.

Taplin, O. (1975). "The title of *Prometheus Desmotes*." *JHS* 95: 184–86.

(1977). *The Stagecraft of Aeschylus. The Dramatic Use of Exits and Entrances in Greek Tragedy*. Oxford.

(1993). *Comic Angels and Other Approaches to Greek Drama through Vase-Paintings*. Oxford.

(2006). "Aeschylus' *Persai* – the entry of tragedy into the celebration culture of the 470s?" in *Dionysalexandros. Essays on Aeschylus and His Fellow Tragedians in Honour of Alexander F. Garvie*, ed. D. Cairns and V. Liapis. Swansea: 1–10.

Telò, M. (2007). *Eupolidis Demi*. Florence.

(2013). "Epic, *nostos*, and generic genealogy in Aristophanes' *Peace*." In *Greek Comedy and the Discourse of Genres*, ed. E. Bakola, L. Prauscello, and M. Telò. Cambridge: 129–52.

Thalmann, W. G. (1984). *Conventions of Form and Thought in Early Greek Epic Poetry*. Baltimore.

Thompson, D. W. (1895). *A Glossary of Greek Birds*. Oxford.

Thompson, G. (1932). *Aeschylus. The Prometheus Bound*. Cambridge.

Thummer, E. (1968). *Pindar. Die Isthmischen Gedichte*. Vol. I. Heidelberg.

(1969). *Pindar. Die Isthmischen Gedichte*. Vol. II. Heidelberg.

Toohey, P. (1996). *Epic Lessons. An Introduction to Ancient Didactic Poetry*. London and New York.

Torjussen, S. (2005). "Phanes and Dionysus in the Derveni Papyrus." *SO* 80: 7–22.

Tortorelli Ghidini, M. (1991). "Due teonimi orfici nel papiro di Derveni." In *Orphisme et Orphée en l'honneur de Jean Rudhardt*, ed. P. Borgeaud. Geneva: 249–61.

Touchefeu-Meynier, O. (1997). "Typhon." *LIMC* 8.1: 147–51.

Trendall, A. D. and Webster, T. B. L. (1971). *Illustrations of Greek Drama*. London.

Treu, M. (1967). Review of Bowra (1964), *Gymnasium* 74: 149–53.

Troxler, H. (1964). *Sprache und Wortschatz Hesiods*. Zurich.

Trumpf, J. (1958). "Stadtgründung und Drachenkampf." *Hermes* 86: 129–57.

Tsagalis, C. (2009). "Poetry and poetics in the Hesiodic corpus." In *Brill's Companion to Hesiod*, ed. F. Montanari, A. Rengakos, and C. Tsagalis. Leiden: 131–77.

(2013). "Typhon and Eumelus' *Titanomachy*." *TC* 5: 19–48.

Tsitsibakou-Vasalos, E. (2010). "Brightness and darkness in Pindar's *Pythian* 3. Aigla-Koronis-Arsinoë and her coming of age." In *Light and Darkness in Ancient Greek Myth and Religion*, ed. M. Christopoulos, E. Karakantza, and O. Levaniouk. Plymouth: 30–76.

Unterberger, R. (1968). *Der gefesselte Prometheus des Aischylos: eine Interpretation*. Stuttgart.

Untersteiner, M. (1954). *Sofisti. Testimonianze e Frammenti. Fasc. III*. Florence.

Vallet, G. (1985). "Pindare et la Sicile." In *Pindare*, ed. A. Hurst. Geneva and Vandoeuvres: 285–327.

Valloza, M. (1989). "Il motivo dell'invidia in Pindaro." *QUCC* 31: 13–30.

Vandvik, E. (1943). *The Prometheus of Hesiod and Aeschylus*. Oslo.

Verdenius, W. J. (1971). "A 'hopeless' line in Hesiod: 'Works and Days' 96." *Mnemosyne* 24: 225–31.

(1972). "Notes on the proem of Hesiod's *Theogony*." *Mnemosyne* 25: 225–60.

(1976). "Notes on the *Prometheus Bound*." In *Miscellanea Tragica in honorem J. C. Kamerbeek*, ed. J. M. Bremer, S. L. Radt, and C. J. Ruijgh. Amsterdam: 451–70.

(1985). *A Commentary on Hesiod. Works and Days, vv. 1–382*. Leiden: Brill.

Vergados, A. (2011). *A Commentary on the Homeric Hymn to Hermes*. Berlin.

Vernant, J.-P. (1974). *Mythe et société en Grèce ancienne*. Paris.

(1979). "A la table des hommes: mythe de fondation du sacrifice chez Hésiode." In *La cuisine du sacrifice en pays grec*, ed. M. Detienne and J.-P. Vernant. Paris: 37–132.

Vian, F. (1952). *Guerre des géants. Le mythe avant l'époque hellénistique*. Paris.

Vogt, E. (1959). "Die Schrift vom Wettkampf Homers und Hesiods." *RhM* 102: 193–221.

Volk, K. (2002). *The Poetics of Latin Didactic. Lucretius, Vergil, Ovid, Manilius*. Oxford.

Wade-Gery, H. T. (1949). "Hesiod." *Phoenix* 3: 81–93.

Walcot, P. (1960). "Allusion in Hesiod." *REG* 73: 36–39.

Walsh, G. B. (1978). "The rhetoric of birthright and race in Euripides' *Ion*." *Hermes* 106: 301–15.

Wassermann, F. M. (1940). "Divine violence and providence in Euripides' *Ion*." *TAPA* 71: 587–604.

Watkins, C. (1995). *How to Kill a Dragon. Aspects of Indo-European Poetics*. Oxford.

Welcker, F. G. (1824). *Die aeschylische Trilogie Prometheus und die Kabirenweihe zu Lemnos: nebst Winken über die Trilogie des Aeschylus überhaupt.* Darmstadt.

(1849). *Der epische Cyclus: oder die homerischen Dichter.* Vol. II. Bonn.

Wessels, A. (1999). "Dike-Drama." In *Das griechische Satyrspiel*, ed. R. Krumeich, N. Pechstein, B. Seidensticker, and R. Bielfeldt. Darmstadt: 98–106.

West, M. L. (1966). *Hesiod. Theogony.* Oxford.

(1967). "The contest of Homer and Hesiod." *CQ* 17: 433–50.

(1978). *Hesiod: Works and Days.* Oxford.

(1979). "The Prometheus trilogy." *JHS* 99: 130–148, reprinted with postscript in M. Lloyd, ed. (2007). *Oxford Readings in Classical Studies: Aeschylus.* Oxford: 359–96.

(1983a). "The Hesiodic Catalogue: Xouthids and Aiolids." *ZPE* 53: 27–30.

(1983b). *The Orphic Poems.* Oxford.

(1985a). *The Hesiodic Catalogue of Women. Its Nature, Structure, and Origins.* Oxford.

(1985b). "The Hesiodic *Catalogue*: new light on Apollo's love-life." *ZPE* 61: 1–7.

(1987). "Ἴαων." *ZPE* 67: 20.

(1990). *Studies in Aeschylus.* Stuttgart.

(1994). "*Ab ovo*: Orpheus, Sanchuniathon, and the origins of the Ionian world model." *CQ* 44: 289–307.

(2000). "*Iliad* and *Aethiopis* on the stage: Aeschylus and son." *CQ* 50: 338–52.

(2001). "Some Homeric words." *Glotta* 77: 118–35.

(2002). "'Eumelos': a Corinthian epic cycle?" *JHS* 122: 109–33.

(2003). *Greek Epic Fragments.* Cambridge, Mass.

(2013). *The Epic Cycle. A Commentary on the Lost Troy Epics.* Oxford.

West, S. (1984). "Io and the dark stranger (Sophocles, *Inachus* F 269a)." *CQ* 34: 292–302.

(1994). "Prometheus orientalized." *MH* 51: 129–49.

Westphal, R. (1869). *Prolegomena zu Aeschylus Tragödien.* Leipzig.

Whittaker, M. (1935). "The comic fragments in their relation to the structure of Old Attic Comedy." *CQ* 29: 181–91.

Wilamowitz-Moellendorff, U. von (1886). *Isyllos von Epidauros.* Berlin.

(1905). "Lesefrüchte." *Hermes* 40: 116–53.

(1914). *Aeschylus-Interpretationen.* Berlin.

(1922). *Pindaros.* Berlin.

(1926). *Euripides. Ion.* Berlin.

(1928). *Hesiodos Erga.* Berlin.

Wilkins, J. (2000). "Edible Choruses." In *The Rivals of Aristophanes*, ed. D. Harvey and J. Wilkins. London: 341–54.

Wilkinson, C. L. (2013). *The Lyric of Ibycus.* Berlin and Boston.

Willcock, M. M. (1995). *Victory Odes: Olympians 2, 7, 11; Nemean 4; Isthmians 3, 4 and 7.* Cambridge.

Willi, A. (2008). *Sikelismos: Sprache, Literatur und Gesellschaft im griechischen Sizilien (8.–5. Jh. v. Chr.).* Basel.

Wilson, A. M. (1977). "The individualized chorus in Old Comedy." *CQ* 27: 278–83.

Wilson, N. G. (2007). *Aristophanis Fabulae*. Vol. 1. Oxford.

Wilson, P. (1980). "Pindar and his reputation in antiquity." *PCPS* 26: 97–114.

Wind, R. (1971). "Bacchylides and Pindar: a question of imitation." *CJ* 67: 9–13.

Winnington-Ingram, R. P. (1983). *Studies in Aeschylus*. Cambridge.

Winter, J. G. (1925). "A new fragment on the life of Homer." *TAPA* 56: 120–29.

Wolff, C. (1965). "The design and myth of Euripides' Ion." *HSCP* 69: 169–94.

Woodbury, L. (1972). "Apollo's first love: Pindar, *Pyth.* 9.26 ff." *TAPA* 103: 561–73.

 (1982). "Cyrene and the ΤΕΛΕΥΤΑ of marriage in Pindar's ninth Pythian Ode." *TAPA* 112: 245–58.

 (1986). "The judgment of Dionysus: books, taste, and teaching in the *Frogs*." In *Greek Tragedy and Its Legacy: Essays Presented to D. J. Conacher*, ed. M. Cropp, E. Fantham, and S. E. Scully. Calgary: 241–57.

Wright, M. (2012). *The Comedian As Critic: Greek Old Comedy and Poetics*. London.

Wüst, E. (1967). "Pindar als geschichtsschreibender Dichter." Ph.D. dissertation Tübingen.

Wyckoff, E. (1946). "Pindar *Pythian* 2. 52–56." *CPh* 41: 160–62.

Xanthou, M. G. (2013). "Pind. P. 3.25 M. post S. καλλιπέπλου λῆμα Κορωνίδος: among literary representation, ethological description and *circumlocutio cum colore epico*." *QUCC* 105: 53–76.

Yalouris, N. (1986). "Le mythe d'Io: les transformations d'Io dans l'iconographie et la littérature grecque." In *Iconographie classique et identités régionales: Paris, 26 et 27 mai 1983*, ed. L. Kahil, C. Augé, and P. Linant de Bellefonds. Paris: 3–23.

 (1990). "Io I." *LIMC* 5.1: 661–76.

Young, D. C. (1968). *Three Odes of Pindar. A Literary Study of Pythian 11, Pythian 3, and Olympian 7*. Leiden.

 (1983). "Pindar *Pythians* 2 and 3: inscriptional ποτέ and the 'poetic epistle'." *HSCP* 87: 31–48.

Yunis, H. (1988). *A New Creed: Fundamental Religious Beliefs in the Athenian Polis and Euripidean Drama*. Göttingen.

Yziquel, P. (2001). "Le drama satyrique eschyléen." *CGITA* 14: 1–22.

Zacharia, K. (1995). "The marriage of tragedy and comedy in Euripides' *Ion*." In *Laughter Down the Centuries*. Vol. II, ed. S. Jäkel and A. Timonen. Turku: 45–63.

 (2003). *Converging Truths: Euripides' Ion and the Athenian Quest for Self-Definition*. Leiden.

Zagdoun, M. A. (1992). "Kyrene." *LIMC* 6.1: 167–70.

Zanetto, G. (1987). *Aristophane. Gli Uccelli*. Milan.

Zannini Quirini, B. (1987). *Nephelokokkygia. La prospettiva mitica degli Uccelli di Aristofane*. Rome.

Zeitlin, F. I. (1986). "Configurations of rape in Greek myth." In *Rape*, ed. S. Tomaselli and R. Porter. Oxford: 122–51.

(1996). *Playing the Other. Gender and Society in Classical Greek Literature.* Chicago.

Zetzel, J. E. G. (1995). *Cicero. De Re Publica.* Cambridge.

Zimmerman, B. (1983). "Utopisches und Utopie in den Komödien des Aristophanes." *WJA* 9: 57–77.

(1991). "Nephelokokkygia. Riflessioni sull'utopia comica." In *Carnevale e utopia nella Grecia antica*, ed. W. Rösler and B. Zimmermann. Bari: 55–101.

(1993). "Aristophanes und die Intellektuellen." In *Aristophane*, ed. J. M. Bremer and E. W. Handley. Geneva and Vandoeuvres: 255–86.

Ziogas, I. (2011). "Ovid as a Hesiodic poet: Atalanta in the *Catalogue of Women* (fr. 72–6 M–W) and the *Metamorphoses* (10.560–707)." *Mnemosyne* 64: 249–70.

(2013). *Ovid and Hesiod. The Metamorphosis of the Catalogue of Women.* Cambridge.

Zuntz, G. (1993). "Aeschyli Prometheus." *HSCP* 95: 107–11.

# Index Locorum

# Subject Index

Achilles, 9, 83, 113–17, 191
Aeschylus
   *Suppliants*, 153
   *Persae*, 166
   in Syracuse, 164–67
aetiology, 7–8, 43, 48, 52, 55, 61, 78, 88, 94, 112,
   136, 147, 155, 175
Aetna, 53–63, 145–47
Ajax, 24–25, 105, 112–13
Alcidamas, 4–5, 181
Alcmene, 12, 89, 176, 196, 220
*alētheia*, 19–25
Alope, 196
Antilochus, 117
Archilochus, 30, 92, 179–80, 183–85,
   229
Aristaeus, 79–81
Aristophanes
   *Birds*, 192–222
   *Frogs*, 181–82, 185–88
Asclepius, 64–65, 77
Atalanta, 11, 82–84

Bacchylides
   Epinician Ode 3, 35–42
   Epinician Ode 5, 26–35
Basileia, 211, 215–20

Centaurus, 92–96
*Certamen Homeri et Hesiodi*, 187
Chiron, 8–9, 64, 86, 114–18, 150, 160,
   188–92
colonization, 78
Coronis, 64–77, 90
cosmogonies, 202–9
Cratinus
   *Archilochoi*, 179–81, 183–84
   *Chirones*, 188–90
   *Ploutoi*, 123, 223–24
Cyrene, 77–90

Deinomenes, 53
dilogy, 123–27

*eidolon*, 98–102
*elpis*, 159
Endymion, 96–97
Epicharmus
   *Pyrrha* or *Promatheus*, 133–34, 166–67
epinician poetics, 17–42
Eumelus
   *Titanomachy*, 150
Euphorion, 123–24, 127
Euripides
   *Wise Melanippe*, 171

fame, 34–35, 40

genealogies, 10–12, 52, 66, 82, 88, 94–96, 167–78
Gigantomachy, 150, 193–97, 211, 220–21
Great Flood, 133–34, 167

Heracles, 11–13, 81, 105, 112–13, 145, 150–51, 153,
   160, 218, 220
hero-cult, 5, 14, 19, 42
Hesiod
   *Aegimius*, 12, 154–55
   *ainos* of the hawk and the nightingale, 40–42
   *Astronomia*, 8, 67
   biographical traditions, 1–6; see also, poetic
     contests; *Certamen Homeri et Hesiodi*
   *Chironos Hypothekai*, 9, 13, 15, 30, 75, 114–18,
     188–92
   didactic poetry, 7–9, 114–21, 185–92
   genealogical poetry, 10–12, 14, 52, 65–91,
     94–96, 154–59, 170–78, 219–20
   *Katabasis of Peirithous*, 13, 112–13
   *Megala Erga*, 8, 75, 192
   *Melampodia*, 8, 13
   *Ornithomanteia*, 8, 67, 209
   Panhellenic poet, 13–16, 62–63, 228–29

CPSIA information can be obtained
at www.ICGtesting.com
Printed in the USA
LVHW011714150821
695370LV00016B/1431

9 781316 615041